Assessment for Decision

EDITOR
Donald R. Peterson

EDITORIAL BOARD

Cary Cherniss

Daniel B. Fishman

Cyril M. Franks

Morris Goodman

Sandra L. Harris

Arnold A. Lazarus

Charles A. Maher

Stanley B. Messer

Stanley Moldawsky

Peter E. Nathan

Milton Schwebel

G. Terence Wilson

Robert L. Woolfolk

VOLUME I

ASSESSMENT FOR DECISION

EDITED BY

Donald R. Peterson and Daniel B. Fishman

RUTGERS UNIVERSITY PRESS

New Brunswick and London

"Huntsman, What Quarry?" is excerpted from "Upon This Age, That Never Speaks Its Mind" by Edna St. Vincent Millay. From *Collected Poems* (Harper & Row). Copyright © 1939, 1967 by Edna St. Vincent Millay and Norma Millay Ellis. Reprinted by permission.

Library of Congress Cataloging-in-Publication Data

Assessment for decision.

(Rutgers symposia on applied psychology;
v. 1)
Includes index.
1. Psychology, Applied—Methodology.
2. Evaluation. I. Peterson, Donald R.
(Donald Robert), 1923–   . II. Fishman,
Daniel B. III. Series.
BF636.A76 1987   150'.28'7   87-4544
ISBN 0-8135-1246-8
ISBN 0-8135-1247-6 (pbk.)

Copyright © 1987 by Rutgers, The State University
All Rights Reserved
Manufactured in the United States of America

Contents

List of Figures

List of Tables

Series Preface

This is the first in a series of symposia on applied psychology sponsored by the Graduate School of Applied and Professional Psychology of Rutgers University. Our aim is to identify issues that need to be addressed if psychological knowledge is to be brought into the public benefit, to identify scholars who know most about those issues, to bring the scholars together in a situation that encourages each participant to inform and be informed by the works of the others, to integrate their ideas into the most coherent statement the various contributions allow, and to present the results of the deliberations in a series of books.

The isolation of investigators in psychology is often deplored. Isolation in applied psychology is especially deplorable, because the aim of application is not discrete discovery but the coordination and use of the most advanced knowledge available for the sake of the people we are trying to help. Yet, in fact, much of the leading research in applied psychology is done by one investigator, or at most a small group, working alone in one institution, away from others whose conceptions, strategies, or findings might improve the research and advance the body of knowledge as a whole.

Symposia can be useful in reducing isolation. We believe symposia can be particularly helpful if the topic to be addressed is carefully defined, if participants are carefully chosen, if the participants know in advance what their colleagues will bring to the meeting, and if earnest attention is given to the integration of materials following the conference. The format of our symposia is designed to meet those conditions. Choice of issue is determined by the Editorial Board, made up of the senior faculty of our school. One or more members of the board assume responsibility for organizing the conference. Once the topic is selected, a general approach is defined and major subtopics are delineated. Then efforts begin to select leading contributors in each area. Nominations are obtained from the Editorial Board, other local scholars, and from distinguished investigators at other universities. Writings of nominees are reviewed and final selections are made by the editors of each volume, usually after consultation with specialists in the various areas to be considered. For the first two symposia, discussants were chosen prior to the conference and were asked to comment on the various contributions; discussants will probably participate in most future symposia.

A statement outlining the goals and structure of the symposium is sent to each participant. Each author is asked to prepare a draft of his or her statement well in advance of the meeting, and draft chapters are circulated to participants and discussants. The conference then ensues over a three-day period, during which authors present their views, discussants savage the ideas of the authors, lively conversations, both formal and informal, take place among those present, and the authors either oppose the ideas they have heard or begin some kind of accommodation. The entire process is taxing. At times it is disturbing. But it is also stimulating enough to be described accurately by one participant as an "intellectual feast."

Upon return to their home institutions, the authors have an opportunity to revise their statements in light of the discussions they have just experienced and in response to any further suggestions the editors may be brave enough to offer. When the revised chapters are received, the task of integrating the entire body of material descends upon the volume editors, who take as much time as is needed to bring it all together. The job is very different from the usual publication of conference proceedings. We hope the results will be more useful.

Two symposia have now taken place, the third is near at hand as these remarks are written, and plans for the fourth are well advanced. The first symposium, suggested by Fishman around some ideas that had long interested Peterson, was directed toward psychological assessment. This is a topic of central concern in applied psychology, but one in which prevailing conceptions seemed to us misguided and the most commonly used procedures of limited practical use. The second symposium, organized by Stanley Messer, Robert Woolfolk, and Louis Sass, was concerned with hermeneutic interpretation as an epistemological basis for personality theory and psychotherapy. The philosophical foundations of psychological investigation have been shaking lately. The structures of Logical Positivism and Operationism appear to be flawed, not so much because they are weak as that they are ill-suited to psychological construction. The editors of the hermeneutics symposium gathered a distinguished group of philosophers and metatheoreticians in psychology to consider the forms a new foundation might take.

It is interesting that a series on applied and professional psychology has begun with two volumes on the epistemology of psychological inquiry. One might expect us to be discussing licensure or third-party payment for the practice of psychotherapy. Perhaps some day we shall. For the survival of our profession, these matters are not trivial. However, when our Editorial Board began to consider issues of the greatest importance for applied psychology, we were quickly led to questions of a most fundamental order. What kinds of knowledge do we need? How can we obtain it? Exploration of those questions led us through some difficult passages, but the voyages were interesting, and we believe we have opened up some new areas for others to explore.

The third symposium, which will take place about the time this book appears, is entitled "Cognition and Education." The conference was organized by Charles Maher, Milton Schwebel, and Nancy Fagley, and addresses an issue no less formidable than understanding the central cognitive processes through which intellectual development occurs. The fourth symposium, to be organized by Sandra Harris and Jan Handelman, is tentatively entitled "Life-Threatening Behavior: Aversive vs. Nonaversive Interventions." The topic is interesting not only for technical and scientific reasons, but has important ethical, legal, and humanitarian implications as well. Two additional topics are under consideration for symposia to follow. How much our efforts will contribute to knowledge in these areas will be for others to decide, but no one is likely to accuse us of undue modesty in our choice of issues.

Preface

Readers accustomed to books on assessment that are restricted to particular classes of procedures or to particular aspects of individuals such as cognitive processes or "personality" may be puzzled by the range of topics covered in this book. What is a chapter that describes a computer-assisted program for rehabilitating stroke victims doing in the same book with a chapter that shows how to improve the productivity of process-design engineers in a chemical plant? And what are those chapters doing before and after others concerned with psychophysiological processes and behavioral medicine, management of treatment programs in mental hospitals, classification of prisoners in Alabama, parental behavior and child aggression, team performance of airline cockpit crews, and the organization of community mental health centers? Answer: All are concerned with the assessment of psychological processes in guiding decisions that affect human lives. The chapters share other qualities as well. The authors have served on the line. They have had to face conditions as nature presents them rather than reducing and distorting conditions to reach the necessary simplifications of experiment. They have met common problems and confronted common issues. They have dealt with the problems in ways that required intelligence, knowledge, skill, and years of hard work. In the meetings described in the series preface, they shared their experiences and their ideas with each other. Now they do the same for readers of this book.

The first chapter shows that applied psychology began as assessment but has shifted over the past half century to an emphasis on intervention, often unexamined and ill-advised. At the same time, the range of application has broadened enormously, extending now from biopsychological processes through the actions of individuals and groups to the functions of organizations. Lest ambition exceed competence, efforts to help others must be based on dependable information. The collection and application of useful information require an assessment technology that goes far beyond, and is in some ways radically different from, traditional approaches to psychological assessment. The second chapter defines a technological-managerial paradigm within which the needed technology might be developed. Basic dimensions of useful assessment systems are outlined and a generic process is proposed for developing assessment technologies at any of the levels and for any of the populations and problems with which psychologists are typically concerned.

Discussion proceeds through eight chapters that represent, in the view of the editors and their consultants, some of the most exciting yet sturdy work now in progress for the practical study of psychological functioning. In selecting contributors, we sought work over a wide range of settings and populations that bore the common mark of excellence in regard to conceptual soundness, innovative quality, respect for data, and practical utility. In the third chapter, Buffery describes a system of brain function therapy that integrates the probes of neuropsychological assessment with systematic procedures to stimulate brain function. Information is used to help patients help themselves get better, instead of telling them where their lesions are in a language they cannot comprehend. In the following chapter, Katkin describes a wide range of methods for studying psychophysiological processes, shows how seriously these methods can be misused, indicates the kinds of research needed to develop more effective procedures, and cautiously suggests some ways the procedures might be employed in behavioral medicine. Then Gordon Paul summarizes his landmark research on the assessment and modification of client and staff functioning in residential treatment settings. Here we see some of the results of a project, over 15 years in the making and still in progress, that can improve the humane benefits and decrease the financial costs of treatment, and can do so dependably because it is founded on an assessment system that was constructed with scrupulous care. Following that, Fowler discusses the Alabama prison project, in which he and his colleagues designed and applied a new system for assessing and reclassifying all the inmates of Alabama prisons. As a result of their efforts, the few truly dangerous prisoners were kept away from the brutalized but helpless many at no reduction in prison security.

At the small group level, Patterson and Bank describe work of the last 20 years with the families of aggressive children. The slow but systematic process of conceptualizing functionally important variables, designing ways of assessing the variables, evaluating the methods and redefining constructs within a theoretically coherent and practically useful conception is illustrated with recent data from Patterson's research. Hackman and Helmreich show that many airline crashes are due neither to "pilot failure" nor mechanical dysfunction but to failures in communication and adaptive cooperation among members of cockpit teams. They then discuss the vicissitudes of assessing team performance of airline cockpit crews when the measures usually taken in the air transport field are of individual performance and the appraisal of team function is impeded both subtly and crassly by such overriding organizational influences as the demands of a pilots' union.

Broskowski is admired by community psychologists for his success in managing community mental health centers. In his account, we learn the harsh realities of assessment and decision-making in not-for-profit human service organizations, and we gain the benefit of his wisdom in identifying factors that impede or inhibit the use of formal assessment systems at the organizational level. Gilbert draws on his knowledge of learning, his pioneer ventures in programmed instruction, and over 20 years of experience as a performance engineer to describe a system for assessing performance at work. His proposals for establishing performance standards, profiling behavior, and changing environments to aid productive function seem applicable to any setting in which people have jobs to do and accomplishments to produce.

Each presentation is discussed by a line practitioner, someone working in the field, responsible for using procedures of the kind the author presents. The discussants are as concerned with the practical utilities of the methods as with their technical merits. Their statements often go beyond commentary to independent contributions in their own right. In the final chapter, the editors return to the conceptions of decision-focused assessment with which the book began. Each of the eight assessment systems is described within the general framework, and a generic structure for the design of assessment methodologies is demonstrated. Common issues confronting those who would design practically useful assessment procedures are identified, and some promising approaches to recurring problems are summarized. Finally, the contributions in this book are linked with the general literature in decision theory and psychological assessment.

The book is intended for people interested in assessing human functions to guide practical decisions in natural settings. Psychologists have traditionally been most active in that enterprise, although other disciplines have also been involved. Graduate students in professional psychology constitute a primary audience. If there is any topic professional psychologists need to master more thoroughly than others, it is psychological assessment. We believe this book will require them to question some common presumptions about assessment and lead them toward more profitable lines of inquiry than they might otherwise pursue. Students, teachers, and investigators with various research interests may also profit from these accounts of field investigation, as well as from the methods that have evolved there. Administrators, managers, any professionals who are concerned with the uses of information in decision-making should find at least some of the contents interesting. Authors have written in plain English. Although some technical complexities are required to match the inherent complexities of the material under consideration, there is nothing in this book that cannot be understood by a bright undergraduate student taking courses in personality assessment or tests and measurement.

Financial support for the symposium was provided by a grant from the matching gifts program of Transaction Publishers/John Wiley and sons and by Rutgers University. Charlotte Schulman served as staff assistant for the project. All of us who took part in the symposium are grateful for her patient, steady work.

Contributors

EDITORS

Daniel B. Fishman
Professor of Psychology
Graduate School of Applied and
  Professional Psychology
Rutgers University
New Brunswick, New Jersey

Donald R. Peterson
Dean and Professor of Psychology
Graduate School of Applied and
  Professional Psychology
Rutgers University
New Brunswick, New Jersey

AUTHORS

Lew Bank
Research Associate
Oregon Social Learning Center
Eugene, Oregon

Anthony Broskowski
Executive Director
Northside Community Mental
  Health Center
Tampa, Florida

Anthony W. H. Buffery
Research Fellow
Corpus Christi College
University of Cambridge, U.K.

Daniel B. Fishman
Professor of Psychology
Graduate School of Applied and
  Professional Psychology
Rutgers University
New Brunswick, New Jersey

Raymond D. Fowler
Dean, School of Psychology
University of Alabama
University, Alabama

Thomas F. Gilbert
Performance Engineering Group
45 Schoolhouse Lane
Morristown, New Jersey

J. Richard Hackman
Professor of Psychology
Yale University
New Haven, Connecticut

Robert L. Helmreich
Professor of Psychology
University of Texas
Austin, Texas

Edward S. Katkin
Chair, Department of Psychology
State University of New York
Buffalo, New York

William D. Neigher
Assistant Director
St. Clare's Hospital Community
  Mental Health Center
Denville, New Jersey

Gerald R. Patterson
Senior Research Scientist
Oregon Social Learning Center
Eugene, Oregon

Gordon L. Paul
Cullen Distinguished Professor
  of Psychology
University of Houston
Houston, Texas

Donald R. Peterson
Dean, Graduate School of
  Applied and Professional
  Psychology
Rutgers University
New Brunswick, New Jersey

DISCUSSANTS

Christopher R. Barbrack
Associate Professor of Psychology
Graduate School of Applied and
  Professional Psychology
Rutgers University
New Brunswick, New Jersey

Edna Kamis-Gould
Chief, Bureau of Research and
  Evaluation
Division of Mental Health and
  Hospitals
Department of Human Services
State of New Jersey
Trenton, New Jersey

Victor M. Kline
Director, Organization
  Development and Training
Johnson & Johnson Corporation
McNeil Consumer Products
  Company
Fort Washington, Pennsylvania

Harvey J. Lieberman
Chief of Service
South Beach Psychiatric Center
Staten Island, New York

William D. Neigher
Assistant Director
St. Clare's Hospital Community
  Mental Health Center
Denville, New Jersey

Nathaniel J. Pallone
Academic Vice President and
    University Professor of
    Psychology
Rutgers University
New Brunswick, New Jersey

Frederick Rotgers
Staff Psychologist
New Jersey State Parole Board
Trenton, New Jersey

Jeanne Wurmser
Executive Director
Children's Psychiatric Center
Eatontown, New Jersey

Assessment for Decision

Upon this gifted age, in its dark hour
Falls from the sky a meteoric shower
Of facts . . . they lie unquestioned, uncombined
Wisdom enough to leech us of our ill
Is daily spun; but there exists no loom
To weave it into fabric. . . .

From "Huntsman, What Quarry?"
by Edna St. Vincent Millay

CONCEPTUAL FOUNDATIONS

Assessment is not a very popular topic among professional psychologists these days. Clinicians are preoccupied with therapies. Community psychologists are busy with preventive interventions. Yet assessment is the core of disciplined practice. Only by carefully discriminating appraisal can appropriate treatments be chosen. Only through close evaluation can the effects of intervention be gauged. In the first chapter, Peterson reviews the history of assessment in professional psychology, and shows that applied psychology was almost exclusively limited to assessment for the first half-century of its development. With the rapid expansion of clinical and counseling psychology after World War II, emphasis shifted to treatment. At the same time, the scope of applied psychology was broadly extended. Interventions reached beyond individuals to groups, organizations, and communities. These shifts require more attention to assessment than before, not less, but Peterson argues that the general topic of assessment has been neglected in recent years and that the functionally useful methods required for responsible practice are poorly formed. In the closing section of the chapter, some proposals are offered to guide development of an improved assessment technology.

In the second chapter, Fishman and Neigher probe more deeply into fundamental assumptions underlying psychological assessment. Assessment is a knowledge-seeking enterprise. Sooner or later, the epistemological foundations of psychological inquiry must be examined if effective improvements are to be made. The authors argue that the paradigm of theory-driven basic research, which has dominated psychology until recent times, rests on logically questionable premises and has yielded poor returns in substantive knowledge. A different approach is proposed, namely, a technological-managerial paradigm that begins in the problems of the real world rather than the theories of investigators and leads to particular solutions to particular problems rather than general laws of nature. Although no universal principles are sought in the technological approach, strategies developed in solving one problem may be useful in solving others. Indeed, the authors propose that the problem-solving process in decision-focused assessment is much the same whether one is studying individuals, groups, or organizations. The steps required to develop a decision-focused assessment system are described; they serve as a general framework within which the assessment systems presented in the rest of the book can be considered.

Chapter 1

The Role of Assessment in Professional Psychology

DONALD R. PETERSON

When people think of psychology as a profession they are likely to think first of psychotherapy. In fact, three surveys (Callan et al., 1986; Garfield & Kurtz, 1976; Peterson et al., 1982) show that professional psychologists currently spend more time doing psychotherapy than any other single activity.[1] Often, behavior change based on learning principles is proposed either as an alternative or as a complement to conventional psychotherapy. Some of the most active theoretical controversies in our field revolve about the distinction between psychodynamic and behavioral views of psychological process and of means for reducing psychological distress (e.g., Arkowitz & Messer, 1984; Wachtel, 1977). Still more broadly, professional psychology may be seen as preventive action in communities, averting the causes of human dysfunction rather than curing ailments (e.g., Albee, 1982; Sarason, 1981). All of these conceptions of professional activity, however, carry in common an emphasis on intervention. Within these views, whether they are psychodynamic or behavioral, individual or social, meliorative or preventive, the goal of professional action is change, and the main job of the practitioner is to fix things so that people can function better than before.

It was not always thus. The earliest applications of psychology were in assessment rather than treatment. For many years "mental testing" was nearly the only activity practicing psychologists were allowed to perform. In rushing to escape the restrictions of that role, however, professional psychologists may have abandoned their strongest heritage

5

and forsaken their most powerful contributions to the public. Assessment is the core of systematic practice. Without assessment, treatments are prescribed by whim or fashion. Assessment is the key to sound research. Only if influences and effects are properly appraised can their relationships be determined. For psychologists, assessment offers an opportunity for contributions that complement rather than compete with those of other professions. There is no reason to suppose psychologists do psychotherapy any better or worse than psychiatrists, social workers, counselors, or for that matter intelligent, caring non-professionals (Strupp & Hadley, 1979). Psychologists have no special purchase on research. Despite the emphasis on research in their training, most professional psychologists do not publish so much as a single study (Kelly & Goldberg, 1959; Levy, 1962). The medical faculties of first-rate psychiatry departments are just as busy investigating the causes and cures of psychiatric disorders as are the clinical faculties of psychology departments. When other professions whose entry levels have traditionally been subdoctoral move to doctoral levels of training, as is now occurring in social work and nursing, it is training for research that sets the doctoral degree apart from the others. What psychologists can do that is uniquely suited to their tradition and especially emphasized in their training is to examine the conditions that trouble others, to provide informed appraisals of those conditions, to help decide where changes may be needed and how they may be brought about, and to evaluate the effects of any changes they and others may have contrived. Assessment for decision in planning and evaluation is the theme of this symposium. In this chapter, I suggest that assessment, broadly conceived, conceptually and operationally linked with intervention, and truly placed in the service of the public, may be the most useful of all the activities psychologists can perform.

ASSESSMENT IN THE BEGINNINGS
OF PROFESSIONAL PSYCHOLOGY

Administrators required to make decisions about people have been assessing human performance for many centuries. In 1115 B.C., the emperor of China subjected his officials to job sample tests in the basic arts of archery, horsemanship, music, writing, and arithmetic (DuBois, 1970). In the sixteenth century A.D., a Spanish physician, Juan Huarte, wrote a treatise on the assessment of human abilities for educational planning. Later translated into English as *The Tryal of Wits, Discover-*

ing the Great Difference of Wits Among Men and What Sort of Learning Suits Best with Each Genius, the book and the methods proposed in it found favor in Elizabethan England (McReynolds, 1975).

These early efforts scarcely qualify as the works of professional psychologists since psychology did not yet exist as an identifiable discipline. Once psychology began, however, with the establishment of Wilhelm Wundt's laboratory at Leipzig in 1879, practical applications were soon attempted, and the first applications came in the assessment of human functions. In England, Francis Galton adapted the psychophysical methods of Weber and Fechner to the measurement of individual differences in weight discrimination, pitch threshold, mental imagery, and reaction time. As an intellectual forebear of the eugenics movement, Galton hoped to use tests such as these as guides to selection in improving the human stock (Galton, 1883).

Responsibility for developing applied psychology is usually attributed to James McKeen Cattell, one of Wundt's early students. After working briefly with Galton in England, Cattell returned to the United States in 1888 and soon afterward established a psychological laboratory at the University of Pennsylvania. Although he identified himself primarily as an experimentalist throughout his career, Cattell had grand visions for the practical use of psychological knowledge, and saw "mental tests" as the technical mainstay of applied psychology. In 1892, Cattell was replaced by Lightner Witmer as director of the Pennsylvania laboratory. Four years later, Witmer established the first psychological clinic at the University of Pennsylvania. Work at the clinic was devoted mainly to the assessment of learning disabilities in children, though evaluations were closely linked with remedial consultation and uses of assessment in preventive planning were clearly foreseen in Witmer's writings (Witmer, 1907).

The practical problems of "slow-learners" also led to construction of the Binet-Simon scale in 1905, its revision in 1908, and further revision, standardization, and redefinition by Terman in 1916. By the time the United States entered World War I in 1917, psychologists had already established a reputation for employing scientific methods in assessing human abilities. Use of the Army Alpha and Beta tests and widespread publicity concerning the apparently limited mental ability of American males (the average mental age of the American soldier was gauged at 13.5 years) drew applied psychology to the attention of the public and brought some measure of respectability within the scientific community.

The following two decades saw a spectacular rise in the production of psychological tests. Besides intelligence tests, many kinds of achievement tests, ability tests, and aptitude tests were invented; along with the personality and interest tests that also flourished between the two world wars, they formed the main stock in trade for the professional psychology of the time.

World War II brought a new call for assessment procedures, not only in America but in other countries as well. In Great Britain, the Raven Progressive Matrices test was widely used for classification of enlisted military personnel. Situational tests and interviews patterned after those devised earlier by German military psychologists were used to select British officers. In the United States, massive assessment programs were undertaken on several fronts. The Office of Strategic Services devised a program of situational tests for selection and placement of Secret Service operatives that Wiggins (1973) regards as one of the milestone studies in psychological assessment. Air force psychologists devised batteries of tests for selecting pilots, bombardiers, and navigators and subjected their instruments to more thorough validation research than is typically possible under peacetime conditions. Reisman has remarked that "hardly a male adult of military potentiality within the United States escaped psychological testing" (Reisman, 1966, p. 271) during these years, and he estimated that 60 million standardized tests were administered to 20 million persons in 1944.

During the war, psychologists also joined medical personnel in treating psychiatric casualties. In doing so, they gained some credibility as prospects for training in the treatment of emotional disorders. Before World War II, however, the clear accomplishments of professional psychologists lay almost entirely in the fields of assessment. Their roles in intervention were yet to be formed.

THE TURN TO TREATMENT

After the war, a serious shortage was seen in the number of professionals qualified to help people with psychiatric problems. One out of three men drafted for American military service had been rejected as psychologically unfit. Nearly half of the medical discharges from the army were based on diagnoses of neuropsychiatric disability. According to the estimates of the time, at least 2 million veterans would need psychological help by the end of the war.

For at least 20 years, psychologists had been pressing for rights to treat as well as diagnose people with psychological problems. They had made some headway in counseling, as long as their activities were restricted to vocational and educational issues, and in helping children through the child guidance movement. They had gained the ideological support of the founder of psychoanalysis, the original and still dominant form of psychotherapy available to practitioners. In a statement psychologists are fond of quoting, Freud said: "Psycho-analysis is not a specialized brand of medicine. I cannot see how it is possible to dispute this. Psycho-analysis falls under the head of psychology; not of medical psychology in the old sense, nor of psychology of morbid processes, but simply of psychology" (Freud, 1927, p. 207).

Regardless of social need, qualifications of competitors, or ideological argument, organized psychiatry held a firm grip on the right to practice psychotherapy. Only physicians, they said, should treat the mentally ill. Facing national crisis, however, the psychiatrists themselves acknowledged their insufficiency. At the time, the American Psychiatric Association claimed fewer than 3,000 members. Responding to the public need and in a spirit of respect born of wartime cooperation, psychiatrists and psychologists worked together to plan training programs for both their disciplines.

In 1946, as Kirsch and Winter have said, "the Veterans Administration created modern clinical psychology" (Kirsch & Winter, 1983, p. 13). Stipends were provided for trainees. Jobs were available for graduates. Consultation fees were offered to university faculty members. Clinical programs were developed in most major universities. Within four years, some 1,500 graduate students were becoming clinical psychologists in over 50 doctoral programs.

The inclusion of psychotherapy as a responsibility of clinical psychologists was clear though circumscribed. Besides the primary task of "diagnosing personality characteristics," clinical psychologists were also to have therapeutic duties "within the medical framework" and "under the direction of the responsible neuropsychiatrist" (Miller, 1946, p. 184). This was less than the privilege of independent practice some psychologists had sought, but more than they had ever had before, and was decisive among the influences that would soon make clinical psychology the dominant professional specialty within the discipline and psychotherapy the dominant activity of clinicians.

A gentle force was added to the move toward psychotherapy by the contributions of Carl Rogers. Until Rogers came along, the therapies psychologists had at their disposal were borrowed from other disciplines. Despite Freud's protest, psychoanalysis was seen as a medical specialty. The "Neo-Freudian" therapies of Jung, Rank, Adler, Horney, and Sullivan were all developed by psychiatrists. Although redefinitions of personality and psychotherapy in the language of learning were soon to be attempted (Dollard & Miller, 1950; Mowrer, 1950), no psychologist before Rogers had suggested a way to do psychotherapy that could be learned, practiced, and identified with the discipline of psychology itself. At first, Rogers emphasized the nondirective character of effective counseling as he saw it, in contrast with the advice and interpretation that dominated most other treatment techniques (Rogers, 1942). Later, he went further in conceiving positive regard, empathy, and genuineness on the part of the therapist as important conditions and then as necessary and sufficient conditions for therapeutic benefit (Rogers, 1951, 1957).

Throughout, Rogers discredited assessment as a useful clinical practice. Indeed, he maintained that tests and other diagnostic operations interfered with the intimacy and authenticity that alone could help clients realize the best of their human potentials. At the same time, clinical assessment techniques came under attack from researchers. In study after study, the reliabilities of projective tests were shown to be poor. Experts could not even agree in interpreting statistically derived "objective" questionnaires (Little & Schneidman, 1959). The tests psychologists had spent so long designing appeared to provide trivial increases over the information easily gained from demographics and a brief interview (Sines, 1959). In a classic monograph, Paul Meehl (1954) showed that mechanical formulas did better than expert clinicians in predicting many forms of socially important behavior, and recommended that clinicians turn their talents toward research in developing better formulas or toward psychotherapy as a way of helping others (Meehl, 1956). Clinicians did not stop giving tests, but the foundations of practice in test-based personality assessment were shaken, and many professionals turned to psychotherapy as a saleable and satisfying alternative.

THE BEHAVIORAL SHIFT IN PROFESSIONAL PSYCHOLOGY

But psychotherapy had troubles of its own as a basis for psychological practice. In 1952, Eysenck surveyed literature then available on the effects of psychotherapy and concluded that psychotherapy offered no greater benefit than simple custodial care or no treatment at all. Not long after, Levitt (1957) compared various psychotherapies for children with several control conditions where no treatment was offered, and concluded that psychotherapy with children had no more effect than the natural process of growing up for an equal period of time. The major psychotherapies of the time were slow, inefficient, based on personality theories of dubious scientific merit, and were increasingly seen by critics as ineffective.

Learning-based alternatives for the treatment of special problems had been available for many years. As early as 1924, Mary Cover Jones had shown that a child's fear of animals could be extinguished by gradual exposure to the animal (Jones, 1924). In 1933, the Mowrers devised a conditioning technique for treating enuresis that is still the most effective treatment available for enuretic problems (Mowrer & Mowrer, 1938). Theoretical bases for understanding complex psychological processes in terms of cognition, emotion, action, and learning had already been provided in the writings of Mowrer (1950) and Dollard and Miller (1950), but these formulations consisted largely of translations of psychodynamic theory into the language of experimental psychology. They did not provide new ways of treating human disorders.

One of the first clear statements of a psychological treatment procedure that was based on experimentally tested principles of learning, that described treatment techniques in enough detail to allow clinicians to employ them, and that offered evidence for the effectiveness of the methods was Wolpe's *Psychotherapy by Reciprocal Inhibition,* which appeared in 1958. Critics later found fault with Wolpe's theoretical formulation, questioned the pertinence of the experiments on which he supposedly based treatments, and noted flaws in his outcome research. For all that, the treatments Wolpe proposed were eagerly tried by clinicians dissatisfied with the psychotherapies they had been using, and the effects of some of the methods, especially systematic desensitization of phobias, were soon documented (Lang et al., 1965; Paul, 1966).

Even earlier, the use of operant conditioning procedures in treating adults (Skinner et al., 1953) and in training children (Bijou, 1955) had begun to stir the behavior modification movement. The main tenets of behavior modification were simple but the implications were profound. Whatever the causes of behavior disorder might be, the task of the clinician was to change behavior for the better, and the theory and technology through which behavior change could be accomplished was the psychology of learning. Early formulations based strictly on the stimulus-response psychology of radical behaviorism were soon extended to encompass cognitive and emotional behavior. Within 15 years, the theoretical structure for a comprehensive psychology of behavior modification had been defined (Bandura, 1969; Kanfer & Phillips, 1970), a behavioral conception of psychopathology had been articulated (Ullmann & Krasner, 1969), a wide array of techniques for treating a wide range of problems had been developed (Lazarus, 1971), a new shelf of journals devoted to behavior therapy had been established, an interdisciplinary, international association for the advancement of behavior therapy had been organized, and annual reviews were needed to help researchers and practitioners stay abreast of rapidly growing developments in the field (Franks & Wilson, 1973).

Advances in behavioral assessment followed advances in treatment. Assessment and treatment were inherently linked in the concept of functional analysis of behavior (Skinner, 1953). Functional analysis begins with systematic observation and recording of behavior. From these observations, base rates of changeworthy behavior are established. Interventions are then introduced, both as treatments and as independent variables in the experimental study of behavior. Effects on dependent variables (i.e., the "target" behaviors to be changed) are observed, and through application of various single-subject designs, the effects of various components of treatment can be determined. Implementation may be complex, but the logic of functional analysis is simple and clear.

A strong goad to seek alternatives to traditional psychodynamic theories and therapies came through Walter Mischel's book *Personality and Assessment* (1968), which showed that the intercorrelations among different measures of hypothetically identical traits were much lower than commonly conceived, and that behavior was more strongly dependent on situational influences than was assumed in most trait theories. Independently and simultaneously, Peterson (1968) presented similar arguments regarding situational influences on behavior, defined interactions of persons with situations rather than personal traits as a focus for clinical assessment, and extended the logic of functional analysis to cognitive-affective behavior and to the functions of groups and organizations. A general rationale and a substantive outline for behavioral assessment were suggested by Kanfer and Saslow (1969). A model for research on the assessment of psychological competence in a behavioral framework was presented by Goldfried and D'Zurilla (1969). Before long, several texts on behavioral assessment had appeared (Ciminero et al., 1977; Hersen & Bellak, 1976) and behavioral approaches to the study of psychological function took their place alongside testing and psychodynamically directed interviewing in curricula for training clinical psychologists. The behavioral movement spread to other specialties as well. Behavioral approaches to counseling (Krumboltz, 1966) and classroom management (O'Leary & O'Leary, 1972) were proposed. Numerous systematic investigations of the effects of behavioral treatment showed quite convincing results (Kazdin & Wilson, 1978; Rachman & Wilson, 1980).

The place of behavioral psychology in the larger profession is still uncertain. Some practitioners, satisfied with psychoanalytic theory and comfortable with their practices, simply ignore the behavioral views. Others acknowledge the importance of behavioral positions, but see them as incompatible with those of psychoanalysis (Messer & Winokur, 1980). Still others seek reconciliation and rapprochement (Goldfried, 1982; Wachtel, 1977). Whatever the outcome of the dialectic may be, no one doubts that behavior psychology has affected psychological practice fundamentally over the past 20 years, and some regard it as the sturdiest methodological and conceptual foundation upon which a cumulative psychology can be constructed (e.g., Staats, 1983).

THE SOCIAL SHIFT IN PROFESSIONAL PSYCHOLOGY

Group methods for treating psychological problems were first justified on grounds of efficiency. If one therapist could see eight patients with similar problems at the same time, effectiveness was multiplied eightfold. If, as proposed by such early leaders as Bender (1937) and Slavson (1943), all members of the group became mutually helpful co-therapists, benefits might increase exponentially. Sociograms of most early group therapy sessions, however, would probably have revealed a "star" pattern of interaction, with the most influential exchanges occurring between the professional therapist and each of the individual patients in the group. Not until later conceptions and methods took hold was the "group" in group therapy actually treated as a functional unit in its own right rather than as a collection of individuals who happened to meet together with a therapist. The conceptions and methods were those of the encounter group movement and of family therapy.

During the turbulent 1960s, a lot of talk was heard about alienation in modern American society. Gaps were seen between one generation and another, between men and women, between races, between the powerful few and the less powerful many. People, it was said, had lost the ability to communicate with one another, to touch one another in emotionally meaningful ways, and thereby to experience fully their own true selves.

In fact, the transformations of society that began with the Industrial

Revolution had damaged many of the caring communities through which intimacy and a sense of belonging were naturally provided in earlier times. The church had lost its place as an ever-present force in the lives of most people. The change from a rural, agricultural society to an urban, industrial society had moved people from the cooperative security of the family farm to the competitive work of business and industry and the social isolation of apartments and single-family homes. The stability of the nuclear family itself was threatened by a rising divorce rate. *Homo sapiens* apparently lived in tribal groups from the beginning of human existence. Close communities were maintained in one form or another through all the ages of evolutionary experience until the most recent. In twentieth-century America, it was said, we had lost our social moorings. With that loss went emotional meaning and personal identity.

Until the 1960s, most people seemed to endure the dreaded anomie in solitary despair. Then arose group leaders in the West to offer hopes of encounter. The earlier "sensitivity training" of the National Training Laboratories was no longer seen as a vehicle for greater organizational effectiveness but as a general means for helping human beings express themselves authentically and understand one another empathically. The humanistic concepts of Rogers (1961, 1970) and Maslow (1962) furnished a rationale for the movement. Buttressing concepts and new methods came from Gestalt therapy (Perls, 1969) and Transactional Analysis (Berne, 1966). By the end of the decade, some 75 "growth centers" were operating in the United States. The oldest of these, Esalen, had over 50,000 participants in 1969 (Yalom, 1975). Werner Erhard's est seminars were soon to have many more. Despite differences among the many varieties of encounter groups, they shared many characteristics. All encouraged intensive, highly emotional group experience. All encouraged self-disclosure, openness, and confrontation. Experiencing was valued; talking about experience was not. All promised an emotional touch with others and with oneself that ordinary experience could not provide.

Encounters and assessment never had much to do with each other. To many leaders of encounter groups, formal assessment was antithetical to the fundamental aim of the movement, which was to put people in immediate touch with one another. This may have been dangerous policy. Early testimonials about the effects of group experience were mainly positive (Bach, 1967), but later studies showed damaging outcomes as well (Lieberman et al., 1973). The main effect of the encounter group movement on psychology was to force an awareness of the importance of emotion and intimacy upon a discipline that had come to pride itself on cold objectivity. Many psychologists took part in encounter sessions either as trainers or as participants. In doing so they expressed their own yearning for closeness with others, and helped move psychology beyond its concern for the individual to a recognition of the inherently social nature of human experience.

The shift in emphasis beyond the individual to the group was also accelerated by the development of family therapy. Practitioners in child guidance clinics recognized early that the psychological treatment of children could not proceed effectively without involving parents, but the treatment of the family group as the unit of central concern awaited other developments. These came in several forms from several sources. In the Mental Research Institute at Stanford, Bateson, Jackson, Haley, Weakland, and others proposed that psychopathologies, even such severe ones as schizophrenia, are not diseases borne by patients but patterns of behavior and communication that originate in and are maintained by the family (Bateson et al., 1956). In 1958, Nathan Ackerman published *The Psychodynamics of Family Life*, the first book on the diagnosis and treatment of disturbed families. At the National Institute of Mental Health, Bowen and Wynne began treating the entire families of schizophrenics. Whitaker in Atlanta and Minuchin, Haley, and Montalvo in Philadelphia tried their own novel way of treating families and constructed their own versions of family systems theory to rationalize and guide the interventions of practitioners. All the approaches designated the family rather than the person as the unit of fundamental concern, adhered to some variant of open systems theory as a theoretical framework, and focused intervention on alteration of interactional patterns within the family.

How much family therapy is going on these days is difficult to judge, but no one doubts that the quantity is large. All the mental health disciplines—psychiatry, psychology, social work, and nursing—include family therapy within their domain, and an independent profession of marital and family counseling has recently been established. A professional association, the American Association of Marriage and Family Counselors, has been formed. A large literature has appeared within a short time. Gurman and Kniskern (1978) note that nine new journals related to marital and family therapy were introduced in the 15 years from 1963 to 1978. Within this period, family therapy has become firmly established as body of theory and practice, though its base in research and systematic evaluation is generally acknowledged by the leaders themselves to be weak.

Assessment of family systems is performed clinically in all forms of family therapy. Somehow or other, therapists have to determine where boundaries fall, where the lines between enmeshment and disengagement are drawn, and where the resources of the family can be redirected to improve family functioning. In some formulations (e.g., Haley, 1976) strategic guidelines for assessment are quite clearly specified. A large body of techniques for use in research on families has also been amassed. However, the research techniques are seldom used in clinical practice by family therapists who work within the framework of systems theory, and the clinical techniques have rarely been subjected to any form of psychometric appraisal, so the reliability and validity of the procedures remain almost entirely unexamined.

In behavioral forms of family intervention, by contrast, assessment is closely linked with change, and the dependability of the assessment methods themselves is an issue of concern. This is true not only for therapists who operate within strictly behavioral forms (e.g., Stuart, 1976) but for those whose definitions of psychological process are more broadly extended (e.g., Gottman, 1979; Patterson, 1982). In the work of Patterson and his colleagues, for example, an assessment technology is required for planning and evaluating treatment and for research and theoretical development as well. As in the history of psychodynamic and behavioral approaches to individuals, "family systems" and behavioral approaches to families have gone their ways mainly in isolation. In some regards the viewpoints may be incompatible. However, integrative formulations have been attempted (e.g., Alexander & Barton, 1976; Birchler & Spinks, 1980; Feldman, 1979), and both approaches share the powerfully significant feature of focus on interpersonal processes rather than only on individuals in conceptualizing, investigating, and managing human problems.

A third force in the "socialization" of professional psychology, probably the most influential so far, is the development of community psychology. Sooner or later, all the mental health professions have had to recognize that treating severely disturbed mental patients one by one is a losing battle. The professions can never produce enough practitioners to do the job, especially if they wait until the problems are fixed and rigid before they offer their ministrations. How much better we all will be if disorders are prevented before they have to be cured. How much better we all will be if we can get at the causes of human problems rather than tinker ineffectually with the long-term effects of a poorly functioning society.

Community organization, along with case work and group work, has been a mission of social work from the start of the profession. Public health nursing was devoted from the start to preventive action in communities. "Social psychiatry" appeared in the lexicon of psychiatry at least as early as 1917 (Bell & Spiegel, 1966). Psychology caught on later. The term "community psychology" was coined at the Boston Conference in 1965 (Bennett, 1965) to designate what some had already heralded as the "third revolution" in managing mental disorders (Hobbs, 1964). In the first revolution, Pinel struck the chains from the insane, declaring them ill. In the second revolution, Freud showed that neuroses were diseases like *no* others, caused and treated by psychological influences. Now, in the third revolution, the origins of mental illness were seen in a dysfunctional society. Any psychologist who wanted to help people in a widespread and lasting way was advised to turn his or her attention toward the community in which human problems arise and through which, given effective social change, the problems might be averted.

Several beliefs pervade the thinking of community psychologists. Aims of prevention predominate over those of treatment. The positive improvement of social competence is as important as the relief of distress. Social and community (systems-level) interventions are emphasized more strongly than individually directed actions. Practitioners reach out to people in the community rather than wait for people in trouble to come to them; they feel that people will be helped more in the long run by encouraging community involvement through consultation than by direct services to individuals. Since many human problems are related to general social conditions such as racial prejudice and poverty, which are beyond the reach of professional intervention, community psychologists need to work with others toward social reform wherever reforms appear to be feasible. The knowledge required for informed community intervention is more likely to come from naturalistic, ecologically representative investigations than from controlled laboratory research (Bloom, 1973; Cowen, 1973; Korchin, 1976).

These are brave ideas. In the wave of social activism that swept the country in the 1960s, community psychology quickly became a major force in the profession. By 1969, 1,500 books and articles had been written on the topic, and by 1973 three journals were devoted to it. A Division of Community Psychology, by now claiming over 1,500 members, was added to the American Psychological Association. Although the militant enthusiasms of the 1960s have largely been replaced by a mood of sober reappraisal (cf. reviews by Bloom, 1980, and Iscoe & Harris, 1984), no one doubts that community psychology has gained a firm position in the discipline, and that the emphasis it requires on a sociological view of human behavior has extended the range of our profession.

Along with community intervention came program evaluation. Other professions evaluate programs too, but psychologists have taken so strong an interest in the field that program evaluation now bids to become a professional specialty in its own right (Cronbach et al., 1980; Perloff et al., 1976; Sechrest et al., 1982). By this move as much as by efforts toward social change, professional psychology has brought organizations and communities, as well as groups and individuals, within its compass.

OTHER CHANGES IN PROGRESS
AND IN PROSPECT

Predicting the future of any profession is risky. Simple projections of prior trends or of one's own fond wishes will not do, because political and economic influences, themselves difficult to predict, can exert forces of such overwhelming power that all internal inclinations or trends of the near historical past seem trivial by comparison. Who foresaw in 1940 the effect the Veterans Administration programs of 1946 would have on clinical psychology? Who foresaw the effects postwar governmental grant programs would have on research in the field? The best we can do is form a set of tentative contingency propositions in attempting to forecast the future. If a program of National Health Insurance is enacted and if psychologists gain access to third-party payment for proffer of psychotherapy as a health service, professional psychologists will continue to devote large fractions of their time to psychotherapy. If public distrust of "social programs" can be reversed by more active public education regarding the benefits of effective programs, some deceleration in the decline of support for social programs may be accomplished. Yet, despite the risks of prediction, predict we must if we are to prepare students for the future and if we are to provide the public the goods it needs.

Some futures are more likely than others. Over the next 10 years, for example, it is clear that many more graduates of doctoral programs in psychology will find employment in professional work than in academic teaching and research. Educational institutions in psychology will produce at least 3,000 new doctoral graduates per year during the next decade (Stapp et al., 1981). Psychologists currently hold slightly more than 15,000 academic positions in four-year colleges and universities. Given the time most current faculty members entered their positions, an annual attrition rate of 4% appears generous. Few new programs will develop in higher education, since no projections suggest increases in enrollment and governmental supports for education are declining. Reductions in support for social and behavioral sciences have been especially severe. No more than 600 new PhDs will therefore be needed each year to fill academic vacancies. The remaining 2,400 graduates will find employment elsewhere. The most obvious locations will be professional positions of various kinds.

What kinds of professional work will they do and where will they do it? These questions are more difficult to answer. It is unlikely that psychotherapeutic services for the "mentally ill" will occupy as much professional time as they have in the past. As Fox (1982) has suggested, devoting 90% of our efforts toward serving the needs of the 10% – 15% of the population with diagnosable (hence reimbursable) mental illness seems an unwise deployment of limited resources. More urgent social needs and more abundant professional opportunities appear to lie in the field of "health psychology" broadly defined (Elliott, 1983; Fox, 1982; Matarazzo, 1980).

At least in developed countries, "lifestyle disorders" have largely replaced infections as the leading causes of death (Brady, 1977). Overeating, smoking, excessive use of alcohol, failure to exercise, and maladaptive reactions to stress are associated with heart disease, cerebrovascular disease, cancer, accidents, and several pulmonary diseases such as asthma and emphysema. These are all medical disorders, but psychological factors are involved as partial determinants and as potential components of treatment. Provision of short-term, carefully focused psychological services can shorten recovery time for cardiac patients (Gruen, 1975), reduce the length of hospitalization for surgical patients (Olbrisch, 1977), and in general reduce costs of medical care (Cummings & Follette, 1976; Rosen & Weins, 1979). Although the use of psychological procedures in preventive medicine is not well established (Kaplan, 1984), some behavior change procedures appear promising. The health care industry is vastly larger than the mental health industry, and health care receives far stronger public acceptance and economic support. The field of general health care thus presents a much larger social need and possibly a greater opportunity for effective service than the more limited field of mental health.

How many psychologists we need to address the behavioral health problems that confront us depends in part on the effectiveness of the services we contrive and in part on our success in placing those services where they will do the most good. No one seems to be asking psychologists to take part in the job of preventive medicine. Some entrepreneurial assertion will be required. Given even a few reasonably effective procedures and relatively polite forms of professional enterprise, however, it is obvious that the 32,000 currently registered health care providers in psychology will not begin to meet the need. The field of "behavioral medicine" has grown rapidly since the term first appeared in 1973. As in the fields of behavior therapy, family therapy, and community psychology, books and journals have appeared at a rapid rate, organizations of practitioners and researchers have been formed, and training programs have been established. All institutional indicators suggest that health psychology is already active as a professional specialty in our field, and several indicators suggest that it will become larger and more firmly established in the future.

Another change that has been going on since the beginning of professional psychology is a general expansion of the scope of the field. Professional psychology began as testing, added psychotherapy after World War II, added behavior modification, group methods, and community psychology in the 1960s and 1970s, and is now moving rapidly into the field of general health care. As each new function developed, it was usually proposed as an alternative to prior practice. Carl Rogers insisted (nondirectively, of course) that psychologists stop diagnosing the mental illnesses of patients and start providing therapeutic environments for clients. Behavioral approaches to treatment were advanced as alternatives to evocative psychotherapy. Family therapists proposed that the treatment of identified patients as individuals was a mistake and required that the family be treated as a system. Preventive community interventions have usually been proposed as replacements for individual meliorative treatments. Each new movement has attracted a group of enthusiasts who advance their own views militantly, oppose the views of the reactionary majority with varying degrees of intellectual contempt, and grow impatient when others do not come around to their views.

Most practicing psychologists, however, have not been swayed by the rhetoric of revolutionary leaders nor even by their data. Clinical psychologists did not stop giving tests when they started doing psychotherapy. Psychotherapists did not all switch to behavioral methods when behavior therapy came along. The charge into the community has not taken all professional psychologists away from individual treatment. The current emphasis on general health care will not stop psychologists from attending to mental health problems. Most practicing psychologists regard themselves as eclectic, ready to suit their practices to the differing needs of different clients and ready to incorporate new methods into their professional repertoires if they are convinced the changes are worth the cost. The field as a whole has not shifted radically from one view to another. It has simply grown larger and more diverse. Each new practice has been added to those before. Uneasy efforts toward conceptual integration have followed every technical advance, but conceptual unity has not been attained.

According to the claims of its educators, the domain of professional psychology is now approximately isomorphic with the universe of human experience. In the course of a recent self-study of schools of professional psychology (Callan et al., 1986) the mission statements of 29 members, associates, and affiliates of the National Council of Schools of Professional Psychology were examined. Objectives varied somewhat. Some schools emphasized work with individuals more than community intervention; others reversed the emphasis. The objectives of some schools were very broad; others were rather narrow. Taken as a whole, however, the aims of modern American professional schools seem ambitious if not downright grandiose. In aggregate, professional psychology is envisioned as the development and application of knowledge in the assessment and improvement of human function at the psychobiological, individual, group, organizational, and community levels; through direct service in all its forms, consultation in various modes, and public education; for the benefit of people of all ages, dispositions, and cultural backgrounds; and in all settings (mental health, medical and health maintenance, educational, corporate, military, and governmental) in which human conditions might be improved through application of psychological principles and procedures. The mission statements of professional schools typically claim that the procedures employed in accomplishing these objectives are, or should be, based in disciplined knowledge.

Few will contest the urge to extend professional psychology beyond the narrow limits imposed by its history as a testing trade or as a mental health profession. A compelling proposal for a more diverse discipline has recently been offered by Levy (1984). The "human services psychology" he outlines requires knowledge and skill in various modes of intervention over several levels of concern, from biopsychology to the community. The size of the field as Levy conceives it is therefore not much different from the domain as envisioned by the designers of professional schools. As Levy recognizes, however, extension of services carries risk of overextension. We may oversell poorly tested products. We may promise more than we can deliver. Adverse public reaction to the social programs of the 1960s should tell us how serious these mistakes can be. If we are to avoid the errors of the past, interventions must be planned rationally and wherever possible based on data rather than intuition. Any changes we attempt must be carefully appraised. All this requires an assessment technology whose current condition should cause us considerable concern.

SOME COMMENTS ON THE STATE OF ASSESSMENT TECHNOLOGY IN PROFESSIONAL PSYCHOLOGY

Ever since psychology broke away from philosophy a hundred years ago, researchers have been struggling to establish the field as a basic science. Comparing knowledge then with the knowledge that appears in any modern text will show that we have made some progress along this line. As Bevan (1976), Parloff (1980), Fishman and Neigher (1982), and others have pointed out, however, the eagerness among psychologists to advance as science may have led us to ignore our responsibilities for direct benefits to the larger society. No one can dispute successfully the importance of basic research. No one can require legitimately the immediate practical application of all research. Yet the worship of research for its own sake in modern American universities needs to be questioned.

Paul Meehl (1984b) has recently written a paper entitled "The Seven Sacred Cows of Academia: Can We Afford them?" In the paper, he lays out a set of beliefs that appear to be accepted by most academics without question, whose implementation costs a lot of money, but which may be, and very likely are, false. One of the propositions is, "Most research published by college professors is worthwhile." The average journal article in social science is read by fewer than 50 people. The most frequently read research articles in psychology may be seen by a maximum of 1,500 people (Darley, 1966). The problems of poor dissemination and low impact are not limited to the soft sciences. Enrico Fermi, upon hearing a colleague describe some unexciting but methodologically sound studies in physics as "bricks in the edifice of science," is reputed to have said that most of them were "just bricks lying around in the scientific brickyard" (Meehl, 1984a). The distinguished historian of science, Derek J. de Solla Price, after studying citation patterns in scientific journals, estimated that approximately 10% of published articles are not cited at all and 50% are cited fewer than five times in the ensuing decade. His report ends with the following lament. "I am tempted to conclude that a very large fraction of the alleged 35,000 journals now current must be reckoned as merely a distant background noise and as very far from central or strategic in any of the knitted strips from which the cloth of science is woven" (Price, 1965, p. 515). Over the 20 years since Price conducted his analysis, the number of scholarly and professional journals published worldwide has approximately doubled. It is likely that the sheer increase in the volume of written material has weakened still further the impact of most of the material that is put into print. These conditions, along with the haughty attitudes of scientists who pursue their esoteric interests aloof from the "noisy yammerings of the secular world" (Pàrloff, 1980) has turned much of the public against the work the scientists themselves consider so important. "These research projects are like exotic, expensively mounted butterfly collections, hidden away in vaults and only exhumed from time to time to display to other collectors of the rare and unusual in mutual reaffirmation of their elite status" (Representative Barbara Mikulski, 1979, quoted in Fishman & Neigher, 1982, p. 533).

The general public expects psychology to be useful. Those who represent the public and control our resources increasingly demand that psychology be useful now. Basic science, by itself, will not provide the needed applications. A profession linked as loosely to science as most of our practices are today will not provide dependably useful, cumulative improving applications. As Fishman and Neigher (1982) have argued and as they will propose further in the next chapter of this book, successful application of scientific knowledge requires a bridging technology. Before chemistry and physics can be employed for public benefit, the disciplines of engineering have to be established. Before the life sciences can be used to improve human health, the technologies of medicine have to be formed. Before psychological knowledge can be used to help people function more effectively, a technology of application must be developed.

Psychologists have been slow to realize that they need a technology, and the technologies they have produced so far are not well developed. Certainly the assessment technology currently available to practitioners leaves much to be desired. General appraisal of the state of psychological assessment across a full range of professional applications is impossible to accomplish here. Just one of the instruments (the Minnesota Multiphasic Personality Inventory) in one of the classes of procedures (tests) required for useful psychological assessment at just one level (individual) has inspired over 5,000 books and articles. When evaluative reviews of limited aspects of assessment are attempted, the conclusions of reviewers often vary widely. Anyone who reads Korchin and Schuldberg's (1981) article on the future of assessment in clinical psychology, for example, will receive the impression that continuing the kind of research that has filled our journals in the past will produce not only the technology we need but the basic scientific knowledge we all desire. Reading Rorer and Widiger's (1983) review of personality structure and assessment, on the other hand, will suggest that psychology is "burdened with an outmoded philosophy and a distorted view of science" that render currently accepted methodologies useless. My own views can claim no greater credibility than anybody else's. There are some areas of assessment methodology, such as neuropsychology and psychophysiology, that I am not qualified to evaluate. I am not closely familiar with professional specialties other than clinical psychology, as the emphasis in this chapter clearly reveals. In areas in which I have followed the literature in a fairly earnest way and have attempted some contributions of my own, however, namely personality assessment, behavioral assessment, and the assessment of interpersonal process, I believe our assessment technology is weak.

I recently had occasion to review two new textbooks in personality assessment. Both were revisions of earlier works. Comparing each book with its earlier edition provided an interesting opportunity to examine advances in personality assessment over the past 15 years. I concluded that enormous amounts of research on projective techniques had produced no new evidence of their validity or utility. My once-favored devices, structured personality tests, had also produced enormous literatures and an entirely new technology for automated interpretation, but no new studies had appeared to show that they were any more useful than before. Behavioral assessment, which I helped pioneer, offered greater promise, but the knowledge about generalizability and utility required for informed use of behavioral methods is still more a prospect than an accomplishment (Peterson, 1983).

In the field that has engaged all of my research effort over the past 10 years, the assessment of interpersonal behavior, I guarantee that our assessment methodology sorely needs improvement. Most practitioners doing family therapy do not even seem to realize that assessment is needed. The methods they employ, largely ad hoc interviews and simulations, are used unsystematically with no questions raised about dependability or generalizability, much less with data to show the merits of the methods. Progress has recently been made in conceptualizing interaction process in terms that lend themselves to sound assessment (e.g., Gottman, 1979; Kelley et al., 1983; Patterson, 1982). The assessment procedures of a few investigator-clinicians are beginning to show the qualities required of a well-developed technology (cf. Patterson, this volume). Capturing the subtleties of interpersonal process in ways that are both sensitive and dependable is an exceedingly difficult task, however, and no scholar familiar with the field will doubt that present methods are badly in need of improvement. I suspect the same can be said for assessment in the other areas to be considered in this book.

For all their flaws, however, the assessment technologies that psychologists can provide are the most promising to be seen on the scientific and professional horizons. At least we are aware of our problems. At least we recognize the need for improvement. Improving the technology of assessment over the full range of action in which professional psychologists are now engaged is a task in which academic and professional psychologists can work together to help the people who pay our bills. Every solid theoretical contribution can guide our conceptions. Every ecologically representative investigation can furnish needed facts about psychological process. One hundred years of work in assessment have given psychology a base of experience, conception, and strategy no other discipline can match.

Merely increasing the literature on presently available assessment procedures is not enough. Five thousand more reports of scales, scoring keys, and automated interpretive routines for the Minnesota Multiphasic Personality Inventory (MMPI) will not release us from the limits imposed by the basic data themselves. Structured personality tests evoke limited classes of verbal behavior in response to limited classes of verbal stimuli elicited at a single time and pertinent to inference of putatively stable personality traits typically treated as if they were independent of the environmental conditions under which psychological dispositions are expressed. No amount of sophisticated fiddling with test data will alter those constraints. Exner's (1974) comprehensive scoring system for the Rorschach test represents a decided technical advance over the several less consistent and reliable procedures previous investigators have employed, but so far I have seen no evidence to show that Exner's scales allow clinicians to infer psychodynamic characteristics with greater validity or predict behavior outside the test situation with greater accuracy than before. Rorschach protocols are still based on verbal responses to verbal instructions related to 10 pieces of stiff cardboard that are dyed in unusual ways. If practical decisions that affect human lives are to be based on information that is truly germane to those decisions, basic changes in conceptions and strategies of assessment are needed, not just growing piles of new techniques or ever bigger mountains of research on the same old procedures.

TOWARD MORE USEFUL PSYCHOLOGICAL ASSESSMENT

If psychological assessment is to become more useful than it has been in the past, basic changes are required in traditional approaches to the task. As I have indicated in several previous statements (e.g., Peterson, 1968, 1979), the following considerations appear fundamental.

1. *The ultimate goal of psychological assessment is to help people.* Most standard references (e.g., Anastasi, 1976; Cronbach, 1970; Wiggins, 1973) define psychological assessment very generally as the systematic collection of information about individual differences. Uses of information in predicting behavior are then noted, and the further use of predictions to inform decisions is ordinarily stipulated as the aim of assessment. The title of this book suggests that we have accepted traditional concepts as a framework for our own discussions.

If the public benefits of assessment are to be improved, however, a change of focus is required. Defining assessment as the collection of information about individual differences directs attention to the aims of the *assessor.* Psychologists are interested in predicting behavior, for their own purposes and to aid administrative decisions of executives in organizations. It is not always clear, however, that a second-grade girl who has just had her IQ tested will benefit from the information, or that a male adolescent whose test results suggest a high risk of delinquency will be better off because a predictive statement to that effect has entered his file at school. Defining the aims of assessment as the description and prediction of behavior to aid rational decision directs attention toward the objectives of the examiner. If assessment is to be used for the good of others, more emphasis must be placed on risks and benefits to the people who are being assessed.

My cardiologist recently suggested that I undergo a coronary arteriogram. I had experienced some mild chest pains during strenuous exertion (swinging a scythe to clear high grass from a pasture) and this, along with a history of vaguely similar episodes and some equivocal results from electrocardiographic tracings during a stress test, led my physician to propose a more invasive but more precise examination.

Coronary angiography requires insertion of a catheter through a large artery in the leg, pushing the tube through the arteries to the heart, injecting some dye, and use of X-ray or related machinery to provide a visual display of the flow of blood through the arterial system that supplies blood to the heart muscle. The procedure is a triumph of modern medical technology. There is no question about its value as a tool in the science and practice of medicine. The immediate question that concerned me, however, was whether or not to go along with my physician's proposal to employ the procedure in my case. The more general question was, What considerations guide a decision of this kind?

To the physician, benefits fall heavily on the side of performing the exam. With the information, she would be able to predict my behavior (evaluate risks of coronary infarction) more accurately than before. Given that prediction, decisions about treatment (medication, possible by-pass surgery) could be based on presumably sound, scientific data. Besides, as physician in charge of catheterization, she would receive a high cut of the financial proceeds. She would also be less liable to litigation should I suffer a heart attack and initiate a malpractice suit, claiming that she should have known I was endangered.

But what would be the risks and benefits to me? For an otherwise healthy man my age, the mortality rates are low. However, about 5% of patients suffer heart attacks or other complications during the examination. The procedure is expensive, over $1,500 on the average, once admission charges, hospital costs, and the fees of the physician and radiologist are taken into account. My insurance carrier is not very generous in paying for elective diagnostic procedures, so much of the charge would be paid from my own pocket. Above all, it was not at all clear to me that I needed the information angiography would provide to reach the decisions that matter to me. I already knew that some occlusion had occurred in my coronary arteries. Given my age, sex, occupation, dietary history, and above all the experience of angina, I could not imagine that the arteriogram would be entirely clear. Suppose it showed some occlusion. What then? Would I consider by-pass surgery? I strongly suspect that large numbers of unnecessary by-pass operations are recommended each year, with cloudy angiograms as a documentary base. Doctors gain from these; patients lose. Were there other measures I might take with or without arteriographic examination? Of course there were. I could walk two miles a day instead of one, take off some extra weight, control my diet, and reduce the stress of my work schedule. To me, the balance of advantage fell against the exam. I decided at least to defer coronary arteriography until I had given more conservative measures a chance to improve my health.

Similar questions need to be raised about the uses of psychological assessment. Who gains from it? In a later chapter of this book, Gordon Paul notes that about 25% of staff time in residential treatment centers for mentally disabled people is devoted to "documentation." People working in mental hospitals spend one-quarter of their time recording information of one kind or another and moving the information around in one way or another. Who benefits from all the paper work? Do people get better because of it? Paul shows convincingly that they do not in traditionally managed psychiatric institutions. I suspect that comparable conditions hold for other populations and other settings. More than 20 years ago, Meehl (1960) reported that 83% of psychotherapists who had been surveyed on the values of psychological assessment did not consider the personality tests commonly employed in clinical practice to be useful guides for treatment. There is no reason to suppose that figure would be different today. The revolutionary character of Gordon Paul's work flows from the radical premise with which it begins. The fundamental aim of a residential treatment center, says Paul, is *treatment*. He then seeks the kinds of information needed to help the staff help the clients function more effectively. From neuropsychological examination to the study of corporate operations, traditional assessments have rarely been useful in helping those who are assessed, as Buffery in the one case and Gilbert in the other will make clear in following chapters of this book. All too often, assessment practices are driven by the needs of the assessors, not the needs of the assessed. The ultimate aim of assessment is not to predict behavior, not to derive rational decisions, not to measure dependent and independent variables so that investigators can do research, publish reports, and gain academic promotions. The ultimate aim of assessment is to help people.[2] The value of assessment would be improved enormously if everyone who ever set out to study any other person, group, or organization first asked a brief series of questions: Will the appraisal I am about to conduct really help the people I am examining? If not, why am I doing it? What might I do that would help people? How can I gain the information I need to accomplish that aim?

2. *The most useful assessments in psychology are linked with change.* Focus on assessees rather than assessors as the ultimate beneficiaries of assessment information leads to another proposition. Assessment operations increase in value to the extent that they are linked systematically with change procedures. The consumers of assessment data do not ordinarily seek the services of psychologists unless they are considering some kind of change. Either something is wrong and needs

to be corrected, or something is not working as well as it might and needs to be improved. Emphasis on the connection between assessment and change has not characterized most assessment efforts in the past, but is strongly represented in this book. In the third chapter, Buffery notes that patients who have suffered brain damage do not need neuropsychological examinations so much to determine the location and exent of brain damage as to guide programs of rehabilitation. Psychophysiological assessment is of less value in judging the guilt or innocence of criminal suspects than in guiding the health-giving regimes of behavioral medicine (Katkin, Chapter 4). Psychological assessment in mental health settings is most useful when it is specifically geared to treatment (Paul, Chapter 5). Fowler and his colleagues were asked to develop a classification system for Alabama prisoners not to serve the correctional bureaucracy but to relieve the assaults and other inhumanities prisoners were suffering (Chapter 6). Patterson studies interaction patterns in families not only to elaborate scientific constructs but to reduce aggressive behavior among children and adolescents (Chapter 7). Hackman and Helmreich are trying to assess team performance of airline cockpit crews in hope of reducing the risk of deadly crashes (Chapter 8). Complexities and ambiguities aside, Broskowski employs performance indicators to evaluate the function of mental health centers most valuably to improve the effectiveness of the organizations (Chapter 9). Assessing performance in the workplace is useful to the extent that it is employed in improving performance and increasing productivity (Gilbert, Chapter 10).

Even decisions that appear to carry no prospect of change gain value if they are considered in light of the inevitability of change in the human process, and if they are directed toward conditions that facilitate or impede constructive change. Assessment for decision in a child custody case, for example, is not aimed directly toward treatment of the child. However, the welfare of the child is the issue of prime concern for court decision, and assessment directed toward the prospective influence of alternative environments on the psychological development of the child will be more useful to the judge than any characterization of personality dynamics can possibly be. Since constructive change is the aim of most if not all psychological assessment, assessment programs that are linked systematically with change procedures are likely to carry the highest values to consumers.

3. *The design and evaluation of change programs require study of psychological function over time.* This means more than measurement of trait or state variables on more than one occasion. The move from

the study of conditions to the study of processes requires a fundamental shift in perspective. A neurosis is not constructively viewed as a condition caused by some set of historical antecedents. A neurosis is more usefully regarded as a pattern of recurrent aversive actions developed through repeated interactions between a person and his or her environment, and subject to change if the patterns of interaction are altered. A faltering corporation is most constructively seen, not as an entity endangered by adverse economic conditions, but as a living organization in which some functional processes are not working as well as they might. In general, psychological change procedures are most powerfully conceived as influences deliberately brought to bear on the continuing functional processes of living systems so as to deflect the courses the systems would follow if additional influences were not exerted. In all cases, at all levels, intervention can be seen as the interruption of natural process.

In order to determine where and how to introduce an intervention, as well as to determine any effect the intervention may have, it is essential first to study the process by which the system functions. Attempts toward psychological treatment of depression, for example, must begin with study of the depressive episodes experienced by the patient. The situations in which episodes begin, the ensuing interactions of thought, feeling, and behavior, and the courses of episodes to their various conclusions must all be described. It is not enough to know how depressed the patient is, nor even the particular symptom syndrome the patient displays. Marital counseling with couples who fight a lot does not benefit greatly from aggregate measures of marital satisfaction or role relations. Interventions are more profitably guided by detailed study of recurrent interaction patterns through which the initiating circumstances, the processes of communication, and the outcomes of conflicts can be described.

The basic data for studies of process are events observed in sequence over time. The appropriate investigative designs for most of the questions that arise are those of single-subject inquiry, whether the subjects are persons, groups, or organizations. The appropriate procedures for analyzing data are those of sequential probability and time series analyses. A fitting metaphor is the motion picture rather than the still photograph. The change in perspective required to examine process rather than condition is as fundamental as the difference between Aristotelian and Galilean modes of thought brought to the attention of twentieth-century psychologists by Lewin (1935). Aristotle viewed a ball on a string as a stationary mass suspended between two opposing forces, the attraction of the earth pulling in one direction and the constraint of the string pulling in the other. Galileo considered what happens when a ball is pushed. The ball begins to swing in a regular way. The latter view and not the former led to the laws of pendular motion and eventually to the physics and the engineering technology upon which the Industrial Revolution was based.

4. *The scope of assessment in applied psychology must be broad enough to include all functionally significant influences.* Applied science begins in the problems and opportunities of natural events. Nature is taken as it comes, in all its complexity. In the case of living systems, functional processes are examined as they occur. All influences that affect the natural course of events to a significant degree must be taken into account. Contextual influences, if they affect the processes under consideration to any material degree, cannot be seen as extraneous.

Extending the bounds of inquiry to include all important sources of variation, as responsible professional inquiry requires, sets professional assessment apart from scientific measurement in important ways. If environmental influences affect behavior as much as internal dispositions do, environmental influences may not be ignored in comprehensive, practically useful psychological inquiries. If behavior studied at one level is materially affected by influences that arise at another level, the latter influences must be taken into account. Thus, if the effective conduct of a neuropsychological rehabilitation program depends on the active cooperation of at least one member of a patient's family, assessment for rehabilitation planning cannot be restricted to neuropsychological functioning alone, but must be extended to include the availability of family supports. If a clinician working with an individual patient within a behavioral framework sees undeniable clinical evidence of the operation of unconscious mental processes in determining the pattern of symptomatology the patient displays, the clinician is ethically bound to take those influences into serious account, whatever his or her prior theoretical predilections may be, and whatever laboratory studies may purport to show about the occurrence or nonoccurrence of unconscious processes. If the study of communication patterns among members of airline cockpit crews suggests that team performance depends in part on implicit rules that govern the larger organization in which the team operates, practically useful assessment requires study of organizational function as well as team performance. If the success of a program initiated by leaders of a community mental health center requires acceptance and support of the surrounding community, planning the program must include appraisal of prospects of community support.

Some year ago, Cronbach and Gleser (1965) wrote cogently about the "bandwidth-fidelity" dilemma in psychological assessment. Applying an analogy from Shannon's information theory of electronic communication, they suggested that the scope and accuracy of assessment in psychology are inversely related. Given constrained investments of time and effort, one can study phenomena within a narrow range precisely, or phenomena over a broad range inexactly, but the goal of precise measurement over a broad range is unattainable.

Fiske (1978) has declared that psychology will never become a true science until basic data are based on observations rather than interpretations of events and until observations among multiple observers are interchangeable, that is, until reliability coefficients of the usual kind approach 1.0. Now and then, reproducibility at this level is attained in practical, decision-focused assessment (cf. Paul, this volume). More often, however, practitioners studying complex phenomena over the full range needed to accommodate the influences that affect the processes they are examining are forced to settle for interpretations and approximations. This does not necessarily mean that they are going "soft." It only means that the demands of application are not entirely the same as those of science, and that anyone who takes on the job of assessing functional processes as they occur in nature will usually have to act on some data that fall short of the ideals of precision a science may require.

5. *The referent for practically useful assessment is behavior in natural settings.* Study of functional processes as they occur in nature demands that people, groups, and organizations be observed in their natural environments. This is true by definition, and would not be worth mentioning were it not for the fact that most psychological assessment as currently conducted in professional psychology is not directed toward the study of behavior in natural surroundings. Artificial stimuli, such as tests, are employed in unusual situations, such as the offices of practitioners, to obtain samples of behavior from which inferences are drawn about behavior in natural settings.

Unless the link between test behavior and behavior outside the test situation is strongly formed, that is, unless the generalizability of test behavior has been carefully mapped, this is risky practice. Tests, interviews, and other restricted samples of behavior may offer very efficient means of estimating behavior over wide ranges of the natural environment. The use of tests as estimates of behavior in natural settings is only justified, however, to the extent that relations between test and nontest behavior are known.

In respect to ecological validity in regard to reproducibility, demands for broad scope ordinarily require compromise. Perfect reliability can be attained in principle and is sometimes approached in fact. Complete knowledge about generalizability can never be obtained in principle. Until at least some facts about generalizability are known, however, there is no substitute for direct observation in natural settings. All estimates must be taken cautiously.

6. *For practical assessment, use of multiple measures is necessary in principle.* As anyone who has tried it will attest, the study of functional processes in natural settings is a formidable task. Standard procedures designed for research or the measurement of static characteristics are usually irrelevant or inadequate, so special methods must often be constructed ad hoc. If any confidence is to be placed in the new procedures, their psychometric qualities must then be appraised (see Gordon Paul's discussion of the "four R's" of utility evaluation in Chapter 5). Although some aspects of psychometric quality can be examined with only one procedure as a data source (e.g., internal consistency as a way of estimating replicability, some components of relative cost), most of the qualities that matter in gauging the practical utility of a method (representativeness, relevance) cannot be studied unless at least two procedures are employed.

Even the most carefully conducted observational methods, centered on important aspects of behavioral process under ecologically representative conditions, cannot alone provide the information required to appraise the quality of the methods themselves. All sciences are indeterminate, but the problems of indeterminacy are particularly severe in psychology because human beings appear to react more strongly to observation than do other animal species or physical objects, and the unavoidable reactivities of observational intrusion are bound to influence findings. Furthermore, most observational procedures are restricted to explicitly observable behavior. To the extent that covert activities such as thoughts and feelings influence behavioral outcomes or are themselves regarded as significant aspects of psychological process, direct observational coding procedures omit important information, a condition that is less forgivable in professional inquiry than it is in science. In principle, there is no escape from the need for multiple data sources in developing practically useful assessment methodologies.

It is commonplace to urge those developing assessment procedures to employ "converging operations" in "triangulating" the phenomena they are trying to measure. This is helpful advice, but often leads to consternation when measures do not converge as expected. When that happens, any of several conditions may prevail. Among major alternatives, the measures themselves may be unreliable, the operations on which they are based may be improperly linked with the constructs they were designed to measure, or independent constructs may be involved. Empirical choice among those alternatives cannot be made except by comparing propositions based on multiple data sources. In developing useful assessment methodologies, the demand for at least two operations per construct cannot be avoided.

7. *Progressive improvement of assessment technology is advanced by grounding operations in sensible conceptions of functional process.* Every procedure ever used to study behavior began in some conception of human nature, however simple or elaborate the conception might have been. Even the psychometric products of "dust bowl empiricism," such as the MMPI, were derived from prior conceptions—in the case of the MMPI, from the system of psychiatric classification on which the nine clinical scales of the original instrument were based. If the proposals offered above have any merit, however, some conceptions are preferable to others as bases for a more useful assessment technology. The more promising conceptions are those linking functional processes of behavior to change in the natural environment. The conceptions may be very simple, though their basic premises are often contrary to common belief or ordinary practice. The functional conception that undergirds Paul's highly successful social learning program for long-term psychiatric residents, for example, is that systematic social reinforcement of alternatives to "crazy" behavior will reduce rates of the latter and increase rates of socially acceptable behavior. No one who knows anything about the psychology of learning would dispute that principle nor call for another demonstration of its validity. The value of Paul's treatment program lies in its reversal of common hospital practice, in which sane behavior, unremarkable and hence untroublesome to the staff, is typically ignored, and displays of crazy behavior are systematically reinforced by increased attention from the staff (Paul & Lentz, 1977). A common parental response to child aggression is erratic physical punishment. Patterson has shown that the aggressive actions of children and the responses of parents are systematically related in mutually coercive patterns that maintain or increase child aggression, which reduces when parental actions change (Patterson, 1982). In Patterson's work as in Paul's, assessment technologies were initially inspired

by relatively simple conceptions of behavior. Enormous investments of time and effort were then required to develop suitably dependable and useful procedures. Once those investments were made, however, the conceptions on which the procedures were based could be refined (cf. the "bootstrapping" process discussed by Patterson in Chapter 7).

Psychology has not settled on a single paradigm within which its inquiries may proceed and its conceptions develop. The theoretical antinomies that divide the field, the methodological divergences that lead one set of investigators in one direction and others in a different direction, clearly place psychology at a preparadigmatic stage as Kuhn (1962) views evolution of the natural sciences. Indeed serious questions can be raised about the very idea of a single paradigm for psychology (e.g., Koch, 1981). Perhaps we are doomed by the nature of our subject matter to wallow forever in an aparadigmatic or multiparadigmatic morass. For all that, some conceptions lend themselves readily to the aims of practical assessment. The general conceptions of social behavior articulated by Bandura (1977), Kelley et al. (1983), and others furnish a reasonably sturdy framework within which assessment methodologies of the kinds to be presented in this book can be articulated. The assessment and treatment strategies of Arnold Lazarus (1981) are coordinated with a relatively simple, straightforward conception of psychosocial behavior. It seems possible that the psychodynamic but not traditionally psychoanalytic formulations of Kohut (1977), Schafer (1976), and others will furnish the conceptual groundwork for an assessment methodology to illuminate the darker corners of mental process with less murk and mess than the earlier theories produced. A general and powerful conception of psychological process in human development is seen in the interactional perspective represented most persuasively by Magnusson and his colleagues (Magnusson, 1985, in press; Magnusson & Endler, 1977). The emphases on longitudinal study, on observation and description of person-situation interactions, and on integration of observations over multiple systemic levels in Magnusson's designs are important not only for basic research but for the construction of practically useful assessment methods.

The substantive specificity of the concepts that ground a useful assessment methodology need not be closely refined. The concepts need only tell the investigator where to look, not what the search will reveal. If conceptions are sensibly chosen at the beginning, if assessment technologies are developed with persistence and care, and if the conceptions are continually tested and revised as data suggest, theory and practice gain from each other.

8. *If psychologists do not develop more useful assessment procedures on their own initiative, others will require it of them.* Whether psychologists devote their energies to the development and application of a technology of assessment will be determined only in part by their own inclinations. Pressures imposed by the larger society will also play a part. At the very time assessment procedures came into full use by American psychologists to select pilots during the Second World War, the German assessment program for selecting air force officers was abandoned. According to Fitts (1946) the German program was opposed by Prussian and Nazi generals alike. The Prussians thought long family traditions of military service should offer access to the officer elite. The Nazis wanted to reward membership in Hitler youth groups. To the Germans, either historical condition mattered more than tested aptitude.

Here, today, the age of accountability is upon us. All decisions require assessment. Even maintaining the status quo in a treatment program, a system for selecting corporate managers, or any other form of deliberate human action is based on the implicit appraisal that operating routines are superior to alternatives. More and more, in our place and time, decisions must be publicly justified, and justifications based on dependable facts are credited more than expert opinions. Political and economic demands to show what we are doing are strong and growing stronger. Limited as our present methods may be for assessing human function, they are better than any available alternatives. If we are honest about our limits and creative in our efforts to improve, there is reason to believe we can offer methods for studying human behavior that are more useful than any known before in aiding the decisions our society requires.

NOTES

1. The distribution of activities is skewed in the direction of psychotherapy and away from other activities by the preponderance of clinical psychologists in professional psychology. In other specialties, different allocations of time are seen. School psychologists, for example, still devote most of their attentions to the individual assessment of exceptional students (Smith, 1984). Throughout this chapter, major emphasis is placed on clinical psychology, the largest and most conspicuous of the specialties in professional psychology. Not everything that is said about clinical psychology holds equally for other fields of application, though most of the issues addressed are of concern to the profession as a whole.

2. Conflicts often arise when one person, group, or organization is examined at the behest of another. Assessment of prisoners in correctional settings, for instance, will not always work to the benefit of each and every inmate. Conflicts of these kinds are not resolved by pious injunctions to help people. It seems likely, however, that ethical decisions in balancing costs and benefits among competing constituents will be reached more fairly if a prior shift has occurred away from the aims of the investigator toward the aims of consumers.

REFERENCES

Ackerman, N. (1958). *The psychodynamics of family life.* New York: Basic Books.

Albee, G. W. (1982). The uncertain direction of clinical psychology. In J. R. McNamara & A. G. Barclay (Eds.), *Critical issues, developments, and trends in professional psychology.* New York: Praeger.

Alexander, J. F., & Barton, C. (1976). Behavioral systems therapy for families. In D. H. L. Olson (Ed.), *Treating relationships.* Lake Mills, Iowa: Graphic Publishing.

Anastasi, A. (1976). *Psychological testing* (4th ed.). New York: Macmillan.

Arkowitz, H., & Messer, S. B. (1984). *Psychoanalytic therapy and behavior therapy: Is integration possible?* New York: Plenum.

Bach, G. R. (1967). Marathon group dynamics: II. Dimensions of helpfulness: Therapeutic aggression. *Psychological Reports, 20,* 1147–1158.

Bandura, A. (1969). *Principles of behavior modification.* New York: Holt, Rinehart & Winston.

Bandura, A. (1977). *Social learning theory.* Englewood Cliffs, N.J.: Prentice-Hall.

Bateson, G., Jackson, D. D., Haley, J., & Weakland, J. H. (1956). Toward a theory of schizophrenia. *Behavioral Science, 1,* 251–264.

Bell, N. W., & Spiegel, J. P. (1966). Social psychiatry: Vagaries of a term. *Archives of General Psychiatry, 14,* 337–345.

Bender, L. (1937). Group activities on a children's ward as methods of psychotherapy. *American Journal of Psychiatry, 93,* 151–173.

Bennett, C. C. (1965). Community psychology: Impressions of the Boston conference on the education of psychologists for community mental health. *American Psychologist, 20,* 832–835.

Berne, E. (1966). *Principles of group treatment.* New York: Oxford University Press.

Bevan, W. (1976). The sound of the wind that's blowing. *American Psychologist, 31,* 481–489.

Bijou, S. W. (1955). A systematic approach to an experimental analysis of young children. *Child Development, 26,* 161–168.

Birchler, G. R., & Spinks, S. (1980). Behavioral-systems marital and family therapy: Integration and clinical applications. *American Journal of Family Therapy, 8,* 6–28.

Bloom, B. L. (1973). The domain of community psychology. *American Journal of Community Psychology, 1,* 8–11.

Bloom, B. L. (1980). Social and community intervention. *Annual Review of Psychology, 31,* 111–142.

Brady, J. P. (1977). Concluding remarks. In R. B. Williams & W. D. Gentry (Eds.), *Behavioral approaches to medical treatment.* Cambridge, Mass.: Ballinger.

Callan, J., Peterson, D. R., & Stricker, G. (Eds.). (1986). *Quality in training professional psychologists: A national conference and self study.* Washington, D.C.: National Council of Schools of Professional Psychology.

Ciminero, A. R., Calhoun, K. S., & Adams, H. E. (Eds.). (1977). *Handbook of behavioral assessment.* New York: Wiley.

Cowen, E. L. (1973). Social and community interventions. *Annual Review of Psychology, 24,* 423–472.

Cronbach, L. J. (1970). *Essentials of psychological testing* (3rd ed.). New York: Harper & Row.

Cronbach, L. J., Ambron, S. R., Dornbusch, S. M., Hess, R. D., Hornik, R. C., Phillips, D. C., Walker, D. F., & Weiner, S. S. (1980). *Toward reform of program evaluation.* San Francisco: Jossey-Bass.

Cronbach, L. J., & Gleser, G. C. (1965). *Psychological tests and personnel decisions* (2nd ed.). Urbana: University of Illinois Press.

Cummings, N. A., & Follette, W. T. (1976). Brief psychotherapy and medical utilization: An eight-year follow-up. In H. Dorken & associates (Eds.), *The professional psychologist today: New developments in law, health insurance, and health practice.* San Francisco: Jossey-Bass.

Darley, J. G. (1966). Information exchange problems in psychology. *Proceedings of 1965 Congress, International Federation for Documentation.* Washington, D.C.: Spartan Books.

Dollard, J., & Miller, N. (1950). *Personality and psychotherapy.* New York: McGraw-Hill.

DuBois, P. H. (1970). *A history of psychological testing.* Boston: Allyn & Bacon.

Elliott, C. H. (1983). Behavioral medicine: Background and implications. In C. E. Walker (Ed.), *The handbook of clinical psychology: Theory, research, and practice.* Homewood, Ill.: Dow Jones-Irwin.

Exner, J. E. (1974). *The Rorschach: A comprehensive system.* New York: Wiley.

Eysenck, H. J. (1952). The effects of psychotherapy: An evaluation. *Journal of Consulting Psychology, 16,* 319–324.

Feldman, L. B. (1979). Marital conflict and marital intimacy: An integrative psychodynamic-behavioral-systemic model. *Family Process, 18,* 69–78.

Fishman, D. B., & Neigher, W. D. (1982). American psychology in the eighties: Who will buy? *American Psychologist, 37,* 533–546.

Fiske, D. W. (1978). *Strategies for personality research.* San Francisco: Jossey-Bass.

Fitts, D. M. (1946). German applied psychology during World War II. *American Psychologist, 1,* 151–161.

Fox, R. E. (1982). The need for a reorientation of clinical psychology. *American Psychologist, 37,* 1051–1057.

Franks, C. M. & Wilson, G. T. (1973). *Annual review of behavior therapy: Theory and practice* (Vol. 1). New York: Brunner/Mazel.

Freud, S. (1927). *The problem of lay analysis.* New York: Brentano's.

Galton, F. (1883). *Inquiries into human faculty and its development.* London: Macmillan.

Garfield, S. L., & Kurtz, R. (1976). Clinical psychology in the 1970s. *American Psychologist, 31,* 1–9.

Goldfried, M. R. (1982). *Converging themes in psychotherapy: Trends in psychodynamic, humanistic, and behavioral practice.* New York: Springer.

Goldfried, M. R., & D'Zurilla, T. J. (1969). A behavior-analytic model for assessing competence. In C. D. Spielberger (Ed.), *Current topics in clinical and community psychology* (Vol. 1). New York: Academic Press.

Gottman, J. M. (1979). *Marital interaction: Experimental investigations.* New York: Academic Press.

Gruen, W. (1975). Effects of brief psychotherapy during the hospitalization period on the recovery process in heart attacks. *Journal of Consulting and Clinical Psychology, 43,* 223–232.

Gurman, A. S., & Kniskern, D. P. (1978). Research on marital and family therapy: Progress, perspective, and prospect. In S. L. Garfield & A. E. Bergin (Eds.), *Handbook of psychotherapy and behavior change: An empirical analysis* (2nd ed.). New York: Wiley.

Haley, J. (1976). *Problem-solving therapy.* San Francisco: Jossey-Bass.

Hersen, M., & Bellak, A. S. (Eds.). (1976). *Behavioral assessment: A practical handbook.* New York: Pergamon.

Hobbs, N. (1964). Mental health's third revolution. *American Journal of Orthopsychiatry, 34,* 1–20.

Iscoe, I., & Harris, L. C. (1984). Social and community interventions. *Annual Review of Psychology, 35,* 333–360.

Jones, M. C. (1924). The elimination of children's fears. *Journal of experimental psychology, 7,* 382–390.

Kanfer, F. H., & Phillips, J. S. (1970). *Learning foundations of behavior therapy.* New York: Wiley.

Kanfer, F. H., & Saslow, G. (1969). Behavioral diagnosis. In C. M. Frank (Ed.), *Behavior therapy: Appraisal and status.* New York: McGraw-Hill.

Kaplan, R. M. (1984). The connection between clinical health promotion and health status: A critical overview. *American Psychologist, 39,* 755–765.

Kazdin, A. E., & Wilson, G. T. (1978). *Evaluation of behavior therapy: Issues, evidence, and research strategies.* Cambridge, Mass.: Ballinger.

Kelley, H. H., Berscheid, E., Christensen, A., Harvey, J. H., Huston, T. L., Levinger, G., McClintock, E., Peplau, L. A., & Peterson, D. R. (1983). *Close relationships.* New York: Freeman.

Kelly, E. L., & Goldberg, L. R. (1959). Correlates of later performance and specialization in psychology: A follow-up study of the trainees assessed in the VA Selection Research Project. *Psychological Monographs, 73* (12, Whole No. 482).

Kirsch, I., & Winter, C. (1983). A history of clinical psychology. In C. E. Walker (Ed.), *The handbook of clinical psychology: Theory, research, and practice.* Homewood, Ill: Dow Jones-Irwin.

Koch, S. (1981). The nature and limits of psychological knowledge: Lessons from a century qua "science." *American Psychologist, 36,* 257–269.

Kohut, H. (1977). *The restoration of the self.* New York: International Universities Press.

Korchin, S. J. (1976). *Modern clinical psychology: Principles of intervention in the clinic and community.* New York: Basic Books.

Korchin, S. J., & Schuldberg, D. (1981). The future of clinical assessment. *American Psychologist, 36,* 1147–1158.

Krumboltz, J. D. (Ed.). (1966). *Revolution in counseling: Implications of behavioral science.* Boston: Houghton Mifflin.

Kuhn, T. S. (1962). *The structure of scientific revolutions.* Chicago: University of Chicago Press.

Lang, P. J., Lazovick, A. D., & Reynolds, D. J. (1965). Desensitization, suggestibility, and pseudotherapy. *Journal of Abnormal Psychology, 70,* 395–402.

Lazarus, A. A. (1971). *Behavior therapy and beyond.* New York: McGraw-Hill.

Lazarus, A. A. (1981). *The practice of multimodal therapy.* New York: McGraw-Hill.

Levitt, E. E. (1957). The results of psychotherapy with children: An evaluation. *Journal of Consulting Psychology, 21,* 189–196.

Levy, L. H. (1962). The skew in clinical psychology. *American Psychologist, 17,* 244–249.

Levy, L. H. (1984). The metamorphosis of clinical psychology: Toward a new charter as human services psychology. *American Psychologist, 39,* 486–494.

Lewin, K. (1935). *A dynamic theory of personality.* New York: McGraw-Hill.

Lieberman, M. A., Yalom, I. D., & Miles, M. B. (1973). *Encounter groups: First facts.* New York: Basic Books.

Little, K. B., & Schneidman, E. S. (1959). Congruencies among interpretations of psychological test and anamnestic data. *Psychological Monographs, 73* (6, Whole No. 476).

Magnusson, D. (1985). Implications of an interactional paradigm for research on human development. *International Journal of Behavioral Development, 8*, 115–137.

Magnusson, D. (in press). *Individual development and adjustment.* Hillsdale, N.J.: Erlbaum.

Magnusson, D., & Endler, N. S. (1977). *Personality at the crossroads: Current issues in interactional psychology.* Hillsdale, N.J.: Erlbaum.

Maslow, A. H. (1962). *Toward a psychology of being.* Princeton, N.J.: Van Nostrand.

Matarazzo, J. D. (1980). Behavioral health and behavioral medicine: Frontiers for a new health psychology. *American Psychologist, 35*, 807–817.

McReynolds, P. (1975). *Historical antecedents of personality assessment.* In P. McReynolds (Ed.), *Advances in psychological assessment* (Vol. 3). San Francisco: Jossey-Bass.

Meehl, P. E. (1954). *Clinical versus statistical prediction: A theoretical analysis and a review of the evidence.* Minneapolis: University of Minnesota Press.

Meehl, P. E. (1956). Wanted—a good cookbook. *American Psychologist, 11*, 263–272.

Meehl, P. E. (1960). The cognitive activity of the clinician. *American Psychologist, 15*, 19–27.

Meehl, P. E. (1984a). Are faculty salaries held down by faculty dogmas? Unpublished paper, University of Minnesota.

Meehl, P. E. (1984b). The seven sacred cows of academia: Can we afford them? Unpublished paper, University of Minnesota.

Messer, S. B., & Winokur, M. (1980). Some limits to the integration of psychoanalytic and behavior therapy. *American Psychologist, 35*, 818–827.

Miller, J. G. (1946). Clinical psychology in the Veterans Administration. *American Psychologist, 1*, 181–189.

Mischel, W. (1968). *Personality and assessment.* New York: Wiley.

Mowrer, O. H. (1950). *Learning theory and personality dynamics.* New York: Ronald.

Mowrer, O. H., & Mowrer, W. A. (1938). Enuresis: a method for its study and treatment. *American Journal of Orthopsychiatry, 8*, 436–447.

Olbrisch, M. E. (1977). Psychotherapeutic intervention in physical health. *American Psychologist, 32*, 761–777.

O'Leary, K. D., & O'Leary, S. G. (1972). *Classroom management: The successful use of behavior modification.* New York: Pergamon.

Parloff, M. B. (1980). Psychotherapy and research: An anaclitic depression. *Psychiatry, 43*, 279–293.

Patterson, G. R. (1982). *Coercive family process.* Eugene, Oreg.: Castalia.

Paul, G. L. (1966). *Insight versus desensitization in psychotherapy: An experiment in anxiety reduction.* Stanford: Stanford University Press.

Paul, G. L., & Lentz, R. J. (1977). *Psychosocial treatment of chronic mental patients: Milieu versus social-learning programs.* Cambridge, Mass.: Harvard University Press.

Perloff, R., Perloff, E., & Sussna, E. (1976). Program evaluation. *Annual Review of Psychology, 27,* 569–594.

Perls, F. S. (1969). *Gestalt therapy verbatim.* Lafayette, Calif.: Real People Press.

Peterson, D. R. (1968). *The clinical study of social behavior.* New York: Appleton-Century-Crofts.

Peterson, D. R. (1979). Assessing interpersonal relationships in natural settings. *New Directions for Methodology of Behavioral Science, 2,* 33–54.

Peterson, D. R. (1983). Clear pictures of a dreary landscape. *Contemporary Psychology, 28,* 784–785.

Peterson, D. R., Eaton, M. M., Levine, A. R., & Snepp, F. P. (1982). Career experiences of doctors of psychology. *Professional Psychology, 13,* 268–277.

Price, D. J. de S. (1965). Networks of scientific papers. *Science, 149,* 510–515.

Rachman, S. J., & Wilson, G. T. (1980). *The effects of psychological therapy* (2nd enlarged ed.). New York: Pergamon.

Reisman, J. M. (1966). *The development of clinical psychology.* New York: Appleton-Century-Crofts.

Rogers, C. R. (1942). *Counseling and psychotherapy: New concepts in practice.* Boston: Houghton Mifflin.

Rogers, C. R. (1951). *Client-centered therapy.* Boston: Houghton Mifflin.

Rogers, C. R. (1957). The necessary and sufficient conditions of therapeutic-personality change. *Journal of Counseling Psychology, 21,* 95–103.

Rogers, C. R. (1961). *On becoming a person.* Boston: Houghton Mifflin.

Rogers, C. R. (1970). *Carl Rogers on encounter groups.* New York: Harper & Row.

Rorer, L. G., & Widiger, T. A. (1983). Personality structure and assessment. *Annual Review of Psychology, 34,* 431–464.

Rosen, J., & Weins, A. (1979). Changes in medical problems and the use of medical services following psychological intervention. *American Psychologist, 34,* 420–431.

Sarason, S. B. (1981). An asocial psychology and misdirected clinical psychology. *American Psychologist, 36,* 827–836.

Schafer, R. (1976). *A new language for psychoanalysis.* New Haven: Yale University Press.

Sechrest, L., Ametrano, I. M., & Ametrano, D. A. (1982). Program evaluation. In J. R. McNamara & A. G. Barclay (Eds.), *Critical issues, developments, and trends in professional psychology.* New York: Praeger.

Sines, L. K. (1959). The relative contributions of four kinds of data to accuracy in personality assessment. *Journal of Consulting Psychology, 23,* 483–492.

Skinner, B. F. (1953). *Science and human behavior.* New York: Free Press.

Skinner, B. F., Solomon, H. C., & Lindsley, O. R. (November 1953). Studies in behavioral therapy. Status Report I. Waltham, Mass.: Metropolitan State Hospital.

Slavson, A. R. (1943). *An introduction to group therapy.* New York: Commonwealth Fund.

Smith, D. K. (1984). Practicing school psychologists: Their characteristics, activities, and populations served. *Professional Psychology, 15,* 798–810.

Staats, A. W. (1983). *Psychology's crisis of disunity: Philosophy and method for a unified science.* New York: Praeger.

Stapp, J., Fulcher, K., Nelson, S. D., Pallak, M. S., & Wicherski, M. (1981). The employment of recent doctorate recipients in psychology. *American Psychologist, 36,* 1211–1254.

Strupp, H. H., & Hadley, S. W. (1979). Specific vs. nonspecific effects in psychotherapy: A controlled study of outcome. *Archives of General Psychiatry, 36,* 1125–1136.

Stuart, R. B. (1976). An operant interpersonal program for couples. In D. H. L. Olson (Ed.), *Treating relationships.* Lake Mills, Iowa: Graphic.

Ullmann, L. P., & Krasner, L. (1969). *A psychological approach to abnormal behavior.* Englewood Cliffs, N.J.: Prentice-Hall.

Wachtel, P. L. (1977). *Psychoanalysis and behavior therapy: Toward an integration.* New York: Basic Books.

Wiggins, J. S. (1973). *Personality and prediction: Principles of personality assessment.* Reading, Mass.: Addison-Wesley.

Witmer, L. (1907). Clinical psychology. *Psychological Clinic, 1,* 1–9.

Wolpe, J. (1958). *Psychotherapy by reciprocal inhibition.* Stanford: Stanford University Press.

Yalom, I. D. (1975). *The theory and practice of group psychotherapy* (2nd ed.). New York: Basic Books.

Chapter 2

Technological Assessment: Tapping a "Third Culture" for Decision-Focused Psychological Measurement

DANIEL B. FISHMAN and WILLIAM D. NEIGHER

Applied psychological assessment can be defined as the organized collection and use of psychological and social information to guide decisions. Many of these decisions consist of choices about the development, management, and evaluation of psychological and social programs for change at the psychobiological, individual, group, and organizational levels of human behavior. Other decisions consist of administrative, legislative, legal, judicial, and policy choices in which no change is formally planned. All decisions require information of some kind, and it is to provide putatively useful information that assessment systems are designed.

Decision-focused assessment systems can be compared, contrasted, and evaluated within a typology bounded by three dimensions: (1) the epistemological paradigm, which underlies the development and ongoing operation of the system; (2) the "process" of assessment, which typically consists of a generic series of sequential, cyclical, problem-solving steps; and (3) the "content" of assessment, which involves the particular types of psychological and social variables being assessed by a system.

In this chapter, we propose a model, called the Technological Assessment in Psychology (TAP) model, for improving decision-focused assessment. The model is based on three propositions, each associated primarily with one of the above dimensions, and numbered accordingly. The propositions are:

1. A review of the accomplishments of traditional, "theory-driven," "basic" research in psychological assessment, together with recent philosophical critiques of the logical positivist epistemology underlying this research, justifies adopting a different, technologically focused paradigm for applied assessment.

2. Applying the technological perspective to the decision-making process reveals new operating procedures for closing the link between data and decisions.

3. The generic, problem-solving steps in decision-focused assessment across content areas are such that the process of developing a technology-oriented assessment model in one area has much to offer the process of developing a model in another domain.

THE NEED FOR A NEW
EPISTEMOLOGICAL PARADIGM

The Basic Research Paradigm: Problematic Epistemology

The first proposition calls for a "paradigm shift" (Kuhn, 1962) in the epistemology underlying assessment. Epistemology is the branch of philosophy that investigates the origin, nature, methods, and limits of human knowledge. An epistemological theory sets forth the criteria upon which the relevance and validity of a particular body of knowledge are judged. A central thesis in epistemology is that there are no given criteria for judging the truth value of propositions. Various coherent epistemological frameworks can be defined (natural science is only one), and the evaluator of any statement's truth value can choose among these systems. To a substantial extent, the truth or falsity of a statement depends upon the epistemological system chosen, rather than the content of the statement itself. In the end, an individual or group's ability to persuade others of the merit of adopting an epistemological system determines whether others will accept it. For example, imagine a 1980s research psychologist being transported by time machine to fifth-century Rome and trying to "sell" a natural science epistemology as the best means of determining a statement's truth!

This idea of the dependence of all knowledge upon basic assumptions that cannot be proved by logic or sense experience has recently been highlighted by two articles. One is by Kimble (1984), who, following the work of C. P. Snow (1964), empirically demonstrates the existence of two different epistemological cultures within psychology itself. These consist of a "scientific" and a "humanistic" culture, which are contrasted on such differential epistemological assumptions as determinism versus indeterminism, objectivism versus intuitionism, nomothetic versus idiographic laws, and elementism versus holism.

The other article is by Krasner and Houts (1984), who summarize criticisms of the notion that science is free of "subjective" epistemological and other value assumptions. We quote their excellent summary:

> The argument for the value neutrality of science was founded on pivotal assumptions about epistemology and ethics developed in the logical positivist philosophy of science (Ayer, 1959). The epistemological assumption of objectivism alleged that observation provided unassailable knowledge—the knowledge of "facts" and "raw data." By separating science into observation language and theoretical language, progress was to be guaranteed through adhering to the rules of formal logic (Suppe, 1974), and the history of science was construed as a story of progress towards unbiased, objective knowledge. In addition, classical meta-ethical questions such as what norms and standards are of value were judged unanswerable because what is knowable consists of what is given as "raw data" in observation. . . .
>
> The claim that observation provided only theoretically neutral, objective knowledge units was challenged both by scientists and by philosophers. Heisenberg (1958) pointed to the implausibility of "objective" observation, and Toulmin (1953) showed how theory and assumptions logically precede observation. Moreover, Hanson (1958) cogently argued that there could be no neutral observation language. Therefore, the fundamental assumption of objectivism is untenable, because it is neither physically nor philosophically possible to obtain knowledge without first choosing some assumptive framework. This framework is undetermined by observations; rather it constitutes the hermeneutic context for generating "facts" and giving meaning to observations (Heelan, 1983). (pp. 840–841)

Other psychologists who began with strong identifications with the scientific culture are also eloquent about the "subjectivity" of science as one of a number of possible epistemologies human beings can adopt. Woolfolk and Richardson (1984) criticize the views of behavior therapists that their discipline consists of valuatively "neutral," "objective" knowledge because it is based upon scientific psychology. They regard the widespread acceptance of science as the ultimate source of knowledge as an implicit feature of the more general world view of "modernity" and argue that behavior therapy and behavioral science are themselves embedded in a world of culturally determined conceptual categories and intersubjective meanings.

Gergen (1973, 1982, 1985) was well known as an experimental social psychologist when, in 1973, he wrote a provocative paper, "Social Psychology as History," which developed ideas critical of traditional scientific psychology. In 1982 he claimed that psychology had become resensitized to science as "a human construction rather than a pawn of nature," and to knowledge generally, including scientific knowledge, as "derived from value-interested conceptual standpoints rather than accurate mappings" (Gergen, 1982, p. 207). In a later statement, Gergen (1985) labeled the new epistemological perspective "social constructionism," and summarized its difference from logical positivism as follows: "Social constructionism views discourse about the world not as a reflection or map of the world [as in logical positivism], but as an artifact of communal interchange" (p. 266).

In such an atmosphere of philosophical relativism, how can one choose among competing epistemologies? In these choices as in others, there are no incontestible rules. The history of the philosophy of science suggests, however, that the primary determinant of the adoption of epistemic systems has been the persuasiveness of the systems as expressed in rhetorical argument by advocates of various views. Weimer (1977) regards science as a rhetorical transaction, "not as a sure road to truth." Gergen (1982) points out that the logical positivist position, with its ultimate reliance upon individual sense data, "places the locus of knowledge . . . in the minds of single individuals." With the breakdown of reliance upon the logical positivist epistemology, we become dependent upon persuasive, rhetorical interactions among groups to determine truth:

> It is not the internal processes of the individual that generate what is taken for knowledge, but a social process of communication. It is within the process of social interchange that rationality is generated. Truth is the product of the collectivity of truth makers. Thus, . . . knowledge is no longer the exclusive property of a cloistered profession deploying an arsenal of sophisticated and rarefied methods. . . . [Rather,] knowledge is a communal creation. *Interpersonal* colloquy is necessary to determine "the nature of things." (p. 207)

The Basic Research Paradigm: Problematic Accomplishments

In an earlier article (Fishman & Neigher, 1982), we argued that the public's considerable support of American psychology—to the tune of over $2 billion per year—is in large part contingent upon societal expectations that psychology, unlike other academic disciplines such as the classics and literary criticism, will have a significant impact on important real-life problems, such as nuclear conflict, pollution, energy-resource depletion, urban decay, crime, isolation among the elderly, and low industrial productivity. Similar arguments have been made by authors such as Bevan (1976) and Wertheimer et al. (1978). Psychology will ultimately be judged by the public on the basis of the field's pragmatic accomplishments in reducing significant social and psychological difficulties, not because it is philosophically the royal road to truth. Public esteem and financial support will follow public judgment of practical effect.

What, then, have been the substantive, practical achievements to date of the theory-based research paradigm, the epistemological model that has overwhelmingly dominated natural science-based psychology since its inception (Fishman & Neigher, 1982)? In our 1982 article we concluded that:

> When the overall substance and quality of psychology's basic research accomplishments are critically reviewed against the criteria of this [the theory-based research] paradigm, the result is a very disappointing one; there is an embarrassing lack of established empirical findings that meet the criteria, as numerous well-known psychologists have discussed (e.g., Cronbach, 1975; Epstein, 1980; Greenwald, 1976; Koch, 1959; Levine, 1974; Wachtel, 1980). (p. 539)

A quote from one of these references is illustrative. Koch (1959), as editor of a seven-volume study focusing on the state of psychological learning theory, concluded: "Consider the hundreds of theoretical formulations, rational equations and mathematical models of the learning process that we have accrued; the thousands of research studies. And *now* consider that there is still no wide agreement, even at the crassest descriptive level, on the empirical conditions under which learning takes place" (p. 731). Staats's (1983, 1984) consideration of the role of this paradigm draws a similar conclusion: "In the face of all of [theory-based research] psychology's efforts, its thousands of studies conducted with scientific finesse, its hundreds of theories, its hundreds of tests, experimental designs, apparatuses, data analysis methods, and so on, those who systematically study sciences are of the opinion that psychology is a would-be science, a pretender to science." (1983, p. 3).

Reviewers in other areas have reached similar conclusions. In the study of personality (Sechrest, 1976), risk-taking (Cartwright, 1973), cognition (Newell, 1973), and social behavior (Mayo, 1977), thousands of studies have yielded meager knowledge. A particularly vivid and dismal picture of psychology's theory-based research accomplishments emerges from a special section in the 15th anniversary issue of *Psychology Today* (Nessel, 1982). Eleven distinguished psychologists, "the best minds in the field," were asked to describe what each considered to be "the most significant work in psychology over the past decade and a half." Their answers to this question are summarized in a *New York Times* editorial ("Smart apes, or Dumb?" 1982):

The results are astonishing: it would seem that there has been none [i.e., no significant work]. "Significant work" implies work generally agreed to be important, but the 11 Best Minds in psychology agree on hardly anything. Stanley Milgram of the City University of New York hails the teaching of sign language to apes as an enduring recent achievement. But another contributor, Ulric Neisser of Cornell, cites as important the evident *failure* to teach sign language to apes.

B. F. Skinner, alleging himself not well informed of recent progress in other fields of psychology, recounts the advances in behavioral psychology, which he pioneered. But two other sages, Jerome Bruner of the New School for Social Research and Richard Lazarus of Berkeley, laud the escape from Skinnerian psychology as the most significant accomplishment.

Almost the only recent achievement hailed by more than one contributor is the discovery of endorphins. . . . This is certainly an interesting development, but the credit belongs to pharmacologists and physiologists; psychology had little to do with it.

Perhaps because of the apparent difficulty of naming significant work, two of the Best Minds [Bernice Neugarten and Philip Zimbardo] make no effort to do so.

The failure of the 11 psychologists to agree on almost anything evinces a serious problem in their academic discipline. Physicists or biologists asked the same question would not concur on everything but there would be a substantial commonality in their answers. Can psychology be taken seriously as science if even its leading practitioners cannot agree on its recent advances? . . . Mature sciences [should] possess a certain level of agreement as to what has been accomplished and what constitutes a fruitful research program.

Perhaps the results of such a survey of psychology's "best minds" justifies some legislators' view of "psychology as an intellectual boondoggle undeserving of the research appropriations given other scientific fields" (Hill, 1981, p. 18E); or, to put it more flamboyantly, in the words of one such legislator, Ohio's Representative John Ashbrook: The social and behavior sciences constitute "the foolish fringe folly of researchers who use tax money like the dilettante squanders his inheritance" (Hill, 1981, p. 18E). Talk about rhetorical grounds for the ultimate acceptance or rejection of a "science"!

The Technological Program-Building Alternative

Emotionality aside, these major epistemological and substantive problems in the basic, theory-driven research paradigm argue for giving at least equal time in our field to other approaches. One alternative is to adopt a "qualitative/hermeneutic" paradigm. The distinction between the "quantitative/natural science" and "qualitative/interpretive" paradigms has been elaborated in social science generally by several scholars (e.g., Arkowitz & Messer, 1984; Gergen, 1982; Kimble, 1984). The differentiation has been framed for program evaluation specifically in terms of the contrast between quantitative and qualitative evaluation (e.g., Cronbach et al., 1980; Morell, 1979; Patton, 1980a, 1980b; Reichardt & Cook, 1979). Patton's (1978) summary of the distinction is particularly clear and succinct:

> Evaluation research is dominated by the . . . natural science paradigm of the hypothetico-deductive methodology. This dominant paradigm assumes quantitative measurement, experimental design, and multivariate parametric statistical analysis to be the epitome of "good" science. This basic model for conducting evaluation research comes from the tradition of experimentation in agriculture, which gave us many of the basic statistical and experimental techniques most widely used in evaluation research. . . .
>   By way of contrast, the alternative to the dominant hypothetico-deductive paradigm is derived from the tradition of anthropo-

logical field studies. Using the techniques of in-depth, open-ended interviewing and personal observation, the alternative paradigm relies on qualitative data, holistic analysis, and detailed description derived from close contact with the targets of study.

The hypothetico-deductive, natural science paradigm aims at prediction of social phenomena; the holistic-intuitive, anthropological paradigm aims at understanding of social phenomena. (pp. 203–204)

The present book will generally be limited to assessment systems that have been developed in a natural science paradigm. Within this paradigm it is possible to distinguish further between two epistemological models: one involving "pure science" and basic research, and one involving "applied science" and "technology" (Azrin, 1977; Broskowski, 1971; Broskowski & Schulberg, 1974; Bunge, 1974; Fishman & Neigher, 1982; Gilbert, 1978; Johnson et al., 1979; Morell, 1979; Neigher & Fishman, 1985; Price & Cherniss, 1977). These epistemologies can be differentiated with regard to the general goal they serve. In a basic research paradigm, the purpose is theory building and description. In a technological paradigm, the purpose is managerial decision-making.

According to the basic research paradigm, an ideal psychological project parallels the best research models from the biological and physical sciences. A controlled, laboratorylike experiment is conducted to test hypotheses derived from abstract psychological theory in a methodologically rigorous manner that controls for experimenter bias and variables "extraneous" to the target hypotheses. In the technological paradigm, by contrast, an ideal psychological project parallels the best action-oriented models from engineering and the field of research and development. A conceptually coherent program is designed to address a significant social or psychological problem within a real-world context in a manner that is feasible, effective, and efficient (Broskowski, 1971; Fishman & Neigher, 1982; Gilbert, 1978).

Consideration of the basic research paradigm evokes such terms as "pure science," "hypothetico-deductive methodology," "experiment-focused research," and "general theory-driven research," or just "theory-driven research." The technological paradigm, on the other hand, calls up such terms as "applied science," "problem-focused research," "program building," "research and development," and "performance engineering." Each of these terms has its own connotations and surplus meaning, and unfortunately none of them is exactly correct in expressing what we have in mind. The terms closest to our intended meaning are "basic, theory-driven research" (or simply "basic research"), to designate the emphasis on knowledge generation and general theory building in the pure science paradigm; and "technological program building" (or simply "technology"), to designate the emphasis on problem solution and practical program building in the applied science paradigm.

As a final note on terminology, the term "theory-driven" associated with basic research is not meant to imply a view of technology as atheoretical or antitheoretical. Rather, the function of conceptualization varies for each approach. In basic research, the emphasis is upon developing general theories with universal laws about psychological and social reality. In technology, the emphasis is upon developing program-oriented, working theoretical models within the context of particular organizations, cultures, and historical times.

Bevan (1980) describes the individualistic, esoteric, "dogma eat dogma" nature of the Cartesian view of research associated with the basic research paradigm. For the Cartesian investigator, "doing science is like running a race, and one's colleagues in the field can therefore only be viewed as strong competitors. . . . The public is perceived as having only one role, that of patron" (Bevan, 1980, p. 790). In contrast, the Baconian view, which is associated with the technological paradigm, stresses that science is a "cooperative activity within a professional community marked by a clear-cut division of labor but bound by a single shared altruistic commitment to the promotion of human welfare" (Bevan, 1980, pp. 780–781).

Other differences between basic, theory-driven research and technological program building help clarify the distinction. Basic research usually involves individualistic investigators who use an epistemology of logical positivism and laboratorylike settings in an effort to derive general descriptive laws about human behavior. Technological research, on the other hand, involves mission-oriented groups of investigators who employ an epistemology of pragmatic social constructivism and real-world settings to derive particular, decision-focused and change-oriented knowledge about specific programs. As will be shown below, the two models also vary as to the incentives they create for the development of formal information systems, with basic research typically generating low incentives, and technological research, high incentives.

In bringing these models to bear on the understanding of decision-focused assessment, an important complexity must be kept in mind. We do not mean to imply that two qualitatively distinct natural science epistemologies are found in psychology. In actuality, the basic research and technological paradigms form the end points of a continuum, which includes a range of mixed epistemologies. However, it is still useful to speak in terms of *relative* differences between epistemologies in the degree to which they are located closer to or farther from the "pure" basic research versus the "pure" technological end points of the continuum. (It should be noted that this argument also applies to the difference between qualitative/hermeneutic and quantitative/natural science epistemologies discussed above.)

We propose that pursuing a technological, program-building aim within a quantitative, natural science epistemology has much to recommend it. In fact, we claim that much fine work has already been done along these lines, but in order to give it "scientific credibility" and get it published, psychologists have felt compelled to clothe their work in the trappings of basic research rather than technology. In the culture of academic scholarship, it is hard to gain scientific respectability unless the emphasis of a psychologist's work is upon general laws, as opposed to the derivation of particular knowledge, or upon conceptual and methodological innovation, as opposed to the maintenance and replication of previously proven programs. Azrin (1977), one of the few psychologists who has attained the double goal of scientific credibility and technological effectiveness, still laments:

> I should warn those who decide to embark on this exciting adventure [finding psychological solutions for human problems] that this outcome emphasis in psychology is not likely to lead to professional recognition. When male psychologists tell me of their knowledge of my toilet training method, further questioning usually reveals that they learned of it from their wives who used it to train their children. Or they learned of the training methods for retarded persons because they were asked to consult at the institution and discovered the procedure in use. Or they took their psychology class to a mental hospital to view catatonics as described in the textbooks, but instead found patients busily occupied and receiving tokens. (p. 148)

Azrin's (1977) summary of his work makes a strong case for approaching traditional "scientific" psychology from a technological point of view:

> Experimental psychology provides a methodology for the scientific evaluation of causes of behavior. Reinforcement theory pro-

vides concrete principles for changing behavior. In spite of the substantial psychological knowledge accumulated about specific psychological problems, scientific evaluation of actual treatment procedures has been surprisingly lacking. The present approach tried to develop new treatments for many different psychological problems, based on a reinforcement theory rationale and evaluating the treatments in controlled experiments *in field settings.* The research strategy was *outcome oriented and consumer directed.* While I started with reinforcement concepts, such concepts were not capable of generating all the procedures needed to solve the practical problem. Other reinforcement procedures and *new emergent concepts* were required to solve the problem. (p. 148, italics added)

Azrin concludes his summary by emphasizing the importance of the principles of the quantitative/natural science model when it comes to method. However, when it comes to substance, he stresses the importance of pragmatic success with specific problems in specific situations, *not* the importance of theory-derived general laws, as required by the theory-driven, basic research paradigm:

A prerequisite in this [my] strategy was scientific rigor regarding objective specification of the procedures, quantitative and objective specification of the behavioral outcome, controlled experimental evaluation, a conceptual foundation for the procedures, and the primacy of data over speculation. Beyond that, the strategy was to increase outcome benefits to the consumer, including such dimensions as the speed, degree, and durability of the benefit, as well as cost, consumer acceptability, and population generality. (p. 148)

The strong need for a more idiographic, individual, case-oriented perspective in the field of quantitative psychology is persuasively argued by Barlow et al. (1984). These authors review the literature and document the claim that not only do practitioners not do traditional, quantitative research, they do not even consume it. They conclude that the typical group experiment in clinical psychology is not appropriate to the subject matter at hand, and that bridging the gap between research and practice involves a focus on the individual case, including systematic, quantitative, naturalistic measurement procedures that are tailored to, and implemented in, the context of the single case.

A final example of the advantages of the technological, as opposed to the basic research, paradigm can be seen in the area of data reliability. In a recent paper, Burstein et al. (1985) catalogue a variety of technical faults in the data collection involved with social program evaluation. They conclude that problems of data unreliability are widespread in evaluation studies, and that this can "eviscerate the refinements in evaluation technology that have occurred in recent years." In analyzing this problem (Neigher & Fishman, 1985), we argue that one of the major causes of poor reliability is the dominance of the basic, theory-driven research paradigm in the evaluation field. As presently practiced, the basic research paradigm contains relatively few consistent, positive motivational incentives for reliable and accurate data collection for those individuals who are involved in the research process. In contrast, we contend that the technological program-building paradigm tends to generate many more such incentives, and that thus one advantage of the technological paradigm is its greater encouragement of data reliability. A summary of our arguments, based upon the distinctions between basic research and technology, follows:

1. Data that are an end in themselves for real-world description tend to create a higher incentive for reliability than data that are only a means for the testing of abstract, theoretical hypotheses.

2. Focus on developing situation-specific knowledge requires attention to the specifics of data more than does focus on deriving general psychological laws.

3. There is a high incentive to produce reliable raw data when the data themselves, rather than summaries of the data, are under direct accountability.

4. Formal information systems used over long periods of time are employed by more individuals in more situations than short-term and less formal information systems. Thus, the collective effort that goes into creating and clarifying the former tends to be greater than the collective effort that goes into the latter.

5. Data directly connected to decisions for action have more serious and immediate practical effects than data connected primarily to knowledge creation per se. For this reason, unreliability in the former tends to generate more concern and corrective response than unreliability in the latter.

Table 2.1 presents a brief summary of some of the contrasts among the three different epistemological paradigms we have been discussing—the basic research, technological, and hermeneutic. A more de-

TABLE 2.1
Summary of Illustrative Differences among
Three Epistemological Paradigms

Paradigm characteristic	Basic research paradigm	Technological paradigm	Hermeneutic paradigm
1. Underlying epistemology	Logical positivism	Social constructionism	Social constructionism
2. Primary type of data	Quantitative	Quantitative	Qualitative
3. Primary mode of research	Nomothetic	Idiographic	Idiographic
4. Primary goal of research	Derivation of theory-based, general psychological laws through laboratory experiments	Solution of context-specific, practical psychological problems	Qualitative understanding of context-specific psychological events and processes
5. Primary use of empirical information generated	Formal theory development	Assistance for lay decision makers in arriving at their decisions	Addition to a cumulative body of commentary about human experience & behavior
6. Primary sites of research	Specially created settings: laboratories, college classrooms	Natural settings	Natural settings
7. Exemplars in psychology	Animal experiments to test Hullian learning theory; correlational studies to test personality trait theory	Market research; standardized educational tests, such as the SATs; behavior therapy token economies	Qualitative interpretation of the Rorschach; interpretation in psychoanalytic therapy; psychohistory
8. Exemplars outside psychology	Natural sciences (physics, chemistry & biology)	National economic indicators; U.S. census; financial accounting data; sports statistics	Investigative reporting; interpretive history; literary criticism

TABLE 2.1 (*continued*)

Paradigm characteristic	Basic research paradigm	Technological paradigm	Hermeneutic paradigm
9. Primary modes of communication	Publication in esoteric, highly technical journals	Written reports to lay decision makers concerning their programs & policies	Publication in academic journals & media such as *New York Times Magazine*
10. Need for complex, quantitative management information systems	Low need: Experiments generate relatively small amounts of quantitative data	High need: Performance indicators about complex, real-world settings generate large amounts of quantitative data	No need: Quantitative data are not relevant within the paradigm

tailed outline of the differences between the technological approach, advocated in this chapter, and the basic research approach, which currently dominates psychological inquiry, is contained in Table 2.2. (Specific sources for the ideas summarized in this table include this chapter, Peterson's chapter in the present volume, and the following: Azrin, 1977; Bevan, 1980; Ceci & Walker, 1983; Fishman & Neigher, 1982; Gergen, 1982; Gilbert, 1978; Morell, 1979; Neigher & Fishman, 1985; and Windle & Neigher, 1978.)

CONNECTIONS BETWEEN DATA AND DECISIONS

The second proposition underlying the Technological Assessment in Psychology (TAP) model specifies that applying the technological perspective to the decision-making process reveals new operating procedures for tightening the link between data and decisions. As implied in Tables 2.1 and 2.2, there is a strong contrast in the approach to assessment derived from the basic, theory-driven research paradigm, which emphasizes the internal validity of assessment data, and that derived

TABLE 2.2

Contrasting Characteristics of Pure and Applied Science

Pure science (basic research)	Applied science (technology)
A. Epistemology: Logical positivism vs. social constructionism	
1. Tied to an epistemology of logical positivism, according to which reality is "discovered" in the scientific laboratory	1. Tied to an epistemology of social constructionism, according to which reality is "constructed" through social interaction
B. Individualistic/esoteric vs. public mission orientation	
2. Driven by the individual social scientist's desire to prove a particular theory with which he or she is identified	2. Driven by goals articulated by lay decision makers to reduce some social or psychological problem
3. Emphasis on what is scientifically intriguing among social scientists	3. Emphasis on what is socially important to nonscientist decision makers
4. Tradition of academic freedom	4. Tradition of public mission orientation
5. Emphasis on publication in esoteric, highly technical journals	5. Emphasis on communication with lay program decision makers
6. Emphasis on specialized language and communication with individuals who share the same specialized training	6. Emphasis on common language and communication with the lay public and lay decision makers
7. Researcher orientation: ultimate goal of assessment is to collect information about individual differences	7. Consumer orientation: ultimate goal of assessment is to help people
8. Assessment for the sake of description per se is completely acceptable	8. The most useful assessments in psychology are linked with change
9. Focus on process, upon how the world works	9. Focus on results, upon how the world can be improved
C. Laboratory vs. "real-world" emphasis	
10. Emphasis on knowledge relating to controlled, laboratory conditions	10. Emphasis on knowledge relating to actual program conditions "in the field"

TABLE 2.2 *(continued)*

Pure science (basic research)	Applied science (technology)
11. Investigations are designed to eliminate or minimize the effects of conditions that do not bear on the theoretical propositions with which the studies began	11. Investigations begin with the problems and opportunities of natural events; nature is taken as it comes, in all its complexity
12. Artificial stimuli, such as tests, are employed in unusual situations, such as research laboratories	12. Study of functional processes as they occur in nature demands that people, groups, and organizations be observed in their natural environments
13. Emphasis on hypothesis-testing: findings of "no significance" are discouraged	13. Emphasis on the systematic, standardized observation and classification of natural phenomena
14. Emphasis on theoretical relevance of concepts, i.e., on construct validity	14. Emphasis on practical relevance of concepts, i.e., on face validity
15. Generally not linked to real-world decision-making, except perhaps for policy decisions	15. Almost always linked to real-world decision-making
16. Response simplicity	16. Clinical significance
17. Stimulus and laboratory simplicity	17. Situational complexity
18. Subject homogeneity	18. Population heterogeneity
19. Single variables	19. Systems approach
20. Objective apparatus measures	20. Subject preferences
21. Emphasis on theoretical payoff: goal is theory-based knowledge	21. Emphasis on pragmatic payoff: goal is to reduce high-priority social and psychological problems in the most cost-effective and ethical manner

D. *Goal of theory development per se vs. action*

22. Emphasis on deriving general statements about human behavior, i.e., on general knowledge	22. Emphasis on deriving particular evaluations and understandings of specific programs, i.e., on situation-specific knowledge

TABLE 2.2 *(continued)*

Pure science (basic research)	Applied science (technology)
23. Emphasis on developing general theories with universal laws about social and psychological reality	23. Emphasis on developing working theoretical models within the context of particular organizations, cultures, and historical times
24. Emphasis on understanding and process: how living systems work	24. Emphasis on outcome: how living systems can be changed and improved
25. Emphasis on statistical significance	25. Emphasis on practicality and cost benefits
26. Emphasis on implication	26. Emphasis on application
27. Emphasis on data-based conclusions	27. Emphasis on data-based decisions

E. *Innovative approaches to general laws*
  vs.
Ongoing replication of particular, quality-controlled programs

28. Goal is to derive universal laws	28. Goal is to derive topical principles, specific to a particular time, place, and culture
29. Innovation emphasis: stress on conceptual and methodological innovation	29. Replication emphasis: stress on maintaining proven programs and replicating them in new situations
30. Emphasis on creativity in research design	30. Emphasis on quality control of established programs
31. The rare, "five star Parisian restaurant" model: emphasis on demonstrating "basic" causal relationships and change programs under "ideal," laboratory-like procedures	31. The "McDonald's hamburgers" model: emphasis on the feasibility of replicating present programs in new situations under real-world constraints
32. Assessor's reward and basis of recognition: peer-reviewed publication about new knowledge concerning general psychological laws	32. Assessor's reward and basis of recognition: identification with and/or partial responsibility for the successful management of a particular program

TABLE 2.2 *(continued)*

Pure science (basic research)	Applied science (technology)

F. Lower vs. higher incentive for formal information systems

33. Emphasis on operational definitions individually tailored to the hypotheses being investigated by a particular organization

33. Emphasis on operational definitions standardized across a large number of organizations (e.g., the federal Bureau of Labor Statistics)

34. Short-term focus of data collection: data are typically gathered in the context of a short-lived, single experiment; if experiment is successful, no need to continue it

34. Long-term focus of data collection; data are typically gathered in the context of ongoing monitoring and evaluation for continuing operational management

35. Data collector held externally accountable for summary statistics only: such statistics alone are sufficient for manuscript acceptance

35. Data collector held externally accountable for raw data; e.g., the outside examination of a business's "audit trail" in evaluating its accounting activities

36. Exemplar of data collection: a particular data system designed for a particular study testing a certain theory about the determinants of attitude change

36. Exemplars of data collection: standardized educational tests, national economic indicators, and life insurance actuarial statistics

37. It follows from items 33–36 that, generally, only short-lived information systems are needed; thus, large investment in cost-efficient and effective management information systems is *not* typically warranted

37. It follows from items 33–36 that, generally, long-lived information systems are needed; thus, large investment in cost-efficient and effective management information systems *is* typically warranted

NOTE: The two columns for each item should be viewed as the end points of a continuum. Varying "blends" are possible all along the continuum.

from the technological paradigm, which stresses the real-world context of assessment data and its pragmatic effects. In the following section of this chapter, we discuss some of the many variables and processes, other than intrinsic technical merit, which help determine the extent to which assessment data are linked to decisions.

Historically, the technology of program evaluation grew out of a mixture of social science research, data-based management, and policy formation as these developed in real-world politics. Program evaluation was thus born of a marriage between the basic research and technological paradigms. With such a combination of parents, many observers expected program evaluation research to be embraced eagerly by an information-consuming society, seeking to make more rational, better decisions and to improve programs and organizations. The initial optimism helped stimulate the government to sponsor social program evaluations, whose support went from almost nothing in 1960 to about $180 million in 1980.

However, by the early and mid 1970s, experts started to agree that the results of the "great evaluation experiment" were very disappointing. Wholey et al. (1970) concluded that "the recent literature is unanimous in announcing the general failure of evaluation to affect decision-making in a significant way" (p. 46). Carol Weiss (1972) viewed underutilization as one of the foremost problems in evaluation research: "Evaluation research is meant for immediate and direct use in improving the quality of social programming. Yet a review of evaluation experience suggests that evaluation results have not exerted significant influence on program decisions" (pp. 10–11). Cohen and Garet (1975) found that "there is little evidence to indicate that government planning offices have succeeded in linking social research and decision-making" (p. 19). Finally, Deitchman (1976) concluded that "the impact of the research on the most important affairs of state was, with few exceptions, nil" (p. 390).

In another paper (Neigher & Fishman, 1985), we have argued that the reason for the initial utilization failure in program evaluation was the predominance of the basic, theory-driven research over the technological paradigm in actual evaluation practice. Cronbach and his associates (Cronbach, 1980) set forth similar arguments, pointing out that until recently, "highly controlled summative studies" had been regarded as the ideal type of evaluation. They conclude that not until the middle and late 1970s have we seen full recognition that politics and science are both integral aspects of evaluation. . . . Evaluators who see themselves as fearless seekers after truth come to feel that they have been assigned walk-on parts in a political pageant. . . . The evaluator venturing into the political arena can no longer be guided solely by the habits of thought of the scientist (Frankel, 1976). The political sensitivity he acquires ought to be used in addition to, and not in place of, his training in impartiality. (pp. 35, 47, 71)

In response to the utilization failures in program evaluation projects, investigators and conceptualizers in the field have been stimulated to study systematically the nature of the managerial and political policy context of program planning and decision-making, and to develop new models of evaluation that attempt to link data with decision-making, as in Scriven's (1967, 1972) "formative" (vs. "summative") and "goal-free" (vs. "goal-oriented") evaluation; Patton's (1978) "utilization-focused evaluation"; Gold's (1983) "stakeholder-based evaluation"; and Wholey's (1983) "evaluability assessment." In fact, one of the models is simply called the "decision-making model of evaluation," in which "the evaluation is structured by the decisions to be made" in order "to supply information on these particular decisions" (House, 1978, p. 4). In addition, a large literature has developed on the process by which new social science innovations, including new assessment data, are either adopted, directly or indirectly, or rejected by individuals, small groups, or organizations who are in decision-making and managerial roles (e.g., Beyer & Trice, 1982; Davis & Salasin, 1978; Rich, 1979), although it should be noted that much of this literature is based primarily upon a basic, theory-driven research paradigm as opposed to a technological paradigm.

In sum, then, within the field of program evaluation, whose mission is decision-focused assessment, initial attempts to link data and decisions were largely unsuccessful, in part because of the primary emphasis on "good" science, together with simplistic and generally undeveloped ideas and observations about the process of decision-making. Subsequent work has highlighted the need to pay much more systematic attention to the traditionally "nonscientific," pragmatic aspects of the decision-making process, that is, to the more technological aspects of linking data to decisions. The remainder of this section is devoted to an illustration of the types of technologically relevant variables that have been studied and proposed as important determinants of the extent to which assessment data are linked to decisions. Two groups of variables are reviewed: A-VICTORY variables, identified in a major review of the "planned change" literature by Davis and Salasin (1978), and Data-Based Decision-Making (DBDM) variables, derived from our own study and experience in management roles.

Davis and Salasin's A VICTORY model

Davis and Salasin's (1978) model consists of an eight-step, quantifiable approach to decision determinants. Their model focuses particularly on decisions to adopt organizational innovations, such as a new system for directly linking systematic, quantitative "performance indicator" data to formal decision-making. Using the acronym A-VICTORY, they selected the following variables as particularly important in determining closeness of linkage:

A bility, the capacity of the organization to implement and evaluate the decision

V alues, the accord between the values inherent in the innovation and those of the adopting organization

I nformation, the adequacy of the information about the innovation

C ircumstances, the specific features of the organizational environment

T iming, the organization's readiness to consider and implement the innovation or change

O bligation, the felt need within the organization to attempt to change

R esistances, those factors that play an inhibiting role

Y ield, the payoff to the actors in the decision-making process

The A-VICTORY system, as part of a decision determinant analysis procedure, allows organizations to look at the likely sources of resistance to the making of data-based decisions, and to act accordingly.

Data-Based Decision-Making (DBDM)

The Davis and Salasin factors are important in understanding decision-making at the organizational level. However, diffusion of responsibility for decision-making exists even in the most hierarchical organizational structures. Ultimately, individuals who bear the responsibility for decision-making face personal consequences for their decisions. In recognition of this fact, and to complement the Davis and Salasin perspective, we have identified the following factors as important in determining the probability that a particular decision maker's choice will be data based. (1) *Perceived data relevance:* Does the decision maker perceive the data as influencing the target decision? (2) *Value consonance:* How do the data fit with the decision maker's own values? (3) *Perceived incentives:* Does the decision maker perceive, in the organization, rewards for DBDM, ranging from financial rewards to heightened self-esteem? (4) *Perceived organizational precedents:* Does the decision maker perceive organizational precedents for DBDM? (5) *Risk to decision maker:* Does using the data set involve personal risk from inside or outside the organization, such as demotion, job loss, or litigation? (6) *Risk to decisional recipients:* Do those affected by the decision bear risks (such as patients in health-related settings, where risk can inhibit a decision maker's use of available data)? (7) *Disclosure:* Will there be public disclosure of the decision? (8) *Reversibility:* Can the decision maker "take back" organizational or individual commitments, such as a demonstration project that has an experimental phase (high reversibility) or the full-scale distribution of a new product or a widely publicized disclosure (low reversibility).

In sum, a close, effective link between scientific, quantified data and practical decision-making requires systematic attention to many non-scientific, political, contextual variables in the decision-making process—variables that have been illustrated by the A-VICTORY and DBDM decision models

A GENERAL PROCESS FOR DEVELOPING TECHNOLOGICAL ASSESSMENT SYSTEMS

The third proposition that underlies the TAP model is that the problem-solving process in decision-focused assessment is much the same whether one is assessing individuals, groups, or organizations, and regardless of the particular content with which assessment is concerned. For this reason, the process of developing an assessment system in one domain may contribute to the development of assessment systems in other domains.

In his definitive book on living systems theory, Miller (1978) differentiates seven types of living systems: the cell, organ, individual organism, group, organization, society, and supranational system. Miller demonstrates that all these systems can be conceptualized in terms of the same structures, functions, and terms. For example, he shows how any of these systems can be viewed as consisting of the same three types of subsystems: (a) those that process both matter-energy and information, like a "boundary" or a "reproducer" subsystem; (b) those that only process matter-energy, like an "ingestor" or a "distributor" subsystem; and (c) those that only process information, like a "memory" or a "decider" subsystem. Miller proposes that in all living systems, performance indicators are necessary "to monitor the many subsystem and systemwide variables that fluctuate constantly in the system." Broadly defined, performance indicators are selective, quantitative statistical measures, collected in a regular and ongoing manner, which can summarize the performance of a particular type of living system. For example, in the individual human physiological system, measures such as blood pressure, white blood count, metabolic rate, and muscle tone are quantitative indicators that assess how well the system is meeting its goal of physical health; in the world of the business organization, performance indicators tend to be variations of the "bottom line," for example, production cost per item, gross sales, net profit, and return on investment.

Miller points out that all systems take in or collect from outside themselves some type of information, which is used in some manner to make decisions about issues internal to the system and about issues relating the system to its outside environment. Because of this commonality across systems, Miller argues, both on conceptual and empirical grounds, that knowledge about the data-to-decisions link at one level is highly likely to yield useful information about those links at other levels.

In line with Miller's conception, we propose that the following assessment-related ideas can apply to each systems level: (1) To tie data to decisions one must first select a limited set of performance indicators, directly linked to the relevant decision, from the system in question (this selection is based in part upon the values and priorities of the decision makers); (2) frequently, there are no perfectly valid single measures of the performance indicators in question, so multiple measures of each indicator may be necessary; (3) relating data to decisions involves developing formal ways to resolve discrepancies among multiple measures of the same performance indicators; and (4) relating data to decisions typically involves developing formal ways to apply a wide range of performance indicators to a relatively small range of decisional alternatives.

Besides the systems level at which assessment is conducted, assessment may vary according to the types of settings within which inquiries are made (e.g., medical, mental health, military, business, and correctional facilities), and according to the kinds of processes to be examined (e.g., perceptual-cognitive functions, physiological processes, individual actions, interpersonal transactions, and organizational outcomes measured by behavioral products). Across all these variations, however, a common strategy can be employed in the design of technological assessment operations.

Most conceptions of decision-focused assessment assume that its process can be divided into sequential steps. A complete sequence of 25 steps, which are clustered into five major stages, A–E, is outlined below:

A. *Conceptualizing the decision to be made*
1. Identify the type of decision to be made.
2. Describe the decision context and decision-maker culture. The context of the decision, its meaning to the relevant decision makers, the values and culture of the decision makers with regard to issues such as quantified data, formal decision models, and a deliberate versus a quick decision-making process—these and similar issues must be taken into account in understanding the nature of the type of decision for which the assessment system is to be employed.
3. Summarize any relevant research that helps to clarify Steps 1 and 2, to construct the conceptual model in Step 4, or to develop the data system in Step 5.
4. On the basis of Steps 1–3, construct a conceptual model for understanding the nature of the decision to be made.

B. *Developing a data methodology linked to the decision*
5. On the basis of Steps 1–4, develop a model of data collection, scoring, and application. This model provides a rationale and operationalized set of procedures for deciding: (a) what particular types of data to collect with what specific methods, (b) what procedure to use

for data sampling, (c) how the data will be scored and summarized, and (d) how the scores will be explicitly linked to the target decision-making process being addressed. This model is then implemented, evaluated, and revised in the steps below.

C. *Pilot-testing the methodology*

6. Select a pilot-test setting and collect an appropriate sample of data.

7. Score the data and summarize the scores for the application of decision rules.

8. Evaluate the data's quality, that is, its reliability and validity. If these are unacceptable, make revisions in Steps 5–7 until acceptable data quality is attained.

9. Use the data in Step 8 to make specific, practical decisions in the pilot-test setting.

10. Evaluate the impact of the data upon decisions.

11. Feed back the results of Step 10 for the revision and refinement of steps 1–9.

12. Try additional pilot tests until the data are found to be of both acceptable quality and usefulness in decision-making.

13. Replicate the successful pilot test at least once before proceeding to subsequent steps.

D. *Implementing the methodology at full scale*

14. Develop an operational plan for extending the successful pilot tests to a full-scale implementation. This plan should incorporate Steps 1–13, together with a consideration of any revisions that are required in going from a pilot test to a full-scale implementation.

15. Implement the operational plan.

16. Evaluate the operational plan by cycling through Steps 8 and 10 for the data in Step 15.

17. Based upon the results of Step 16, make any revisions needed.

18. Routinize the operational plan, with ongoing monitoring of it through the periodic repetition of Steps 16 and 17.

E. *Disseminating the methodology at full scale*

19. Replicate the full-scale implementation in Steps 15–18 at least once.

20. Review the professional literature on the dynamics of technology diffusion and dissemination, and apply the principles in this literature to the intended dissemination context.

21. On the basis of Steps 1–20, develop an operational plan for dissemination.

22. Implement the operational plan.
23. Evaluate the operational plan by cycling through Steps 8 and 10 for the data in Step 22.
24. Based upon the results of Step 23, make any revisions needed.
25. Routinize the operational plan, with ongoing monitoring of it through the periodic repetition of Steps 23 and 24.

Over a range of assessing operations, some of these steps may be emphasized more than others, and in some cases the complete process may be truncated for practical reasons. However, unless decisions are adequately conceptualized, unless data systems, linked with decisions, are developed, tested, and implemented, and unless successful and generalizable systems are disseminated, assessment will be less useful than it can be. Those who aspire to develop assessment systems would do well to heed the entire series of steps before slighting some of the considerations as a matter of choice or practical necessity.

SUMMARY: BROTHER, CAN YOU PARADIGM?

Epistemology

For many years, the epistemological paradigm of basic, theory-driven research has dominated psychology, including the field of decision-focused assessment. In recent times, this paradigm has come under increasing attack, based both upon philosophical critiques of the logical positivism underlying the paradigm and sobering reviews of the paradigm's substantive accomplishments. Some critics, such as Gergen (1982), have responded by turning away from quantitative, natural science approaches completely and advocating a qualitative, interpretive epistemology for psychology. Our proposal is less extreme. We have argued that the improvement of decision-focused assessment requires a paradigm shift to an alternative quantitative epistemology, that of technology, in the form of our TAP model.

Tables 2.1 and 2.2 contrast the basic research and technological paradigms. In summary, basic research involves individualistic investigators who use a philosophy of logical positivism and laboratorylike settings in an effort to derive general descriptive laws about human behavior. The technological model involves mission-oriented groups of investigators who employ a philosophy of social constructionism and real-world settings to derive particular, decision- and change-oriented knowledge about particular programs.

We have pointed out that the paradigms contrasted in Table 2.2 can be viewed as end points of a continuum, and that many points along the continuum are represented in the work of different psychologists. However, we have argued that the basic research paradigm still predominates the field. Our call for a paradigm shift toward technology, then, is actually a call for a more even balance in the value and attention that is paid to the technological end of the continuum by applied psychologists in general, and particularly by those concerned with decision-focused psychological assessment.

The Process Structure of Decision-Focused Assessment

Our analysis of the process of decision-focused assessment yielded 25 discrete steps, which can be clustered into five sequential stages: (a) conceptualizing the decision to be made, (b) developing a data methodology linked to the decision, (c) pilot-testing the methodology, (d) implementing the methodology at full scale, and (e) disseminating the methodology at full scale.

A review of the basic research paradigm (see Table 2.2) with regard to the 25 steps reveals that only 5 of the steps are addressed by the paradigm—specifically, Step 4 (construct a conceptual model for understanding the nature of the decision to be made), Step 5 (develop a data methodology linked to the decision), and Steps 6–8 (pilot-test the data methodology and evaluate its reliability and validity). This incomplete connection between the basic research paradigm and the steps of decision-focused assessment is not surprising, because the research paradigm was designed to investigate general psychological laws that most clearly reveal themselves in controlled, laboratory settings. In contrast, the technological paradigm addresses all of the 25 process steps, because this paradigm was explicitly designed to carry out programs in complex, natural settings.

Since the technological paradigm, unlike the basic research paradigm, values and explicitly addresses all the process steps, it directs our attention to the many variables—other than intrinsic "technical merit"—that help determine the extent to which assessment data are linked with decisions. Without paying careful attention to these variables, the connection between a psychologist's assessment data and the decision-making process is typically not made. To illustrate the nature of these variables, we reviewed two sample groups of them: Davis and Salasin's (1978) A-VICTORY model and our own DBDM model.

The Perspective of General Systems Theory

General systems theory is a very useful perspective in developing decision-focused assessment methods for at least two reasons. First, as discussed in the previous section, general systems theory provides the rationale for using effective procedures to solve problems developed at one level of decision-focused assessment in order to generate effective procedures for solving those problems at other levels. Two of the examples we cited of cross-level issues are: (a) the need to develop formal ways to resolve discrepancies among multiple measures of the same construct, and (b) the need to take large numbers of measurable variables and focus and summarize them so that they are linked with a limited number of decisional alternatives.

A second way in which general systems theory is useful in developing decision-focused assessment methods relates to understanding the context and culture of decision-making. As systems theorists (e.g., Bronfenbrenner, 1979; Miller, 1978) point out, human behavior typically takes place in a context involving multiple systems levels. Thus, behavior in a particular setting is usually performed by one or more individuals who have specific neuropsychological and psychophysiological subsystems and who are embedded in a specific small group, such as a work team or family. In addition, the individual and the group are embedded in a larger culture, and are frequently also embedded in a specific organization, such as a corporation or public agency at work, a church or synagogue, a political party, a recreational group, and so forth.

This multiple-system-level aspect of behavior has a particularly important bearing on an early step in the process of developing a decision-focused assessment system—namely, that of understanding the context of the target decisions and the nature of the decision-maker culture. A full understanding of these contextual and cultural issues must explicitly consider each system level involved—the relevant individual decision makers, the small groups in which they function, and the organizational culture and larger culture in which they are embedded.

The technological paradigm is more closely compatible with general systems theory than the basic research paradigm. Technology stresses naturalistic, real-world contexts in all their complexity, whereas basic research typically focuses upon a few variables, usually at only one systems level, and tries to control variables at the other levels.

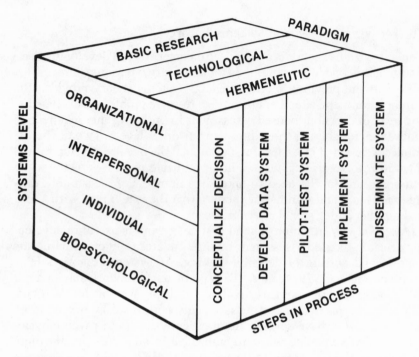

FIGURE 2.1. Three Dimensions of Decision-Focused Assessment

A Typology of Decision-Focused Assessment

Figure 2.1 outlines the three dimensions of decision-focused assessment as discussed in this chapter and offered as a framework for describing particular assessment models in the remainder of the book. As shown in the figure, the dimensions create a 3×4×5 matrix within which any assessment system can be described. The figure also suggests that any assessment system can be viewed from at least 60 different perspectives! There is no escape from the complexity of the natural world.

The Organization of This Book

We have argued that decision-focused assessment has a distinct process structure, and that this structure is better matched to a technological than to a basic research paradigm. We have also argued that decision-focused assessment has a close affinity with general systems theory, and again, the technological paradigm is more closely compatible with this theory than is the basic research paradigm.

The next eight chapters of this book describe illustrative, sophisticated systems of decision-focused assessment, together with discussions of the systems by selected psychologists who are sample decision maker/consumers of them. The systems were chosen with the above themes in mind. First, the systems are based upon conceptual and methodological models from the technological side of the epistemological continuum outlined in Table 2.2. Second, as shown in Figure 2.1, the systems were chosen to reflect four different levels articulated in the general systems theory of human behavior: the biopsychological, individual, interpersonal, and organizational levels. Further discussion of these systems in the context of the general themes discussed in the present chapter will be given in the book's summary chapter.

We hope this book will encourage readers to consider the TAP paradigm as a "cultural alternative" to the basic research and qualitative-interpretive paradigms. We believe that the increasing adoption of TAP will enhance psychology's effectiveness in decision-focused assessment.

REFERENCES

Arkowitz, H., & Messer, S. B. (Eds.). (1984). *Psychoanalytic therapy and behavior therapy: Is integration possible?* New York: Plenum.

Ayer, A. J. (1959). *Logical positivism.* New York: Free Press.

Azrin, N. H. (1977). A strategy for applied research: Learning based but outcome oriented. *American Psychologist, 32,* 140–149.

Barlow, D. H., Hayes, S. C., & Nelson, R. O. (1984). *The scientist practitioner: Research and accountability in clinical and educational settings.* Elmsford, N.Y.: Pergamon.

Bevan, W. (1976). The sound of the wind that's blowing. *American Psychologist, 31,* 481–489.

Bevan, W. (1980). On getting in bed with a lion. *American Psychologist, 35,* 779–789.

Beyer, J. M., & Trice, H. M. (1982). The utilization process: A conceptual framework and synthesis or empirical findings. *Administrative Science Quarterly, 27,* 591–622.

Bronfenbrenner, U. (1979). *The ecology of human development.* Cambridge, Mass.: Harvard University Press.

Broskowski, A. (1971). Clinical psychology: A research and developmental model. *Professional Psychology, 2,* 235–242.

Broskowski, A., & Schulberg, H. C. (1974). Clinical research and development: A model training program. *Professional Psychology, 5,* 133–139.

Bunge, M. (1974). Towards a philosophy of technology. In A. C. Michalos (Ed.), *Philosophical problems of science and technology.* Boston: Allyn & Bacon.

Burstein, L., Freeman, H. E., Sirotnik, K. A., Delandshere, G., & Hollis, N. (1985). Data collection: The Achilles Heel of evaluation research. In P. H. Rossi, H. F. Freeman, & L. Burstein (Eds.), *Improving data collection reliability in program evaluation.* Beverly Hills, Calif.: Sage.

Carnap, R. (1928). *Der Logische Aufbau der Welt.* Berlin: Welkreis Verlag.

Cartwright, D. (1973). Determinants of scientific progress: The case of research on the risky shift. *American Psychologist, 28,* 222–231.

Ceci, S. J., & Walker, E. (1983). Private archives and public needs. *American Psychologist, 38,* 414–423.

Cohen, D. K., & Garet, M. S. (1975). Reforming educational policy with applied social research. *Harvard Educational Review, 45,* 17–41.

Cronbach, L. J. (1975). Beyond the two disciplines of scientific psychology. *American Psychologist, 30,* 116–127.

Cronbach, L. J., Ambron, S. R., Dornbusch, S. M., Hess, R. D., Hornik, R. C., Phillips, O. C., Walker, & Weiner, S. S. (1980). *Toward reform in program evaluation.* San Francisco: Jossey-Bass.

Davis, H. R., & Salasin, S. E., (1978). Strengthening the contribution of social R & D to policy-making. In L. E. Lynn (Ed.), *Knowledge and policy: The uncertain connection.* Washington, D.C.: National Academy of Sciences.

Deitchman, S. (1976). *The best-layed schemes: A tale of social research and bureaucracy.* Cambridge, Mass.: MIT Press.

Epstein, S. (1980). The stability of behavior: II. Implications for psychological research. *American Psychologist, 35,* 790–806.

Fishman, D. B. & Neigher, W. D. (1982). American psychology in the eighties: Who will buy? *American Psychologist, 37,* 533–546.

Frankel, C. (Ed.). (1976). *Controversies and decisions: The social sciences and public policy.* New York: Russell Sage Foundation.

Gergen, K. J. (1973). Social psychology as history. *Journal of Personality and Social Psychology, 26,* 309–320.

Gergen, K. J. (1982). *Toward transformation in social knowledge.* New York: Springer-Verlag.

Gergen, K. J. (1985). The social constructionist movement in modern psychology. *American Psychologist, 40,* 266–275.

Gilbert, T. F. (1978). *Human competence: Engineering worthy performance.* New York: McGraw-Hill.

Gold, N. (1983). Stakeholder and program evaluation: Characterizations and reflections. In A. S. Bryk (Ed.), *Stakeholder based evaluation.* San Francisco: Jossey-Bass.

Greenwald, A. G. (1976). An editorial. *Journal of Personality and Social Psychology, 33,* 1–7.

Hanson, N. R. (1958). *Patterns of discovery.* Cambridge: Cambridge University Press.

Heelan, P. A. (1983). *Space-perception and the philosophy of science.* Berkeley: University of California Press.

Heisenberg, W. (1958). *Physics and philosophy.* New York: Harper & Row.

Hill, G. (1981). Of mice and men and now computers. *New York Times,* August 30, p. 18E.

House, R. (1978). Assumptions underlying evaluation models. *Educational Researcher, 7,* 4–12.

Johnson, J. H., Williams, T. A., Giannetti, R. A., Klinger, D. E., & Dittmer, H. E. (1979). The auto repair shop model: A vehicle for the transmission of management technology. *Professional Psychology, 10,* 373–380.

Kimble, G. A. (1984). Psychology's two cultures. *American Psychologist, 39,* 833–839.

Koch, S. (1959). Epilogue. In S. Koch (Ed.), *Psychology: A study of a science* (Vol. 3). New York: McGraw-Hill.

Krasner, L., & Houts, A. C. (1984). A study of the "value" systems of behavioral scientists. *American Psychologist, 39,* 840–850.

Kuhn, T. S. (1962). *The structure of scientific revolutions.* Chicago: University of Chicago Press.

Levine, M. (1974). Scientific method and the adversary model: Some preliminary thoughts. *American Psychologist, 29,* 661–677.

Mayo, C. (1977, November). *Toward applicable social psychology.* Presidential address to the New England Psychological Association. Worcester, Mass.

Miller, J. G. (1978). *Living systems.* New York: McGraw-Hill.

Morell, J. A. (1979). *Program evaluation in social research.* Elmsford, N.Y.: Pergamon.

Neigher, W. D., & Fishman, D. B. (1985). From science to technology: Reducing problems in mental health evaluation by paradigm shift. In P. H. Rossi, H. F. Freeman, & L. Burstein (Eds.), *Improving data collection reliability in program evaluation.* Beverly Hills, Calif.: Sage.

Nessel, J. (1982). Understanding psychological man: A state-of-the-science report. *Psychology Today, 16,* 40–59.

Newell, A. (1973). You can't play 20 questions with nature and win. In W. G. Chase (Ed.), *Visual information processing.* New York: Academic Press.

Patton, M. Q. (1978). *Utilization-focused evaluation.* Beverly Hills, Calif.: Sage.

Patton, M. Q. (1980a). *Qualitative Evaluation Methods.* Beverly Hills, Calif.: Sage.

Patton, M. Q. (1980b). Making methods choices. *Evaluation and Program Planning, 3,* 219–228.

Price, R. H., & Cherniss, C. (1977). Training for a new profession: Research as social action. *Professional Psychology, 8,* 222–231.

Reichardt, C. S., & Cook, T. D. (1980). "Paradigms lost": Some thoughts on choosing methods in evaluation research. *Evaluation and Program Planning, 3,* 229–236.

Rich, R. F. (1979). Editor's introduction. *Knowledge: Creation, Diffusion, Utilization, 1*, 3–5.

Schlick, M. (1939). *Problems of ethics*. New York: Prentice-Hall.

Scriven, M. (1967). The methodology of evaluation. In R. W. Tyler, R. M. Gagne, & M. Scriven (Eds.), *Perspectives in curriculum evaluation*. AERA Monograph Series on Curriculum Evaluation No. 1. Chicago: Rand McNally.

Scriven, M. (1972). Pros and cons about goal-free evaluation. *Evaluation Comment, 3*, 1–7.

Sechrest, L. (1976). Personality. In M. R. Rozenszweig & L. W. Porter (Eds.), *Annual Review of Psychology, 27*, 1–28.

Smart apes, or dumb? (1982, May). *New York Times.*

Snow, C. P. (1964). *The two cultures and a second look*. London: Cambridge University Press.

Staats, A. W. (1983). *Psychology's crisis of disunity: Philosophy and method for a unified science*. New York: Praeger.

Staats, A. W. (1984, August). *Scientific chaos is not science: A proposal to solve psychology's disunity*. Invited address to the American Psychological Association. Toronto, Canada.

Suppe, F. (1974). *The structure of scientific theories*. Urbana: University of Illinois Press.

Toulmin, S. (1953). *The philosophy of science*. London: Hutchinson.

Wachtel, P. L. (1980) Investigation and its discontents: Some constraints on progress in psychological research. *American Psychologist, 35*, 399–408.

Weimer, W. B. (1977). Science as a rhetorical transaction: Toward a nonjustificational conception of rhetoric. *Philosophy and Rhetoric, 10*, 1–29.

Weiss, C. H. (Ed.). (1972). *Evaluating social action programs*. Boston: Allyn & Bacon.

Wertheimer, M., Barclay, A. G., Cook, S. W., Kiesler, C. A., Koch, S., Riegel, K. F., Rorer, L. G., Senders, V. L., Smith, M. B., & Sperling, S. E. (1978). Psychology and the future. *American Psychologist, 33*, 631–647.

Wholey, J. S. (1983). *Evaluation and effective public management*. Boston: Little, Brown.

Wholey, J. S., Scanlon, J. W., Duffy, H. G., Fukumotu, J. S., & Vogt, L. M. (1970). *Federal evaluation policy: Analyzing the effects of public programs*. Washington, D.C.: The Urban Institute.

Windle, C., & Neigher, W. D. (1978). Ethical problems in program evaluation: Advice for trapped evaluators. *Evaluation and Program Planning, 1*, 97–108.

Wittgenstein, L. (1922). *Tractatus logico-philosophicus*. London: Routledge & Kegan Paul.

Woolfolk, R. L., & Richardson, F. C. (1984). Behavior therapy and the ideology of modernity. *American Psychologist, 39*, 777–786.

ASSESSING BIOPSYCHOLOGICAL
FUNCTION

We now begin descriptions of assessment systems at each level of organization with which applied psychology is concerned. Buffery starts with a presentation of brain function therapy, an approach to clinical neuropsychology that links assessment with individually designed rehabilitation programs for people who have suffered cerebral damage. Brain function therapy as "probe" examines how well the brain is working. The extent and severity of dysfunctions are determined; functions served by intact brain tissue are mapped. Brain function therapy as "bombardment" presents to the patient a complex set of stimuli engineered to encourage maximum recovery of functions controlled by injured parts of the brain, as well as shifts in control to intact contralateral parts of the brain. Under supervision of a "caring team" of professionals and with the help of family members, the testing and rehabilitation routines can be individually programmed for a personal computer. Frequent, home-based sessions, managed directly by the patient and his family, can be conducted in this way, promising greater benefits than the usual weekly visits to a neuropsychologist, speech therapist, or other professional.

Buffery's chapter is discussed by Christopher Barbrack. When Barbrack is not teaching, writing, or meeting other academic responsibilities as a Rutgers faculty member, he practices psychology. One of his recent professional projects has been to develop a neuropsychological assessment and rehabilitation service at a private, multiservice clinic. He therefore views Buffery's proposals not only from the perspective of a scholar but from the position of a practitioner who needs to put a practically useful program into operation. His comments on the limits as well as the merits of brain function therapy deserve close consideration. As Barbrack notes and as Buffery acknowledges, the procedure involves a new combination of ideas and techniques, of equipment and personnel. The rationale is intriguing and preliminary reports of effect are encouraging, but the data base required for general professional use is only beginning to form.

In Chapter 4, Katkin describes the main procedures used in psychophysiological assessment. He reviews major findings on psychophysiological response in mental disorders, especially anxiety, schizophrenia, and sociopathy. He notes, however, that by far the most widespread use of psychophysiological assessment procedures to guide practical decisions is in government and industry. Paraprofessional polygraphers are routinely asked to appraise security risks of employees in the Department of Defense. Lie detection techniques are widely used by commercial employers to ferret out dishonesty among workers. After reviewing research on the accuracy of these procedures, Katkin discusses the conceptions and misconceptions upon which practical uses of psychophysiological assessment are commonly based. Since physiological responses are rooted in biological organ structures, they are often considered more "real" than behavioral or cognitive responses. The author examines the logic of this idea and argues that psychophysiological assessment techniques may be more properly employed as measures of physiological functions than of complex biopsychosocial processes such as lying or stress. He concludes with a discussion of psychophysiological assessment in behavioral medicine, and indicates the kinds of research needed to bring the technology into more effective use.

William Neigher, coauthor with Daniel Fishman of Chapter 2, doubles as discussant of Katkin's statement. Neigher's primary employment is as an administrator in an acute-care general hospital. He has recently taken responsibility for developing and marketing a division of behavioral medicine in the hospital, and writes from that experience in his comments on Katkin's chapter. To survive economically, hospital administrators must bring market considerations into their plans, along with concerns for the clinical effectiveness and the research base of any practices they offer the public. The financial attractiveness of some programs, such as those in stress management, pain control, and biofeedback, may lead to misuse. Practitioners are advised to heed the cautions of critics like Katkin lest they oversell products of dubious merit. At the same time, they should realize that many clinical services with weak foundations in basic research may responsibly be offered to patients desperate for help of any kind, as long as the limits of knowledge about the service are accurately described. New patterns of research funding that provide seed money for technological innovation, prototype development, and commercial adoption offer promising means to encourage some of the research whose need Katkin has emphasized.

Chapter 3

The Promotion of Neuropsychological Rehabilitation: The Role of the Home-Based Personal Computer in Brain Function Therapy

ANTHONY W. H. BUFFERY

After asserting his belief that neuropsychology had traditionally lacked a therapeutic emphasis, Lishman (1975) commented, "It is a fascinating subject of enormous theoretical importance, but it seems often to be oriented in directions other than helping people to get better" (p. 259). Even when neuropsychologists have directed their work toward problems in clinical practice the emphasis has been upon assessment rather than treatment. Much effort has gone into developing tests alleged to be sensitive to the presence of damage in the central nervous system (CNS) and to the localization of such damage (for review see Lezak, 1983). However, advances in medical technology appear to cast many psychological procedures into obsolescence. In particular, the emergence of more discriminative radiological techniques may make neuropsychological assessment designed to determine the presence, locus, and extent of CNS damage of less use and interest than before. At the present time, clinical neuropsychology is becoming more concerned with decisions regarding the design of rehabilitation programs. Therein lies its rationale as a discipline and its future as a profession (Buffery, 1977).

In this chapter a brief review of clinical neuropsychology precedes a description of the clinical neuropsychologist as rehabilitation scientist (Buffery & Burton, 1982). Particular attention will be paid to the development of brain function therapy (BFT) and the implications of its promotion through the use of home-based personal computers. Finally the role of neuropsychological assessment in contributing toward decisions regarding the planning and evaluation of patient-specific rehabilitation programs is examined.

THE STATE OF THE ART IN NEUROPSYCHOLOGICAL ASSESSMENT AND REHABILITATION

Despite an extensive literature describing the history of attempts to apply the methods and skills of psychology to the problems of the neurological patient, the question of whether clinical neuropsychology can be regarded as a distinctive substantive discipline has remained open. This is primarily so because the administration of psychological tests to patients suffering from neurological disorders cannot in itself be a methodology, or even of heuristic value, unless performed within the context of a theory and applied in ways that produce important consequences. Without a theory of neuropsychological function and dysfunction and the consequent generation of testable hypotheses, the quantification of the degree of impairment amounts to little more than "test bashing the brain bashed," and neurological patients, like all patients, expect more from an investigation than a description of what they already know in a language that they cannot understand. Not unreasonably, a patient assumes that the results of an inquiry will contribute toward decisions and strategies for treatment. After all, the patient is there to get better, not merely to provide data.

In 1870 Fritsch and Hitzig criticized the prevailing practice in neurological examinations of judging the intellectual status of a patient by informal inquiry and called for more objective and standardized measures of mental function. This call was finally answered in 1905 when Binet and Simon formally tested retarded and brain-damaged children in Paris. In 1907 Bekhterev founded the Psychoneurological Institute in what is now Leningrad (see Bekhterev, 1905–1907), and in 1909 Burt published the results of his then acclaimed experimental tests of intelligence in London. In 1934 Strauss and Savitsky wrote somewhat prematurely: ". . . the day has passed when the neuropsychiatrist can ask the injured person a few questions and as a result of a brief interview form an opinion as to the intactness of all the psychological processes, the patient's adaptive capacity and his personality make-up" (p. 911). This was premature because in 1939 Rylander could still criticize psychiatric evaluations of the mental state as being "a tangled skein of objective observations and subjective opinions" (p. 50). He recommended their replacement by more uniform psychological measures, thereby permitting meaningful comparisons of results among patients.

The introduction of psychometric tests to assess the intellectual, cognitive, motor, and personality characteristics of the neurological patient may be seen as an extension of clinical psychology but does not in itself represent a discipline of clinical neuropsychology. For though such tests provided useful baselines and indeed repeatable measures for the efficacy of intervention, the introduction of standardized psychometry into neurology at first merely encouraged the comparison of groups of patients at the expense of the individual case study. Further, the addition to the number of CNS-damaged patients by the casualties of warfare only reinforced the group analysis approach. Because of the idiosyncratic nature of the dysfunctioning subsequent upon similar CNS lesions in different people, the further the clinician moves from data derived from single case studies, the less relevance the neuropsychological measures have to the rehabilitation of the individual patient (Buffery, 1974). The investigation of groups of CNS-damaged patients has academic merit, but its practical importance should be judged by the degree to which the findings influence clinical practice and a particular patient's prognosis. Very few studies adopting the group comparison approach have had such an influence, with exceptions such as the studies of Milner (1971) on brain surgery in epileptic patients and of Newcombe (1969) on patients with missile wounds to the brain. In general, greater relevance to clinical issues has been achieved by single-case-study neuropsychological research, particularly in the area of amnesia (e.g., Milner et al., 1968; Shallice & Warrington, 1970; Weiskrantz & Warrington, 1975). For single-case-study methodology see Davidson and Costello (1969), Shapiro (1970), and Yule and Hemsley (1977). For its use within clinical neuropsychology see Shallice (1979) and Walsh (1985).

The main difference between traditional clinical psychology and clinical neuropsychology in their approaches to the assessment of a neurological patient is that the former tests for evidence of an "organic syndrome" (e.g., loss of the "abstract attitude," Goldstein, 1952) whereas the latter tests for signs of the etiology, locus, and nature of the dysfunctioning (see Walsh, 1978). Both disciplines were at first limited to assessment for assessment's sake, frequently using tests that were neither appropriate for, nor standardized upon, neurological populations. Eventually more specific neuropsychological tests emerged, but they usually amounted to little more than quantified versions of informal procedures from clinical neurology. Some clinical psychologists administered such tests but usually without the training in neurology that would have allowed informed and useful interpretation. Gradually those clinical psychologists not specializing in neurological dysfunctioning concentrated their skills upon other classes of patients for whom their standardized psychometries were at least appropriate.

As noted in the first chapter of this book, clinical psychologists caring for behaviorally or psychiatrically disturbed patients have long since added therapeutic techniques to their psychometrics. Behavioral therapeutic techniques were derived largely from experimental studies of the learning process and appeared particularly promising as a systematic means of changing behavior (Feldman & Broadhurst, 1976; Franks, 1984; Rachman & Wilson, 1980). Buffery (1977) suggested that the clinical neuropsychologist could do the same for neurologically damaged patients and should be encouraged to develop appropriate therapies to promote recovery of brain function, drawing on the expanding knowledge concerning the influence of learning upon the development and regeneration of the nervous system (reviewed by Buffery, 1985; Finger, 1978; Fletcher & Satz, 1983; Gaze & Keating, 1974; St. James-Roberts, 1979, 1981; Satz & Fletcher, 1983; Smith, 1983). But the therapeutic role of the clinical neuropsychologist would have poor foundations if built upon assessment procedures that were simply inappropriate applications either of the psychometrics of clinical psychology or the informal guess work of clinical neurology. New tests were required. Recently, two major contributions to neuropsychological assessment have appeared. First, Reitan and colleagues modified and expanded Halstead's test batteries (see Boll, 1981; Reitan & Davison, 1974). Then Golden and colleagues modified and standardized Christensen's (1975a, 1975b, 1975c) formulation of Luria's clinical skills (see Golden, 1981a; Golden et al., 1978). Although they offer some advantages over previous methods, these contributions have not generally been sensitive to individual idiosyncrasies of neurological dysfunction or clearly related to strategies for personal rehabilitation (Buffery & Burton, 1982).

WHITHER CLINICAL NEUROPSYCHOLOGY?

The promise of clinical neuropsychology lies in the bringing together of neuropsychological theory with sensitive techniques of diagnosis for neurological dysfunction and patient-specific strategies for learning and relearning (Buffery, 1977). Further, as will be shown below, the boundary between assessment and rehabilitation can be developed from an interface into an interaction. At present, however, many of the tests administered by clinical neuropsychologists are time consuming, of little intrinsic interest, and of no apparent relevance to patients' perceptions of their own problems. These tests do not usually provide scores that clearly indicate the nature and the rate of the information that the patient can handle, nor do they help specify the particular difficulties experienced. It is impossible to gain insights into strategies for recovery from the mere listing of the results of such tests. In consequence, the efforts of professional therapists, of the family, and indeed of the patient in question to promote rehabilitation have rarely drawn upon the potentially useful information camouflaged by the numbers and jargon of the clinical neuropsychologist's typical report. Usually the professional therapists are overworked and the families of patients are overwhelmed, so that they are unable to monitor and promote a neurological patient's rehabilitation without interruption or distraction. By the nature of his or her condition, a patient has a considerable amount of time to spare, but this usually becomes time to kill. Patients sit in idle despair, waiting for the next consultation or hospital visit. Such episodic treatment is anathema to the enhancement of CNS recovery. The patients are frustrated by their inability to help themselves get better. They lose their belief in the possibility of recovery and then their motivation to improve. Many become clinically depressed. Such additional problems to the patient's original CNS damage are, at least in part, the result of ill-conceived therapeutic intervention and are clearly counterproductive to its aims.

In short, the quality of various hospital-based therapies could be improved. This might be achieved by the creation of "caring teams," the professional balance of which would be defined by the nature of the patient-specific program of rehabilitation undertaken (Buffery, 1983). Such programs would incorporate, and be partly derived from, sensitive, motivating and disability-relevant techniques of neuropsychological assessment and retraining, with an emphasis upon home-based self-help (for further reading see Diller & Gordon, 1981; Filskov & Leli, 1981; Matthews, 1981).

Miller (1978, 1980, 1984) distinguishes usefully between two goals for the therapeutic intervention: the restitution and the amelioration of neuropsychological function. Restitution implies the full or partial restoration of function, that is, function as a means. Amelioration implies assistance to perform despite handicap, that is, function as an end. Miller (1984) states that: ". . . amelioration is a much more sensible and potentially attainable goal than restitution for a psychological intervention directed at the management and rehabilitation of brain-injured subjects" (p. 79). It is possible, however, that the goals of amelioration and restitution can be combined. Miller's statement disregards recent insights into the regenerative and compensatory capacities of the CNS (reviewed by Marshall, 1984), and overlooks the possibility that a patient's response to "amelioration" could be improved if built upon a maximized "restitution." Viewed in this way, a neurological patient is not necessarily a candidate for one of these two approaches to neuropsychological therapy, but rather relatively suited at different times and to different degrees to either approach, or to combinations of both. Acknowledging the unique complexity and changing nature of the neurological patient's predicament gives strength to the argument for less rigid techniques of neuropsychological assessment and retraining, and for the reorganization of the various and separated therapeutic disciplines into caring teams.

Powell (1981) asserts that behavior therapy is the single most promising approach to the retraining of overt and covert skills among neurologically impaired patients. Yates (1970) has defined behavior therapy as

the attempt to utilize systematically that body of empirical and theoretical knowledge which has resulted from the application of the experimental method in psychology and its related disciplines (physiology and neurophysiology) in order to explain the genesis and maintenance of abnormal patterns of behaviour; and to apply that knowledge to the treatment or prevention of these abnormalities by means of controlled experimental studies of the single case, both descriptive and remedial. (p. 18)

Most contemporary behavior therapists regard behavior as being comprised of at least three interrelated systems: overt activity, cognition, and physiology. These systems do not refer to the "brain" per se. Even in Yates's (1970) textbook on behavior therapy "brain" is not indexed, and reference to neural processing or to brain-damaged people is minimal. Yet, as Powell (1981) points out, it is known from the work of neuropsychologists (e.g., Luria, 1966, 1973) that the brain is the controller of overt activity, which is planned by the frontal lobes in conjunction with modality-specific processing centers; the brain is the seat of cognition, elaborating and interpreting the information arriving at the cortex from the sense organs, forming images and drawing upon memories;

and the brain is the ultimate receptor and governor of physiological states, as mediated by the limbic system and the brain-stem activating systems. Consequently, behavior therapy, with its tripartite goal of changing overt activity, cognition, and physiology, implicitly modifies the functioning of almost every region of the brain. It is therefore a natural development and a legitimate aim for behavior therapy to modify the brain directly. Buffery (1977) coined the phrase brain function therapy (BFT) for this extension of behavior therapy. It is the claim of this chapter that BFT has considerable potential to assist in the rehabilitation of people with CNS damage, particularly when presented in the context of a caring team of therapists and experienced intensively by the individual through home-based self-administration under hospital-based monitoring.

But, if a therapeutic paradigm (behavior therapy) can be said to have become intrigued by the brain, can it also be said that a brain science (neuropsychology) has become intrigued by the idea of therapy? Until recently apparently not. Textbooks on neuropsychology have typically paid little attention to therapy (see Lezak, 1983; Reitan & Davison, 1974; Walsh, 1978; Williams, 1979). However, since the work of Luria and his colleagues (Luria, 1963, 1970; Luria et al., 1969; Luria & Tsvetkova, 1964) there has been growing interest in neuropsychological rehabilitation (see Filskov & Boll, 1981; Kolb & Whishaw, 1980). Two particularly useful books focus on this topic (Miller, 1984; Powell, 1981) from a broader vantage point than that of Golden (1981a, 1981b) with his emphasis upon the Halstead-Reitan and Luria-Nebraska test batteries. There is reason to hope that the implications of BFT will further both interest and research in neuropsychological rehabilitation.

BRAIN FUNCTION THERAPY

Overview of BFT

The aim of brain function therapy (Buffery, 1977; Buffery & Burton, 1982) is to influence the course of learning, and in particular of relearning, in the cerebrum itself. BFT is a treatment technique that can focus knowledge from many disciplines upon the particular rehabilitation requirements of a neurologically damaged person through the technology of an appropriately programmed personal computer (Benjamin & Buffery, 1984). It would do so under the general supervision of a team of rehabilitation scientists, such as speech therapists, physiotherapists, and occupational therapists, who themselves would work closely with colleagues from the medical, nursing, psychiatric, psychological, and social services and, most importantly, with members of the patient's family. The particular pattern for the organization and balance of such a "caring team" would be governed by the changing nature of the person's difficulties, their stage of treatment, and the degree to which BFT was home-based and self-administered. Throughout, however, the key role of orchestrating the contributions from the various professional disciplines and from the family would fall to the clinical neuropsychologist, who would also assist in the creation of patient-specific assessment and rehabilitation tasks in the form of "software," utilizing knowledge from psychology, neurology, and personal computer technology.

The principles underlying brain function therapy will be introduced in relation to the treatment of a particular stroke patient. Further details of this case are reported by Buffery and Burton (1982). This will be followed by proposals for enhancing neuropsychological rehabilitation by modifications of BFT in the light of recent advances. Finally, further possibilities for BFT are considered.

The Recent Past of BFT

Clearly lateralized neural structures necessary to subserve the perception and production of speech are found not only in the adult human brain (Geschwind & Levitsky, 1968), but at birth (Witelson & Pallie, 1973) and even as early as the 18th gestational week (Wada et al., 1975). Buffery (1968, 1971a) proposed that the typical left-sided cerebral predominance for language functions in human adulthood is acquired through interaction between primarily audio-verbal and visuo-verbal stimuli with innate, species-specific, lateralized and linguistically predisposed neural structures. This proposal was elaborated by Buffery and Gray (1972) and later revised by Buffery in 1974, 1976, 1978, and 1981a. Any approach to the promotion of recovery of cerebral function following cerebral trauma must consider the implications of these innate structural asymmetries of the brain and their related functional counterparts (Berent, 1981; Kinsbourne, 1981; Zangwill, 1960).

A Case Study

The neurological patient was a university-educated, right-handed gentleman who had suffered extensive damage from a series of strokes in his mid-forties to his left and language-predominant cerebral hemisphere. BFT commenced two years after his last cerebral trauma, by which time, according to the accepted view on the efficacy of various therapies for a patient of this age and with such a severe language disability, posttraumatic recovery should have reached an asymptotic level. In consequence, no significant improvement would be expected for measures of recovery from various difficulties in language comprehension and expression after brain damage, including the expected, and commonly accepted, relationship of posttraumatic to pretraumatic performance (see Kertesz & McCabe, 1977). The procedure was intended to monitor the damaged brain's ongoing patterns of functional recovery (BFT as "probe") and to present a task, the processing of which would accelerate the rate of this functional recovery toward a higher asymptotic level of posttraumatic performance than would otherwise have been predicted (BFT as "bombardment").

Figure 3.1 shows a single trial from the most advanced task experienced by the patient. Multiple stimuli were presented separately but simultaneously to the auditory, visual, and tactile (i.e., haptic or active-exploration-by-touch) modalities. The patient was instructed to keep his gaze fixed on the center of a tachistoscopic screen. By naming a number that would appear in the center of the screen he could validate adherence to this instruction. His main task, however, was to discriminate semantically among the various stimuli he received by identifying the stimulus that was different in meaning from the other two. He could show that he had done so by naming the "odd word out." In this trial, the printed word LAD was presented by tachistoscopic exposure for the "titrated" duration (Buffery, 1974), of 150 msec to the left visual hemifield (and thereby initially to the right cerebral hemisphere). Simultaneously, the plastic letters forming the word BOY were presented for dichaptic perception by the left hand (and thereby initially to the right cerebral hemisphere) in conflict with the right hand's palpation of a neutral stimulus (a sponge). At the same time, the spoken word "TOY" was presented by the dichotic listening technique to the left ear (and thereby initially to the right cerebral hemisphere) in conflict with the right ear's reception of a neutral stimulus ("white noise").

The correct vocal response is "6 TOY" because the word TOY is the "odd word out" in meaning and the accurate naming of the number six validates the trial. Figure 3.1 illustrates a stage in BFT in which there is a one-trial attempt to "bombard" the patient's functionally less appropriate, though structurally sound, right cerebral hemisphere with a "language" task, rather than to "probe" the patient's functionally more appropriate, though damaged, left cerebral hemisphere. The rationale for these methodologies may be found in the work of Buffery, 1971b,

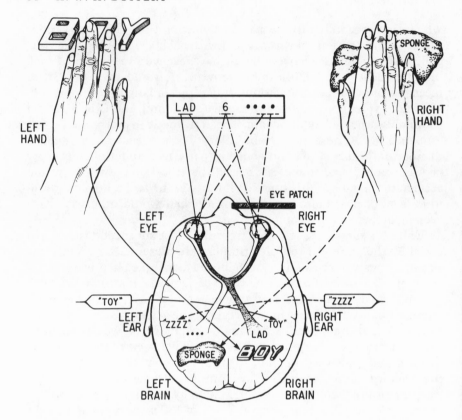

FIGURE 3.1. Lateralized Cross-Tri-Modal Semantic Discrimination Task Used in Brain Function Therapy

1974, 1976; Geffen et al., 1973; Hubel and Weisel, 1959; Lehmann, 1968; and Witelson, 1974, 1977.

In this original investigation of BFT principles, no personal computer or caring team was involved, and the clinical trial was hospital-based. After the use of BFT as a probe to establish the nature of the damaged brain's hemispheric potential for language function, this particular patient experienced BFT as bombardment to the right cerebral hemisphere. Had damage been less extensive in the left it is probable that the patient would have received bombardment to that cerebral hemisphere, for although language shift to the right can occur, according to Rasmussen and Milner (1975) most "natural" recovery appears to be mediated by intact portions of a damaged but language-predominant cerebral hemisphere. The encouragement of a "right shift" for language was deemed necessary for the patient under discussion. He worked through one sensory modality at a time (visual, V; auditory, A; tactile, T) with progressively more difficult verbal material for recognition and then comparison (from upper- and lower-case single letters to words). Then the simultaneous pairing of different sensory modalities was introduced (V/A; V/T; A/T) again progressing from single letters to words. Finally, the simultaneous cross-tri-modal semantic discrimination task was achieved as shown in Figure 3.1. Different words were used for each trial of a 36 trial session, with each sensory modality having a target "odd word out" in meaning on 12 occasions at random. Similarly, "fixation" numbers from 1 to 9 were used on 4 occasions at random. Throughout treatment a trial was discounted and repeated at the end of the session if the fixation number was not reported or incorrectly identified.

Over a period of 30 months, 3 or 4 sessions were conducted per week, each approximately one hour in length. Multimodal presentation was predicted to be more relevant to the goals of BFT in this case because of the evidence relating cross-modal skill to language development (see Chapanis, 1977; Davenport, 1977; de Moore et al., 1985; Locke & Buffery, 1982; O'Connor & Hermelin, 1978). It was hypothesized that the characteristics of the verbalizable stimuli and the requirement for a cross-modal "serial" processing would modify the usually "spatial holistic" processing bias of the right cerebral hemisphere to produce a patterning of neural substrate more appropriate for language skill. Evidence supporting this possibility is derived from the research of developmental neurologists and others (e.g., Isaacson, 1976; Stein et al., 1974; Teuber, 1975).

Figure 3.2 summarizes the patient's progress on the BFT task together with parallel psychometric assessment from February 1976 until August 1978. The bar diagrams at the left show the percentage correct of cross-tri-modal semantic discriminations presented initially to the left or right cerebral hemisphere, averaged for three consecutive days within one week of a month. The psychometric scores were obtained from one of those same three days. The tests employed for psychometric assessment were the Wechsler Adult Intelligence Scale (WAIS) and the Wechsler Bellevue Intelligence Scale (WB 1 and 2) yielding verbal (V) performance (P) and full scale (F) IQ scores, the Wechsler Memory Quotient (MQ), the Logical Memory (LM) test for immediate and delayed memory for prose, and the Rey Osterrieth (RO) test that requires copying and delayed reproduction of an abstract design. Performance on the LM and RO

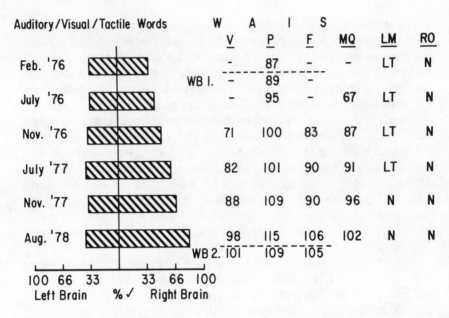

FIGURE 3.2. Changes in Performance of a Stroke Patient Undergoing Brain Function Therapy

tests is designated in Figure 3.2 as normal (*N*) or indicative of left temporal lobe damage (*LT*).

Performance on the cross-tri-modal semantic discrimination task was at the chance level of 33% level of accuracy for each cerebral hemisphere when probed by BFT in February 1976. By August 1978 the functionally more appropriate, but structurally damaged, left cerebral hemisphere was still at chance level, but the functionally less appropriate, but structurally sound, right cerebral hemisphere was at around an 80% level of accuracy, despite the fact that both hemispheres had been equally bombarded. Performance on standardized psychometric and neuropsychological tests also improved from February 1976 to August 1978, particularly on those tests with a strong verbal component, such as WAIS *V*, MQ, and LM. Performance on more spatial tasks, such as the WAIS *P* and RO, remained stable or showed a little improvement. Thus, the patient's enhanced "serial" processing skill, normally subserved predominantly by the left cerebral hemisphere, was not at the expense of the "spatial holistic" processing capacity of the right cerebral hemisphere. Improvement on the Wechsler Bellevue 1 and 2 IQ tests was impressive, particularly from wb1 *V* in February 1976 (unmeasurable) to wb2 *V* in August 1978 (101) since they are equated, but different intelligence scales and the improvement could not be due simply to a practice effect. Some research workers have implied that an improvement of impaired skills in a brain-damaged patient could not occur to such a degree in a mid-40-year-old man between 2 and 4½ years after severe cerebral trauma (cf. Kertesz & McCabe, 1977). Perhaps this belief has arisen more because of the relative impotency of our therapeutic interventions than because of a progressive functional rigidity in the neurophysiology of our patients. If this is so, there is more hope for the neurological patient than anticipated and more challenge for the rehabilitation scientist than is commonly appreciated (see also Blumstein, 1981; Castro-Caldas & Botelho, 1980; Cleeland, 1981; Johnson et al., 1977; Seron, 1982).

Possibilities

How might bft be improved and extended with particular reference to the patient described above, given our present knowledge and new technology? To begin with, from observations at the time and from subsequent studies, the tactile modality seemed to be redundant for this particular "language comprehension" treatment. Indeed, Code (1980, 1982), in another single case study of bft, increased right cerebral hemisphere involvement for phonemic discrimination and for auditory verbal retention and recognition after using left ear dichotic listening "bombardment" alone presented for 35 minutes twice weekly for 28 weeks. In parallel with this bft, Code's patient improved upon the Porch Index of Communicative Ability (pica). All this was achieved in spite of the patient's age (37 years), severity of disorder (left hemisphere cerebrovascular accident, or cva); and delay in commencing bft (after 4 years of conventional speech therapy). Buffery (in preparation) has found significant improvement in spatial skills following bft bombardment of the functionally less appropriate, but structurally sound, left cerebral hemisphere in a 48-year-old patient 18 months after a right cva using only visual and tactile cross-modal "difficult to verbalize" stimuli. It seems probable, therefore, that the patient described in the previous section would have improved in semantic discrimination skills as much from an audio-visual cross-modal bft as he did from the audio-visual tactile variation. This would lend itself to combining dichotic listening with visual hemifield presentation under the control of a home-based personal computer. The patient-specific software for the personal computer could be designed and supervised by a clinical neuropsychologist in close cooperation with a caring team of appropriate professional and family members. Further, and perhaps most important of all, instead of a therapeutic regime that consisted of 3 or 4 hospital-based one-hour sessions per week commencing 2 years after cerebral trauma and lasting for 130 weeks, BFT might have achieved better, or at least the same language benefits, for the brain-damaged patient, from 3 home-based one-hour sessions per day, 5 times per week, commencing a week or so after cerebral trauma and lasting for approximately only 26 weeks.

Other advantages would be derived from home-based, computer-assisted assessment and treatment. The loaned, hired, or purchased personal computer could be programmed by software (disc or casette) that was not only patient-specific in task format (e.g., discrimination, memory, or problem solving) and content (e.g., easy-to-verbalize or difficult-to-verbalize visual, auditory, or tactile stimuli, Buffery 1971b, 1974, 1976) but also in terms of the nature of response required (e.g., key-press, patterned movements or even vocalization, the latter using voice recognition units for shaping impaired speech). Further, the accuracy and latency of such responses could be recorded by the same software components that presented the task, thus facilitating subsequent analyses by the clinical neuropsychologist and by other appropriate members of the caring team. The particular task could be programmed as "paced" or "self-paced" and "titrated" in difficulty according to fluctuations in the ongoing level of performance (Buffery, 1964, 1965, 1966). This would ensure relatively few errors and thereby help maintain the patient's interest and motivation. The next level of BFT tsk would be selected and programmed according to the quality of performance. Throughout, progress in the area of the original neuropsychological dysfunctioning would be monitored and charted, both as a record of therapeutic intervention and as a source of feedback for the patient and family.

Regarding the general utility of BFT, in addition to the studies by Code (1980, 1982) and Buffery (in preparation) reported above, the efficacy of certain of its constituent procedures have been well exemplified in the area of developmental learning disorders. Bakker et al. (1981) utilized "hemisphere-specific" stimulation to improve the reading performance of dyslexic boys. Nineteen poor readers, along with appropriate controls, were divided into two groups according to the "balance model" of dyslexia (Bakker, 1979). Relative ear-advantage for speech recognition was measured by the dichotic listening technique; P-type dyslexics showed a left ear advantage suggesting an overdevelopment of right cerebral hemisphere involvement with language, and L-type dyslexics showed the reverse. Progressively more complex verbal tasks were then presented tachistoscopically to the right visual hemifield (i.e., to the left cerebral hemisphere) of the P-type dyslexics, and to the left visual hemifield (i.e., to the right cerebral hemisphere) of the L-type dyslexics. Separately, the dichotic listening technique was used to feed spoken language into the right ear (i.e., to the left cerebral hemisphere) and light classical music into the left ear (i.e., to the right cerebral hemisphere) of the P-type dyslexics. This was reversed for the L-type dyslexics (see Van den Honert, 1977). These separate visual and auditory "hemisphere-specific" stimulations were experienced over 16 sessions of 40 minutes each, 2 sessions per week. The results suggested that reading ability was significantly improved following visual and auditory verbal stimulation of the right cerebral hemisphere in the L-type dyslexics and of the left in the P-type. That this improvement was due to subtle modification of hemispheric functional asymmetry was supported by the finding of correlated changes in the degree of asymmetry of evoked potentials recorded from the temporal and parietal lobes during the tasks (Bakker et al., 1980). Had the visual and auditory "hemisphere-specific" stimulation occurred simultaneously, thereby encouraging cross-modal information processing, it is likely that Bakker et al., (1981) would have produced greater shifts in the degree of hemispheric functional asymmetry and more significant improvements in reading ability. This general methodology has proved most successful in the design of computer games, and consequently, appropriately programmed BFT should be apposite for the training of impaired or absent skills in children (Anderson & Buffery, 1983; Bodley & Buffery, 1984; Boll & Barth, 1981; Buffery, 1981b; Field & Buffery, 1984; Matheson & Buffery, 1982; Robinson et al., 1985; Rourke, 1981).

Barbrack (personal communication, 1984) has pointed out the implications of home-based brain function therapy for the community-centered clinic where other aspects of neuropsychological assessment would also take place (see also Malloy, 1984). The hospital-based caring team would, of course, be in close contact with the various behavioral scientists working in such clinics. The dynamics of patient management together with libraries of BFT software could become even more personal given this further decentralization of neuropsychological rehabilitation. Further, the "networking" of similar or complementary neurological patients through their personal computers and/or via the community clinic would certainly relieve feelings of isolation and possibly contribute to the general well-being of all involved. After all, technology is only a means to an end, and the end only comes in sight for the patients when they feel themselves to be whole people again, fulfilled within a family, within a community, and within society, at one with themselves and with others.

NOTE

The author wishes to thank the Master and Fellows of Corpus Christi College, Cambridge, for the award of a Senior Research Scholarship in 1984, and in particular Dr. Christopher Andrew and Dr. Richard Bainbridge. The technical assistance of Dr. Herman Hauser and Dr. John Horton of Acorn Computers Limited, Cambridge; and advice on software from Geraint Wiggins, Peter Dickman, and Ben George are gratefully acknowledged. Dr. Hugh Fairweather, the Middlesex Polytechnic, and the Institute of Psychiatry, London, facilitated the writing of this chapter. Dalia Buzin gave invaluable help in editing the final version. Numerous friends, relations, and colleagues in the U.K. and U.S.A. provided necessary support.

REFERENCES

Anderson, V. M., & Buffery, A.W.H. (1983). Personality changes after head injuries in children: A neuropsychological approach. *Proceedings of the 7th annual brain impairment workshop, 1982.* Melbourne, Australia: University of Melbourne Press.

Bakker, D. J. (1979). Hemispheric differences and reading strategies: Two dyslexias? *Bulletin of the Orton Society, 29,* 84–100.

Bakker, D. J., Licht, R., Kok, A., & Bouma, A. (1980). Cortical responses to word reading by right- and left-eared normal and reading-disturbed children. *Journal of Clinical Neuropsychology, 2,* 1–12.

Bakker, D. J., Moerland, R., & Goekoop-Hoefkens, M. (1981). Effects of hemisphere-specific stimulation on the reading performance of dyslexic boys: A pilot study. *Journal of Clinical Neuropsychology, 3,* 155–159.

Bekhterev, V. M. (1905–1907). *Fundamentals of brain function* (7 vols.). St. Petersburg.

Benjamin, T., & Buffery, A.W.H. (1984). Brain Function Therapy (BFT): Theory, microcomputer techniques, clinical practice and home-based rehabilitation. *Proceedings of the 8th annual brain impairment conference, 1983.* Newcastle, Australia: University of Newcastle Press.

Berent, S. (1981). Lateralization of brain function. In S. B. Filskov & T. J. Boll (Eds.), *Handbook of clinical neuropsychology.* New York: Wiley.

Binet, A., & Simon, T. (1905). Methodes nouvelles pour le diagnostic du nouveau intellectual des anormaux. *L'anee Psychologigue, 11,* 191–244.

Blumstein, S. E. (1981). Neurolinguistic disorders: Language-brain relationships. In S. B. Filskov & T. J. Boll (Eds.), *Handbook of clinical neuropsychology.* New York: Wiley.

Bodley, A., & Buffery, A.W.H. (1984). Intellectual deficits in spina bifida children with and without hydrocephalus. *Proceedings of the 8th annual brain impairment conference, 1983.* Newcastle, Australia: University of Newcastle Press.

Boll, T. J. (1981). The Halstead-Reitan neuropsychology battery. In S. B. Filskov & T. J. Boll (Eds.), *Handbook of clinical neuropsychology.* New York: Wiley.

Boll, T. J., & Barth, J. T. (1981). Neuropsychology of brain damage in children. In S. B. Filskov & T. J. Boll (Eds.), *Handbook of clinical neuropsychology.* New York: Wiley.

Buffery, A.W.H. (1964). *The effects of frontal and temporal lobe lesions upon the behaviour of baboons.* Unpublished PhD thesis, University of Cambridge.

Buffery, A.W.H. (1965). Attention and retention following frontal and temporal lesions in the baboon. *Proceedings of the 73rd Annual Convention of the American Psychological Association* (Chicago), pp. 103–104.

Buffery, A.W.H. (1966). Some effects of bilateral frontal and temporal lesions upon the behaviour of baboons. *Proceedings of the 18th International Congress of Psychology (Moscow).* Symposium 10: 77–83.

Buffery, A.W.H. (1968). Evidence for the asymmetrical lateralization of cerebral function. *Bulletin of the British Psychological Society, 21,* 29.

Buffery, A.W.H. (1971a). Sex differences in the development of hemispheric asymmetry of function in the brain. *Brain Research, 31,* 364–365.

Buffery, A.W.H. (1971b). An automated technique for the study of the development of cerebral mechanisms subserving linguistic skill. *Proceedings of the Royal Society of Medicine, 64,* 919–922.

Buffery, A.W.H. (1974). Asymmetrical lateralization of cerebral functions and the effects of unilateral brain surgery in epileptic patients. In S. J. Dimond & J. G. Beaumont (Eds.), *Hemisphere function in the human brain.* London: Elek Science.

Buffery, A.W.H. (1976). Sex differences in the neuropsychological development of verbal and spatial skills. In R. Knight & D. J. Bakker (Eds.), *The neuropsychology of learning disorders: Theoretical approaches.* Baltimore: University Park Press.

Buffery, A.W.H. (1977). Clinical neuropsychology: Review and preview. In S. J. Rachman (Ed.), *Contributions to medical psychology* (Vol. 1). Oxford: Pergamon.

Buffery, A.W.H. (1978). Neuropsychological aspects of language development: An essay on cerebral dominance. In N. Waterson & C. Snow (Eds.), *The development of communication.* London: Wiley.

Buffery, A.W.H. (1981a). Male and female brain structure and function. In N. Grieve & P. Grimshaw (Eds.), *Australian women: Feminist perspectives.* Melbourne: Oxford University Press.

Buffery, A.W.H. (1981b). Visual memory in epileptic children. In A. R. Neasdale,

C. Pratt, R. Grieve, J. Field, D. Illingworth, & J. Hogben (Eds.), *Advances in child development: Theory and research*. Perth: University of Western Australia.

Buffery, A.W.H. (1983). Nemesis to nightingale: The rehabilitation of medicine by the medicine of rehabilitation. *6th annual oration to the Royal Melbourne Hospital*. Melbourne: Royal Melbourne Hospital Press.

Buffery, A.W.H. (1985). Concerning the recovery of human brain functions. *Proceedings of the 6th annual brain impairment conference, 1981*. Sydney, Australia: University of New South Wales Press.

Buffery, A.W.H. (in preparation). Promoting 'spatial' skills in the left cerebral hemisphere by brain function therapy (BFT) after damage to the right.

Buffery, A.W.H., & Burton, A. (1982). Information processing and redevelopment: Towards a science of neuropsychological rehabilitation. In A. Burton (Ed.), *The pathology and psychology of cognition*. London: Methuen.

Buffery, A.W.H., & Gray, J. A. (1972). Sex differences in the development of spatial and linguistic skills. In C. Ounsted & Taylor, D. C. (Eds.), *Gender differences: Their ontogeny and significance*. Edinburgh: Churchill Livingstone.

Burt, C. (1909). Experimental tests of general intelligence. *British Journal of Psychology, 3*, 94–177.

Castro-Caldas, A., & Botelho, M.A.S. (1980). Dichotic listening in the recovery of aphasia after stroke. *Brain and Language, 10*, 145–151.

Chapanis, L. (1977). Language deficits and cross-modal sensory perception. In S. J. Segalowitz & F. A. Gruber (Eds.), *Language development and neurological theory*. New York: Academic Press.

Christensen, A. L. (1975a). *Luria's neuropsychological investigation*. New York: Spectrum.

Christensen, A. L. (1975b). *Luria's neuropsychological investigation: Test cards*. New York: Spectrum.

Christensen, A. L. (1975c). *Luria's neuropsychological investigation: Manual*. New York: Spectrum.

Cleeland, C. S. (1981). Biofeedback as a clinical tool: Its use with the neurologically impaired patient. In S. B. Filskov & T. J. Boll (Eds.), *Handbook of clinical neuropsychology*. New York: Wiley.

Code, C. (1980). Hemispheric specialization retraining in aphasia with dichotic listening. Paper presented at Aphasia Therapy Summer Conference, Cardiff School of Speech Therapy, Cardiff, U. K.

Code, C. (1982). Hemisphere specialization retraining in aphasia: Possibilities and problems. In C. Code & D. Muller (Eds.), *Aphasia therapy*. London: Edward Arnold.

Davenport, R. K. (1977). Cross-modal perception: A basis for language? In D. M. Rumbaugh (Ed.), *Language learning by a chimpanzee: The Lana project*. New York: Academic Press.

Davidson, P. O., & Costello, C. G. (Eds.). (1969). *N = 1: Experimental studies of single cases*. New York: Van Nostrand Rheinhold.

de Moore, D., Buffery, A.W.H., & Nienhuys, T. (1985). A deficit in the non-verbal visual-tactile cross-modal skill of deaf children. *Proceedings of the 2nd national child development conference.* Melbourne, Australia: Institute of Early Child Development Press.

Diller, L., & Gordon, W. A. (1981). Rehabilitation and clinical neuropsychology. In S. B. Filskov & T. J. Boll (Eds.), *Handbook of clinical neuropsychology.* New York: Wiley.

Feldman, M. P., & Broadhurst, A. (Eds.). (1976). *Theoretical and experimental bases of the behaviour therapies.* London: Wiley.

Field, D., & Buffery, A.W.H. (1984). Visual memory in children with spina bifida. *Proceedings of the 8th annual brain impairment conference, 1983.* Newcastle, Australia: University of Newcastle Press.

Filskov, S. B., & Boll, T. J. (Eds.). (1981). *Handbook of clinical neuropsychology.* New York: Wiley.

Filskov, S. B., & Leli, D. A. (1981). Assessment of the individual in neuropsychological practice. In S. B. Filskov & T. J. Boll (Eds.), *Handbook of clinical neuropsychology.* New York: Wiley.

Finger, S. (Ed.). (1978). *Recovery from brain damage.* New York: Plenum.

Fletcher, J. M., & Satz, P. (1983). Age, plasticity, and equipotentiality: A reply to Smith. *Journal of Consulting and Clinical Psychology, 51*(5), 763–767.

Franks, C. M. (Ed.). (1984). *New developments in behavior therapy: From research to clinical application.* New York: Haworth Press.

Fritsch, G., & Hitzig, E. (1870). On the electrical excitability of the cerebrum. In G. von Bonin (Ed.), *Some papers on the cerebral cortex.* Springfield, Ill.: Charles C. Thomas. (1960 translation of German paper.)

Gaze, R. M., & Keating, M. J. (Eds.). (1974). Development and regeneration in the nervous system. *British Medical Bulletin, 33*(2, Whole Volume).

Geffen, G., Bradshaw, J. L., & Nettleton, N. C. (1973). Attention and hemisphere differences in reaction time during simultaneous audio-visual tasks. *Quarterly Journal of Experimental Psychology, 25,* 404–412.

Geschwind, N., & Levitsky, W. (1968). Human brain: Left-right asymmetries in temporal speech region. *Science, 161,* 186–187.

Golden, C. J. (1981a). A standardized version of Luria's neuropsychological tests: A quantitative and qualitative approach to neuropsychological evaluation. In S. B. Filskov & T. J. Boll (Eds.), *Handbook of clinical neuropsychology.* New York: Wiley.

Golden, C. J. (1981b). *Diagnosis and rehabilitation in clinical neuropsychology.* Springfield, Ill.: Charles C. Thomas.

Golden, C. J., Hammeke, T., & Purisch, A. (1978). Diagnostic validity of the Luria neuropsychological battery. *Journal of Consulting and Clinical Psychology, 46,* 1258–1265.

Goldstein, K. (1952). The effects of brain damage on the personality. *Psychiatry, 15,* 245–260.

Hubel, D. H., & Weisel, T. N. (1959). Receptive fields of single neurons in the cat's striate cortex. *Journal of Physiology, 148,* 574–591.

Isaacson, R. L. (1976). 'Recovery'(?) from early brain damage. In T: D. Tjossem (Ed.), *Intervention strategies for high risk infants and young children.* London: University Park Press.

Johnson, J. P., Sommers, R. K., & Weider, W. E. (1977). Dichotic ear preference in aphasia. *Journal of Speech and Hearing Research, 20,* 116–129.

Kertesz, A., & McCabe, P. (1977). Recovery patterns and prognosis in aphasia. *Brain, 100,* 1–18.

Kinsbourne, M. (1981). The development of cerebral dominance. In S. B. Filskov & T. J. Boll (Eds.), *Handbook of clinical neuropsychology.* New York: Wiley.

Kolb, B., & Whishaw, I. Q. (1980). *Fundamentals of human neuropsychology.* San Francisco: W. H. Freeman.

Lehmann, R. A. (1968). Motor co-ordination and hand preference after lesions of the visual pathway and corpus collosum. *Brain, 91,* 525–538.

Lezak, M. D. (1983). *Neuropsychological assessment* (2nd ed.). New York: Oxford University Press.

Lishman, W. A. (1975). Remarks in *Outcome of severe damage to the nervous system. CIBA Foundation symposium no. 34.* Amsterdam: Elsevier-North-Holland.

Locke, M., & Buffery, A.W.H. (1982). Cross-modal skill in deaf children. In G. A. Broe & R. L. Tate (Eds.), *Brain impairment.* Sydney, Australia: University of Sydney Press.

Luria, A. R. (1963). *Recovery of function after brain injury.* New York: Macmillan.

Luria, A. R. (1966). *Higher cortical functions in man.* London: Tavistock.

Luria, A. R. (1970). *Traumatic aphasia.* The Hague: Mouton.

Luria, A. R. (1973). *The working brain: An introduction to neuropsychology.* Harmondsworth, England: Penguin Books.

Luria, A. R., Naydin, V. L., Tsvetkova, L. S., & Vinarskaya, E. N. (1969). Restoration of higher cortical function following local brain damage. In P. J. Vinken & G. W. Bruyn (Eds.), *Handbook of clinical neurology* (Vol. 3). Amsterdam: North-Holland.

Luria, A. R., & Tsvetkova, L. S. (1964). The programming of constructive activity in local brain injuries. *Neuropsychologia, 2,* 95–107.

Marshall, J. F. (1984). Brain function: Neural adaptations and recovery from injury. *Annual Review of Psychology, 35,* 277–308.

Matheson, M., & Buffery, A.W.H. (1982). Auditory verbal information processing in epileptic children. In G. A. Broe & R. L. Tate (Eds.), *Brain impairment.* Sydney, Australia: University of Sydney Press.

Matthews, C. G. (1981). Neuropsychology practice in a hospital setting. In S. B. Filskov & T. J. Boll (Eds.), *Handbook of clinical neuropsychology.* New York: Wiley.

Miller, E. (1978). Is amnesia remediable? In M. M. Gruneberg, P. E. Morris, & R. N. Sykes (Eds.), *Practical aspects of memory.* London: Academic Press.

Miller, E. (1980). Psychological intervention in the management and rehabilitation of neuropsychological impairments. *Behaviour Research and Therapy, 18,* 527–535.

Miller, E. (1984). *Recovery and management of neuropsychological impairments.* Chichester, England: Wiley.

Milner, B. (1971). Interhemispheric differences in the localization of psychological processes in man. In A. Summerfield (Ed.), *Cognitive psychology.* British Medical Bulletin, 27, 272–277.

Milner, B., Corkin, S., & Teuber, H. L. (1968). Further analysis of the hippocampal amnesic syndrome: 14 year follow-up study of H. M. *Neuropsychologia, 6,* 215–234.

Molloy, M. P. (1984). Microcomputers: A new perspective in cognitive rehabilitation. *Proceedings of the 8th Annual Brain Impairment Conference, 1983.* Newcastle, Australia: University of Newcastle Press.

Newcombe, F. (1969). *Missile wounds of the brain.* Oxford: Oxford University Press.

O'Connor, N., & Hermelin, B. (1978). *Seeing and hearing and space and time.* London: Academic Press.

Powell, G. E. (1981). *Brain function therapy.* Aldershot, England: Gower Publishing.

Rachman, S. J., & Wilson, G. T. (1980). *The effects of psychological therapy* (2nd enlarged ed.). New York: Pergamon.

Rasmussen, T., & Milner, B. (1975). Clinical and surgical studies of the cerebral speech areas in men. In K. Zulch, O. Creutzfeldt, & G. C. Galbraith (Eds.), *Cerebral localization.* Berlin: Springer-Verlag.

Reitan, R. M., & Davison, L. A. (Eds.). (1974). *Clinical neuropsychology: Current status and applications.* Washington, D.C.: V. H. Winston.

Robinson, B., Buffery, A.W.H., & Hinchcliff, L. (1985). Intellectual development and the cerebral lateralization of verbal and spatial audio-visual cross-modal skills in boys and girls. *Proceedings of the 2nd National Child Development Conference, 1982.* Melbourne, Australia: Institute of Early Child Development Press.

Rourke, B. P. (1981). Neuropsychological assessment of children with learning disabilities. In S. B. Filskov & T. J. Boll (Eds.), *Handbook of clinical neuropsychology.* New York: Wiley.

Rylander, G. (1939). *Personality changes after operation on the frontal lobes: A clinical study of 32 cases.* Copenhagen: Munksgaard.

St. James-Roberts, I. (1979). Neurological plasticity: Recovery from brain insult and child development. In H. W. Reese (Ed.), *Advances in child development and behaviour.* New York: Academic Press.

St. James-Roberts, I. (1981). A re-interpretation of hemispherectomy data without functional plasticity of the brain: 1. Intellectual function. *Brain and Language, 13,* 31–53.

Satz, P., & Fletcher, J. M. (1983). Emergent trends in neuropsychology: An overview. *Journal of Consulting and Clinical Psychology, 49*(6), 851–865.

Seron, X. (1982). The reeducation of aphasics: The problem of the reeducation strategies. *International Journal of Psychology, 17*, 299–317.

Shallice, T. (1979). Case study approach in neuropsychological research. *Journal of Clinical Neuropsychology, 1*(3), 183–211.

Shallice, T., & Warrington, E. K. (1970). Independent functioning of verbal memory stores: A neuropsychological study. *Quarterly Journal of Experimental Psychology, 22*, 261–273.

Shapiro, M. B. (1970). Intensive assessment of the single case: An inductive-deductive approach. In P. Mittler (Ed.), *The psychological assessment of mental and physical handicaps.* London: Methuen.

Smith, A. (1983). Overview or "Underview"? Comment on Satz and Fletcher's "Emergent trends in neuropsychology: An overview." *Journal of Consulting and Clinical Psychology, 51*(5), 768–775.

Stein, D. G., Rosen, J. J., & Butters, N. (Eds.). (1974). *Plasticity and recovery of function in the central nervous system.* New York: Academic Press.

Strauss, I., & Savitsky, N. (1934). Head injury: Neurologic and psychiatric aspects. *Archives of Neurology and Psychiatry, 31*, 893–955.

Teuber, H. L. (1975). Recovery of function after brain injury in man. In *Outcome of severe damage to the nervous system. CIBA Foundation symposium no. 34.* Amsterdam: Elsevier-North-Holland.

Van den Honert, D. (1977). A neuropsychological technique for training dyslexics. *Journal of Learning Disabilities, 10*, 21–27.

Wada, J. A., Clarke, R., & Hamm, A. (1975). Cerebral hemispheric asymmetry in humans. *Archives of Neurology, 32*, 239–246.

Walsh, K. W. (1978). *Neuropsychology: A clinical approach.* Edinburgh: Churchill Livingstone.

Walsh, K. W. (1985). *Understanding brain damage: A primer of clinical evaluation.* Edinburgh: Churchill Livingstone.

Weiskrantz, L., & Warrington, E. K. (1975). The problem of the amnesic syndrome in man and animals. In R. Isaacson & K. Pribram (Eds.), *The Hippocampus* (Vol. 2). New York: Plenum.

Williams, M. (1979). *Brain damage, behaviour and the mind.* Chichester, England: Wiley.

Witelson, S. F. (1974). Hemispheric specialization for linguistic and non-linguistic tactile perception using a dichotomous stimulation technique. *Cortex, 10*, 3–17.

Witelson, S. F. (1977). Early hemisphere specialization and inter-hemisphere plasticity: An empirical and theoretical review. In S. J. Segalowitz & F. A. Gruber (Eds.), *Language development and neurological theory.* New York: Academic Press.

Witelson, S. F., & Pallie, W. (1973). Left hemisphere specialization of language in the newborn: Neuroanatomical evidence of asymmetry. *Brain, 96*, 641–646.

Yates, A. J. (1970). *Behaviour therapy.* New York: Wiley.

Brain Function Therapy: Progress, Problems, and Prospects

CHRISTOPHER R. BARBRACK

The consequences of CNS impairment can be devastating not only for patients (vanPraag et al., 1980) and their families (Rosenthal, 1984) but also for community-based agencies (e.g., public schools, sheltered workshops) that are called upon to provide comprehensive, long-term services to this population. Within and between these impacted levels (i.e., individual patient, family group, and community organization) CNS impairment presents unique and interlocking problems. At any one of these levels, satisfactory solutions are few and far between. Consequently, it is not surprising that comprehensive programs, aimed at resolving problems at all three levels, are virtually nonexistent. Insofar as brain function therapy attempts to address the problem of neuropsychological rehabilitation on all three levels (and then some), it is unquestionably the kind of unique, pioneering effort that warrants widespread consideration from researchers and practitioners alike.

This endorsement should not obscure BFT's preliminary status. Essentially, Buffery has developed the bare outlines of a potentially powerful approach to neuropsychological rehabilitation. BFT is not a finished product and, consequently, is not likely to have an immediate effect on the routine practice of clinical neuropsychology.

In developing his methods, Buffery drew on new scientific information and technologies to create a coherent rehabilitation package. Forged by intellect and creativity, BFT is ready for large-scale experimental analyses, the beginnings of which are foreshadowed by the few case

101

studies presented by Buffery. This experimental stage probably will focus on BFT's major components: assessment, treatment, and service delivery. Accordingly, the following commentary deals with these components in the interest of helping to identify strengths and weaknesses and to delineate directions for future research.

ASSESSMENT

Brain function therapy's approach to assessment relies heavily on "probes," which consist of a series of tasks, of varying types and levels of difficulty, that require the patient to engage in problem-solving activities based on multisensory input. Probes are tailor made for individual patients and are intended to assess each cerebral hemisphere's capacity for change (i.e., plasticity).

In relation to rehabilitation planning, probes seem potentially valuable for at least two reasons. First, probes may detect residual capacity amid an otherwise largely injured hemisphere. Since rehabilitation tends to be more effective when it is aimed at its natural hemisphere, this type of assessment information could be very useful in determining the targets for intervention. Second, because probes are tailor made, they can be calibrated to a very high level of sensitivity and can be targeted accurately within a narrow range of the cerebral cortex. Possessing these characteristics, probes could be useful in the continuous monitoring of patients' responses to various rehabilitation activities over time.

Unfortunately, as Buffery acknowledges, probes have yet to be standardized. Further, the psychometric characteristics of this assessment procedure are not reported. In this regard, Buffery perilously falls back on the trained eye of the experienced clinician as a substitute for technically adequate data. Unquestionably, BFT assessment would be better if it were conducted by a trained clinician using reliable and valid data for decision-making in the rehabilitation process.

In view of BFT's early stage of development, psychometric weakness is not a fatal flaw. However, Buffery should emphasize the need for additional research in this area. Also, more attention should be devoted to clarifying the specific nature of the probe process, for example, how probes are constructed and what the specific connection is between probe data and rehabilitation planning decisions. In short, what decision rules govern BFT assessment procedures?

The development of neuropsychological assessment procedures

continues to outstrip the development of rehabilitation strategies. Although Buffery tends to exaggerate the gap between standardized neuropsychological test batteries and rehabilitation planning, the loose connection between traditional diagnostic procedures and treatment simply cannot be glossed over. Consequently, BFT's emphasis on rehabilitation and on the linkages between assessment and intervention is responsive to one of the most pressing needs in the fledgling field of clinical neuropsychology.

Nevertheless, Buffery should reconsider his severe criticism of standardized neuropsychological test batteries. The reasons for this are twofold. First, data derived from these procedures are beginning to be used in rehabilitation planning (Golden, 1984). Second, clinical neuropsychologists conduct assessments for various reasons. The choice of an assessment strategy may by preferences of referring psychiatrists or neurologists and of the examining clinician. A neuropsychological examination might be conducted for any of the following reasons: (a) to help determine whether a patient's clinical presentation stems from psychological factors, organic factors, or some combination of factors; (b) to help localize sites of potential cerebral injury; (c) to help establish a patient's current pattern of functional strengths and weaknesses; (d) to provide information for information planning; (e) to monitor changes in a patient's status; and (f) to provide data for research purposes. In view of these many and varied "reasons for referral," it is difficult to argue that standardized test batteries have as little value as Buffery suggests. Instead, Buffery should define the scope of BFT assessment's utility. Moreover, he should take account of recent developments wherein traditional batteries, such as the Luria and the Halstead Reitan, are being used for rehabilitative planning (see Christensen, 1984).

INTERVENTION

BFT's approach to rehabilitation involves "bombardment" of the ipsilateral and/or contralateral hemisphere for the purpose of coercing an intact area of the brain to function in place of an impaired area. The "what" and "how" of bombardment are established by repeated use of probe measures. Hence, at least on the surface, BFT mandates an ongoing interplay between assessment and intervention.

As an intervention, BFT can be examined from two perspectives. The first pertains to the evidentiary basis for the effectiveness of BFT as a rehabilitation strategy. In spite of his eloquent advocacy on behalf of BFT's many virtues, Buffery would be the first to admit (Buffery & Burton, 1982) that BFT's data base is meager. In fact, the lack of outcome data probably is BFT's most important shortcoming; the design and implementation of relevant outcome studies are its most pressing need. Until such evidence is obtained, claims about BFT must be modest and circumspect.

In view of this state of affairs, the second perspective is important not only in its own right but to maintain BFT's appeal during the interval when basic empirical studies are being conducted. This perspective pertains to the plausibility of BFT rehabilitation, that is, is there any reason to believe that BFT might be an effective intervention?

The answers to this question are complicated and some may find them unsatisfying. The relevant issues in this area are somewhat clearer when examined in relation to Marshall's (1984) review of work on central nervous system injury and recovery of function. First, Marshall acknowledges the long-established observation that after injury to the CNS, some patients experience the spontaneous recovery of some previously lost functions. Second, he argues that this spontaneous recovery results from a natural, endogenous process, which instigates morphological and neurochemical changes in the CNS such that an intact area is modified to replicate an injured area. This process culminates in the recovery of functioning. Third, concluding with considerable circumspection, Marshall contends that the available evidence suggests that spontaneous recovery of function is most likely to occur in cases of spinal cord injury and/or in very immature organisms in which localization of function has not yet been firmly established. It is noteworthy that although some of the numerous studies cited by Marshall were conducted with human subjects, the vast majority of the available evidence was derived from studies on infrahuman subjects.

BFT theory is consistent with the notion that recovery of function following CNS injury can and does occur. This assumption is essential to BFT. In fact, if recovery of functioning did not or could not occur, then BFT would make no sense. Unfortunately, BFT's next fundamental assumption is on much more tenuous ground. In essence, BFT assumes that if spontaneous recovery can and does occur, then recovery of functioning can be accelerated by deliberate, exogenous intervention (i.e., cortical stimulation). Although there is some clinical evidence to support this position, the evidence is sparse and does not specify the intervening processes that are involved. Finally, though the best evidence for recovery of function relates to spinal cord injuries and to immature organisms, BFT deals with the cerebral cortex and with the impaired adult patient. Here again, there is some clinical evidence to demonstrate this kind of outcome but the data base is meager.

In order to arouse and maintain the interest of researchers and clinicians, Buffery must offer a model of adult brain structure and function, and on the basis of this model, he must identify the nature of cerebral recovery of function and must describe intervening mechanisms involved in this process. There is no reason why this kind of conceptual refinement cannot be undertaken in conjunction with the empirical studies referred to earlier.

The same kind of conceptual and empirical work is needed to support and clarify Buffery's aspiration to integrate BFT and certain principles and techniques of behavior therapy. As is often the case, this integration may be less simple and straightforward than first appears. For example, a considerable body of evidence (e.g., Walrath & Stern, 1980) suggests that various types of CNS impairment have an impact on the effectiveness of various behavioral techniques.

SERVICE DELIVERY

Examined in isolation, many of the components of BFT's approach to service delivery are not innovative. At least the ideas are not new. The virtues of the multidisciplinary team are commonly acknowledged in the rehabilitation field, and the general practitioner is bombarded these days by advertisements for computer-based rehabilitation programs. The importance of the CNS-injured patient's family is also widely recognized (e.g., Rosenthal, 1984). Buffery's contribution resides in his interweaving of these various components into a coherent rehabilitation program. Certainly he should be credited for encouraging active participation of family members in the rehabilitative process. This is a substantial advance over simply helping the family to adjust to the dynamic consequences of an intractable illness.

At this early stage in its development, the main problem with brain function therapy is the lack of a strong data base for professional application. In spite of the social-economic-political appeal of the service delivery package, it is not too soon to question which, if any, of the components of BFT contribute, independently or interactively, to improvement in patient functioning.

REFERENCES

Buffery, A.W.H., & Burton, A. (1982). Information processing and redevelopment: Towards a science of neuropsychological rehabilitation. In A. Burton (Ed.), *The pathology and psychology of cognition.* London: Methuen.

Christensen, A. L. (1984). The Luria method for examination of the brain-injured patient. In P. E. Logue & J. M. Schear (Eds.), *Clinical neuropsychology: A multidisciplinary approach.* Springfield, Ill: Charles C. Thomas.

Golden, C. (1984). Rehabilitation and the Luria-Nebraska neuropsychological battery: Introduction to theory and practice. In B. A. Edelstein & E. T. Couture (Eds.), *Behavioral assessment and rehabilitation of the traumatically brain damaged.* New York: Plenum.

Marshall, J. F. (1984). Brain function: Neural adaptation and recovery from injury. In M. R. Rosensweig & L. M. Porter (Eds.), *Annual review of psychology, 35,* 277–308.

Rosenthal, M. (1984). Strategies for intervention with families of brain injured patients. In B. A. Edelstein & E. T. Couture (Eds.), *Behavioral assessment and rehabilitation of the traumatically brain damaged.* New York: Plenum.

vanPraag, H. M., Lader, M. H., Rafaelson, O. J., & Sachar, E. J. (Eds.). (1980). *Brain mechanisms and abnormal behavior.* New York: Dekker.

Walrath, L. C., & Stern, J. A. (1980). General considerations. In H. M. vanPraag, M. H. Lader, O. J. Rafaelson, & E. J. Sachar, (Eds.), *Brain mechanisms and abnormal behavior.* New York: Dekker.

Chapter 4

Psychophysiological Assessment for Decision-Making: Conceptions and Misconceptions

EDWARD S. KATKIN

The early development of psychophysiology can be attributed largely to the research efforts of clinical psychologists. These psychologists were interested in psychophysiologically relevant aspects of such phenomena as arousal, anxiety, schizophrenia, and psychopathy. For instance, there are virtually no theories of anxiety that do not postulate a psychophysiological component of the response pattern. Recent developments in the fields of behavioral medicine, biofeedback, and health psychology have revived and reinforced a keen interest in psychophysiological assessment among clinicians (throughout this chapter I use the term "clinician" generically to include psychiatrists and other allied mental health practitioners).

Psychophysiological assessment may be defined as the measurement of physiological responses to psychosocial events. As such, the use of psychophysiological techniques is best understood as assessment at the biopsychological level. Although very few clinicians use psychophysiological techniques diagnostically in their office practices, psychophysiological tools are commonly seen in hospital settings and considerable research and theory have been dedicated to the proposition that psychophysiological assessment should enhance diagnosis and treatment.

The most common clinical use of psychophysiological assessment, however, is not in clinical settings, but in the workplace, where meaningful decisions about fundamental character traits such as honesty, morality, trustworthiness, and reliability affect the disposition of individual careers. These decisions are often made by paraprofessional polygraphers on the basis of interpretations of psychophysiological response profiles. Professional psychology generally has deferred to the paraprofessional world of polygraphy and remained aloof from the practical use of, or research upon, the "lie detector."

Psychologists and laypersons alike often assume that because the physiological index of a response reflects some basic biological component, it must be the "real" index of the construct under assessment. It will be argued here that such reification is a misuse of psychophysiological assessment. Psychophysiological assessments may be more useful as indexes of physiological functions than as indexes of psychological functions. The following discussion will address both the process and the content of psychophysiological assessment. In general the discussion will be limited to noninvasive psychophysiological measures of bioelectric signals from the surface of the body.

THE PROCESS OF PSYCHOPHYSIOLOGICAL ASSESSMENT

The most common psychophysiological indexes are electroencephalography (EEG), electromyography (EMG), electrodermography (EDA), electrocardiography (EKG), and assessments of blood pressure (BP) and blood volume (BV). A brief review of the nature of these responses and their measurement techniques will be followed by a discussion of the psychological processes that they are presumed to reflect.

Electroencephalography (EEG)

The EEG assesses small amplitude (20 to 50 microvolt) potentials generated by the brain. Although there are a number of ways to measure these potentials, the most common technique is to use surface electrodes on the scalp. Ever since Hans Berger (1929) first reported the discovery of "brain waves" in human subjects there has been a high degree of agreement about the basic components of the phenomenon. When subjects are quiet, relaxed, and awake, they emit brain waves with a frequency of approximately 8 to 12 Hz and an amplitude of about 50 microvolts. This characteristic resting pattern is known as "alpha." When subjects become more alert, the alpha pattern "desynchronizes" and is replaced by the "beta" pattern of faster frequency, smaller amplitude waves. Conversely, as subjects become more drowsy than they were in the "alpha" state they emit slower (4 to 8 Hz) "theta" waves; as they drift into sleep, even slower (less than 4 Hz) "delta" waves are observed.

This popular description of alpha, beta, delta, and theta waves oversimplifies the actual state of electrical activity in the brain. Usually, the brain generates a complex combination of all the frequencies. Complex Fourier analyses are required to determine the dominant frequency at a given time; typically, the results of EEG measurement are reduced to a description of the percentage of time that a given frequency is present. Thus the literature on EEG data usually reports findings such as "percent alpha."

In addition to assessing the relative dominance of total brain wave activity, it is also possible to assess the degree to which the brain shows discrete changes in electrical activity in response to specific stimulation. This elicited activity is called the "evoked response" or "event related potential" (ERP). In most cases the ERP is so small that it cannot be discerned against the background of ongoing brain wave activity. However, if the same stimulus is presented repeatedly, and if it evokes a lawful response, that response will be set against a background activity that varies randomly from trial to trial. In that case, averaging over a long series of trials should reveal the evoked response. For that reason averaging techniques are usually employed over hundreds of trials of stimulus presentation in order to identify ERPs; the measured ERPs are thus usually referred to as "average evoked potentials," or AEPs.

EEG measurement is one of the only psychophysiological techniques in which there has been extensive standardization of measurement techniques and scoring conventions; the International Federation of the Societies for Electroencephalography and Clinical Neurophysiology has adopted an official electrode placement system (Jasper, 1958). Nevertheless, the development of precise technical standards for measurement resolves only a small part of the difficulty inherent in EEG assessment, for the actual physiological basis of the EEG is still largely unknown (Andersen & Andersson, 1968).

Electromyography (EMG)

Electromyography is the measurement of the electrical activity of muscles. EMG techniques have been developed to measure the activity of small numbers of contractile muscle fibers innervated by a single neuron (referred to as the single motor unit), as well as larger groupings of muscle fibers that are innervated by more than one neuron. Muscle fibers contract when they are stimulated by the release of acetylocholine from a motor neuron; upon contracting they undergo an electro-chemical change similar to that seen in neuronal depolarization; the EMG is a record of this bioelectric change (Geddes & Baker, 1975).

Although the EMG can be used for identifying the specific function of muscles, and it often is used that way diagnostically, its most common psychological application is as an index of physical tension presumed to accompany psychological tension. Indeed, Edmund Jacobson (1938), the developer of "progressive relaxation," relied upon EMG measures as his primary index of relaxation (Hassett, 1978).

Electrodermal Activity (EDA)

The electrodermal response (EDR), sometimes referred to as the galvanic skin response (GSR), is among the most widely used indexes of psychological responsivity, probably because it is simple and relatively inexpensive to use and to quantify. The EDR's widespread use is also based on its uncanny lawfulness. Virtually any form of stimulation results in contingent, easily measured changes in electrical activity of the skin. Also, a mystique about the EDR's validity as an index of emotion has developed. This mystique has been fostered, in part, by the heavy reliance upon its use by professional lie detection experts.

Interest in electrodermal measurement can be traced back to Féré (1888) and Tarchanoff (1890), who discovered that electrical properties of the skin covary with behavioral events. One hundred years later there has been no basic change in technique, only refinement of the electronics. Féré's technique assesses skin resistance (SR), or its reciprocal, skin conductance (SC); Tarchanoff's technique assesses skin potential (SP).

Almost all of the variance in electrodermal assessment can be attributed to the activity of the sweat glands. Electrodermal assessment is focused on electrical activity of the palmar or plantar skin surfaces because these surfaces contain sweat glands that are responsive primarily to psychological experience and not to temperature. Since the palmar and plantar sweat glands are innervated exclusively by sympathetic neurons it is likely that EDA reflects relative activation of the sympathetic division of the autonomic nervous system (ANS).

Electrocardiography (EKG)

The EKG is actually a special form of the EMG, for it measures the electrical activity associated with the contraction of cardiac muscle. The

EKG can be measured by placing electrodes on any two points of the body; however, clinical cardiologists have devised a standard set of electrode placements that include various points on the chest and limbs. By developing a set of actuarial norms concerning the "normal" EKG recorded from each of these points, cardiologists have achieved great success using the EKG as an aid in the diagnosis of cardiac lesions. Behavioral scientists, however, have focused their attention on the relationship between stimulus events and changes in the heart, or pulse, rate. No expensive equipment is required to feel someone's pulse at the wrist. A clinican who wants patients to monitor their own heart rates can probably use self-observed measures of pulse rate with confidence in their reliability and validity (Bell & Schwartz, 1975).

The heart is innervated by fibers from both the sympathetic and parasympathetic divisions of the ANS. In general, activation of sympathetic fibers results in increased heart rate, and activation of the parasympathetic vagus nerve results in decreases of heart rate. It is essential to bear in mind that the primary purpose of the cardiovascular system is to provide oxygen to the body by maintaining a constant flow of blood. Therefore, cardiac changes that accompany behavioral phenomena must be interpreted in the context of the primary homeostatic function of the cardiovascular system.

Blood Pressure (BP)

The contraction of the heart forces blood into the arteries with each beat. Consequently, the pressure within the arteries varies during each cardiac cycle, from a high level during contraction (systole) to a lower level when the heart relaxes (diastole). Blood pressure in the arteries is determined by two major factors: the output of the heart and the resistance of the blood vessels. The output of the heart, in turn, is defined as the product of the heart rate and the volume of blood pumped on a given beat. Any change in any of these factors will result in a change in blood pressure. For instance, a blood pressure increase may result from increased heart rate, increased stroke volume, or increased resistance of the peripheral blood vessels.

Blood Volume (BV)

The total amount of blood flowing through the vascular system at any time is constant, but transient fluctuations in a variety of sympathetic and parasympathetic influences result in different organs receiving differing proportions of the total blood volume. This is particularly evident, for instance, during sexual arousal, when the blood volume in the penis or clitoris increases as a result of vasocongestion. It is equally obvious in embarrassed blushing, in which case the blood volume in the face increases dramatically.

The most popular instruments for the assessment of blood volume are plethysmographs and thermometers. Plethysmograph is a fancy word for any instrument that measures volume in a container; in the field of psychophysiology it usually refers to a device used for the assessment of peripheral blood volume (Cook, 1974). The most commonly used plethysmographs rely upon light transmission through, or light reflectance off, body tissue, a technique known as photoplethysmography. If a light source is focused on a fingertip or an earlobe, for example, the amount of light that will pass through the tissue is inversely related to the density of blood contained therein. If a photocell is placed on the opposite side of the light source, it is easy to get accurate readings of the transitory changes in blood volume. In the event that one wishes to assess blood volume in areas where light cannot be transmitted through the tissue (e.g., the head), a reflectance device can be used to measure the reflected light off the vasculated tissue.

As peripheral blood vessels dilate, the temperature of the skin in which they are embedded will rise. Thus the measurement of peripheral skin temperature is thought to be a rough index of blood volume. Although most of the variance in peripheral vasoconstriction and dilatation may be attributed to homeostatic responses to external temperature changes, it is also the case that within normal limits of external temperature vascular changes often reflect emotional responses. Typically, skin temperature is measured by placing a thermistor over the skin surface and passing small electrical currents through it. A thermistor has the property of changing its electrical resistance systematically as its temperature varies, so that a simple reading of resistance can yield a calibrated measure of skin temperature. The primary advantage of skin-temperature measures rather than plethysmographic measures is their ease of implementation and comparatively low cost.

THE CONTENT OF PSYCHOPHYSIOLOGICAL
ASSESSMENT

Psychophysiological techniques have been applied to problems of assessment in two general settings: mental health and business/government. In mental health settings there has been a general focus, for theoretical reasons, on the use of psychophysiological techniques as an aid in the diagnosis of anxiety, schizophrenia, and sociopathy, with a subsidiary interest in their use as an aid to the evaluation of certain behavior therapeutic effects, particularly systematic desensitization. In business and government there has been extensive application of psychophysiology, specifically addressed to the use of psychophysiological responses as indexes of deception. The private use of polygraphy for personnel screening is a billion-dollar enterprise, and the governmental use of polygraphy for security and investigative purposes is widespread. There is no doubt that the total use of psychophysiological assessment in mental health and medical settings for decision-based assessment is trivial when compared to its use for decision-making in the business/ government sector.

Mental Health

Anxiety. Spielberger (1966) has popularized the distinction between trait and state anxiety. In this dichotomy, trait anxiety is defined as an individual's predisposition to respond to certain perceived threats with a constellation of responses (e.g., behavioral, physiological, and phenomenological), which are, collectively, the anxiety state. This model gives little reason to predict differences in physiological activity among subjects who differ in trait anxiety, unless they are exposed to conditions that will elicit different states of anxiety. A number of empirical investigations have supported this view. Rappaport and Katkin (1972) demonstrated that subjects who were selected from extreme ends of the distribution of a trait anxiety inventory (the Taylor Manifest Anxiety Scale) did not show any differential electrodermal activity during rest; however, when placed in an ego-threatening situation, those subjects high on the trait scale showed significantly greater increases in skin resistance fluctuations than those who scored low on the scale. Earlier studies from the same laboratory had shown that when a severe threat to the body (threat of painful electric shock) was employed, subjects who were high and low in trait anxiety (Katkin, 1965) or prethreat state anxiety (Katkin, 1966) showed similar increases in skin resistance fluctuation rate. These findings are an important reminder that although trait anxious people may be predisposed to respond with state anxiety, under severe circumstances even people who are low in trait anxiety may be induced into an anxious state.

Wolpe (1971) has defined anxiety "as an individual organism's characteristic constellation of autonomic responses to noxious stimulation" (p. 341). He has also suggested that the mechanism by which systematic desensitization succeeds is the "reciprocal inhibition" of these conditioned autonomic responses. Specific tests of this theoretical view have been carried out using psychophysiological measures. The conclusions of two reviews of this literature (Katkin & Deitz, 1973; Mathews, 1971) are quite similar: Psychophysiological research on desensitization leaves no doubt that "the EDR to phobic and nonphobic stimulus objects provides an accurate index of a subject's fear state" (Katkin & Deitz, 1973, p. 369). This is true for real stimulus objects (Barlow et al., 1970), pictures of stimulus objects (Geer, 1966; Wilson, 1967), and imagined stimulus objects (Lang et al., 1970).

Parenthetically, on the basis of the evidence it appears unlikely that progressive relaxation serves as a counterconditioning agent. More likely, progressive relaxation reduces autonomic arousal, thereby facilitating the habituation or extinction of conditioned fear responses (Katkin & Deitz, 1973). This is supported by much evidence, including Katkin and McCubbin's (1969) demonstration that electrodermal orienting responses habituate more rapidly in low states of arousal. There is also no special advantage to the specific relaxation ritual used in systematic desensitization according to the preponderance of evidence indicating that any type of instruction to relax works as well as the specific progressive relaxation instructions preferred by Wolpe (Katkin & Deitz, 1973).

In summary, the application of psychophysiological methods to the study of anxiety and systematic desensitization has been extensive. It appears that electrodermal indexes may have some utility in aiding the differential diagnosis of anxiety states, although they may be of little or no utility in diagnosing trait anxiety. In the case of desensitization, certain tests of theoretical postulates have been made that might not have been possible without psychophysiological methods. Although there are myriad unresolved questions for future research, this is one area in which psychophysiology has made a substantial contribution.

Schizophrenia. Psychophysiological assessment of schizophrenia has focused primarily on electrodermal and electroencephalographic responses. Most of the early psychophysiological research on schizophrenia derived from arousal theory and attempted to test whether schizophrenics were either overaroused or underaroused (see Lang & Buss, 1965). Most of that early research focused on ANS measures rather than CNS measures, partly because of technical ease and partly because of an overriding theoretical assumption that schizophrenia was at least partially caused by limbic system (amygdala, hippocampus, and septum) dysfunction, which is reflected in the ANS (Venables, 1975). Later research, especially in the last decade, has addressed CNS function, with increasing attention being paid to evoked responses (Buchsbaum, 1977; Itil, 1977; Roth, 1977). In addition, there has been a recent surge of interest in the recording of smooth pursuit eye movements (Holzman & Levy, 1977), using a special form of EMG recording known as the electrooculogram (EOG).

The rationale for *electrodermal* assessment of schizophrenia has been summarized elegantly by Venables (1975), who states "that several . . . approaches have produced the idea that what may be at least a partial feature of schizophrenic pathology is a disturbance of limbic system function, and that if this is so, then certain disturbances of autonomic function can be predicted and investigated by psychophysiological techniques" (p. 107). Direct recording from human limbic structures with indwelling electrodes is, in Venables's words, "in general ethically undesirable" (1975, p. 112). Therefore, an appropriate noninvasive index of limbic system activity was sought after. Venables and many other investigators, spurred on primarily by the theorizing of Bagshaw (Bagshaw & Benzies, 1968; Bagshaw et al., 1965), chose the electrodermal component of the orienting response (OR) as their measure of choice. The OR, according to Pavlov, is a generalized response to any change in the environment, irrespective of its significance. According to Sokolov's (1963) elaborate model of the OR, any novel stimulus will elicit unconditional central, motor, and autonomic responses, including phasic changes in SC. With repeated presentations of the same stimulus, a "neuronal model" of that stimulus is generated; as the neuronal model becomes strengthened by repeated exposures, the central, motor, and autonomic responses to stimulus presentation habituate. When the neuronal model is complete, and there is thus no mismatch between it and the stimulus, the OR disappears. Bagshaw and her colleagues, working with primates, found that ablation of the amygdala produced a marked diminution of the skin conductance component of the OR, and that ablation of the hippocampus led to greater resistance to habituation of the SC or OR. Venables and his co-workers postulated, therefore, that close examination of the SC OR and its habituation would be a methodologically sound approach to studying the role of the limbic system in schizophrenia.

At the time that Venables began his research program he was confronted with two conflicting sets of data that had been collected by other investigators. Zahn and his colleagues (Zahn et al., 1968) had found that schizophrenics habituated less than normals; Bernstein

(1964, 1970) had found that schizophrenics habituated more than normals. Substantial data from Venables's laboratory indicated that both sets of data might be right. Approximately 50% of the schizophrenics in Venables's sample failed to respond at all. The remaining 50% tended to be slow habituators. This led to a dichotomous classification of schizophrenics as electrodermal "hyperresponders" and "hyporesponders."

Based upon his research on electrodermal correlates of schizophrenia, and the reports of Mednick (1970) and Mednick and Schulsinger (1968) on prenatal and perinatal factors increasing risk for schizophrenia (presumably via selective anoxia adversely affecting limbic system structures), Venables (1977) established a large, cross-cultural, longitudinal study of children at risk for schizophrenia on the island of Mauritius. From an initial pool of 1,800 three-year-old children, a final longitudinal sample of 200 was selected. These children were all screened on family history, health, obstetric history, behavioral observation of play and parent-child interaction, and finally, electrodermal and EEG patterns.

The children were placed in three categories of electrodermal responsiveness: a normal category, and both hyperresponsive and hyporesponsive categories, as defined earlier by Venables's research on adult schizophrenic populations. The 200 children were then subdivided, with half entering nursery schools and half remaining in the community. A follow-up study about three years later showed that the nursery-school experience had little positive social effect on hyperresponsive and hyporesponsive children, but that it led to substantial improvement in constructive play among the normally responsive children, as compared to the non-nursery-school control group. Furthermore, although the nursery-school experience did not affect the "abnormal" responders as compared to controls, it was noted that, overall, hyper-responders showed considerably more constructive play that hyporesponders. Venables summarized his early findings as follows:

> This very preliminary description of some of the research for this study is presented here to suggest that even in very young children the abnormal hyperresponsive-hyporesponsive dichotomy does appear to be a viable distinction. It is perhaps remarkable in this instance that children selected in a very brief psychophysiological testing procedure at the age of 3 showed distinctive patterns of behavior 3 years later as a result of their experience in the intervening period. It is also not unreasonable to suggest that the sorts of behavior shown are in accord with the patterns that

might be expected to be associated with the psychophysiological types of behavior measured. (Venables, 1977, p. 44)

Unfortunately, some of the subsequent studies from Venables's own laboratory have failed to confirm the basic findings of differential habituation (Patterson & Venables, 1978); thus the current status of the "responder-nonresponder" dimension, like so much in schizophrenia research, remains unclear.

The earliest research on *electroencephalographic correlates* of schizophrenia addressed the identification of resting differences in patterns of brain wave activity. The field has been plagued with a number of interpretive difficulties. For instance, are differences between schizophrenic and normal patterns antecedents or consequents of the disorder? The most carefully controlled studies, taking into account the effects of medication and other important extraneous variables, suggest that schizophrenics manifest reduced levels of alpha and increased levels of fast beta (24 to 33 Hz) waves (Itil, 1977). According to Itil (1977) these are also the patterns that can be induced by psychotomimetic drugs such as LSD-25. Itil also notes that these patterns, along with significant increases in early delta (3 to 4 Hz) waves, are observed in some nonpsychotic children who have been identified as being at high risk for schizophrenia.

A second line of EEG research, on event-related potentials, has emerged during the past decade. This research divides roughly into three areas: analysis of "early" ERPs (occurring within 50 msec of stimulation); "middle" ERPs (occurring between 100 to 200 msec after stimulation); and "late" ERPs (occurring at least 300 msec after stimulation). Middle ERPs have been the subject of the most intense investigation. Buchsbaum (1977) has noted that the middle potentials seem reduced in schizophrenic subjects. Since the negative potential usually seen at about 140 msec after stimulation (N140) is presumed to reflect "stimulus selection" and the positive potential usually seen about 200 msec after stimulation (P200) is presumed to reflect response to novelty, it is inferred that the reduction of these middle potentials in schizophrenia reflects the well-known attentional deficits associated with the disorder.

Early components of the ERP are believed to reflect the neurological integrity of the cortical system, and late components are widely believed to represent the functional, or psychological, integrity of the cortex. In general, studies of the early components show no differences between schizophrenics and controls. Roth (1977) has provided an excellent review of the literature on late ERPs. The data in this realm are clouded by severe methodological problems , but there is some reason to believe that with respect to late evoked potentials, which are generally presumed to reflect expectancy or readiness, schizophrenics show delayed responding. This is not a solid finding, however, and may be an artifact of the inability of the laboratory task to engage the patient's attention. Roth (1977) has raised profound questions concerning not only the current status of evoked potential (EP) research with schizophrenia, but also the conceptual basis for its future:

> In general, the quality of research in the area of EPs and psychopathology is poorer than in experiments designed to answer questions of theoretical interest to psychology. . . . It is not surprising that event-related potentials most influenced by behavior should be sensitive to psychopathology. A more pertinent question is whether they have anything to add to behavioral assessment. (Roth, 1977, p. 116)

Research on *smooth pursuit eye movements* in schizophrenia has a long history. As early as 1908 Diefendorf and Dodge noted that schizophrenics were not as able as normals or other mental patients to track the movement of a swinging pendulum. More than 60 years later, using modern electrooculogram (EOG) techniques, Holzman and his associates (Holzman & Levy, 1977; Holzman et al., 1973; Holzman et al., 1974) reported similar findings. Holzman's group, however, also reported that nonpsychotic first-degree relatives of schizophrenic patients showed similar deviant patterns of smooth pursuit eye tracking. Although Holzman found that nonschizophrenic functional psychotics manifested high rates of deviant eye tracking, the incidence of deviance in first-degree relatives of nonschizophrenic patients was only about 10% whereas for relatives of schizophrenics it was between 40% and 50%.

A variety of theoretical statements deal with these striking data. One popular view is that the deviant eye tracking may represent a genetic marker. This view is strengthened somewhat by the report of Holzman et al. (1977) that deviant eye tracking is more concordant within monozygotic twins than within dizygotic twins. Unfortunately, the twin samples were not perfectly matched, and the data must be accepted as merely suggestive. There have also been a number of questions raised concerning the possible confounding effects of medication, differences in attentiveness, and EOG artifacts. The methodological issues involved in proper quantification of the EOG for such assessment are very complicated (Iacono & Lykken, 1979).

Sociopathy. Although there has been substantial research on psychophysiological assessment of individual differences in sociopathy, only those studies that have used electrodermal indexes have reported any consistently positive findings. A programmatic series of studies by Hare and his colleagues (Hare, 1965; 1968; 1972; 1975; Hare & Craigen, 1974; Hare & Quinn, 1971) has indicated that sociopaths generally tend to show lower levels of skin conductance and fewer skin conductance fluctuations than control subjects.

Most studies of sociopathy are carried out on convicted criminals. Few researchers are addressing the problem of identifying potential sociopaths prior to law-breaking, and any attempts to do so are likely to be faced with some serious confounding problems. Kirkegaard-Sorensen and Mednick (1977) report that the offspring of schizophrenics also demonstrate elevated risk for criminal activity and, in fact, that schizophrenic mothers themselves have a higher than normal crime rate. Thus, research on predictors of risk for sociopathic criminal behavior must be careful to eliminate schizophrenics and potential schizophrenics from their sample. With this in mind, Loeb and Mednick (1977) examined 104 teen-age children of nonschizophrenic families, who had no history of criminal offenses. They administered a psychophysiological examination and conducted an eight-year follow-up study to determine if the electrodermal signs present in known sociopaths (low conductance, nonresponsiveness, and slow response recovery time) would predict criminal behavior. After eight years, seven of the original sample had been convicted of at least two legal offenses. These seven were then matched for sex, age, and social class with another sample of the original population who had not committed offenses; the electrodermal data obtained eight years earlier discriminated the two groups. Most importantly, the offender group had shown the typical pattern of electrodermal activity associated with adult known sociopaths. Although these data appear to support the utility of psychophysiological assessment of sociopathic behavior, there are sufficient null results to warrant extreme caution about conclusions (Siddle & Trasler, 1983).

Business and Government: The Detection
of Deception

Every day, business executives call upon professional polygraphers to
make definitive decisions about a potential employee's truthfulness
concerning his or her past reliability, honesty, or fidelity to the job.
Similarly, the Department of Defense routinely asks polygraphers to
make decisions about the truthfulness with which its employees assert
that they are loyal to the United States and are not security risks. Defense attorneys often appeal to polygraphers to demonstrate that their
clients are innocent of the crimes of which they are accused. In all of
these examples we see more clearly and directly than we ever see in
mental health settings the direct application of psychophysiological
techniques to decision-based assessment.

Most professional polygraphers measure BP, EDA, and respiration to
assess the presence of deception (Orne et al., 1972). Yet it is widely
agreed that no known physiological response is unique to deception
(Lykken, 1981; Orne, 1975). Rather, the polygrapher "diagnoses" deception on the basis of a subject's pattern of autonomic responses to
carefully planned questions that are tailored to each individual under
examination. Although the research literature suggests that the EDR is
the most reliable physiological index of deception (Podlesny & Raskin,
1977), most field assessments continue to employ at least BP and respiration measures in addition to EDA measures.

Although it is commonly assumed that the polygrapher bases his decision about deception on physiological evidence alone, it must be
understood that a considerable amount of subtlety is involved in the
determination of criteria for defining the "deceptive" response. No pattern of psychophysiological activation is uniquely associated with deception. Rather, the polygrapher deals with the assumption that deception is one of a number of possible reasons why an individual may show
autonomic arousal; if all plausible reasons other than deception can be
ruled out, then deception may be *inferred* from the arousal response. In
order to increase the validity of this inference, a number of precautions
are taken. Among these, the most important is the use of the control
question technique. A control question is one that is not particularly
relevant to the issue under investigation, but is presumed to have emotional impact on most subjects. For instance, in an investigation of the
theft of narcotics from a drugstore, an employee may be asked something like, "Other than what you have told me during our interview,
have you ever stolen anything in your life?" Or a control question may

ask, "Have you ever betrayed anyone who trusted you?" The purpose of these questions is to establish individualized norms for a subject's autonomic response to threatening questions. In general, if a subject shows larger responses to crime-specific questions than to control questions, deception may be inferred. Polygraphers also assume that for an innocent subject the control questions are likely to be more threatening than the relevant questions and will elicit larger responses.

An alternative to the control question technique, the Guilty Knowledge Test (GKT), has been proposed by Lykken (1974; 1981). In the GKT the subject is questioned about information not generally known to anybody except the investigators and the culprit. To the innocent, the information is neither significant nor threatening, and should not elicit a large response; to the possessor of "guilty knowledge," the information should be salient and should elicit a large EDR. The following kinds of questions appear in guilty knowledge tests:

1. If you are the thief, you will know where the desk was located in the office in which the theft occurred. Was it (a) on the left, (b) in front, or (c) on the right?

2. The thief hid what he had stolen. Where did he hide it? Was it (a) in the men's room, (b) on the coat rack, (c) in the office, (d) on the windowsill, or (e) in the locker?

Generally speaking, academics have supported the GKT test but workers in the field have ignored it. The problem with the GKT, it is argued, is that there are not a great many incidents in which specific details are relevant to the investigation. Also, it is possible that an innocent might have been present at the scene of the crime and have been identified as a suspect; such a person might fail the GKT.

How effective is polygraphy in accurately detecting deception? Two research approaches to this problem have been reported: field studies and analog studies. Field studies investigate actual polygraph examinations, and in some sense provide the most direct evidence for their validity; however, it is not always easy to judge what the actual or "ground" truth is in a field study (Ben-Shakhar et al., 1982). For these reasons, a number of analog studies have been carried out in which subjects volunteer to commit mock crimes and are then interrogated by polygraphers who are blind to the assignment of "criminal" and "noncriminal" subjects. An extensive review and analysis of the existing literature on field and analog studies has been prepared by the U.S. Congressional Office of Technology Assessment (Office of Technology Assessment, 1983). This report indicates the following with respect to the utility of the polygraph using some version or other of the control question technique for specific-incident criminal investigations. For field studies: Correct guilty detections ranged from 70.6% to 98.6% and averaged 83.6%; correct innocent detections ranged from 12.5% to 94.1% and averaged 76%; false positive rate (innocent persons found deceptive) ranged from 0% to 75% and averaged 19.1%; and false negative rate (guilty persons found nondeceptive) ranged from 0% to 29.4% and averaged 10.2%. For analog studies: Correct guilty detections ranged from 35.4% to 100% and averaged 63.7%; correct innocent detections ranged from 32% to 91% and averaged 57.9%; false positives ranged from 2% to 50.7% and averaged 14.1%; and false negatives ranged from 0% to 28.7% and averaged 10.4%.

There is little doubt that polygraph examinations using the control question technique applied to specific incidents can detect deception at a rate better than chance. Whether one would want to make serious life determinations in view of the observed false positive rates is a political rather than a scientific decision. Nevertheless, there is no other area of applied psychophysiology where we even have access to data such as these.

With respect to validity data on the use of the polygraph for employment and preemployment screening there are no data. The data above, suggesting about 80% correct identifications, are very appealing to businessmen who are concerned with identifying white-collar criminals in their employ. Consequently, polygraph testing is used widely for preemployment screening and for postemployment monitoring in the world of business. Unfortunately, no experimental studies of the predictive validity of polygraph testing for preemployment screening are available, and it is not likely that there will be any soon. In order to carry out such a test experimentally, some employers would have to volunteer to hire blindly an equal number of candidates who passed and failed the polygraph screen, and then evaluate their performance after a specified time period. As it stands, candidates who fail polygraph tests are not hired, nor are they followed up. The employer has no knowledge about how these rejected candidates might have fared in comparison to those who passed and were eventually employed. Nevertheless, belief in the efficacy of the polygraph test is strong, and it continues to be used widely.

Summary

The data on psychophysiological assessment suggest that we are a long way from being able to use autonomic or central nervous system response indexes to make diagnostic decisions with confidence. Even in the area of lie detection, where the criteria are more easily defined and the predictive validity more easily tested, we are plagued with high rates of both false positives and negatives. In the area of mental health assessment the field has not even reached the point where such assessment of validity is feasible. In the next section, some of the epistemological problems inherent in the use of psychophysiology for behavioral assessment will be discussed, and a modest proposal for redirection will be introduced.

EPISTEMOLOGICAL MUSINGS

Why is the record on psychophysiological assessment so dismal and what can be done about it? Obviously, there are no clear answers to such broad questions, but the source of the problem may be found by examining both the methodological shortcomings inherent in psychophysiology and the nature of the questions that are asked.

Methodological Issues

Psychophysiological responses may be quite fragile; for instance, the difference between a "soft" and a "moderately loud" tone may be crucial in predicting electrodermal habituation rate (Katkin & McCubbin, 1969). In addition to simple problems created by variability in stimulus parameters, a number of other methodological problems are specific to psychophysiology.

Measurement artifact. There are two basic varieties of measurement artifact: those specific to one response measure (e.g., proper salt concentration in the electrode paste is crucial for electrodermal measurement, but irrelevant for the EKG), and those which may alter several responses simultaneously (e.g., gross body movement, which will affect most response parameters). Dealing with both of these classes of artifact requires detailed understanding of the nature of the response being recorded, and familiarity with techniques. Proper technique for recording and reducing psychophysiological data requires a substantial artistic talent; practice may not make perfect, but it will surely sensitize the practitioner to sources of artifact. Individual differences in technique are a source of reduced reliability and validity of assessment.

Other sources of artifact are sex, age, and cultural differences among experimenters and subjects, and the complex interactions that result from these differences. Bell et al. (1975) noted that many reports do not even mention the sex of the examiner despite frequent reports of effects of this variable on electrodermal activity. Age and sex of subject present a more complex source of error; with respect to female subjects, practically no researchers in psychophysiology control for menstrual cycle phase, despite observations of central and autonomic changes related to the cycle (Bell et al., 1975). Oral contraceptives, caffeine, nicotine, and various forms of medication constitute other sources of potential measurement artifact. Even ambient changes in the environment itself may have profound, if unexpected, systematic effects on responsiveness. Venables (1977) reported that when he used subjects from tropical climates in a European lab kept at 21° C, the subjects showed an absence of "normal" electrodermal responsiveness; when he raised the temperature 10° C they showed "normal" responsiveness.

Response habituation and long-term assessment. In psychophysiological assessment the phenomenon of response habituation presents difficulties on two levels: physiological and psychological. On the physiological level, even an aversive stimulus such as an electric shock may elicit smaller responses after several trials. A related problem is the effect of previous response on subsequent ones. The magnitude and recovery of electrodermal responses, for instance, are known to be affected by the frequency of prior responses (Bundy & Fitzgerald, 1975). At the psychological level, habituation is perhaps even more difficult to contend with. Surwit et al. (1978) have reported that blood pressure during "baseline" resting sessions is substantially lower than that measured by a physician. Thus, failure to obtain true resting measurements prior to testing may result in attribution of reduced reactivity to a stimulus when psychological habituation to the laboratory or clinic is the real source of the change.

Individual response stereotypy and patterning. Lacey (1956) and his co-workers (Lacey et al., 1953; Lacey & Lacey, 1958) have defined an important methodological issue in psychophysiological assessment: individual response stereotypy. This refers to the tendency of subjects to show maximum responsivity to stimuli in only one particular response modality. One subject, for instance, might be a heart rate responder, and another a blood pressure reactor; another subject might show minimal reactivity in all cardiovascular modes but show maximum responsivity in the skin conductance channel. Lacey and Lacey (1958) reported that some individuals were inconsistent in their patterns of responding, but most showed a degree of consistency across stress situations that differed both in physiological and psychological demands. Individual response stereotypy makes it difficult to assess "the" psychophysiological response. At the least, it suggests the need for recording multiple channels of response data if one is to assess the responsivity of a given individual.

Several solutions for comparing data from different autonomic responses have been proposed, including percent-change scores, standard scores, and range-corrected scores. Yet, there does not appear to be one best way of treating all data. For example, Lykken (1972) found that his range-correction technique was useful for skin conductance measures, but not for heart rate responses. Sersen et al. (1978) pointed out that the amount of stereotypy of autonomic responses depends in part upon the method chosen for standardization of scores and in part upon the stimuli used. Other investigators have suggested that pragmatic considerations such as reliability and validity should determine the method of response analysis for each new situation (Johnson & Lubin, 1972).

One may not always wish to minimize the effects of individual response stereotypy, which may, for example, contribute to an understanding of why some individuals develop a particular psychosomatic disorder. Engel and Bickford (1961) found that essential hypertensives showed maximal blood pressure reponses to several kinds of stress, whereas they did not show large magnitude responses in other autonomic channels.

Finally, mention must be made of the so-called law of initial values described by Wilder (1950), according to which a subject with a high resting level of autonomic activity will show reduced response amplitude to stimulation. This "law" has been used in various arguments alternately to justify both negative and positive findings in psychophysiological research. It has considerable status as methodological caveat, but its virtues are unclear. Depending on whose data are cited, there either is or is not evidence that the law is correct, and there is much reason to suspect that it is not generally applicable to all physiological response measures (Venables & Christie, 1973). Further, to the extent that there is a statistical law of initial values, it remains unclear whether it is determined by homeostatic mechanisms, measurement artifact, or ceiling effects.

Conceptual Issues

In most of the examples discussed so far, physiological assessment was utilized because it was assumed that the construct under scrutiny had either a physiological basis (i.e., limbic system malfunction in schizophrenia) or a physiological component (i.e., autonomic arousal in anxiety). Further, it is often assumed (mistakenly, I believe) that physiological assessment is, by its nature, more valid than behavioral assessment or questionnaire assessments.

The failure of psychophysiological assessment may lie in the fact that there are fundamental flaws in these assumptions. First, it should be noted that the conceptual relationship between the construct and the physiological index is, in most cases, not well understood. Let us examine anxiety as a case in point, for anxiety has been associated with physiological arousal more often than any other psychological construct. Lang (1968; 1969) has popularized the notion of anxiety as a tripartite construct that can be indexed by self-report, motor behavior, and physiological response. His assertion that anxiety is reflected physiologically is not new; such diverse theorists as James (1884), Freud (1936), and Wolpe (1971) have noted this. James went so far as to *define* anxiety as the perception of physiological responses.

Are all three indexes of anxiety equipotential? I think not. If a patient reports a feeling of anxiety and describes the familiar symptoms of dread and sense of impending doom, but shows neither motor signs of anxiety nor physiological arousal, would we consider the patient not anxious? On the other hand, if a patient shows a rapid pulse, elevated skin conductance, and very low percent alpha, but reports no subjective symptoms of anxiety, would we diagnose the patient as anxious? I do not think either diagnosis would be likely. My point here is that the so-called tripartite structure of anxiety is an academic conceit; it has little or nothing to do with the clinical construct under scrutiny. We may not know exactly how to define anxiety, but as the supreme court justice said about pornography, we know it when we see it, and what we see is that anxiety is fundamentally a phenomenological experience. If we are fortunate enough to observe that occasionally there is correspondence between that experience and some physiological activity, that is fine;

but it is foolish to assume that the physiological responsivity defines anxiety. More likely, as James (1884), Schachter and Singer (1962), and Harris and Katkin (1975) have noted, if physiological arousal is involved in determining the presence of anxiety, it is only to the extent that the arousal is subjectively perceived, that is, *experienced.*

In terms of the dichotomy posed between "quantitative-scientific" paradigms and "qualitative-hermeneutic" paradigms it appears that psychophysiological assessment falls somewhere in between. Even in such a cut-and-dried decision-making process as lie detection we see that the physiological index is far from isomorphic with the psychological construct. Every polygrapher knows that there is no physiological correlate of lying—only physiological correlates of subjective responses to the act of lying. In order to use physiological indexes of lying, then, the polygrapher must be as much an intuitive, artistic clinician as a scientific technician. The final decision about a subject's veracity is made on the basis of finely tuned judgments about relative degrees of responsivity to carefully crafted questions that are individualized.

The general conceptual problem, therefore, is that psychophysiological measures are being used to make inferences about psychological processes that may be only tangentially related to them. As long as conceptual and definitional vagueness are part of the psychophysiological relationship there will always be sufficient error of measurement to thwart decision-focused assessment. For these reasons I shall play devil's advocate and take the extreme position that physiological assessment should be reserved for making inferences about physiological function and not psychological function. That is, blood pressure measurements should be used to assess blood pressure responses, not stress; heart rate should be used to assess cardiac activity and not anxiety. To the extent that we are interested in physiological responses to psychosocial events for their own sake, we may be able to develop more accurate and useful decision criteria that may be of value in psychosomatic diagnoses. The emerging field of behavioral medicine provides a context for such developments.

Psychosomatic, or psychophysiological, disorders have been a major area of interest for many decades, but recent theoretical and methodogical developments in health-related psychology have provided new opportunities for the use of psychophysiological techniques, both for diagnosis and treatment. Despite the potential importance of autonomic functions in the diagnosis of psychophysiological disorders, it is a rare physician who employs psychophysiological assessment to aid in evaluation. For example, peripheral blood volume and pulse amplitude measures may contribute to the differential diagnosis of migraine and other vascular headaches. Measures of daily variability in blood pressure responsivity to stimulation may provide more information about hypertensive patients than the current diagnostic procedures 'of interview, self-report, or single blood pressure readings at infrequent intervals.

Recent reports of increased cardiovascular response to stress among individuals with the so-called Type A behavior pattern (Mathews, 1982) suggest that psychophysiological screening for cardiovascular activity may enhance early identification of persons at risk for myocardial disease. Goldband et al. (1979) have proposed a model for evaluating individual differences in proneness to coronary disease based on individual psychophysiological response patterns rather than on traditional personality assessment procedures. The thrust of their position is that if certain behavior patterns, or person-environment interactions, are likely to produce cardiovascular disease, then those patterns must be associated with pathophysiological responses in the cardiovascular system that mediate the behavior-disease relationship. Therefore, psychophysiological assessment of cardiovascular responsivity should facilitate the identification of persons at risk.

A final comment is in order. The relationship between specific psychophysiological reactivity patterns and subsequent disease onset is only beginning to be explored (see Katkin & Manuck, 1985). In order for psychophysiological assessment to be of some decision-making value for identifying individual differences in risk for disease, a great deal of basic parametric research on the reactivity-disease relationship must be done. There is no guarantee that the results of such research will prove to be any more salutary for the ultimate utility of psychophysiological assessment, but it will certainly be interesting.

REFERENCES

Andersen, P., & Andersson, A. A. (1968). *Physiological basis of the alpha rhythm.* New York: Appleton-Century-Crofts.

Bagshaw, M. H., & Benzies, S., (1968). Multiple measures of the orienting reactions and their association after amygdalectomy in monkeys. *Experimental Neurology, 20,* 175–187.

Bagshaw, M. H., Kimble, D. P., & Pribram, K. H. (1965). The GSR of monkeys during orienting and habituation and after ablation of the amygdala, hippocampus, and inferotemporal cortex. *Neuropsychologia, 3,* 111–119.

Barlow, D. H., Agras, W. S., Leitenberg, H., & Wincze, J. P. (1970). An experimental analysis of the effectiveness of "shaping" in reducing maladaptive avoidance behavior: An analogue study. *Behaviour Research and Therapy, 8,* 165–173.

Bell, B., Christie, M. J., & Venables, P. H. (1975). Psychophysiology of the menstrual cycle. In P. H. Venables & M. J. Christie (Eds.), *Research in psychophysiology.* New York: Wiley.

Bell, I. R., & Schwartz, G. E. (1975). Voluntary control and reactivity of human heart rate. *Psychophysiology, 12,* 339–348.

Ben-Shakhar, G., Lieblich, I., & Bar-Hillel, M. (1982). An evaluation of polygraphers' judgments: A review from a decision theoretic perspective. *Journal of Applied Psychology, 67,* 701–713.

Berger, H. (1929). Über das elektrenkephalogramm des menschen. *Archiv für Psychiatrie und Nervenkrankheiten, 87,* 527–570.

Bernstein, A. S. (1964). The galvanic skin response orienting reflex in chronic schizophrenics. *Psychonomic Science, 1,* 391–392.

Bernstein, A. S. (1970). The phasic electrodermal orienting response in chronic schizophrenics: II. Response to auditory signals of varying intensity. *Journal of Abnormal Psychology, 75,* 146–156.

Buchsbaum, M. S. (1977). The middle evoked response components and schizophrenia. *Schizophrenia Bulletin, 3,* 93–104.

Bundy, R., & Fitzgerald, H. (1975). Stimulus specificity of electrodermal recovery time: An examination and reinterpretation of the evidence. *Psychophysiology, 12,* 406–411.

Cook, M. R. (1974). Psychophysiology of peripheral vascular change. In P. A. Obrist, A. H. Black, J. Brener, & L. V. DiCara (Eds.), *Cardiovascular psychophysiology.* Chicago: Aldine.

Diefendorf, A. R., & Dodge, R. (1908). An experimental study of the ocular reactions of the insane from photographic records. *Brain, 31,* 451–489.

Engel, B. T., & Bickford, A. F. (1961). Response specificity: Stimulus-response and individual response specificity in essential hypertensives. *Archives of General Psychiatry, 5,* 478–489.

Féré, C. (1888). Note sur des modifications de la résistance électrique sous l'influence des excitations sensorielles et des émotions. *Comptes Rendus des Séances de la Société de Biologie, 5,* 217–219.

Freud, S. (1936). *The problem of anxiety.* New York: Norton.

Geddes, L. A., & Baker, L. E. (1975). *Principles of applied biomedical instrumentation.* New York: Wiley.

Geer, J. H. (1966). Fear and autonomic arousal. *Journal of Abnormal Psychology, 71,* 253–255.

Goldband, S., Katkin, E. S., & Morell, M. A. (1979). Personality and cardiovascular disorder: Steps toward demystification. In I. G. Sarason & C. D. Spielberger (Eds.), *Stress and anxiety* (Vol. 6). Washington, D.C.: Hemisphere Publishing.

Hare, R. D. (1965). Temporal gradient of fear arousal in psychopaths. *Journal of Abnormal Psychology, 70,* 442–445.

Hare, R. D. (1968). Psychopathy, autonomic functioning and orienting response. *Journal of Abnormal Psychology Monograph, 73,* 1–24.

Hare, R. D. (1972). Psychopathy and physiological responses to adrenalin. *Journal of Abnormal Psychology, 79,* 138–147.

Hare, R. D. (1975). Psychophysiological studies of psychopathy. In D. C. Fowles, (Ed.), *Clinical applications of psychophysiology.* New York: Columbia University Press.

Hare, R. D., & Craigen, D. (1974). Psychopathy and physiological activity in a mixed motive game situation. *Psychophysiology, 11,* 197–206.

Hare, R. D., & Quinn, M. J. (1971). Psychopathy and autonomic conditioning. *Journal of Abnormal Psychology, 77,* 223–235.

Harris, V. A., & Katkin, E. S. (1975). Primary and secondary emotional behavior: An analysis of the role of autonomic feedback on affect, arousal, and attribution. *Psychological Bulletin, 82,* 904–916.

Hassett, J. (1978). *A primer of psychophysiology.* San Francisco: W. H. Freeman.

Holzman, P. S., Kringlen, E., Levy, D. L., Proctor, L. R., Haberman, S. J., & Yasillo, N. J. (1977). Abnormal pursuit eye movements in schizophrenia: Evidence for a genetic indicator. *Archives of General Psychiatry, 34,* 802–805.

Holzman, P. S., & Levy, D. L. (1977). Smooth pursuit eye movements and functional psychosis: A review. *Schizophrenia Bulletin, 3,* 15–27.

Holzman, P. S., Proctor, L. R., & Hughes, D. W. (1973). Eye tracking patterns in schizophrenia. *Science, 181,* 179–181.

Holzman, P. S., Proctor, L. R., Levy, D. L., Yasillo, N. J., Meltzer, H. Y., & Hurt, S. W. (1974). Eye tracking dysfunctions in schizophrenic patients and their relatives. *Archives of General Psychiatry, 31,* 143–151.

Iacono, W. G., & Lykken, D. T. (1979). Electroculographic recording and scoring of smooth pursuit and saccadic eye tracking: A parametric study using monozygotic twins. *Psychophysiology 16,* 94–107.

Itil, T. M. (1977). Qualitative and quantitative EEG findings in schizophrenia. *Schizophrenia Bulletin, 3,* 61–79.

Jacobson, E. (1938). *Progressive relaxation.* Chicago: University of Chicago Press.

James, W. (1884). What is an emotion? *Mind, 9,* 188–205.

Jasper, H. H. (1958). Report of committee on methods of clinical examination in EEG: Appendix: The ten-twenty electrode system of the international federation. *Electroencephalography and Clinical Neurophysiology, 10,* 371–375.

Johnson, L. C., & Lubin, A. (1972). On planning psychophysiological experiments: Design, measurement and analysis. In N. S. Greenfield & R. A. Sternbach (Eds.), *Handbook of psychophysiology*. New York: Holt, Rinehart & Winston.

Katkin, E. S. (1965). Relationship between manifest anxiety and two indices of autonomic response to stress. *Journal of Personality and Social Psychology, 2*, 324–333.

Katkin, E. S. (1966). The relationship between a measure of transitory anxiety and spontaneous autonomic activity. *Journal of Abnormal Psychology, 71*, 142–146.

Katkin, E. S., & Deitz, S. R. (1973). Systematic desensitization. In W. F. Prokasy & D. C. Raskin (Eds.), *Electrodermal activity in psychological research*. New York: Academic Press.

Katkin, E. S., & Manuck, S. B. (1985). *Advances in behavioral medicine*. Greenwich, Conn.: JAI Press.

Katkin, E. S., & McCubbin, R. J. (1969). Habituation of the orienting response as a function of individual differences in anxiety and autonomic lability. *Journal of Abnormal Psychology, 74*, 54–60.

Kirkegaard-Sorenson, L., & Mednick, S. A. (1977). A prospective study of predictors of criminality: A description of registered criminality in the high-risk and low-risk families. In S. A. Mednick & K. O. Christiansen (Eds.), *Biological bases of criminal behavior*. New York: Gardner Press.

Lacey, J. I. (1956). The evaluation of autonomic responses: Toward a general solution. *Annals of the New York Academy of Sciences, 67*, 123–164.

Lacey, J. I., Bateman, D. E., & Van Lehn, R. (1953). Autonomic response specificity: An experimental study. *Psychosomatic Medicine, 15*, 8–21.

Lacey, J. I., & Lacey, B. C. (1958). Verification and extension of the principle of autonomic response stereotypy. *American Journal of Psychology, 71*, 50–73.

Lang, P. J. (1968). Fear reduction and fear behavior: Problems in treating a construct. In J. M. Schlien (Ed.), *Research in psychotherapy* (Vol. 3). Washington, D.C.: American Psychological Association.

Lang, P. J. (1969). The mechanics of desensitization and laboratory studies of human fear. In C. M. Franks (Ed.), *Assessment and status of the behavioral therapies and associated developments*. New York: McGraw-Hill.

Lang, P. J., & Buss, A. (1965). Psychological deficit in schizophrenia: II. Interference and activation. *Journal of Abnormal Psychology, 70*, 77–106.

Lang, P. J., Melamed, B. G., & Hart, J. (1970). A psychophysiological analysis of fear modification using an automated desensitization procedure. *Journal of Abnormal Psychology, 76*, 220–234.

Loeb, J., & Mednick, S. A. (1977). A prospective study of predictors of criminality: 3. Electrodermal response patterns. In S. A. Mednick & K. O. Christiansen (Eds.), *Biological bases of criminal behavior*. New York: Gardner Press.

Lykken, D. T. (1972). Range correction applied to heart rate and GSR data. *Psychophysiology, 9*, 373–379.

Lykken, D. T. (1974). Psychology and the lie detector industry. *American Psychologist, 29,* 725–739.

Lykken, D. T. (1981). *A tremor in the blood: Uses and abuses of the lie detector.* New York: McGraw-Hill.

Mathews, A. M. (1971). Psychophysiological approaches to the investigation of desensitization and related procedures. *Psychological Bulletin, 76,* 73–91.

Mathews, K. (1982). Psychological perspectives on the Type A behavior pattern. *Psychological Bulletin, 91,* 293–323.

Mednick, S. A. (1970). Breakdown in individuals at high risk for schizophrenia: Possible predispositional perinatal factors. *Mental Hygiene, 54,* 50–63.

Mednick, S. A., & Schulsinger, F. (1968). Some premorbid characteristics related to breakdown in children with schizophrenic mothers. In D. Rosenthal & S. Kety (Eds.), *Transmission of schizophrenia.* London: Pergamon.

Office of Technology Assessment. (1983). *Scientific validity of polygraphy testing: A research review and evaluation.* Washington, D.C.: U. S. Government Printing Office, Technical Memorandum OTA-TM-H-15.

Orne, M. T. (1975). Implications of laboratory research for the detection of deception. In N. Ashley (Ed.), *Legal admissibility of the polygraph,* Springfield, Ill.: Charles C. Thomas.

Orne, M. T., Thackray, R. I., & Paskewitz, D. A. (1972). On the detection of deception: A method for the study of the physiological effects of psychological stimuli. In N. S. Greenfield & R. A. Sternbach (Eds.), *Handbook of psychophysiology.* New York: Holt, Rinehart & Winston.

Patterson, T. T., & Venables, P. H. (1978). Bilateral skin conductance and skin potential in schizophrenic and normal subjects: The identification of the fast habituator group of schizophrenics. *Psychophysiology, 15,* 556–560.

Podlesny, J. A., & Raskin, D. C. (1977). Physiological measures and the detection of deception. *Psychological Bulletin, 84,* 782–799.

Rappaport, H., & Katkin, E. S. (1972). Relationships among manifest anxiety, response to stress, and the perception of autonomic activity. *Journal of Consulting and Clinical Psychology, 38,* 219–224.

Roth, W. T. (1977). Late event-related potentials and psychopathology. *Schizophrenia Bulletin, 3,* 105–120.

Schachter, S., & Singer, J. E. (1962). Cognitive, social, and physiological determinants of emotional state. *Psychological Review, 69,* 379–399.

Sersen, E. A., Clausen, J., & Lidsky, A. (1978). Autonomic specificity and stereotypy revisited. *Psychophysiology, 15,* 60–67.

Siddle, D.A.T., & Trasler, G. B. (1983). The psychophysiology of psychopathic behaviour. In M. J. Christie & D. G. Mellett (Eds.), *Psychosomatic approaches to medicine* (Vol. 1). *Behavioural Science Foundations.* London: Wiley.

Sokolov, E. N. (1963). *Perception and the conditioned reflex.* New York: Macmillan.

Spielberger, C. D. (Ed.). (1966). *Anxiety and behavior.* New York: Academic Press.

Surwit, R. S., Shapiro, D., & Good, M. I. (1978). Comparison of cardiovascular biofeedback, neuromuscular biofeedback, and meditation in the treatment of borderline essential hypertension. *Journal of Consulting and Clinical Psychology, 46,* 252–263.

Tarchanoff, J. (1890). Über die galvanischen Erscheinungen an der Haut des Menschen bei reizung der Sinnesorgane und bei verschiedenen Formen der psychischen Tätigkeit. *Pfluger's Archiv Psycholischen, 46,* 46–55.

Venables, P. H. (1975). A psychophysiological approach to research in schizophrenia. In D. C. Fowles (Ed.), *Clinical applications of psychophysiology.* New York: Columbia University Press.

Venables P. H. (1977). The electrodermal psychophysiology of schizophrenics and children at risk for schizophrenia: Current controversies and developments. *Schizophrenia Bulletin, 3,* 23–48.

Venables, P. H., & Christie, M. J. (1973). Mechanisms, instrumentation, recording techniques, and quantification of responses. In W. F. Prokasy & D. C. Raskin (Eds.), *Electrodermal activity in psychological research.* New York: Academic Press.

Wilder, J. (1950). The law of initial values. *Psychosomatic Medicine, 12,* 392.

Wilson, G. D. (1967). GSR responses to fear related stimuli. *Perceptual and Motor Skills, 24,* 401–402.

Wolpe, J. (1971). The behavioristic conception of neurosis: A reply to two critics. *Psychological Review, 78,* 341–343.

Zahn, T. P., Rosenthal, D., & Lawlor, W. G. (1968). Electrodermal and heart rate orienting reactions in chronic schizophrenia. *Journal of Psychiatric Research, 6,* 117–134.

Psychophysiological Assessment: Some Uses and Misuses

WILLIAM D. NEIGHER

Katkin's review is a thorough, concise, helpful framework for viewing conceptual and methodological research issues in psychophysiological assessment. Along with Neal Miller's 1983 chapter on behavioral medicine in that year's *Annual Review of Psychology*, it offers readers an excellent overview of major issues in the field. Katkin's central proposition is accurate and important: "The data on psychophysiological assessment suggest that we are a long way from being able to use autonomic or central nervous system response indexes to make diagnostic decisions with confidence" (Chapter 4, Summary). In spite of these well-placed reservations, however, socially important diagnostic decisions *are* being made daily, in a widespread, wholesale way. The confidence limits associated with those decisions are seldom fully understood in practical applications of psychophysiological assessment by practitioners, and are rarely conveyed to patients or clients.

Katkin has focused on conceptions and misconceptions. I will focus on "uses and misuses" of psychophysiological assessment, both in current practice and in some likely, but undesirable, future developments. My comments develop from my experience as a provider, consumer, and funder of the kinds of psychophysiological assessment Katkin describes.

BEHAVIORAL MEDICINE SERVICES

My primary employment is in an acute-care general hospital as assistant director of mental health services and division director of research and development. I am part of the management team responsible for the hospital and its corporate planning, specifically for initiating, developing, and marketing a division of behavioral medicine. Several theses in Katkin's chapter are illuminated in the light of that experience.

Katkin points out that the limits of psychophysiological assessment may lie mainly in poorly eludicated conceptual relationships between constructs and the physiological indexes used to measure them. In most cases, these relationships are not well understood. Similarly, interventions in behavioral medicine are limited by gaps between knowledge gained from basic laboratory research and the current state of clinical practice in the field. Yet, knowledge or no knowledge, the field of behavioral medicine has grown rapidly and is now very large, as shown by its conceptual scope, the numbers of people affected, and the financial costs involved. By "behavioral medicine," I refer to the entire field of behavioral and biomedical knowledge relative to health and disease as described by Neal Miller: "It involves the integration of relative parts of epidemiology, anthropology, sociology, psychology, physiology, pharmacology, nutrition, neuroanatomy, endocrinology, immunology, and various branches of medicine and public health, as well as related professions such as dentistry, nursing, social work and health education" (Miller, 1983, pp. 2–3). This is a rapidly expanding field. The second volume of *Behavioral Medicine Abstracts* (Taylor, 1981) contains over one thousand articles. The newly formed APA Division of Health Psychology counted 2,419 members in 1984.

The fact that emotions play a role in health should come as no surprise to anyone. Galen estimated that 60% of his patients had symptoms of emotional rather than physical origin. The number is close to the contemporary estimate of 60% to 80% (Shapiro, 1978). One particular application of behavioral medicine, stress management, has become especially popular in recent years. The impact of stress on the cardiovascular system, on the immune system, and on the body's gastrointestinal system has been well documented. The indirect cost of stress-related disorders has been estimated between 17 and 25 billion dollars per year. Not surprisingly, many employers have sought out stress management programs for their employees as one means of reducing employer-share costs of providing health benefits. Some hospitals have been extremely aggressive in marketing employee assistance programs to industry, in competition for a market share against other area hospitals with similar ambitions. Stress management procedures are prominent in nearly all these programs.

Stress management programs have taken many different forms but usually include a combination of several techniques. "Progressive relaxation," introduced by Jacobson in the 1930s, has been one of the earliest and most common procedures. Several of the psychological assessment procedures described in Katkin's chapter are involved in current uses of progressive relaxation. Biofeedback helps patients learn muscular relaxation by providing them with information from instruments that measure EMG, GSR, heart rate, increased alpha waves, or warmth of fingers. Biofeedback is also used in the treatment of muscle contraction headaches, vascular headaches, mixed headaches, Raynaud's disease, fecal incontinence, many neural muscular disorders including myofacial pain and bruxism, various problems that follow muscle tendon transfer, and certain cardiac arrhythmias (Miller, 1983; Schwartz, 1983).

Many hospitals are currently in the process of developing behavioral medicine initiatives for inpatient services and programs. Stress management is often used as part of a marketing strategy. Because the effects of stress are widely recognized and "stress management" has become a popular phrase, stress management programs are often used as "loss leaders" to encourage more extensive employee assistance programs and more profitable inpatient referrals, especially for psychiatric and alcohol-related disabilities. Stress management programs aimed at middle and upper management establish good will and often lead to the referrals the hospitals seek; they are also aimed at the general population, advertised through health fairs and local mailings, and then delivered on a fee-for-service basis if economically sufficient registration is achieved.

Biofeedback, which incorporates many of the psychophysiological assessment techniques that Katkin describes, is most successful with a case mix of limited incidence in acute-care general hospitals. In other areas where it is widely used, the cost effectiveness of biofeedback is questionable. An important problem in medical management is excessive use of medication where prescription does not necessarily work to the benefit of patients. Our hospital has identified two primary areas in which the need is greatest. First, approximately one-third of all medications for pain reduction appear to be unnecessary. Drugs are prescribed at the behest of the patients and not in the best interests of their general recovery. Second, sleep medications are similarly misused, but physicians comply under pressure from patients. These two prescribing problems prolong patients' length of stay and impede recovery. Biofeedback might appear to be a promising alternative to medication in these cases, but from a financial standpoint hospital-based biofeedback is unlikely to be cost effective. The procedures require highly trained staff, a considerable amount of space and equipment, and a quiet environment, all of which are at a premium in most general hospitals. Much more profitable would be the development of ambulatory pain clinics for patients with headache and low back pain. Unfortunately, most individuals who need these services do not fit the definitive diagnostic categories that carry third-party reimbursement for their treatment. A preliminary market analysis shows that biofeedback offered to patients suffering from headache and low back pain would mainly serve the affluent, who can afford to pay on their own.

The uses of psychophysiological assessment in an acute-care general hospital, particularly in behavioral medicine, are thus influenced as much by financial as by clinical factors. Whatever the conceptual status or empirical validity of the methods may be, their uses and misuses are likely to be determined by the economic returns they offer to the health care industry. The best an ethically responsible hospital manager can do is to see that harmful procedures are not allowed, that more promising procedures are honestly advertised, and that every effort is made to bring the benefits of useful procedures to the patients who need them most.

INTEGRATING RESEARCH AND TECHNOLOGY:
GOVERNMENTAL SUPPORT
AND COMMERCIAL ADOPTION

Katkin concludes his chapter with a plea for basic research on the processes underlying psychophysiological assessment. Some recent funding initiatives may provide opportunities for combining basic and applied research with incentives for commercial application. The Small Business Innovation Research (SBIR) Program of the Public Health Service, for example, provides seed money for technical innovations that may lead to prototype development and commercial adoption. As a member of a committee reviewing applications for SBIR grants, I have often found myself in conflict over the competing demands of sound research methodology and potential for commercial application. A strong interest can be seen in extending our current knowledge and technology in the areas of psychophysiological assessment that Katkin describes. Large numbers of proprietary and academically based research and development firms capable of bringing in electrical engineers, software development specialists, and computer hardware specialists to join traditional teams of psychologists and physicians offer exciting possibilities for advancing the field of neural and psychophysiological assessment. We must be concerned, however, with those who will make this new technology available to practitioners marginally qualified to use them. For example, the development of microprocessor-driven assessment systems for physicians' and psychotherapists' offices proposes to automate tests of limited or poor psychometric validity. As Matarazzo has said, "There is a danger that wholesale use of automated tests by people without a knowledge of their limitations will be a disservice to the public. Compounding this danger, the tests have a spurious appearance of objectivity and infallibility as a halo effect from the computer, and their ease of use may cause them to be more widely employed than are current tests" (Matarazzo, 1983, p. 1).

Funding agencies that link basic and applied research with commercial application may stimulate useful research. The lure of financial gain, however, may blind investigators to demands for careful inquiry and cautious interpretation. In funding research as in marketing services, scientific and economic interests are sometimes in conflict. Developing projects that are both rigorous and commercially profitable is not an easy task.

PSYCHOPHYSIOLOGICAL ASSESSMENT: SOME ALTERNATIVE FUTURES

Leading experts on health and mental health care have offered interesting projections about the future of the field. One has said that "sophisticated technology will make possible instantaneous readouts of physiological states, even by telemetry, in real time" (Mannerscheid, quoted in Landsberg et al., 1979, p. 228). Others have offered a scenario in which individuals would be periodically screened by computers and those showing adverse biopsychosocial problems would be automatically called up for early therapy. Records would be transferred across the country through automated medical data banks, and advances in technological assessment would continue to burgeon. Some of these projections have already been realized and others are obsolete.

The issue of rapid accessibility of psychophysiological data must be distinguished from troubling questions about validity and the inferences that clinicians may draw. In this regard, Katkin's basic conceptual concern with our ability to generalize between psychological processes and their physiological concomitants is especially important to note. Just as the third edition of the *Diagnostic and Statistical Manual* of the American Psychiatric Association was in some ways an attempt to "remedicalize" psychiatry, there is a potential for widespread misuse of psychophysiological technologies in an attempt to "medicalize" psychotherapeutic services. The problems are likely to become more serious in the future as diagnoses eligible for third-party reimbursement are constricted in an effort to reduce the costs of mental health care. Assessment technology in general, and biopsychological forms of assessment in particular, may become increasingly attractive to practitioners for purely economic reasons. As Miller has said, the temptations are extreme: "Statement overheard at a recent conference on gastrointestinal diseases. . . 'If you make the mistake of asking the patient how he feels, you will be talking with him for about half an hour, and the most his insurance would pay is $50.00. But if you tell him that you'll give him a complete series of tests, it will only take five minutes of your time and there will be no question about a bill of $250'" (Miller, 1983, p. 5).

If we fail to follow the methodological and conceptual recommendations that Katkin offers us in addressing current shortcomings of psychophysiological assessment, the potential for misuse of this important technology will clearly increase. There are indeed major shortcomings with the current knowledge base for understanding psychophysiological processes and their assessment. There are also serious problems in the application of knowledge to technology and clinical practice. The problems are not unique to psychology. They hold for medicine as well. The Congressional Office of Technology Assessment reports that only 10% to 15% of all general medical procedures have been proven to be demonstrably effective in random clinical trials, and the Federal Drug Administration often labels drugs as "ineffective" even after they have been prescribed for years. The task for psychology, however, is to keep its own house in order. Psychologists and others responsible for the application and reimbursement of psychophysiological assessment bear special obligation to qualify the uses and misuses of these techniques, to inform patients and the public when interventions are "experimental" or have variable outcomes, and to attempt whenever possible to collect and publish data on patient outcomes, especially when results are less than popular expectations might suggest.

REFERENCES

Landsberg, G., Neigher, W. D., Hammer, R. J., Windle, C., & Woy, J. R. (Eds.). (1979). *Evaluation in practice: A sourcebook of program evaluation studies from mental health care systems in the United States* (DHEW Publication No. (ADM) 78–763). Washington, D.C.: U.S. Government Printing Office.

Matarazzo, J. (1983). Computerized psychological testing. *Science, 221,* 1.

Miller, N. E. (1983). Behavioral medicine: Symbiosis between laboratory and clinic. In M. R. Rosenzweig & L. W. Porter (Eds.), *Annual review of psychology* (Vol. 34). Palo Alto, Calif.: Annual Reviews.

Schwartz, M. S. (1983). Biofeedback: Does it really work? For what? And by whom? *Continuing Education,* December: 1087–1098.

Shapiro, A. K. (1978). Placebo effects in medical and psychological therapies. In S. L. Garfield & A. E. Bergen (Eds.), *Handbook of psychotherapy and behavior change: An empirical analysis* (2nd ed.) New York: Wiley.

Taylor, C. B. (Ed.). (1981). *Behavioral Medicine Abstracts, 2,* (Whole Volume).

ASSESSING INDIVIDUAL BEHAVIOR

In the following section of the book, we consider two assessment systems directed mainly toward study of the individual. This is the level of analysis at which most conventional assessment methods in psychology, such as tests of intelligence and personality, have focused. The authors of the next two chapters show, however, that traditional procedures for measuring traits or states are insufficient as bases for the decisions that matter most to the people under study. They also show that carefully designed methods for studying individual behavior can provide information useful at other levels, especially for the design and evaluation of organizational programs.

In Chapter 5, Paul describes the system for assessing client and staff functioning in residential treatment settings that he and his colleagues have constructed over the past 15 years. He begins with a sobering discussion of the high costs and miserable effects of traditional approaches to assessing and treating the "mentally ill." He proceeds with a carefully refined, yet straightforward analysis of the varieties of decisions required in residential treatment settings, and the classes and domains of variables that must be considered if treatment programs are to be conducted rationally. After defining the psychometric conditions that need to be met by any useful assessment system, he presents his own methods for direct observational coding of client and staff behavior. Near-perfect reliabilities are demonstrated. Impressive evidence of validity is shown. The usefulness of the program for many kinds of clients and settings is documented. Use of computers for registering, retrieving, and aggregating data allows ongoing information about staff and client functioning to be used not only for individual treatment planning but for a wide range of administrative decisions.

Harvey Lieberman is chief of a residential treatment service in a state psychiatric hospital. His praise for Paul's contribution is strong, he has used components of the system in his own program, and he is considering implementation of the complete methodology in the future. Lieberman considers Paul's system conceptually bold, technically exemplary, and institutionally revolutionary. Unlike many procedures that are inherently limited to incremental change, Paul's method promises a quantum improvement in the quality of residential treatment. As an admin-

141

istrator, however, Lieberman has a keen appreciation of conditions that need to be met if radical changes are to be made in a organization of the kind he manages. In his commentary, he raises the clinical, technical, and administrative questions that need to be addressed if a program of this scope is to be placed in successful operation.

The exchange between Paul and Lieberman during and after the symposium was difficult in some ways, but the outcome offers a particularly felicitious illustration of the value these kinds of meetings can have. The first draft of Paul's chapter, already longer than most of the others because of the scope and technical complexity of the project, contained little content on administrative implementation of the program. This was just the area in which Lieberman had encountered problems with Paul's methodology, so his initial comments emphasized the practical difficulties of putting the program into effect. Paul then extended his chapter to include a section on implementation and dissemination that countered most of the objections Lieberman had raised. This required Lieberman to revise his discussion from beginning to end. The process was vexing for all concerned, but the outcome was a more complete and persuasive statement than the author had originally presented, and a commentary by the discussant that is useful not only in appraising one particular technology but in planning the installation of any system of the scope and consequence that Paul's methodology represents.

We move from mental health settings to correctional institutions for another illustration of successful decision-focused assessment of individual behavior. Following a court order that declared all prisoners in the State of Alabama subject to cruel and unusual punishment because of universally deplorable conditions in the prisons, faculty and students of the University of Alabama Department of Psychology undertook reclassification of all inmates. Their charge was to develop an assessment system that would place inmates under the least restrictive custody possible and identify those in need of special treatments of various kinds. Fowler's Chapter 6 tells the story of the efforts and accomplishments of the project group. The effects of legal and political influences are vividly described. The importance of the rationale for decision rules is demonstrated. The value of behavioral records in estimating risks of violent behavior is shown. Conflicts between institutional staff, motivated to sustain the status quo, and university psychologists, coming in by court order to change conditions, offer comments on the politics of institutional intervention. The lore of social psychology and the methodology of assessment are both enriched by this account of the Alabama project.

Fowler's chapter is discussed by Frederick Rotgers, a staff psychologist with a state parole board who has had many years of experience in the field of corrections. After remarks on the technical merits and limitations of the Alabama classification project, Rotgers addresses the political issues involved in efforts of this kind. From the view of the larger society, the main purposes of the prison are to segregate, incapacitate, and punish. Rehabilitation and humanitarian decency are lesser concerns. The political vulnerability of prison administrators, whose funding and jobs depend on public support, encourages opposition to the kind of "liberal" program Fowler describes, however rational or successful the program may be.

Chapter 5

Rational Operations in Residential Treatment Settings through Ongoing Assessment of Client and Staff Functioning

GORDON L. PAUL

Residential treatment settings for mentally disabled adults consist of institutions or subunits within other facilities in which clientele reside 24 hours per day to receive treatment. They include public and private mental hospitals and residential schools for the mentally disabled, inpatient units in mental health centers, community residential facilities, and psychiatric units within general hospitals. Within the field of mental health, the populations and programs in residential settings are seriously in need of assistance from psychological science and decision-focused assessment for both research and service. The clientele served in residential facilities are the most severely disabled of all emotionally disturbed and mentally retarded adults receiving treatment or care in either public or private sectors. Few professionals are aware of the degree of suffering or emotional and financial drain on clients and their loved ones in this group of people. Even fewer are aware of the extreme level of disability existing in the long-stay populations of public institutions (Paul, 1984).

Residential treatment settings also pose serious problems for public policy (see Paul, 1978, 1985b, 1986b). They are the most restrictive of client rights with the greatest potential for abuse of all service settings. They are the most subject to impact by distant political and administrative decisions and the most overwhelmed by existing regulations and paper work. For example, at least 25% of clinical staff time and salaries are regularly devoted to fulfilling documentation requirements for ex-

145

ternal agencies. They are also the most dependent on the actions of pre-professional rather than professional staff, to the extent that 40% to 95% of on-line clinical personnel have less formal schooling than a bachelor's degree. Further, they are the most expensive of all mental health services to operate. The daily costs in U.S. state and county hospitals are estimated to average nearly $150 per client by 1987—more than $54,000 per year. Costs in for-profit and not-for-profit private mental hospitals average nearly two-and-one-half times as much as state institutions, with Veterans Administration (VA) neuropsychiatric units and other inpatient units falling in between. Even though "deinstitutionalization" has been the stated policy in the public sector for more than two decades, the dollars spent on the operation of residential facilities are estimated to consume about 70% of the total direct expenditures for public mental health services—nearly 1% of the U.S. gross national product. Thus, the operation of residential treatment facilities and the populations and programs within them constitute some of the most important areas for the discovery and application of science-based knowledge and technology.

THE CONTEXT IN NEED OF DECISION-FOCUSED ASSESSMENT

As I have argued elsewhere (Paul, 1984, 1985b, 1986a), the only valid reason for the existence of residential treatment facilities—their reason-to-be from humanitarian, ethical, professional, economic, or public policy perspectives—*should be* to provide treatment that is effective and cost-efficient for the most severely mentally disabled. The primary goal of residential treatment should be to improve the functioning of clients whose problems are too burdensome or too dangerous to allow treatment elsewhere. Functioning should be improved at least to a level that allows clients to return to less restrictive community settings where improvements could be maintained or further enhanced. Unfortunately, current operations provide little objective data for genuine evaluations of existing programs or their components.

Inadequacies of Current Practices

Inefficient operations and ineffective treatment. The available data point to a woeful inadequacy of most current practices (Paul, 1984, 1985b, 1986b). Even though client participation in such an expensive service as residential treatment can be justified only by the need for the more intensive and extensive treatment presumably provided, work-sample assessments of the way in which clients and staff spend their time in traditional programs clearly show a gross underutilization and inefficient use of resources. For example, the clinical staff in state and VA hospitals average less than 15% of working time with any client contact at all, and clients in those facilities average less than 11% of waking hours in contact with staff. The staffing levels in private mental hospitals and psychiatric units of university and general hospitals are much higher, but staff in these facilities average less than 25% of working time in client contact. The highest average rates of client contact with staff in the latter facilities range from 17% to 22% of waking hours. Thus, the average client observed in traditional residential programs fails to receive any attention at all from staff about 80% to 90% of the time that could be available for treatment; most client time is spent alone, asleep, or inactive. During those hours in which clinical staff in traditional programs could be in direct contact with clients, roughly 75% to 85% of the average staff member's working hours are spent in other activities—mostly doing paper work, attending meetings, and engaging in other "housekeeping" tasks or personal pursuits. Since client and staff time are the major resources available, their inefficient use represents a tremendous opportunity-cost in current practices, a cost that is not at all in keeping with the preferences of most staff, clients, or family members. The opportunity-cost of chemotherapy is also substantial, since 20% to 90% of the dollars currently spent on psychotropic drugs are estimated to be supporting ineffective and possibly harmful treatment. These drug costs alone represent 1% to 5% of the total operating expenditures of different residential facilities.

Although isolated treatment programs exist that are efficient and effective, the failure of current practices at the national level is reflected in the numbers of clients who are chronically institutionalized for at least a year, who fill about 60% of beds in state mental institutions. The extensive efforts toward deinstitutionalization and shorter lengths-of-stay have resulted in massive reductions in state and county hospital beds, but with parallel increases in mental health centers, community residential facilities, and use of beds in general hospitals and in correctional facilities. Although nearly 80% of admissions to state hospitals are now released in less than three months, readmission rates have climbed from 25% to 80% over the past 25 years and the long-stay population has been increasing again since 1979. The percentage of admissions who are readmissions at VA hospitals is nearly

86%. Private hospitals, where third-party payments determine much of the clientele, average nearly 70% readmission rates. The "revolving door" phenomenon of multiple readmissions is equally apparent in mental health centers and general hospitals in which much shorter lengths of stay are typical—reflecting the failure of current short-term crisis stabilization, chemotherapy, and aftercare programs to improve or maintain the functioning of significant numbers of clientele. In fact, the *majority* of admissions to acute treatment units are now accounted for by the "revolving door."

More than two-thirds of discharged clients still demonstrate serious problems in functioning, less than 25% return to full-time employment, and the "homeless mentally ill" who wander the streets have become a national disgrace. The best predictors of postdischarge client functioning after receiving residential treatment are still measures of preadmission functioning over most programs. The best predictor of future hospitalization is still past hospitalization. Both of these statistical relationships indicate a relative lack of positive impact (i.e., variance accounted for) of current residential treatment practices. Indeed, direct monitoring of residential programs in one of the better funded state mental health systems found clientele were simply being processed rather than effectively treated; at the time of client discharge, roughly a third were worse, a third were better, and a third were unchanged from their level of functioning at entry.

An estimated 70% or more of clientele are kept for too long or too short a time in residential settings for optimal use of resources, representing excessive human and financial costs. Exposés of various sorts regularly report long-standing intolerable conditions and occasional blatant atrocities in residential settings. Overall, current practices in residential treatment settings appear woefully inadequate to ensure legal, ethical, and humane conditions for either clientele or staff or to fulfill the goal of providing effective, let alone cost-efficient treatment. Such inadequacies are further evidenced by the rapid growth of grassroots advocacy and support groups of ex-clients and/or family members who are clearly communicating the human and financial costs of ineffective practices and outrage with the status quo.

Displacement of effective treatment by the current context and culture. Numerous commentators have described the context, culture, and manner of decision-making in current human service bureaucracies and mental health systems in general, as well as residential treatment organizations in particular (see Paul, 1978, 1985b; Paul & Lentz, 1977). These factors, including the absence of information required to support rational planning, evaluation, or day-to-day clinical activities, are strong contributors to the inadequacies in most current residential practices—if not the major bases for the continuing, sorry state of affairs. Space prohibits even a cursory summary of these factors. Rather, the reader is referred to the above sources for detailed descriptions and analyses, as well as to earlier works by Peterson (1968), Tornatzky et al. (1980), Saper (1975), and Ullmann (1967). Broskowski's description of the complex, instable, ambiguous, and reactive context of decision-making in mental health centers in Chapter 9 of this book is consistent with the detailed analyses of specific factors that contribute to the displacement of effective treatment as a goal in residential settings by other commentators. Similarly, his description of current organizational decision-making within the "qualitative/hermeneutic" dimension of the assessment typology presented in Fishman and Neigher's chapter in this book (Chapter 2, Figure 2.1)—with either no decision-focused assessment data or only exceptionally fallible, easily obtained indicators, which are far removed from the phenomena of interest—appears characteristic of current practices at all levels in residential treatment settings. Tornatzky et al. (1980) colorfully summarize the consequences of these practices in describing large human service bureaucracies as "bumbling giants" in which attempts to maintain a faltering hold on rationality and predictability occur in a world that has become irrational and unpredictable, with incentives often rewarding inefficiency or, at best, perpetuation of the status quo.

A Major Technological-Methodological Obstacle

Most policy makers, funders, and administrative and clinical staff involved with residential treatment are concerned and caring people who are neither malevolent nor stupid; in principle, they, as well as clientele and their loved ones, subscribe to high-quality, cost-effective treatment. How then could such woefully inadequate decision-making and treatment practices come to pass? I have argued elsewhere that a major technological-methodological obstacle—the absence of an objective, practical assessment technology that can provide the information needed for the rational operation of residential treatment facilities (Paul, 1978, 1979, 1985b, 1986b)—has allowed the current condition to develop and continue. None of the typical practices in these facilities, or in the overall systems of service of which they are a part, include even the fundamental considerations described by Peterson in Chapter 1 of this book for useful, decision-focused, functional assessments.

All rational decision-making requires that choices among courses of action be based on the probable gains and losses offered by each alternative. "Assessment" goes on even if it is subjective and unrecognized because rational choices imply comparisons and predictions among relevant phenomena (see Paul et al., 1986a; Wiggins, 1973). Formal decision-focused assessment is, thus, critically important to the provision of good management and services and to the conduct of good research. The absence of such information allows current practices to be determined by subjective predilection, tradition, ideological "correctness," least-energy expenditure, political self-protection and self-enhancement, and simple cost containment, rather than by quality, effectiveness, and cost efficiency. The consequences for clients, staff, and society are costly.

OVERVIEW AND CONCEPTUAL PARADIGM

Guiding Concepts and Collaboration

As a clinical psychologist with one foot in the academic-scientific world and the other in the world of mental health service providers, with clinical-research, training roles, and administration (as head of residential units and aftercare programs) bridging the two, I have had the opportunity over the past 20 years to view the above problems from many perspectives. For the last several years, a major portion of my time has been devoted to a task analysis of the varieties of decisions required for the rational operation of residential treatment facilities and the information needed to support such decision-making. The guiding conceptualizations that have been most useful are decision theory and generalizability theory as presented by Cronbach and Gleser (1965), Cronbach et al. (1972), and Wiggins (1973), as well as my own formulations of assessment needs derived from the "ultimate question" for clinical research and practice (see Paul, 1969, 1985a; Paul & Lentz, 1977; Paul et al., 1986a). My colleagues and I have also been engaged for more than 17 years in a research and development program, which, in addition to basic questions regarding theoretical principles relevant to psychoses and intervention procedures, has focused on practical, exportable technologies for comprehensive treatment and assessment, especially within residential facilities.

The "R&D" program has resulted in a cost-effective multifaceted assessment system, which appears to fulfill the majority of the most important technological-methodological information needs for the rational operation of residential treatment facilities for the full range of adult mentally disabled populations and programs (Paul, 1979, 1986a, in press a).

Overview of the Chapter

In the remaining pages, I hope to familiarize the reader with the major outcomes of the above analyses and R&D program. The gist of the decision problems, the domains and classes of variables within which information is needed, and the level of detail required for common information across clients and staff will be presented for orientation. The guidelines for determining the quality and potential value of data obtained by different assessment strategies will then be noted. Application of these guidelines shows that a nontraditional approach to assessment is best for supporting the most important decisions relating to residential treatment facilities. That approach then forms the core of a comprehensive paradigm for the integrated application of assessment strategies. Only a skeletal outline of these recommendations can be provided, as an entire volume is needed to fully develop the logic and details of analysis, the specific nature of the differing approaches to assessment, and the comprehensive paradigm (Paul, 1986a). I will then describe the core assessment system and its components—the Computerized TSBC/SRIC Planned-Access Observational Information System. A sampling of reliability and validity evidence and a few comments on practical implementation, dissemination, and costs compared to current practices will also be noted. The brief description of the TSBC/SRIC (Time-Sample Behavioral Checklist/Staff-Resident Interaction Chronograph) system will synopsize a series of materials that provides the full information for implementation and documentary evidence of utility for "real-world" decisions. This evidence has led me and my colleagues to be quite optimistic about the promise of the TSBC/SRIC system to provide a basis for residential treatment facilities that not only would improve the quality, effectiveness, and cost efficiency of operations but that would allow service programs to approach the status of an applied science.

"Dimensions of Decision-Focused Assessment"

The dimensions of decision-focused assessment presented by Fishman and Neigher in Chapter 2 of this book, and summarized in their Figure 2.1, provide a common framework for discussing the diverse content covered in other chapters. Although my experience, as well as my reading of the same literature, does *not* result in corresponding conclusions regarding the basis for either the general lack of progress or the differential incentives for reliable and accurate data collection and use (see Paul, 1985a, 1985b, 1986b), Fishman and Neigher have undertaken a massive task and have provided a genuine contribution in explicating a number of factors that are often implicit or ignored. The material presented in this chapter is quite compatible with their general logic, conceptualizations, and the relative importance placed on different aspects of assessment technology and its link to decision-making. However, several differences in approach should be noted at the outset regarding the fit of the work presented in this chapter within their assessment typology.

Content and systems level. My analysis of decision problems has been undertaken for multiple-systems levels regarding the entirety of operational decisions in and about residential treatment programs and populations, rather than for a single set of decision problems as in the Fishman-Neigher typology. As a result of this focus, and the somewhat unique characteristics of the task of residential treatment facilities, different sources of information and methods of assessment have more and less potential value for different classes of variables and for different decision problems. A major outcome of the analysis of decision problems at multiple-systems levels, combined with the nature of those decisions, is that *ongoing, trustworthy,* and *comparable* information of *common relevance* to decision-making for *all* clientele, staff, and treatment programs is of primary importance for these settings. Specific assessment strategies that are unique to a single client or staff member, such as those described by Buffery in Chapter 3 and Katkin in Chapter 4 of this book, are also clearly important; however, such strategies are high in cost and may be sequentially triggered on the basis of information gathering on common classes of variables (see Paul et al., 1986a, 1986b, for explication).

This means that the primary focus of information gathering in residential treatment settings should be on individual clientele, staff members, and their environments, but that aggregations of those data can provide most of the information needed for small groups and treatment units, and for higher organizational entities as well. That is, the same assessment data ideally fulfill multiple-systems levels of the Fishman-Neigher typology. Similarly, as noted below, the types of variables and processes of relevance include the characteristics of people and envi-

ronments, as well as individual and interpersonal functioning and interactions among the classes.

Problem-solving process. The best fit within the Fishman-Neigher
typology occurs within this problem-solving process dimension. All
stages and steps of their typology have been and continue to be addressed in the work summarized in this chapter, albeit not always in
the linear and sequential way suggested. The assessment system to be
described has proceeded through all five stages of conceptualization,
development, pilot-testing, implementation, and the beginnings of dissemination. Current and future efforts are simultaneously being devoted to ongoing implementation and to preparation of the materials
necessary for widespread and efficient dissemination, with all of Fishman and Neigher's 25 steps being accomplished and/or "in process."
However, given the space limitations of a single chapter, description of
these aspects of process (see Paul, in press a) must be forsaken for description of the outcomes.

Epistemology. The poorest fit within the Fishman-Neigher typology
occurs in the epistemological-paradigm dimension. The analyses and
instrumentation presented below and the work of our clinical-research
group in general have purposely blurred this dimension of their typology, at times emphasizing one aspect and at times another. We have
never placed the paradigms in opposition—preferring to advance both
basic and applied work whenever possible. In fact, on the list of contrasting characteristics of pure and applied science in Table 2.2 of their
chapter, we not only represent a mid-point blend of the continua, but
usually emphasize the end points of each at different times for different
purposes.

The analysis of decision problems and information needs is clearly
undertaken from a "quantitative/natural science" perspective, but
the emphasis is on identification and development of assessment technologies that can serve "technological" managerial, clinical, and professional decision-making *and* both applied and "basic" scientific-
research purposes. Although the TSBC and SRIC assessment instruments
were originally designed only to fulfill scientific research needs, their
development into the TSBC/SRIC system was undertaken to fulfill the
majority of the most important ongoing decision-support needs for all
levels of decision-making in practical operations. The TSBC/SRIC system is based on the quantitative/natural science approach to information gathering and evaluation of data quality; however, the data obtained may be employed as a basis for both qualitative and quantitative
interpretation and decision-making. Thus, assessment technologies are

viewed as tools to aid all decision makers by providing trustworthy information that has comparable meaning over time, people, and settings. Such information is needed to aid individual clients and their loved ones, to aid the clinical staff in serving individual clients, to aid unit and facility directors in managing operations, to aid state, county, or corporate authorities in developing and monitoring overall programs in a system of service, and to aid researchers in fields related to mental disabilities (Paul et al., 1986a; Weinstein, 1975).

Decisions Required for Rational Operations

Rational operations at the level of the individual clinical staff member and the individual client, the unit or facility director and their aggregate treatment units, or central-office management and the facilities under them all require the ongoing monitoring of actions and effects. In rational operations, activities are performed, performance and effects are assessed, that information is fed back and compared to the desired goals, and changes in activity are made in response to that feedback. Although a multitude of separate, ongoing decisions are required in the operation of residential treatment facilities, a limited number of categories of decision problems can account for most of them. Such decisions typically involve actions regarding clients and staff, or their characteristics, actions, or interactions. These categories and client or staff focus of action are summarized in Table 5.1 (see Paul et al., 1986a, for details).

The first two categories focus on the individual client or staff member. *Placement and disposition* decisions have to do with getting people into a facility, assigning them to treatment units, and determining whether to retain, discharge, or transfer them—whether clients or staff. The next level of decisions involve *problem identification and description* for clientele, to identify their assets and the excesses and deficits that got them into the facility in the first place, to establish treatment goals, and to develop an initial treatment plan. Parallel to the latter class of decisions for clients are decisions concerning *staff development and utilization*. Decisions within this category are required any time that there is specification or change in programs and procedures, in time or responsibilities of staff, or for personnel actions involving salaries, tenure, evaluation, promotion, and evaluation of training.

After the first two categories, the decision problems relate to both clients and staff, and the same kinds of data are required. Management

TABLE 5.1
Varieties of Decisions Required for the Rational Operation
of Residential Treatment Facilities

Regarding clients	Regarding staff
1. *Placement & disposition* Admit Assign to treatment programs Retain, discharge, transfer	1. *Placement & disposition* Hire Assign to treatment programs Retain, discharge, transfer
2. *Problem identification & description* Identify assets, excesses, deficits Establish treatment goals Establish initial treatment plan	2. *Development & utilization* Specification or change in treatment Specification or change in staff time or responsibilities Personnel actions
3. *Concurrent monitoring of operations* Desired change occurring?	Prescribed treatment being carried out?
If not ⟶ modify & reevaluate ⟵ If not	
4. *Absolute & comparative program evaluation* Intended population served? Desired change attained (as well as other effects)?	Intended treatment programs employed? Nature of treatment implementations (as efficient, cost effective as others?)
If not ⟶ modify & reevaluate ⟵ If not	
5. *Legal & ethical regulation & documentation* Documentation of all above Compliance with external standards	Documentation of all above Compliance with external standards
6. *Specific research questions* Measurement/control of 1, 2, 3, & 4 above Questions of specific focus	Measurement/control of 1, 2, 3, & 4 above Questions of specific focus

SOURCE: Adapted from Paul (1985b).

decisions simply need the information to be aggregated over individuals for each unit or facility. For *concurrent monitoring of operations*, rational procedures would determine if desired changes are occurring for individual clients and specified client groups, and if prescribed treatment programs are being carried out by individual staff, treatment teams, or full treatment units on an hour-by-hour, day-by-day, week-by-week basis. If desired procedures or changes were not occurring, that information would signal the need for modification of staff actions and reevaluation of client changes. Concurrent monitoring should comprise the majority of ongoing decisions for rational operations, but is the least attended to in most current practices. *Absolute and comparative program evaluations* are also essential for effective treatment. Are clientele served as intended? Are desirable or undesirable changes occurring in each unit and as compared to others? Are staff implementing intended programs? Are there similar or different programs across units or facilities? Is the nature of implementation cost effective on an absolute basis? Are some programs more cost effective than others? Rational operation of residential treatment facilities would base funding allocations and program specifications on such data. If the intended effects were not occurring, changes would be introduced with ongoing reevaluations. The major difference between program evaluations and concurrent monitoring is that the former always involve aggregated group data over longer time periods, whereas the latter involves detailed individual and group data on an hourly, daily, or weekly time frame.

Legal and ethical regulation and documentation are also extremely important in the operation of residential treatment programs. Not only do staff employees need to be managed and protected, but the client population is at risk for a number of reasons. The information needed for regulatory bodies and for determination of compliance with external standards should be the same as that required for rational operation in the other decision categories—it just has to be documented and retrievable. Unfortunately, the great majority of mental health organizations currently spend most energies on generating paper documentation only, without the resulting data accurately reflecting what actually occurs, and with minimal contribution to the other decisions. The last category of decisions—*specific research questions*—is, in fact, not a requirement for rational operation of residential treatment facilities. However, if the data were available for the other categories of decisions, contributions to basic and applied science regarding the understanding and amelioration of mental and behavioral disabilities could be regularly made as part of ongoing operations, rather than as a separate, often disruptive and expensive, activity.

VARIABLES THAT SHOULD BE ASSESSED TO SUPPORT RATIONAL DECISIONS

Domains and Classes of Variables

Several years ago I proposed the "ultimate question(s)" to be answered by research on clinical interventions: "What treatment, by whom, is most effective for this individual with that specific problem, under which set of circumstances, and how does it come about?" (Paul, 1969, p. 44). That question, and the domains and classes of variables encompassed within it, was originally focused on research needs for evaluating psychotherapies and later elaborated with design considerations emphasizing psychosocial treatment more broadly defined. The applicability of the domains and classes of variables has since been expanded and applied to pharmacological treatments and both residential and in-community psychosocial programs, and to the operation of mental health facilities and systems (see Paul, 1985a; Paul et al., 1986a). It is from these domains and classes of variables that information is needed to support rational actions for the categories of decision problems listed in Table 5.1. The domains are *clients, staff,* and *time.*

Within the client (or patient or resident) domain, three classes of variables are necessary targets for nearly all categories of decision problems: (a) Problem behaviors—those aspects of client motoric, emotional, or ideational functioning that are distressing to the client or others and that result in decisions to enter or remain in the treatment facility. This class of variables includes the assets, deficits, and excesses in client functioning that should be the focus of treatment efforts. (b) Relatively stable personal-social characteristics—those attributes other than problem behaviors on which clients may differ that can define role behavior and/or interact with responsiveness to treatment or client compatibility with various groups. Demographic characteristics, educational and vocational history, physical status, psychiatric diagnosis, personality traits, and expectancies regarding treatment are examples of variables within this class. (c) Physical-social life environments—those settings and events outside of the treatment facility that provide intercurrent experiences that can affect treatment goals and outcomes and that provide the external settings for the occurrence of problem behaviors. Examples of variables within this class include economic and social resources, family, friends, and work and school situations.

Within the staff (or therapist) domain, three classes of variables are also necessary targets for nearly all categories of decision problems: (a) Therapeutic techniques—those aspects of clinical staff performance through which improvements in client functioning are attempted. These include discrete somatic treatments, such as drugs or electroconvulsive therapy, and planned or unplanned psychosocial procedures defined by the nature, frequency, content, and timing of verbal and nonverbal staff actions. (b) Relatively stable personal-social characteristics—those attributes other than therapeutic techniques on which clinical staff may differ that can influence the effectiveness of treatment for given clients, problem behaviors, and settings. Demographic characteristics, personality traits, education, experience, prestige, physical status, theoretical orientation, and attitudes and opinions are examples of variables within this class. (c) Physical-social treatment environment—the immediate residential environment where treatment occurs. Variables in this class are important because they may interact with those in other classes to influence treatment effectiveness. Ward size, staff-client ratios, reputation, atmosphere, and activity schedules are examples of potentially important variables here.

The third domain, time, serves to further specify the "set of circumstances" for assessing other classes of variables and the nature of information needed for different decisions. Fiske (1978) called attention to both the importance and relative neglect of time in traditional assessment operations. The time to which assessment information applies, the length of time between assessments, and the relationship of variables to each other over time are all important characteristics to be considered for assessment information to support rational decision-making (see Paul et al., 1986a, 1986b).

Level and Target of Information Needed
for Different Decisions

The level of information desired for a specific decision within each class of variables can range from the highly detailed (e.g., frequency of bizarre verbalizations, milligrams per kilogram dosage of a neuroleptic, or number of chairs in a sitting room) to broader and more global units (e.g., the presence or absence of delusions, chemotherapy, or group cohesion). Similarly, the focal targets or subjects about whom information should be available can range from each individual client or staff member to aggregations over client and staff groups within a unit or facility, depending on the decision problem.

The level of common information required from each class of variables within the client and staff domains for the decision problems in residential treatment facilities is summarized in Table 5.2. Although space precludes much discussion of that summary, a few points are needed to understand it. In particular, the "detailed" levels in Table 5.2 for common assessment over all clients, staff, and programs are molecular but not microscopic in terms of the system levels and processes of the Fishman-Neigher assessment typology. Information on client and staff functioning of common relevance for the general case focuses on typical performance in natural situations, covering detailed behaviors, actions, and interactions in given real-life situations and classes of situations. More microscopic information would be needed for decisions unique to specific individuals, and might be gathered through neurological or neuropsychological exams; biological studies; specific tests of cognitive, physiological, or motor functioning in response to standard stimuli; or instructed performances to evaluate specific skills or environmental contingencies. Status evaluations of the biological integrity and functioning of individuals beyond standard physical exams and monitoring of general health, as well as maximum-performance tests of specific abilities, proficiences, and achievements, are not general information needs; they are unique to sequential questions about specific individuals. Such status evaluations would, however, be triggered by appropriately gathered common information on assets, deficits, and excesses of typical functioning (see Paul et al., 1986b).

Although all six classes of variables in Table 5.2 are important for decision-making, *client problem behaviors* and *staff therapeutic techniques* are the most important for all decisions, since they define functioning for both process and outcomes. These classes of variables are also differentiated from the other four classes because they consist of transitory phenomena, which could and should change over time, in varying situations, and in relationship to environmental events and to one another. The other four classes of variables are important ones, but function primarily as moderator or blocking variables for most decision problems. They also consist of more or less stable phenomena, which generally change slowly or not at all; if they do change, they do so abruptly and obviously on infrequent occasions and remain relatively stable thereafter. The differences among the phenomena result in different demands for their assessment, as described later. Unfortunately,

TABLE 5.2

Level of Information Needed from Client and Staff Domains for Different Categories of Decisions in Residential Treatment Facilities

	Domains and classes of variables for which information is needed			
	Client domain			
	Problem behaviors		Personal-social characteristics	
Category of decision problem	Individual	Aggregate	Individual	Aggregate
Placement and disposition:				
Client initial admission/ assignment	global	global	global	global
Client terminal discharge/ placement	detailed	(global)[a]	detailed	(global)[a]
Staff initial hiring/ assignment		global		global
Staff terminal discharge/ placement		global		
Problem identification/ description (& initial treatment plan)	detailed		detailed	
Staff development/utilization		global		
Concurrent monitoring	detailed	detailed	detailed	
Program evaluation: absolute/ comparative		global		global
Legal & ethical regulation/ documentation	detailed/ global	detailed/ global/ (global)[a]	detailed/ global	detailed/ global/ (global)[a]
Specific research questions	detailed/ global	detailed/ global/ (global)[a]	detailed/ global	detailed/ global/ (global)[a]

SOURCE: Reprinted from Paul ed. (in press a).
Note: Table entries reflect the level of information needed from classes of variables for the individual client or staff member or from the aggregate client or staff group within the residential unit of focus.
[a](global) refers to information needed from possible posttransfer or postplacement programs when clients are placed in other residential settings, rather than discharged to independent circumstances.

**Domains and classes of variables
for which information is needed**

Client domain		Staff domain				
External life environment		Therapeutic techniques		Personal-social characteristics		Intramural treatment environment
Individual	Aggregate	Individual	Aggregate	Individual	Aggregate	Aggregate
global	global		global		global	global
detailed	(global)[a]		detailed/ (global)[a]		(global)[a]	detailed/ (global)[a]
	global	detailed	global	detailed	global	global
		detailed	detailed	detailed	detailed	detailed
detailed			detailed			detailed
		detailed	detailed	detailed	detailed	detailed
detailed		detailed	detailed	detailed	detailed	detailed
	global		global		global	global
detailed/ global	global/ (global)[a]	detailed	detailed/ global/ (global)[a]	detailed	detailed/ global/ (global)[a]	detailed/ global/ (global)[a]
detailed/ global	detailed/ global/ (global)[a]	detailed/ global	detailed/ global/ (global)[a]	detailed global	detailed/ global/ (global)[a]	detailed/ global (global)[a]

in many current practices, data on personal-social characteristics, such as personality traits, attitudes, and opinions of clients and staff, or client psychiatric diagnoses are mistakenly used as if they reflected the transitory phenomena within the classes of client problem behaviors and staff therapeutic techniques. If the detailed information required for timely concurrent monitoring of individual clients and staff is collected and stored on an ongoing basis, the same data may be summarized into more global categories and/or aggregated over individuals and retrieved for most other decision problems involving either individuals or groups (see Table 5.2).

THE POTENTIAL UTILITY OF FORMAL ASSESSMENT STRATEGIES

The "Four Rs" of Assessment Procedure Utility

Since the sheer volume of information suggested by Table 5.2 for operation of residential treatment facilities could easily be overwhelming, a means of determining the potential utility of different assessment approaches is required for the selection and development of appropriate strategies. Anything less than perfect, error-free measurement of all components of information relevant to a particular decision—an impossible task in most circumstances—represents generalizations and inferences from obtained data that may be fallible in coverage of one or more facets of content, people, occasions, and assessors. Based on an analysis of the information needs and the nature of decision problems in residential treatment settings from the perspective of decision theory and generalizability theory, Paul et al. (1986a) suggested that the potential value of an assessment strategy will be determined by the *Replicability*, *Representativeness*, *Relevance*, and *Relative* cost of obtained data—the "Four Rs" of assessment procedure utility.

Replicability refers to the trustworthiness or dependability of the information obtained—the generalizability, reliability, and accuracy over the assessor (observer) facet—that is, the degree to which identical information is encoded and recorded by different observers or assessors at the same time, or by the same observer or assessor at different times. The greater the replicability, the greater the trustworthiness of the information and the greater the potential value of the assessment procedure. *Representativeness* refers to the adequacy of an assessment procedure or technology in covering the information desired for a particular decision problem. This adequacy is traditionally indexed as criterion-related, construct, or content validity. However, the potential validity of obtained information for a particular decision is a function of the extent to which sampling over the facets of people, content, and occasions is representative of all the information on which a decision would ideally be based. For work-sample assessments that representatively cover all facets included in the decision criterion, the potential utility of the obtained data reduces to its replicability. In general, the greater the adequacy in sampling appropriate facets, the greater the representativeness of the obtained information for particular decisions and the greater the potential value of the assessment procedure. *Relevance* refers to the appropriateness of the information to a variety of decision problems—the range of application of the same data set to many different decisions. The greater the number of decisions to which the obtained information can contribute, the greater the relevance to overall decision-making and the greater the potential value of the assessment procedure. *Relative cost* refers to the expense of an assessment procedure in comparison to alternatives that could provide equally useful information. Costs include direct costs of assessment staff and materials, indirect and offset costs of clinical and management staff time to collect, process, and use the information, and differences in start-up and ongoing maintenance expenditures. Relative costs must also take into account the value placed on possible outcomes as a result of having the information—both dollar values and qualitative judgments. "Net" relative costs, thus, consist of comparative direct, indirect, and offset costs, less the dollars potentially saved by the information obtained, less the value of potential gains in treatment effectiveness, less the value of potential assurance of legal, ethical, and humane operations. Application of the Four Rs in combination, to evaluate the potential utility of different assessment strategies, results in a reasonably straightforward decision rule: The lower the relative costs *and/or* the greater the replicability, representativeness, and relevance of the information obtained, the lower the net relative costs, and the greater the potential value of an assessment approach.

QICS and DOC Approaches to Formal Assessment

Paul et al. (1986b) define *formal assessment* as "a systematic procedure for observing the characteristics of people, their environment, and their behavior within that environment and describing those characteristics with the aid of a numerical scale or category system" (p. 27). Two primary approaches to formal assessment by standardized instruments emerged from a detailed analysis of when, what, how, and by whom observations are obtained, systematized, and recorded or encoded into numerical scales or categories. They are: (a) reports about observations in response to questions posed orally, in print, or by apparatus on Questionnaires, Inventories, Checklists, and Scales (QICS) and (b) Direct Observational Coding (DOC) of information at the time and place of occurrence. Although there are many important differences between QICS and DOC approaches, and variations within each, the most important ones appear in the characteristic procedures for assessing the transitory phenomena of typical functioning. QICS methods are the traditional ones in which retrospective, interpretive recordings of past observations are obtained on a single occasion. One relatively self-contained instrument provides all information for decision makers at a single sitting, with the permanent record consisting of the observer's or assessor's inferences and judgments about past actions, interactions, characteristics, and events, reconstructed at the time of formal information gathering. In contrast, DOC methods employ trained observers who immediately record observations obtained at the time and place of occurrence on multiple occasions. The permanent duplicative record consists of the observer's direct transcriptions of actions, interactions, and other characteristics or events in the categories of a coding system on each of many brief occasions of observation, with little or no interpretation or inference. Information provided for decision makers is then derived by mechanical summation of data over occasions of observation and over categories.

In contrast to the characteristic DOC assessment of transitory phenomena, noted above, variants of DOC procedures may be employed to obtain brief, sequential, duplicative recordings within a single occasion as part of a structured interview, medical examination, or other assessment of the biological or physical status of people or environments. Such single-occasion assessments may also include variants of QICS procedures, in which immediate rather than delayed recording of the assessor's own judgmental interpretations are obtained. In fact, it is quite possible for structured interviews and other single-occasion interactive assessments within residential treatment facilities to employ combined procedures. With combined procedures, some subparts record respondent reports with traditional QICS methods, and other subparts provide objective and evaluative recordings of status at the time of assessment, respectively, with DOC and QICS variants.

Although exhaustive observation of all people, content, and occasions relevant to decision-making has long been recognized as the desirable but unattainable ideal for formal assessment of typical behavior, QICS approaches have been the tradition in all settings, including residential treatment applications—when formal assessment has been used at all. DOC approaches have a long and confused history of research applications, but were seen as unfeasible and impractical for operational use beyond brief research studies (Hartmann, 1982). This was primarily because DOC procedures require explicit sampling of occasions and people by trained observers. Such information gathering produces tremendous amounts of recorded data, which must be systematically combined to be useful for decision makers and requires that the targets of assessment be accessible to observation. Residential treatment facilities are unique from the standpoint that the people and treatment environments on whom information is desired are accessible to observation, essentially, on a continuous basis. Further, the development and widespread availability of high-speed computers has brought about rapid evolutionary changes in QICS approaches and revolutionary advances in formal assessment. The low-cost availability of electronic computers now make standardized DOC approaches feasible and practical for ongoing operational use in residential treatment facilities.

The Maximum Potential Utility Assessment Paradigm

Application of the Four Rs of assessment procedure utility resulted in an illuminating analysis and, some would say, drastic recommendations (Paul, 1986c; Paul et al., 1986b; Paul & Mariotto, 1986). Specifically, the great majority of current assessment and documentation practices in residential treatment facilities have very little potential utility for assisting decision makers—whether they are clinical and professional staff, administrators and managers, regulators, or clientele and their loved ones. Rather, nontraditional DOC systems have the highest potential utility for providing needed facts on the most important classes of variables—client problem behaviors and staff therapeutic techniques—and they are the *only* ones that can provide the specificity of information in these classes that is required for ongoing concurrent monitoring.

However, even with carefully designed and precisely implemented procedures that are conceptually relevant to the content of interest, multiple source-method assessment strategies are required to provide the information to support rational operations. This is because each practical strategy differs in the quality of data obtained and each has limits on the sampling of one or more facets for at least one decision category. Consequently, Paul and Mariotto (1986) detail a comprehensive paradigm for the integrated application of practical assessment strategies that has maximum potential utility for providing all the common information needed to support rational decisions for all categories of problems (see Table 5.2). That paradigm includes three recommended primary or central strategies to provide the best quantity and most important common information in both staff and client domains. Four secondary strategies are recommended to provide information on moderator variables and for specific limited decisions when data are not available from primary strategies as well as to provide converging evidence.

The role of multiple-occasion DOC strategies. Nontraditional multiple-occasion DOC methods constitute two of the three primary strategies of the recommended paradigm. DOC methods, almost by definition, are superior with regard to the potential replicability of obtained data, since observers are trained and monitored in the use of duplicative encoding and recording procedures. QICS methods are much more subject to error from fallible information-processing characteristics and/or the imprecision of natural language (Fiske, 1978). In addition, multiple-occasion DOC systems are the only practical assessment strategies that can obtain ongoing information on every client and staff member within a residential program with highly representative coverage of transitory content and occasions for any of the information needs and decision problems listed in Table 5.2. Noncomplex DOC instruments (compiled multivariate systems) employed by trained clinical staff—with data collection integrated with their regular clinical and administrative duties—can schedule observations based on the occurrence of specified events to provide "100% event recording" of certain important transitory phenomena (e.g., Paul & Shelite, in press; Redfield, 1979). In both client problem-behavior and staff therapeutic-technique classes, behavior that is totally setting-dependent and low-frequency critical events (e.g., client assaults and consequent staff responses; administration of drugs and other biomedical techniques) can be accurately and practically monitored only in this way. A more radical departure from usual approaches involves DOC systems with even greater potential utility—namely, direct multivariate systems applied on stratified hourly time-sampling schedules by full-time independent noninteractive observers. The latter DOC strategy, therefore, constitutes the core of the comprehensive paradigm as the "number one" primary strategy, supplemented by clinical-staff compiled multivariate DOC systems as the "number two" primary strategy (see Paul & Mariotto, 1986).

The TSBC/SRIC system represents the most fully developed of the direct multivariate systems for coverage of either the client or staff domains (Fiske, 1979; Paul, 1986a; Rhoades, 1981). It is enough to note here that ongoing hourly time sampling with direct multivariate DOC systems provides detailed time- and situation-specific information on the psychosocial functioning of every client and staff member within a treatment program from the moment of entry through the moment of departure. As mentioned earlier, the resulting data base is the only one that allows the timely analytic decisions required for concurrent monitoring of individuals or groups with high, unbiased representativeness of people, content, and occasion facets. In addition, the same data base allows the retrieval and combination of detailed content into more global higher-order categories, and aggregation over any combination of clients or staff, occasions, or time periods. Consequently, this assessment strategy is of exceptionally high relevance to overall decision-making, since the same data set can contribute trustworthy and representative information for all aggregate information needs on client problem behaviors and staff therapeutic techniques listed in Table 5.2. It can also contribute trustworthy and representative information on individual information needs on those classes of variables for all decision categories after initial assignment to a treatment unit. Further, on-line observers, who need only be high-school-level personnel, and the computer free clinical staff from much of the time previously spent simply on documentation as well as increasing the efficiency of staff utilization. Therefore, as noted at the end of the chapter, offset costs combined with the exceptionally high replicability, representativeness, and relevance of obtained data result in the DOC strategy being exceptionally advantageous in net relative cost when compared to any alternative, including nearly any practice in current residential operations.

The role of more traditional single-occasion assessment strategies. Multiple-occasion DOC methods have the highest potential utility for providing the most important facts on which to base rational operations. Direct-multivariate DOC systems that obtain hourly data on all clientele and staff as the core of assessment practices, supplemented by compiled-multivariate DOC systems that obtain 100% data on specific events, can provide complete round-the-clock information with computer summarization of all relevant public events in residential treatment facilities with the minimum practical dross rate. However, more traditional single-occasion QICS methods, DOC and QICS variants, and interactive assessments involving combined procedures have higher potential utility for gathering other needed information. Strategic application of these procedures with particular sources of information are recommended to supplement DOC systems as part of total assessment practices in the comprehensive paradigm (see Paul & Mariotto, in press).

Since these assessment methods are more or less traditional ones with which most readers are familiar, the outcome of the potential utility analyses will only be noted for orientation. Mainly these strategies are favored only for gathering information that is impossible or impractical to obtain with multiple-occasion DOC methods. Such information includes any phenomena that are not accessible to direct observation, including activities and events occurring outside of the purview of ongoing residential programs (e.g., those occurring before entry or after departure; nonpublic acts or intimacies) and private events of staff, clients, or clients' significant others (e.g., expectations, sensations, opinions, evaluative judgments). Any single-occasion assessment of transitory phenomena can only provide a momentary "snapshot" of status and is quite costly since each individual decision requires new data-gathering for information to be timely. In contrast, stable phenomena, whether accessible to direct observation or not, are often more efficiently assessed by single-occasion procedures with relatively long intervals between assessments. The information obtained from ongoing DOC systems focused on client problem behaviors and staff therapeutic techniques can also contribute information needed in the other four classes of variables listed in Table 5.2. The only exclusions are variables in the external life environment for clients in independent circumstances (rather than other residential or day-care settings), and individual information needs for initial placement and disposition decisions.

In general, most single-occasion procedures are recommended only as secondary strategies in the comprehensive paradigm. Information abstracted from archival records by independent noninteractive observers, or clerical staff working in that capacity, has potential utility for formalizing much of the information on physical characteristics and concrete demographic characteristics for all four classes of relatively stable variables. Single-occasion DOC and QICS variants employed by clinical staff or independent observers and brief standardized QICS instruments employed by clinical staff have the greatest potential utility for completing the information needed on the physical and social characteristics of the intramural treatment environment. Due to the stable nature of these variables, single assessments every several months, or when external events signal a change, can provide a data set that is relevant to all decision problems. Traditional QICS methods employed as self-report devices by clinical staff have the greatest potential utility for completing the information needed on staff-personal-social characteristics. Such data collected from each staff member at entry, departure, and when other events signal a change may also be relevant to all decision problems.

Structured interviews and other brief, sequential interactive assessments employing combined procedures with clientele and their significant others have the highest potential utility, as an overall strategy, for gathering the remainder of information needed in the client domain, when those assessments are conducted by trained clinical staff who also have treatment responsibilities (as distinct from independent interactive assessors). Consequently, this interactive sequential strategy constitutes the third primary strategy of the recommended paradigm. Structured interviews, with respondent reports recorded on QICS instruments, and status assessments by clinical staff recorded on DOC and QICS variants, are the best means of obtaining the individual information needed for all three classes of variables at the point of client initial admission/assignment. Such interviews are also best to obtain more detailed information on private events and nonobservable phenomena at the point of problem identification/description and terminal discharge/placement considerations. Although these assessments are exceptionally costly in terms of professional staff time, the overall yield of information in all three classes of variables in the client domain increases the relevance of the strategy beyond the replicability and representativeness of any single class of data. Such data on stable phenomena may fulfill most information needs for all categories of decisions. Combined procedures within brief interactive occasions on a weekly or bi-weekly basis, integrated with clinical contacts scheduled for other purposes, can also provide some useful information for concurrent monitoring on client health status and on client and staff private events.

The replicability of information on transitory phenomena obtained with the third primary strategy and the representativeness of content and occasions coverage are low to moderate at best. Nevertheless, staff, clients, and clients' significant others are the only sources of information for some phenomena. Additionally, the perspective of involved participants must be included for ethical and humanitarian reasons at several points of operation. Dissatisfaction or concerns that appear from the above sequential strategy should be given major importance for investigatory actions, either to examine information from other sources or to introduce changes that might resolve such concerns. Critical-decision points involving placement and disposition or other terminal decisions, such as the application of irreversible biomedical treatment techniques, should only be undertaken with converging evidence from the perspective of involved participants, as well as the most accurate information available from DOC systems. Although structured interviews are intrusive on other activities and expensive due to the high cost of professional staff time, such status assessments at standardized time points (including postdischarge follow-up) can contribute information from multiple perspectives to program evaluation, as well as to decision-making for individuals.

Excessive costs due to inappropriately frequent or infrequent applications of client status assessments via structured interviews, or of single-occasion assessments of less stable phenomena within the classes of client and staff personal-social characteristics and the intramural treatment environment, can also be reduced when ongoing DOC systems provide the core of assessment practices. That is, the more trustworthy continuous data from DOC systems can trigger the application of multiple-perspective status assessments of individual client functioning, and alert decision makers to points where more detailed sequential assessments unique to individual clientele or staff members are needed. Similarly, the ongoing DOC data can signal some changes in conditions that would trigger additional single-occasion QICS assessments of client or staff satisfaction and morale. Thus, such DOC systems, as the core of assessment practices within a comprehensive integrated paradigm, can increase the potential utility of more traditional assessment procedures, as well as provide direct information with the highest potential utility themselves.

THE COMPUTERIZED TSBC/SRIC PLANNED-ACCESS OBSERVATIONAL INFORMATION SYSTEM

The TSBC/SRIC system is the multifaceted assessment technology resulting from the R & D program of our clinical-research group, and the one recommended as the core strategy of the comprehensive paradigm to improve the quality, effectiveness, and cost efficiency of residential treatment operations. The system's components are two observational instruments on which the overall system is based—the Time-Sample Behavioral Checklist (TSBC) and Staff-Resident Interaction Chronograph (SRIC). As direct multivariate systems, themselves, these instruments possess all of the advantages and limitations described earlier for such DOC systems, essentially providing ongoing work-sample assessments of functioning for all clientele and staff from the moment of entry to the moment of departure (see Paul, 1986c).

Overview of the System in Operation

Staffing and organizational structure. Full-time, independent, non-participating, technician-level observers who are trained in objective and nonreactive data collection on both instruments are the heart of the system. In the standard and most cost-effective installation observers are "on-the-floor" in the residential environment of a single unit approximately half the time, coding low-inference instances of actions, interactions, and other characteristics of every client and staff member—including settings and contexts—through hourly sampling over all client waking hours, seven days per week. Except for huge treatment units or wards (e.g., 120 beds), the same cadre of observers provides coverage of two or more units in multiple-unit facilities. Because observers are required to make only immediate, low-inference "present-absent" judgments, their reliability and objectivity (replicability) has regularly equaled or exceeded that of measurement in the natural sciences. For those familiar with common problems in research applications of DOC procedures, let me note that neither clients nor staff have shown reactivity to being observed in ongoing applications of the system and that observers themselves have been free of drift or bias due to expectancy, familiarity, or typicality effects. This is probably because observers are "ever present" on an unpredictable schedule from the point of view of clients and staff, and are required to reach a criterion of 100% act-by-act replicability on a full-day's observational schedule before they are certified to collect data, with ongoing monitoring of replicability by both direct and indirect procedures insuring maintenance. Effective observer training procedures and materials have been developed and tested for both the SRIC (Licht, et al., 1980) and the TSBC (Power et al., 1982), with about two months of full-time training required for observers to reach criterion on both instruments.

Organizationally, observers function as clinical support staff, with an office independent of any of the clinical units in multiple-unit facilities. All TSBC/SRIC data collection, monitoring for replicability, processing (except for computer input), distribution, and consulting on interpretation are handled by the observational staff, who report to a TSBC/SRIC facility coordinator through a BA-level supervisory observer. The position of the facility coordinator varies as a function of the particular organization, but should be a bright professional-level individual with

data management, quality assurance, or clinical-administrative responsibilities above the level of a treatment unit director in multiple-unit
facilities. A well-trained doctoral-level professional with both clinical
and scientific expertise is ideal. In a typical installation of two to six
treatment units averaging 20 to 50 beds each, about six hours per week
would be required from the facility coordinator to supervise operations
after initial training and installation. Such functions in single-unit facilities would likely require about an hour per week. Although the
exact numbers of observational staff required varies somewhat as a
function of the physical plant, and consequent travel time within and
between treatment sites and units, a typical initial implementation
would need three technician-level on-line observers with high-school
educations and one BA-level supervisory observer to provide complete
coverage of two 20- to 50-bed treatment units. Additional treatment
units could usually be incrementally added to the system with an average full-time equivalent (FTE) of two on-line observers per unit, including a single supervisory observer for up to 11 or 12 high-school-level
personnel. All clinical staff and relevant administrative and management personnel must be trained in interpretation and use of data from
the system, so that computer reports can be quickly interpreted and entered in appropriate records (i.e., in 5 to 10 minutes). In addition at least
one senior clinical staff member on each treatment unit is designated a
TSBC/SRIC "expert," who provides ongoing consultation on interpretation and trains new staff.

A computer terminal and video screen or microcomputer on each
treatment unit in which the TSBC/SRIC system is installed allows each
day's observational data to be entered into computer files by night-shift
clinical staff while clients are sleeping. Data are coded for confiden-
tiality with regular monitoring of input accuracy by the observational
staff. Computer programs store, retrieve, and combine the extensive
and detailed information from discrete TSBC and SRIC observations into
scores and indexes at detailed and global levels, allowing both "narrow-
band" measurement of behavior-in-situation and "broad-band" coverage with psychometric combinations of data. The total system also
contains computer programs that allow the retrieval of the continuous
observational data on all clients and staff to be combined and sorted
with information on client movement and outcomes and with biographical, fiscal, and personnel files, which are directly entered in computer files by clerical personnel as part of regular processing of clients
and staff. Thus, data collection for administrative, regulatory, and program evaluation purposes comes from the same operations that are

needed to support clinical functions, rather than as a separate time-consuming set of operations. Because observers and the computer provide the majority of ongoing data and documentation needed for rational operations, the cost efficiency of the system is enhanced by replacing costly nonutilitarian practices and improving the use of clinical staff. The increased staff efficiency is such that all staffing for the system can usually be maintained through reallocation of existing funded positions and duties rather than requiring added positions. For comparison purposes, the total staffing for unitized intensive treatment residential programs, which I have personally run or recently proposed, ranges from 71.0 FTES per 100 clients average-daily-census (ADC) for long-stay chronic units to 91.7 FTES/100 ADC for mixed units (2/3 acute beds, 1/3 chronic beds), *including* observers needed for the full TSBC/SRIC system and *all* clinical and administrative staff for two to five decentralized treatment units. More detail on implementation and cost-benefit analyses will be noted at the end of the chapter.

Computer reports and data base. Once the TSBC/SRIC system is installed and the staff is trained, several types of reports can be accessed or initiated directly from the on-unit terminal or microcomputer. Unique or "special searches" can be initiated to answer particular questions about individual staff or clientele, groups or subgroups, over any specified activity or time period on any variable on the observational instruments or in the biographical files for nearly any of the decision problems listed in Table 5.1. These special searches may be scanned over the video screen with interactive questioning of the data file and hard-copy reports obtained for whatever information is desired as a permanent record. The system also regularly provides standard weekly summary reports on the functioning of every individual client and staff member and on the aggregate treatment unit for concurrent monitoring, as well as a series of three "quality assurance reports," for a time period of two weeks to a year or more, for program evaluation and regulatory purposes.

The observational instruments have now been tested for feasibility and generalizability in multi-institutional studies covering the full range of adult intramural programs and populations in public mental hospitals, community mental health centers, and community residential facilities. To our surprise and delight, the feasibility, exceptional replicability, and validity for the range of decision problems were found to hold up under all conditions. In our original application, the instruments collected ongoing and complete data on all clients and staff of 2 different 28-bed residential units of a large community mental health center for a period of nearly 4½ years; data were originally used only for scientific research purposes, with gradual development for use of different components to support ongoing clinical and administrative decision-making, resulting in a full-scale pilot test for all decision problems for a period of 12 to 18 months (Paul & Lentz, 1977). Ongoing full-scale implementations with further development and testing of staff training procedures, computer report formats, modes of data processing and distribution, and approaches to consulting were later undertaken with 5 units in 2 different facilities over a 7-year period and in a third hospital for more than a year at the time of this writing. In addition, normative data and interpretive users' manuals based upon full-week observational samples of more than 1,200 clients and 600 staff in 36 different treatment units located in 17 different institutions will soon be available. These data cover treatment units ranging from 8 to 120 beds, both open and locked, with individual staff responsibility ranging from 1 to 120 clients. Staff range from aide-level personnel through MDs and PhDs employing one-to-one, group, and unit-wide treatment modalities. Programs cover rational-emotive, behavioral, psychodynamic, milieu, biological, social-learning, eclectic private-practice, and custodial orientations. The normative client group ranges in age from 18 to 99 years covering all diagnostic groups including alcohol and substance abuse, mentally retarded, and "mentally ill" with acute, chronic, and revolving-door residential histories and lengths of stay ranging from 3 days to 59 years.

A few highlights of the nature of the information available through the TSBC/SRIC system may help to clarify the optimism of its developers concerning the potential for improving the quality, effectiveness, and cost efficiency of residential treatment programs and facility operation. A full description of the nature and uses of the system, cost-effective implementation procedures and requirements, and supporting evidence requires several volumes for complete explication. A five-part series will provide personnel-training information, including videotape observer training programs and users' manuals for clinical and management staff (Paul, 1986a, in press b,c,d,e). Although the use of information from the system can be relatively easily learned by both clinical and management staff, its multifaceted nature requires about 28 hours of training for clear understanding, plus an additional 8 hours for higher-level organizational applications. Without the full series of written materials, it takes a two-day workshop to provide the staff of residential facilities with an adequate understanding of the instruments and the capabilities of the system. Therefore, this presentation will be necessarily restricted. Readers wishing a more thorough review of the TSBC/ SRIC system before the entire set of implementation volumes and materials are available may consult descriptions and uses in the literature, particularly articles by Engel and Paul, Fiske, Licht, Mariotto, and Power in a special issue of the *Journal of Behavioral Assessment* (Paul, 1979), and publications by Engel and Paul (1979, 1981), Licht (1979, 1984), Licht et al. (1980), Paul (1980, 1981), Paul and Lentz (1977), Power (1979, 1984), and Power et al. (1982).

The Time-Sample Behavioral Checklist

The TSBC is the primary DOC system for providing information on the nature and amount of client functioning; TSBC data are also obtained on staff as well. The format for computer summaries of TSBC information on individuals or groups is presented in Figure 5.1. The actual size of printed summaries is at least an 8½- by 11-inch sheet, allowing direct entry and documentation of client TSBCs into clinical records, thus saving staff time and paper work. Standard weekly reports are regularly provided for each individual and for aggregates over individuals for each treatment unit (means and standard deviations). Special reports may be obtained in this format for individuals and subgroups from the continuous data file, sorted on any code or higher-order score, time, behavior setting, or biographical data.

Of course a single observation has little or no meaning beyond identifying the location and activity of each individual at a particular time. It is the relative frequency of occurrence or nonoccurrence over multiple observations—usually 50 to 100 per week for each client—that provides a remarkably thorough picture of an individual's activities and functioning. The full set of information in this format is usually of use only for clinical purposes with the individual client and for individual staff time management, with aggregate data and administrative applications using only a small portion of the total report. However, after training, staff readily learn which data are important for their particular use and prefer to have the full set in order to follow up hypotheses and obtain an overall gestalt of actual activities.

The three columns of x.xxx in each section of the TSBC format in Figure 5.1 represent the numbers provided by the computer program. Under the "curnt state" column in the left and middle sections, the numbers reflect the proportion of observations or percentage of time during which each code occurred for the person's *current status*—that time period covered by the specific TSBC summary. Each current status

TIME-SAMPLE BEHAVIORAL CHECKLIST (TSBC):

POR	HOS	INDEX/BEHAVIOR	CURNT STATE	CHANGE FROM ENTRY	L.WK
		CONCURRENT ACTIVITIES:			
	(AP)	WATCHING OTHERS	x.xxx	±.xxx	±.xxx
	(AP)	TALKING TO OTHERS	x.xxx	.xxx	.xxx
	(AP)	LISTENING TO OTHERS	x.xxx	.xxx	.xxx
	(AP)	PLAYING A GAME	x.xxx	.xxx	.xxx
	(AP)	GROUP ACTIVITY	x.xxx	.xxx	.xxx
	(AP)	READING	x.xxx	.xxx	.xxx
	(AW)	WRITING	x.xxx	.xxx	.xxx
	(AW)	HOBBY OR HANDICRAFT	x.xxx	.xxx	.xxx
	(AW)	WORKING	x.xxx	.xxx	.xxx
	(AM)	EATING	x.xxx	.xxx	.xxx
	(AM)	DRINKING	x.xxx	.xxx	.xxx
	(AM)	PERSONAL GROOMING	x.xxx	.xxx	.xxx
	(AE)	SINGING	x.xxx	.xxx	.xxx
	(AE)	SMOKING	x.xxx	.xxx	.xxx
	(AE)	LISTENING TO RADIO, PHONO	x.xxx	.xxx	.xxx
	(AE)	WATCHING TV	x.xxx	.xxx	.xxx
	(A)	OTHER	x.xxx	.xxx	.xxx
		STEREOTYPE (1)/VARIABLE (17)	x.xxx	.xxx	.xxx
		FACIAL EXPRESSION:			
	(AP)	SMILING-LAUGHING W/STIM	x.xxx	±.xxx	±.xxx
	(AP)	GRIMACING-FROWNING W/STIM	x.xxx	.xxx	.xxx
	(A)	NEUTRAL NO/STIMULUS	x.xxx	.xxx	.xxx
	(IS)	NEUTRAL W/STIMULUS	x.xxx	.xxx	.xxx
	(IC)	SMILING-LAUGHING NO/STIM	x.xxx	.xxx	.xxx
	(IC)	GRIMACING-FROWNING NO/STIM	x.xxx	.xxx	.xxx
		STEREOTYPE (1)/VARIABLE (6)	x.xxx	.xxx	.xxx
		SOCIAL ORIENTATION:			
		ALONE	x.xxx	±.xxx	±.xxx
		WITH RESIDENTS (CLIENTS)	x.xxx	.xxx	.xxx
		WITH STAFF	x.xxx	.xxx	.xxx
		WITH OTHERS	x.xxx	.xxx	.xxx
		STEREOTYPE (1)/VARIABLE (4)	x.xxx	.xxx	.xxx
		PHYSICAL POSITION:			
	(A)	SITTING	x.xxx	±.xxx	±.xxx
	(A)	STANDING	x.xxx	.xxx	.xxx
	(A)	WALKING	x.xxx	.xxx	.xxx
	(A)	RUNNING	x.xxx	.xxx	.xxx
	(A)	DANCING	x.xxx	.xxx	.xxx
	(IS)	LYING DOWN	x.xxx	.xxx	.xxx
		STEREOTYPE (1)/VARIABLE (6)	x.xxx	.xxx	.xxx

POR	HOS	INDEX/BEHAVIOR	CURNT STATE	CHANGE FROM ENTRY	L.WK
		CRAZY BEHAVIOR:			
	(IS)	ROCKING	x.xxx	±.xxx	±.xxx
	(IS)	REPET-STEREOTYPIC MOVEMENT	x.xxx	.xxx	.xxx
	(IS)	POSTURING	x.xxx	.xxx	.xxx
	(IS)	SHAKING-TREMORING	x.xxx	.xxx	.xxx
	(IS)	PACING	x.xxx	.xxx	.xxx
	(IS)	BLANK STARING	x.xxx	.xxx	.xxx
	(IC)	CHATTERING-TALKING TO SELF	x.xxx	.xxx	.xxx
	(IC)	VERB DEL-HALLUC-S.THRT	x.xxx	.xxx	.xxx
	(IC)	INCOHERENT SPEECH	x.xxx	.xxx	.xxx
	(IC)	CRYING	x.xxx	.xxx	.xxx
	(IH)	SCREAMING	x.xxx	.xxx	.xxx
	(IH)	SWEARING-CURSING	x.xxx	.xxx	.xxx
	(IH)	VERBAL INTRUSION	x.xxx	.xxx	.xxx
	(IH)	DESTROYING PROPERTY	x.xxx	.xxx	.xxx
	(IH)	INJURING SELF	x.xxx	.xxx	.xxx
	(IH)	PHYSICAL INTRUSION	x.xxx	.xxx	.xxx
	(I)	OTHER	x.xxx	.xxx	.xxx
		STEREOTYPE (1)/VARIABLE (17)	x.xxx	.xxx	.xxx
		AWAKE-ASLEEP:			
		EYES OPEN	x.xxx	±.xxx	±.xxx
	(IS)	EYES CLOSED	x.xxx	.xxx	.xxx
		LOCATION:			
		CLASSROOM-LOUNGE	x.xxx	±.xxx	±.xxx
		TV ROOM	x.xxx	.xxx	.xxx
		CORRIDOR-LOUNGE	x.xxx	.xxx	.xxx
		OWN BEDROOM	x.xxx	.xxx	.xxx
		OTHER BEDROOM	x.xxx	.xxx	.xxx
		ACTIVITY AREA	x.xxx	.xxx	.xxx
		LIVING ROOM/DAY ROOM	x.xxx	.xxx	.xxx
		OFFICE	x.xxx	.xxx	.xxx
		HALLWAY	x.xxx	.xxx	.xxx
		DINING AREA	x.xxx	.xxx	.xxx
		KITCHEN	x.xxx	.xxx	.xxx
		RESTROOM	x.xxx	.xxx	.xxx
		BATHING AREA	x.xxx	.xxx	.xxx
		LAUNDRY ROOM	x.xxx	.xxx	.xxx
		SITTING ROOM	x.xxx	.xxx	.xxx
	(I)	SECLUSION ROOM	x.xxx	.xxx	.xxx
		OFF UNIT	x.xxx	.xxx	.xxx
		STEREOTYPE (1)/VARIABLE (20)	x.xxx	.xxx	.xxx
	(I)	UNAUTH ABS - NO OBSERV	x.xxx	±.xxx	±.xxx
		SICK - NO OBSERVATION	x.xxx	.xxx	.xxx
		AUTHORIZED ABS - NO OBSERV	x.xxx	.xxx	.xxx

SUMMARY INFORMATION & HIGHER-ORDER SCORES

POR	HOS	HIGHER-ORDER SCORES:	CURNT STATE	CHANGE FROM ENTRY	L.WK
	(A)	TOTAL APPROPRIATE BEHAVIOR	x.xxx	±.xxx	±.xxx
	(AP)	INTERPERSONAL INTERACTION	x.xxx	.xxx	.xxx
	(AW)	INSTRUMENTAL ACTIVITY	x.xxx	.xxx	.xxx
	(AM)	SELF MAINTENANCE	x.xxx	.xxx	.xxx
	(AE)	INDIVIDUAL ENTERTAINMENT	x.xxx	.xxx	.xxx
	(I)	TOTAL INAPPROPRIATE BEHAV	x.xxx	±.xxx	±.xxx
	(IS)	BIZARRE MOTORIC BEHAVIOR	x.xxx	.xxx	.xxx
	(IC)	BIZARRE FACIAL & VERBALS	x.xxx	.xxx	.xxx
	(IH)	HOSTILE-BELLIGERENCE	x.xxx	.xxx	.xxx
	(X)	ASSAULT FREQUENCY	xx	xx	xx

PROBLEM-ORIENTED RECORDS: BEFORE ENTRY OR REFERENCE, RECORD "T" FOR TEMPORARY PROBS OR PERMANENT PROB NUMBERS IN "POR" COLUMN AND COMPLETE ID BOX BELOW.

THE "HOS" COLUMN REFERS TO CODES THAT ENTER HIGHER-ORDER SCORES. ALL CODES (A-) OR (I-) ENTER "TOTAL". HIGHER-ORDER SCORES. ALL CODES ENTERING (AP) REQUIRE A "WITH" SOCIAL ORIENTATION. "PLAYING A GAME" ALONE ENTERS (AE).

TYPE OF SUMMARY:

NUMBER OF PEOPLE SUMMARIZED W/DATA=   TOTAL=
PROPORTION OF OBSERVATIONS WITH DATA=
NUMBER OF OBSERVATIONS WITH DATA..=
NUMBER OF OBSERVATIONS WITHOUT DATA=

DATE ADMITTED TO UNIT: / /
DATES SUMMARIZED: (/ - /)

FACILITY/UNIT:

TSBC ID NUMBER:

RESIDENTS NAME

RESIDENTS ID (DEPT)

FACILITY NAME

UNIT/SUBUNIT   DATE

STAFF SIGNATURE

score, thus, reflects an absolute rate of performance or activity, which can be compared to performances at other times or by other persons or groups. For example, a score of .350 on "social orientation: alone" indicates that the person was alone 35% of the time during waking hours, or on a group summary, that the average individual was alone 35% of the time. The last two columns of x.xxx reflect *absolute change* from earlier time periods. The "change from entry" column indicates the change in current status from that observed during the first week of the person's entry into the treatment unit, and the "change from l.wk" column indicates the change from the last week preceding the time covered for current status.

In addition to the individual items in the left and middle sections of the TSBC summary, which reflect the codes directly employed by observers for each discrete hourly time-sample, "stereotype(1)/variable (x)" scores reflect the extent to which functioning within the category is limited to a few or single codes (stereotyped), or ranges across several codes (variable). These scores have proven to be important determinates of evaluative judgments of functioning, as well as the absolute levels of behavior indexed by individual codes and higher-order scores.

The right section of the TSBC format in Figure 5.1 provides higher-order scores and information necessary to identify and interpret the summary, as well as space for documentation of review by specified clinical staff, if the summary is to be entered into clinical records. This upper right section provides the information on current status and change for higher-order combinations of the discrete codes, grouped by adaptive and maladaptive functioning, and for "assault frequency," which is obtained through 100% event-recordings by clinical staff. These higher-order scores are the first level of examination for individual clinical decision-making. Aggregated over individuals, they are often the only information of interest for program evaluation and managerial purposes, although "location" and "social orientation" codes are of interest for time management, as are "facial expression" codes for monitoring the affective tenor of a unit.

Although TSBC higher-order scores are parallel to the more global ones that are typically obtained from standardized QICS instruments (e.g., rating scales and structured interviews), the TSBC higher-order scores are computer-calculated by summing the actual occurrence of discrete individual codes. The individual component codes entering higher-order scores are readily identified by common entries in the "hos" column. Thus, normative comparisons of the abolute levels and change for higher-order classes of functioning may be followed by analytic examination of discrete components for precision targeting and monitoring of interventions. Absolute rate comparisons for all scores may be made to local groups or to normative data for overall institutional samples and successful discharge samples of clientele. The significance of change is also noted for guidance.

The remaining columns on the TSBC summary sheet are the blanks headed by "por." These blanks are provided for easy integration of the TSBC sheet into *problem oriented records*, allowing direct identification and monitoring of progress for targeted client assets and problems in a standard format.

The documented replicability and utility of TSBC data are wide ranging (Paul, in press b). The trustworthiness of the information at both detailed and global levels has been exceptional. For example, the interobserver intraclass replicability coefficients obtained for one day observations over the entire multi-institutional normative-feasibility sample ranged from $r = .90$ to 1.00 for individual codes, with the median r exceeding .98. The lowest one-day replicability for higher-order scores was $r = .95$. Conservative estimates of interobserver replicability for a week's observations found the lowest intraclass coefficient for individual codes to exceed $r = .97$, whereas all higher-order scores were equal to or greater than $r = .99$. The discriminations among individual clients reflect differences in discrete codes ranging from weekly performances of "none" to 91.7% of the time, with even larger spreads for higher-order scores. Higher-order scores have shown excellent discriminations in expected directions among client groups whose level and nature of functioning are fairly well established (e.g., good-bad premorbid competency, acute-chronic institutionalization, oriented-disoriented mental status, delusional-nondelusional, organic-nonorganic, etc.), often providing further clarifications of the nature of disordered functioning that make a great deal of theoretical sense.

Concurrent and predictive studies have found exceptional convergent and discriminant validities for TSBC scores. In fact, weekly TSBC higher-order scores account for about all of the reliable variance in scores obtained from standardized QICS instruments during the same time—including several of the best ward rating scales and structured interviews—without problems in shifting anchor-points, which often plague QICS instruments. TSBC scores have also been found to predict which clients achieve successful discharges and their level of functioning in the community up to 18 months after discharge (r's in the .60s & .70s). This is a genuinely unique finding in the residential treatment literature, which provides a basis for normative data that can provide empirical guidance for placement and disposition decisions. Empirical guidelines can, in fact, now identify assets, deficits, and excesses for individual clients as initial problems with objective, measurable goals for concurrent monitoring and triggering of discharge considerations. Over time, each facility can develop discharge and placement norms of their own to provide more precise guidelines for particular settings.

The TSBC has also demonstrated a remarkable sensitivity to change with specified interventions, whether psychosocial or biological—providing information on both intended and unintended effects. Although not established with "hard" scientific evidence, TSBC data have been used clinically in a host of ways, including the prediction of suicidal attempts, interactive goal-setting with clients and families, convincing of community facilities to accept clients with bad reputations, convincing of judges to remove legal restrictions, and many others.

The TSBC was originally developed to provide objective assessment and ongoing monitoring of client functioning, and has been documented to provide most of that client information required for all categories of decisions listed in Table 5.1. Portions of TSBC data on staff have also been found to be particularly useful. Because TSBC observations cover hourly time-samples of all staff as well as clients, data from the "social orientation," "physical position," and "location" categories and from the "working" item provide an excellent picture of the way in which individual staff and staff groups spend their time, whereas data from the "facial expression" category provide an overall picture of staff affect. Many staff are, in fact, surprised to find how they spend their time and use the TSBC for their own goal setting. Additional uses of both client and staff TSBC data as part of the overall TSBC/SRIC system will be noted later.

The Staff-Resident Interaction Chronograph

The SRIC is the primary DOC system for providing information on the nature and amount of interaction between staff and clients in residential settings. In addition to TSBC summaries on each individual client and staff member, and TSBC means and standard deviations for the entire client group and staff group on each treatment unit, the system provides standard weekly reports with SRIC summaries of means and standard deviations over all staff on each treatment unit. The SRIC summaries of the nature and amount of staff activity for the treatment unit as a whole cover the same period as the TSBC summaries. In addition, special reports can be obtained in the same format on individual staff or staff subgroups for any specified period of time, shift, location, or activity (behavior setting and context).

Whereas TSBC observations employ brief discrete-momentary, hourly time-samples of every client and staff member, SRIC observations use a continuous-chronographic, 10-minute observation period of a single staff member, systematically observing all staff members over time at the rate of one or two per hour within each treatment unit. For each SRIC observation, an observer systematically codes all interactions with clients by the target staff member, or absence thereof, during each minute within a matrix of five columns and 21 rows. Ten such matrices are, therefore, coded during each 10-minute observation period. The five columns of the matrix specify the nature of client behavior to which staff responds (appropriate, inappropriate failure, inappropriate crazy, "straight" requests, or "neutral"). The "neutral" client column allows coding of staff initiations and noninteractive activities. The 21 rows of the matrix categorize the nature of the staff member's verbal and non-verbal interactions with clients, as well as noninteractive activities that are job relevant (e.g., preparing drugs, attending staff meetings) or job irrelevant (e.g., personal phone calls, crossword puzzles). Each coding entry, thus, represents a discrete instance of staff behavior in functional relationship to the class of client behavior. SRIC observers also record a variety of other information regarding the number of clients and staff members present during the observation as well as identifying data regarding the behavior setting and context of each observation (activity, time, and location) parallel to that recorded for TSBC observations.

SRIC observations are summarized by first tallying the number of coded interactions for individual clients or client groups in each cell of the 5 × 21 matrix over all 10 minutes of the observation period. These data are then entered into the system computer files to allow summarization of all SRIC observations for a given time period and treatment program, or summarization over specific staff, activities, locations, time periods, or other selected variables.

The format for computer summaries of SRIC information on individuals and groups is presented in Figure 5.2. As with TSBC summaries, the actual size of printed SRIC summaries is at least 8½ × 11 inches, and the xx.xx's in Figure 5.2 represent numbers. In the case of SRIC summaries, the numbers are either "average hourly instances" of activity and percentage calculations, or standard deviations. Although xx.xx's are shown in Figure 5.2 only for one program or one staff member, the format provides for two SRIC summaries on a single sheet "no.-1, no.-2"

STAFF-RESIDENT INTERACTION CHRONOGRAPH (SRIC):

PRODUCTION DATE: / /
REQUESTED BY:
SRIC-ID NO.: NO.-1:
NO.-2:

TYPE OF SUMMARY:

DATES SUMMARIZED: NO.-1: (/ / - / /)
NO.-2: (/ / - / /)

FACILITY/UNIT: NO.-1:
NO.-2:

NO. STAFF: NO.-1:
NO.-2:

NO. OF SRICS SUMMARIZED: NO.-1: xxx
NO.-2:

AVG INCIDENCE/HR FOR A SINGLE OCCURRENCE WITH THIS NO. OF SRICS & STAFF IS: NO.-1: x.xx
NO.-2:

AVERAGE HOURLY INSTANCES OF STAFF ACTIVITY (MEAN)

CATEGORY OF STAFF BEHAVIOR	CATEGORY OF RESIDENT BEHAVIOR TO WHICH STAFF RESPONDED													TOTAL STAFF BEHAVIOR		% OF INTERACTION		CATEGORY OF STAFF BEHAVR
	APPROPRIATE (AP)		INAPPROPRIATE FAILURE (INF)		INAPPROPRIATE CRAZY (INC)		REQUEST (R)		NEUTRAL (N)									
	NO.-1	NO.-2	NO.-1	NO.-2	NO.-1	NO.-2	NO.-1	NO.-2	NO.-1	NO.-2			NO.-1	NO.-2	NO.-1	NO.-2	
POSITIVE VERBAL	xx.xx		xx.xx		xx.xx		xx.xx		xx.xx				xx.xx		x.x		(POS VERBAL)
NEGATIVE VERBAL	xx.xx		xx.xx		xx.xx		xx.xx		xx.xx				xx.xx		x.x		(NEG VERBAL)
POS NONVERBAL	xx.xx		xx.xx		xx.xx		xx.xx		xx.xx				xx.xx		x.x		(POS NONVERB)
NEG NONVERBAL	xx.xx		xx.xx		xx.xx		xx.xx		xx.xx				xx.xx		x.x		(NEG NONVERB)
POS NONSOCIAL	xx.xx		xx.xx		xx.xx		xx.xx		xx.xx				xx.xx		x.x		(POS NONSOC)
NEG NONSOCIAL	xx.xx		xx.xx		xx.xx		xx.xx		xx.xx				xx.xx		x.x		(NEG NONSOC)
POS STATEMENT	xx.xx		xx.xx		xx.xx		xx.xx		xx.xx				xx.xx		x.x		(POS STATMT)
NEG STATEMENT	xx.xx		xx.xx		xx.xx		xx.xx		xx.xx				xx.xx		x.x		(NEG STATMT)
POSITIVE PROMPT	xx.xx		xx.xx		xx.xx		xx.xx		xx.xx				xx.xx		x.x		(POS PROMPT)
NEGATIVE PROMPT	xx.xx		xx.xx		xx.xx		xx.xx		xx.xx				xx.xx		x.x		(NEG PROMPT)
POS GRP REFERENCE	xx.xx		xx.xx		xx.xx		xx.xx		xx.xx				xx.xx		x.x		(POS GP REF)
NEG GRP REFERENCE	xx.xx		xx.xx		xx.xx		xx.xx		xx.xx				xx.xx		x.x		(NEG GP REF)
REFLECT/CLARIFY	xx.xx		xx.xx		xx.xx		xx.xx		xx.xx				xx.xx		x.x		(REFL/CLARIF)
SUGGEST ALTRNATIV	xx.xx		xx.xx		xx.xx		xx.xx		xx.xx				xx.xx		x.x		(SUGGEST ALT)
INSTRUCT/DEMONSR	xx.xx		xx.xx		xx.xx		xx.xx		xx.xx				xx.xx		x.x		(INSTRUC/DEM)
DOING WITH	xx.xx		xx.xx		xx.xx		xx.xx		xx.xx				xx.xx		x.x		(DOING WITH)
DOING FOR	xx.xx		xx.xx		xx.xx		xx.xx		xx.xx				xx.xx		x.x		(DOING FOR)
PHYSICAL FORCE	xx.xx		xx.xx		xx.xx		xx.xx		xx.xx				xx.xx		x.x		(PHYS FORCE)
IGNORE/NO RESPONS	xx.xx		xx.xx		xx.xx		xx.xx		xx.xx				xx.xx		x.x		(IGNORE/NO R)
ANNOUNCE	***		***		***		***		xx.xx				xx.xx		—		(ANNOUNCE)
ATTEND/RECORD/OBS	***		***		***		***		xx.xx				xx.xx		—		(A/R/O)
TOTAL INTERACTION	xx.xx		xx.xx		xx.xx		xx.xx		xx.xx				xxx.xx		x.x		TOTAL INTERAC
% OF INTERACTIONS	xx.xx		xx.xx		***		xx.xx		xx.xx				***	***	***		& OF INTERACT
TOTAL ACTIVITY	***		***		***		***		xx.xx				xxx.xx		***		TOTAL ACTIVIT

NOTE: "% OF INTERACTIONS" COLUMN FOR (ANNOUNCE) (A/R/O) AND "TOTAL INTERACTIONS" REFLECT % OF TOTAL ACTIVITY INSTEAD OF INTERACTIONS. "(IGNORE/NO R) - (N)" CODES ARE NOT INCLUDED IN "% OF INTERACTION" FIGURES.

AVG RESIDENTS PRESENT: NO.-1: xx.x
NO.-2:

CONTACTS/HOUR/RESIDENT: INDIVIDUALLY: NO.-1: x.xx
NO.-2:
IN A GROUP: NO.-1: x.xx
NO.-2:
TOTAL: NO.-1: x.xx
NO.-2:

AVG INTERACTIONS/CONTACT: NO.-1: x.xx
NO.-2:
AVG ATTENTION RECVD BY INDIVIDUAL RESIDENT: NO.-1: xx:xx.xx
NO.-2:

AVG FUNCT RESPONSIBLE: NO.-1: xx.x
NO.-2:

CONTACTS/HOUR/RESIDENT: INDIVIDUALLY: NO.-1: x.xx
NO.-2:
IN A GROUP: NO.-1: x.xx
NO.-2:
TOTAL: NO.-1: x.xx
NO.-2:

AVG INTERACTIONS/CONTACT: NO.-1: x.xx
NO.-2:
AVG ATTENTION RECVD BY INDIVIDUAL RESIDENT: NO.-1: xx:xx.xx
NO.-2:

FIGURE 5.2. Format of Staff-Resident Interaction Chronograph (SRIC) Summary Reports

to allow easy comparisons between individuals, groups, or different time periods.

The top portion of the sric summary format, above the horizontal line, provides identifying information and documentation of the data base of the summary. The part below the bottom horizontal line provides information on the average number of clients ("residents") for whom staff were responsible as well as the amount of attention received by the average client. The specific staff-client interactions and staff activities observed are displayed in the central part of the summary, along with information over total rows and columns. The first five columns and the top 21 rows parallel the 5×21 matrix used to code the raw interactions observed. Thus, a sric summary showing "12.13" in the "appropriate—reflect/clarify" cell represents staff providing an average of 12.13 Rogerian reflections or clarifications per hour in response to clients' (residents') performance of appropriate behavior. By reading across each row in the sric summary, the way in which staff apply the particular type of action to different categories of client functioning becomes apparent. Similarly, reading down each column of the summary shows the way in which different categories of client behavior are responded to by staff—on both absolute and relative levels. The last two columns and bottom three rows within the central portion of the sric summary provide totals of staff and client categories observed in both hourly rate and percentage interaction terms as well as the total average hourly rate of all activities and interactions.

As with the tsbc, the documented replicability and utility of sric data are wide ranging (Paul, in press c). Given the complexity of the instrument, the obtained trustworthiness of the information is particularly impressive. For example, the interobserver intraclass replicability coefficients obtained for one-day's observations over the multi-institutional normative-feasibility sample ranged from $r = .84$ to 1.00 for individual cells of the matrix, with the median interobserver replicability over all cells of the instrument exceeding $r = .99$. Non-doc approaches cannot provide even partial data comparable to that of the sric; therefore traditional concurrent validity studies are impossible. Rather, discriminative and predictive evaluations of the instrument are of major interest. The range of discrimination among individual staff within residential programs and between different programs, based upon full week samples of all staff, is either remarkable or shocking depending on your point of view. For example, across the 30 programs in public mental institutions included in the multi-institutional studies, average hourly rates of staff-client interactions ranged from a low of 42.66 interactions per hour to a high more than ten times that rate (459.23). The average staff member was found to be responsible for as few as 4.31 clients over an entire week in some programs and as many as 32.96 in others. The total attention received by the average client in these programs varied by more than 1,300%. More than fivefold differences were observed across programs in the amount of job-relevant activity not including interactions with clients, whereas the proportion of staff activity spent "goofing off" varied by a factor of 13.5. Even greater discriminations were obtained within individual cells of the SRIC matrix over different treatment programs and for individual staff members within programs.

The SRIC objectively documents the psychosocial activities performed by staff and received by clients, whether those activities are planned or not. That is, the SRIC is relatively value free. The desirability of specific types of interactions must be determined by empirical documentations of effectiveness, legal and ethical guidelines, or by stipulated principles derived from theory or other sources. Where specific treatment principles have been specified, the SRIC has proven its usefulness as an objective criterion for evaluating the effectiveness of staff training and development procedures, and in the concurrent monitoring and documentation of the ongoing conduct of different group therapies and unit-wide treatment programs. When used as a basis for feedback in ongoing staff inservice training and concurrent monitoring, the SRIC has increased staff efficiency from threefold to fivefold in different programs, in terms of the amount of staff-client interactions, while reducing nonprogrammatic "errors" to less than ½ of 1% on a continuing basis. The SRIC has also provided legal/ethical protection to facility staff, individually and as a group, through the documentation of the nature and amount of attention actually received by clients. Thus, SRIC information has served both to defuse unjustified complaints or concerns about treatment programs and to quickly identify and allow remediation of undesirable staff actions. In specific research studies, SRIC data have proven to be of exceptional value in documenting the nature and interactive effects of the planned or unplanned psychosocial environment on specific tests of psychological and sociological factors and psychopharmacological interventions. When used as an objective basis for staff personnel actions, staff morale, acceptance, and overall evaluations of fairness have been dramatically higher than with traditional practices.

Perhaps the most exciting potential of the SRIC is as a "bootstrap" mechanism for improving treatment effectiveness, in addition to ensuring accurate implementation of empirically documented effective programs. Correlations of SRIC data and client TSBC data over time have documented relationships (r's in the .50s to .90s) between specific classes of staff-client interactions and client functioning and improvement—showing that *how* staff interact is more important than *how much* they interact. In addition to the guidance provided by normative data, empirical comparisons of ongoing SRIC summaries obtained from different programs, staff, or time periods that differ in effectiveness within a single program can identify those features of staff-client interaction associated with greater effectiveness or efficiency. Those features may then serve as a basis for positive, precise, in-service training and feedback for the way in which staff should change their functioning to improve services—rather than nonspecific pleas to "do better." In general, staff SRICs and TSBCs have shown excellent utility in providing the great majority of the most important information needed in the staff domain for all decision problems listed in Table 5.1.

Additional System Components and Quality Assurance Reports

In addition to the continuous data file containing client and staff TSBCs and staff SRICs, system computer programs provide for the sorting and timely summarization of data on client, staff, and program functioning in combination with biographical data and information on client movement. A series of three quality assurance summaries support program evaluation and other management decisions regarding treatment units and facilities or answer questions regarding subgroups of clientele or staff within or across programs. Because the data on client and staff functioning are continuous, quality assurance reports may be initiated for any time period desired, from two consecutive weeks through a fiscal year or more (Paul, in press d).

Quality assurance summary no. 1. The format of the first quality assurance summary is presented in Figure 5.3. This report breaks out information from the client TSBC file, grouping clients according to categories of their movements (columns) during the time period being examined. As in previous system summaries, different decision makers are usually interested in only a few pieces of information at any given time, but—after training in interpretation—prefer to have access to the full set. Columns P-1 and P-2 allow ready comparison of two different programs, facilities, or subgroups over the same time period, or two different time periods for a single program, facility, or subgroup. The xx's

FACILITY/UNIT/PROGRAM SUMMARIZED:
P - 1=
P - 2=

PRODUCTION DATE:
PERIOD SUMMARIZED - START:
· END:

QUALITY ASSURANCE SUMMARY NO. 1

TSBC GLOBAL FUNCTIONING & OUTCOME BY CLIENT MOVEMENT

CLIENT DATA		TOTAL SERVED		START PERIOD CONTINUES		IN PERIOD ADDITIONS		END PERIOD CONTINUES		DSCHRG SUCC (DAYS > 30)		DSCHRG FAIL W/I 30 DAYS		DSCHRGED TO INDEP LIV		DSCHRGED BY AMA/AWOL/CT		DSCHRGED TO COM PLC		TRANSFERRED (DEPT/OTHR)		DEATH	
		P-1	P-2	P-1	P-2	P-1	P-2	P-1	P-2	P-1	P-2	P-1	P-2	P-1	P-2	P-1	P-2	P-1	P-2	P-1	P-2	P-1	P-2
CLIENTS: TOT NUMBR		xxx		xxx		xxx		xxx		xxx		xxx		xxx		xxx		xxx		xxx		xxx	
% OF TOTAL		100.0		xxx.x		xxx.x		xxx.x		xxx.x		xxx.x		xxx.x		xxx.x		xxx.x		xxx.x		xxx.x	
ADAPTIVE FUNCTION																							
PROGRAM ENTRY	M	x.xx		x.xx		x.xx		x.xx		x.xx		x.xx		x.xx		x.xx		x.xx		x.xx		x.xx	
	SD	x.xx		x.xx		x.xx		x.xx		x.xx		x.xx		x.xx		x.xx		x.xx		x.xx		x.xx	
START OF PERIOD	M	x.xx		x.xx		x.xx		x.xx		x.xx		x.xx		x.xx		x.xx		x.xx		x.xx		x.xx	
	SD	x.xx		x.xx		x.xx		x.xx		x.xx		x.xx		x.xx		x.xx		x.xx		x.xx		x.xx	
END/TERMINATION	M	x.xx		x.xx		x.xx		x.xx		x.xx		x.xx		x.xx		x.xx		x.xx		x.xx		x.xx	
	SD	x.xx		x.xx		x.xx		x.xx		x.xx		x.xx		x.xx		x.xx		x.xx		x.xx		x.xx	
MALADPTIVE FUNCTION																							
PROGRAM ENTRY	M	x.xx		x.xx		x.xx		x.xx		x.xx		x.xx		x.xx		x.xx		x.xx		x.xx		x.xx	
	SD	x.xx		x.xx		x.xx		x.xx		x.xx		x.xx		x.xx		x.xx		x.xx		x.xx		x.xx	
START OF PERIOD	M	x.xx		x.xx		x.xx		x.xx		x.xx		x.xx		x.xx		x.xx		x.xx		x.xx		x.xx	
	SD	x.xx		x.xx		x.xx		x.xx		x.xx		x.xx		x.xx		x.xx		x.xx		x.xx		x.xx	
END/TERMINATION	M	x.xx		x.xx		x.xx		x.xx		x.xx		x.xx		x.xx		x.xx		x.xx		x.xx		x.xx	
	SD	x.xx		x.xx		x.xx		x.xx		x.xx		x.xx		x.xx		x.xx		x.xx		x.xx		x.xx	
PERCENT ASSAULTIVE																							
PROGRAM ENTRY	%	x.x		x.x		x.x		x.x		x.x		x.x		x.x		x.x		x.x		x.x		x.x	
START OF PERIOD	%	x.x		x.x		x.x		x.x		x.x		x.x		x.x		x.x		x.x		x.x		x.x	
END/TERMINATION	%	x.x		x.x		x.x		x.x		x.x		x.x		x.x		x.x		x.x		x.x		x.x	
FROM PROGRAM ENTRY																							
LENGTH OF STAY (IN DAYS)	M	xxx		xxx		xxx		xxx		xxx		xxx		xxx		xxx		xxx		xxx		xxx	
	SD	xxx.x		xxx.x		xxx.x		xxx.x		xxx.x		xxx.x		xxx.x		xxx.x		xxx.x		xxx.x		xxx.x	
ADAPTIVE FUNCTION																							
LEVEL CHANGE	M	±x.xx		±x.xx		±x.xx		±x.xx		±x.xx		±x.xx		±x.xx		±x.xx		±x.xx		±x.xx		±x.xx	
IMPROVED	%	x.x		x.x		x.x		x.x		x.x		x.x		x.x		x.x		x.x		x.x		x.x	
WORSE	%	x.x		x.x		x.x		x.x		x.x		x.x		x.x		x.x		x.x		x.x		x.x	
MALADPTIVE FUNCTN																							
LEVEL CHANGE	M	±x.xx		±x.xx		±x.xx		±x.xx		±x.xx		±x.xx		±x.xx		±x.xx		±x.xx		±x.xx		±x.xx	
IMPROVED	%	x.x		x.x		x.x		x.x		x.x		x.x		x.x		x.x		x.x		x.x		x.x	
WORSE	%	x.x		x.x		x.x		x.x		x.x		x.x		x.x		x.x		x.x		x.x		x.x	
TOTAL FUNCTION																							
IMPROVED	%	x.x		x.x		x.x		x.x		x.x		x.x		x.x		x.x		x.x		x.x		x.x	
WORSE	%	x.x		x.x		x.x		x.x		x.x		x.x		x.x		x.x		x.x		x.x		x.x	
FROM START OF PERIOD																							
LENGTH OF STAY (IN DAYS)	M	xxx		xxx		xxx		xxx		xxx		xxx		xxx		xxx		xxx		xxx		xxx	
	SD	xxx.x		xxx.x		xxx.x		xxx.x		xxx.x		xxx.x		xxx.x		xxx.x		xxx.x		xxx.x		xxx.x	
ADAPTIVE FUNCTION																							
LEVEL CHANGE	M	±x.xx		±x.xx		±x.xx		±x.xx		±x.xx		±x.xx		±x.xx		±x.xx		±x.xx		±x.xx		±x.xx	
IMPROVED	%	x.x		x.x		x.x		x.x		x.x		x.x		x.x		x.x		x.x		x.x		x.x	
WORSE	%	x.x		x.x		x.x		x.x		x.x		x.x		x.x		x.x		x.x		x.x		x.x	
MALADPTIVE FUNCTN																							
LEVEL CHANGE	M	±x.xx		±x.xx		±x.xx		±x.xx		±x.xx		±x.xx		±x.xx		±x.xx		±x.xx		±x.xx		±x.xx	
IMPROVED	%	x.x		x.x		x.x		x.x		x.x		x.x		x.x		x.x		x.x		x.x		x.x	
WORSE	%	x.x		x.x		x.x		x.x		x.x		x.x		x.x		x.x		x.x		x.x		x.x	
TOTAL FUNCTION																							
IMPROVED	%	x.x		x.x		x.x		x.x		x.x		x.x		x.x		x.x		x.x		x.x		x.x	
WORSE	%	x.x		x.x		x.x		x.x		x.x		x.x		x.x		x.x		x.x		x.x		x.x	

FIGURE 5.3. Format of Quality Assurance Summary No. 1

represent the numbers provided for each client grouping during the period examined. The first two rows show the number of clients in each grouping and their percentage of the total served during the period. Except for "length-of-stay" data, the remainder of the information reflects client functioning derived from the TSBC. Mean TSBC total appropriate behavior ("adaptive function") and total inappropriate behavior ("maladaptive function") for each client grouping are provided for the first week of each client's entry to a program ("program entry"), for the first week of the time period examined ("start of period"), and for the last week of the time period examined or for a client's last week in a program ("end/termination"). Similarly, mean changes in the level of TSBC scores and the percentage of clients showing objective improvement or worsening are provided for each client grouping to the end of the period examined from each client's entry to the programs in question ("from program entry") and from the start of the period examined ("from start of period").

The data provided on client functioning in quality assurance summary no. 1 are intended to answer nearly any formative or summative program evaluation question regarding absolute or comparative efficacy and/or analytic questions for ongoing monitoring. As such, unit and facility directors or higher-level management staff may only be interested in one or two pieces of information—such as the total percentage of clients improved or comparative level differences between discharge successes and failures. Most management, program evaluation, and quality assurance uses of these data only examine a few cells of the report—if things are going well. If things are not going so well or if problems are suggested from other sources, the additional information provides a means of rational hypothesis generation and testing based on objective data.

Quality assurance summary no. 2. The second report in the series is intended to assist in the analytic study of comparative program or treatment team effectiveness as well as to provide information on the nature of clients served. This report presents information on client characteristics prior to program entry that have empirical relationships to outcome in residential treatment. Such information is usually available in most facilities—here, to ease interpretation, it is simply summarized for the same client groupings and time periods included on the quality assurance summary no. 1. These data include the percentage of clients in each grouping in major diagnostic classifications, legal categories (involuntary, incompetent), and admission categories (e.g., transfer, readmission), as well as information on prior admissions, length and type of previous treatment, and usual demographics. If things are going well, these data may be ignored.

Quality assurance summary no. 3. The last report in the series provides information on staff and program characteristics and functioning for the same time periods and the same programs, facilities, or subunits on which the client summaries are obtained. This summary includes demographic characteristics of staff, staff and client turnover rates over the time period examined, and both allocated and actual program census information and client staff ratios over the period and at the beginning and end of the period. Space is also provided to include information on program costs and average drug dosages for the same time period. All of the latter data are obtained from other sources and included in the quality assurance summary to ease interpretation.

The unique information on quality assurance summary no. 3 is derived from staff TSBCs and SRICs. Means and standard deviations are provided on each program for the beginning and ending weeks of the time period examined and for change over the period for several variables. These include the actual client/staff ratios observed as well as the interactions/contact, contacts/hour, and total attention received by the average client. Average staff time spent alone, with clients, with other staff, and with outsiders and average staff time working and on authorized or unauthorized absences are included. Finally, average instances of total activity, total staff/client interactions per hour, the percentage of total activity spent in interactions with clients, and the percentage of both job-relevant and job-irrelevant noninteractive activity are summarized.

Quality assurance summary no. 3 is intended to provide relatively high-level objective information in the staff domain to answer formative and summative program evaluation questions. It is also intended to allow initial generation and testing of hypotheses regarding programmatic differences in staff utilization and functioning that might be related to differential effectiveness identified from client outcome data on quality assurance summary no. 1. As with the other summaries, only a portion of the data would usually be of interest. However, managerial and regulatory decision makers and professional program directors can use the entire system in as much detail as necessary. Various levels of decision makers may wish to examine only the standard summaries of TSBC and SRIC data for ongoing weekly monitoring or the set of quality assurance summaries for program evaluation on a quarterly, semiannual, or annual basis—simply documenting that "good things" are happening. But, if questions or discrepancies occur, the continuing data base allows more and more specific information to be obtained by a further search of full TSBC and SRIC summaries on groups, subgroups, and individuals—down to a specific hour if need be. Thus, rational operations, regulation, and improvement of services can be based on hypotheses generation and testing from objective data rather than from surmise or the differential persuasive abilities of various administrators.

ISSUES IN IMPLEMENTATION AND DISSEMINATION OF THE TSBC/SRIC SYSTEM

The TSBC/SRIC system is recommended as the core of a comprehensive assessment paradigm to serve as a cost-efficient vehicle for improving the quality and effectiveness of services and research in residential treatment facilities. By supplying the information with maximum potential utility for supporting rational decision-making in all categories of problems listed in Table 5.2, these procedures can remove the major technological-methodological obstacle that has allowed the development and continuation of costly, inefficient, and ineffective decision-making and treatment practices of most current operations. The purpose of this chapter is to simply familiarize readers with the nature of the problems and promising technology in order to encourage further study; however, the recommended procedures represent such radical departures from current practices that a few comments on implementation and dissemination must be made so as to clarify practical considerations.

The Diffusion of Innovations Perspective

In Chapter 2 of this book Fishman and Neigher note some of the variables and sources cited in the literature on the diffusion of innovations. This literature is sizable in the field of education and mental health in general and in the area of residential treatment settings in particular (see also: Glaser, et al., 1983; HIRI/NIMH, 1976; Liberman & Phipps, in press; Paul, 1985 b; Rogers, 1983; Stein & Test, 1985; Stoltz, 1981; Tornatzky et al., 1980; Winett, 1985). Although much of this literature consists of creative listings of variables to form mnemonic acronyms (e.g., A VICTORY, CORRECT, HELP SCORES) with conclusions based more on the accumulated wisdom of practitioners and thinkers than of documented facts, a number of commonalities appear that have relevance to the dissemination of the TSBC/SRIC system.

The adoption of innovations. With regard to influences on the adoption of innovations, these commonalities can be most simply summarized in the following way (see Paul, 1985 b). For an innovation to be adopted in practice, it must be judged to be worthwhile by those who have the power to adopt, and the adopters must be *informed* about the need for the innovation and its availability and be *willing* and *able* to undertake its implementation. Those innovations requiring minimal change in current practices and adoption decisions by individual professionals are disseminated rapidly, often being overadopted beyond the scientific data base (e.g., new drugs, surgical procedures, and laboratory tests; office-based treatment and biofeedback techniques; computerized test scoring and interpretation and paper-and-pencil assessment devices). In contrast, those innovations requiring changes in roles, structures, and operating principles as well as organizational adoption decisions are—and probably should be—disseminated slowly, often being actively resisted or avoided (e.g., unit-wide residential and community psychosocial programs; comprehensive management information systems).

Particularly for the latter type of innovation, which requires extended periods of preparation and staff training and, ideally, an operational host site for demonstration of new procedures, the context and culture of residential treatment settings undermine the "informed, willing, and able" triad. Because current cultural forces maintain the status quo and because, outside of structured opportunities, few administrative or clinical staff become informed by reading, (most rely on person-to-person communication and first-hand experience), even worthwhile innovations requiring major changes are unlikely to be considered seriously in the absence of external pressures and/or a strong individual or group within the agency to serve as internal advocate. Such internal advocates, themselves having identified the need for and availability of worthwhile innovations, push others to become informed, willing, and able in spite of the general pull to maintain the status quo. Thus, in addition to the commonalities identified above as influences on the adoption of innovations in residential treatment facilities, I would add two characteristics which are needed by the developers/disseminators of major innovations and by internal advocates—sensitive perseverance and tenacity in the face of adversity.

Possible timelines of the TSBC/SRIC system. The TSBC/SRIC system certainly qualifies as an innovation that requires organizational adoption decisions and fundamental changes in assessment and decision-making practices. To be sure, the R & D effort of our clinical-research group has been subject to unanticipated and uncontrollable political events, which have caused innumerable delays and, on more than one occasion, frustrated attempts to establish demonstration units in the public sector to serve as our own research, dissemination, and training base (see Paul, 1985 b). Given the current context and culture of mental health systems and research funding agencies, such problems may be inevitable for work that is admittedly so far from the "mainstream," or as Fiske (1985) suggests, "main pond," since there is no appreciable movement in the body as a whole.

However, over the 13 years since the TSBC/SRIC system began "going public" through use of data in publications and presentations and through data collection and implementations outside our own treatment units, the interest in adoption has systematically grown. Most residential administrative and clinical staff who have had the opportunity to become "informed" through first-hand, person-to-person participation in a full two-day workshop judged the TSBC/SRIC system to be extremely "worthwhile," and the majority of staff from more than 90% of facilities indicated that their own institution was "willing and able" to adopt it. Inquiries requesting further information have been received from facilities in nearly every state in the U.S. and in several Canadian provinces. Task forces have recommended inclusion of the TSBC/SRIC system as part of regional state-of-the-art service/demonstration/training units in the public mental health system (Menninger & Hannah, in press) as well as implementation in the VA system (Errera, 1985). About 10% of state hospitals and several private hospitals and community centers have already indicated firm plans to adopt one or more treatment units as soon as the necessary implementation materials are available.

All of the interest in adoption of the TSBC/SRIC system has occurred with minimal direct dissemination efforts to date outside of one state. Rather, the majority of requests and adoption plans have come from increasing numbers of concerned "internal advocates" who learned of the work through the literature or at professional meetings, and from a few who received directives to "do something" because of excessive costs, litigation, or public outcries resulting from current practices. Perhaps the appearance of the TSBC/SRIC system is timely because various segments of society are becoming informed about the need to alter the current state of affairs in residential treatment settings so that major changes are more acceptable in principle. Pressures for accountability and cost efficiency from "fiscal conservatives" appear to be escalating in tandem with pressures for improved quality and effectiveness of operations from "social liberals," with the TSBC/SRIC system increasingly identified as a worthwhile vehicle to aid in accomplishing the objectives of those in both groups. In fact, the requests for assistance in implementation became so numerous that our clinical-research group had to stop giving workshops and actively *discourage* adoptions until the published materials are available to appropriately install the system without excessive consultation. If it can't be done properly, it shouldn't be done at all!

Desirable implementation procedures. The commonalities from the diffusion-of-innovations literature and direct experience with implementation of the TSBC/SRIC system point to desirable procedures for proper installation and maintenance, which are detailed elsewhere (Paul, in press b, in preparation d, e). For such fundamental changes in assessment and decision-making practices, considerable time, effort, and preplanning should be expended on the part of facilities in deciding whether to adopt or pilot-test the system in order to minimize the intangible costs of change and maximize the efficiency of implementation. Slow, careful, and systematic implementation should be carried out with sensitivity to the inevitable disruptions and concerns of staff occasioned by any major change in operations, with as much participatory planning and specification of structure as possible. The initial installation in any facility should be limited to two or three treatment units in order to "debug" procedures and pilot-test the overall assessment/decision-making enterprise in local circumstances. Additional treatment units in multiple-unit facilities and in networked single-unit facilities can be systematically added, one at a time, by expanding on the training base provided by the first implementing units.

For the initial installation, a "one-time blitz" implementation could be completed in about 3 months, concurrent with the installation of a treatment program, if a new facility and/or treatment unit were to be opened and all staff were available for planning and training without other ongoing responsibilities. More often, incremental implementations would be undertaken concurrent with continuing provision of clinical services. In the latter case, the initial installation in any facility would require 3 to 6 months of preparation time before data were available for use—the longer preparation being sufficient for the entire comprehensive assessment paradigm as well the TSBC/SRIC system as its core strategy. During this period, a number of mundane tasks must be accomplished, including establishment of an administrative structure; selection or development of job classifications and positions; selection, reallocation, and/or hiring of employees to perform new duties;

familiarization of all levels of personnel and employee organizations with purposes, procedures, and timelines, with continuing communications to maintain their understanding and support; adaptation of computer programs to local equipment and operating systems; preparation of new written policies and procedures; conversion of existing records on current clientele and staff with input to computer files; and identification of existing assessment and documentation practices to be replaced. The last task is critical to the efficiency and rationality of all operations; otherwise staff will continue to be overloaded with previous nonutilitarian practices so that new information would be an added burden rather than an aid in offsetting inefficient activities.

Although the preparatory activities for an initial installation encompass many tasks and require coordinated efforts, the absolute hours are relatively few compared to the more substantial amounts of staff time noted earlier for initial training. By the end of the initial preparatory period all levels of clinical, management, assessment, and support staff must be trained to criteria in the proper collection, monitoring, processing, and interpretation of data from the TSBC/SRIC system. After the initial preparatory period, an additional 3 to 6 months of declining-contact training and consultation would be required for on-unit and management staff to insure proper use of systems data in ongoing applications. Thus, the first unit of an initial installation would usually require 9 to 12 months from the start of the preparatory period before the TSBC/SRIC system was completely implemented. Starting data collection at the same time on two units of an initial installation but lagging clinical staff training on one unit by 3 to 6 months is desirable for efficiency of trainer time and to provide comparative data for evaluating the impact of the installation on the first unit. Since more of the preparatory tasks do not have to be repeated for units after the initial implementation, 6 months should be enough time for the incremental introduction of all procedures and practices of the entire comprehensive paradigm for the second unit of an initial installation and for each additional treatment unit operating under the same administrative auspices.

Net Relative Cost Compared to Current Practices

The current state of affairs in most residential treatment settings is so problematic that some would argue for change at any cost; however, given the constraints within which any treatment facility must operate, a rational decision whether or not to implement new procedures as different as those represented by the TSBC/SRIC system must consider

:he net relative cost in comparison to current operations. Precise esti-
nates can only be accomplished for specific treatment units and facili-
:ies with knowledge of existing staff competencies, physical plant, sup-
)ort services, documentation practices, and clientele to be served *and*
:horough familiarity with the assessment technology, its capabilities,
ind desirable implementation procedures. Although it would be sheer
'olly for me to attempt an estimation of the actual cost of implemen-
:ation of the TSBC/SRIC system, I have elsewhere provided a detailed
lescription of the direct, indirect, and offset cost elements and prospec-
:ive benefits, as well as the entire maximum potential utility assess-
nent paradigm compared to the existing uses of resources and out-
:omes in current practice (see Paul, 1986 b). A brief summary of these
inalyses may help to pinpoint the ways in which the net relative cost of
mplementing the new technology would be much less than continu-
ng the status quo for most residential treatment facilities.

*Offset of maintenance costs by increased efficiency and productiv-
ty.* Aside from the direct benefits expected from basing decisions on
nformation with maximum potential utility, most residential treat-
nent facilities in both the public and private sector could maintain the
:ntire integrated assessment paradigm without increasing marginal
:osts at all—that is, without an increase in the total dollars already
)eing spent on current practices. In general, the overhead and costs of
)ngoing materials, supplies, data-processing equipment, and support
)ersonnel required for maintenance of the new technology would be
nore than adequately handled by the budgetary allocations already de-
/oted to these purposes in the average facility nationwide. By replacing
1onutilitarian forms, computer reports, and data-processing practices
ind by integrating computer input with other duties of clerical and
1ight-shift staff, the ongoing requirements of the TSBC/SRIC system and
)ther assessment strategies of the recommended paradigm are not only
ow cost in absolute terms, but probably cheaper than those of most
:urrent practices. The major offsets, however, would come from the in-
:reased efficiency and productivity of staff. This is largely because the
:SBC/SRIC system staffing and computer summaries provide so much
:omparable and trustworthy information and documentation that real-
ocation of staff positions and increased efficiency and productivity,
:ompared to the way that staff currently spend their time in traditional
)rograms, would more than offset the ongoing direct and indirect costs.

In particular, the inefficient use of staff resources noted at the begin-
1ing of this chapter allows for "cost-free" increases in productive staff
ime. Such efficiencies are obtained by the elimination of unnecessary

paperwork, the reduction of time spent in personal pursuits, the reduction in unnecessarily frequent one-to-one information-gathering contacts, and reductions in the number and length of staff meetings, which are now occasioned by the need for verbal communication of information not available otherwise. The reduction or elimination of these inefficient uses of staff time allows more time to be spent actually providing clinical services, with some positions totally reallocated to observer slots. In fact, *only half* the efficiency previously found with the TSBC/SRIC system through reductions in staff time currently spent on documentation and personal pursuits, alone, would offset *all* continuing direct and indirect staffing costs without an increase in dollars spent in the average facility nationwide, and would produce sizable gains in additional functional time with clients for clinical staff as well. Based upon the most recent nationwide data, such minimal gains in efficiency for existing staff in the average facility would not only support the entire ongoing costs of the new assessment technology, but result in additional "cost-free" increases in staff time devoted to clients that would more than triple current rates in private facilities and quadruple to quintuple current rates in public facilities.

Recovery of start-up costs and continuing benefits through improved quality and effectiveness. There generally is no such thing as a "free lunch," and the front-end investment of a little money and a lot of staff time and effort constitute the price to be paid for the implementation of the TSBC/SRIC system. Since the increased efficiency and productivity of staff are expected to more than offset maintenance costs, an advantageous net relative cost of implementing the new assessment technology is dependent on recouping start-up costs by payoffs from using the obtained information (see also, Alkin & Solomon, 1983). The total direct front-end costs for accomplishing the desirable implementation procedures described earlier for the first two units in an initial installation—all materials, proportional salaries and benefits of all involved staff, and costs of consultants and/or technical support personnel—are estimated to be less than 3.7% and 1.2% of the units' annual budgets, respectively, in average public and private mental hospitals nationwide. The average total direct front-end costs for each added unit after the initial installation are estimated to be less than 1.7% of each unit's annual budget in public facilities and less than 0.8% in private facilities. Even these costs might be offset within budget periods by careful timing in many facilities.

The specific way of achieving economic benefits would obviously vary among facilities by the nature and quality of the overall systems of which they are a part and as a function of the funding mechanisms through which they are supported. Besides the gains noted above, a number of previously unfulfilled but promising clinical and management techniques (e.g., Management by Objectives, Problem Oriented Records) and computerized management information systems (see Hedlund, et al., 1985) can become true decision-support systems by incorporating the new information. However, procedures must be done differently on the basis of the information provided in order to improve practices; no facility should put forth the effort to implement the TSBC/SRIC system, or any other similar innovation, without a proactive focus on maximizing the quality of operations and effectiveness of treatment as the basis for action.

The tangible direct benefits resulting from such proactive decisions based upon the information provided by the new assessment technology would easily recoup the front-end expenditures of implementation in the average residential facility and result in continuing tangible and intangible benefits as well. Recovery of start-up costs and other early benefits could be seen within a fiscal year in many programs with the anticipated savings already documented from the ability of the TSBC/SRIC system to allow precise chemotherapy or increased effectiveness of treatment for long-stay clientele alone. The dollars saved by the increased precision of placement and disposition decisions and the assurance of optimal therapeutic settings with appropriate lengths-of-stay could repay implementation costs in geometric proportions within one to two fiscal years, given the 70% to 86% readmission rates in various facilities and the more than 70% of clientele who are kept for too long or too short a time in any particular facility. Continuing increases in precision and benefits would be expected over time as local norms were developed.

Many additional continuing benefits with long-term payoffs are anticipated as service operations approach the status of an applied science. These include the integration of research and services and the consequent attraction and retention of quality personnel, funding, and added improvements in operating practices. The insurance of legal, ethical, and human operations by the data provided would improve satisfaction and morale, reduce staff turnover, prevent outrageous practices, and avoid litigation. Of course, the avoidance of one malpractice, wrongful-injury, or class-action suit could save enough money to pay for the installation of the TSBC/SRIC system in every unit of every facility of an entire state or corporate organization. Strategic advantages in private facilities would be expected to attract an increased share of the market with consequent increased use of capacity and reductions in per person operating costs. Even greater long-range benefits could be expected in public mental health systems; the increased quality and cost-effectiveness of residential services should allow resources now devoted to ineffective residential settings to be gradually redirected to improve community programs for the ultimate betterment of the entire service system.

Adoption versus Adaptation

The above presentation has focused on the implementation of the full TSBC/SRIC system as the core of comprehensive assessment operations in residential treatment facilities. Given the regularity with which proposals to make "little changes" are received from cost-conscious administrators and/or researchers who are not completely familiar with the system and its capabilities, a few comments are required regarding "adoption" of the system in toto—exactly as it has been developed and tested—versus "adaptation," with various large or small changes.

Limited application of component instruments for other purposes. The individual TSBC or SRIC instruments could, of course, be used for specific, limited research purposes with experimental variations in the type of observer, in the sampling schedule for obtaining observations, or even in the targets or medium to be observed (see Mariotto, 1979). The use of the TSBC and/or SRIC in this way may, in fact, have a wide range of research applications, particularly in providing precision data for the behavioral side of various studies of drug/behavior, brain/behavior, environment/behavior, and behavior/behavior relationships. Similarly, a limited number of additional categories or codes might be added to each instrument and tested to determine if observers could maintain replicability, or "new" higher-order scores might be derived by unique combinations of individual codes for a specific purpose. Even in these limited and explicitly experimental adaptations of the instruments, however, neither the existing category and code definitions nor the components of standard higher-order scores should be changed at all. Neither should the training procedures nor criterion required of observers be changed unless the observers are the subject of study and the data are not intended for other uses. In addition to being a violation of copyright, any change in the latter set of paramaters completely destroys the meaningfulness of the supporting validity evidence for the instruments.

Some limited rather than ongoing use of TSBC/SRIC data could be considered to aid operational decisions in residential or day-care treatment settings and mental health systems. For example, Kohen and Paul (1976) described how a regionally based team of traveling observers could collect weekly data for samples of clientele and staff every other month from a large number of community residential facilities or other treatment units to provide information solely for program evaluation, incentive funding, and regulatory purposes. This application was projected to be quite cost effective and to provide an improved basis for upgrading treatment programs and placement decisions. However, beyond such limited use or use for specific research studies, the TSBC/SRIC system should not automatically be considered as the best assessment approach for any isolated purpose (see Paul, 1986c; Paul et al., 1986b). In fact, the system generally would not be a cost-effective assessment approach for any "one-time" decision, even though the data quality might be the best that is available.

Complete adoption without modification for ongoing implementation. There are circumstances in which the TSBC/SRIC system should not even be considered for ongoing implementation in residential treatment facilities. These include situations in which (a) decision makers are only seeking data for *pro forma* compliance with external regulations and do not intend to base actions and operations on the information obtained and (b) anything less than complete adoption of the total system as it has been developed and tested could not or would not be implemented. In the first circumstance, the implementation would not be cost effective and the decision makers would either be embarrassed or tempted to behave unethically by suppressing data. In the second circumstance, the implementation is unlikely to be cost effective and, more importantly, the information obtained would have unknown utility.

Once the TSBC/SRIC system is properly installed and running with all components as originally developed and tested, information from other sources could be added to computer reports, variations in report formats could be developed and evaluated, sampling variations in report formats could be developed and evaluated, sampling variations for specific units or locations could be compared to the standard schedule, and other potential improvements in processes and procedures could be explicitly tested. However, no modifications of the instruments, sampling schedules, levels and time commitments of personnel, or competency criteria for completion of training and ongoing performance should even be a "glimmer in the mind's eye" in making adoption decisions. The cost-effectiveness of the TSBC/SRIC system is in large part due to the range of application of the total set of quality data provided. Its relative-cost advantages, as well as all of the replicability, representativeness, and validity evidence obtained over 17 years of R & D work, cannot be transferred to other applications that do not maintain the conceptual relevance, strength, and integrity of procedures as developed and tested (see Paul, 1985 a). The introduction of objective data as a basis for decision-making in human service bureaucracies of any sort is a difficult, even revolutionary undertaking. However, the human and financial costs of perpetuation of the status quo seem sufficiently great in the area of residential treatment that we should avoid diluting effective science-based procedures to fit existing practices. Rather, science-based procedures should provide the basis for changing existing practices in rational ways that may improve long-range effectiveness and efficiency, even if it takes a few years and a lot of work.

CONCLUSION

Although this chapter attempted to cover far more ground than is warranted by the space available—for either clear communication on the part of the writer or ease of understanding on the part of the reader— my goals will have been satisfied if a few major messages come through: (a) The populations and programs served by residential treatment settings are among the most important of those for whom behavioral science should be seeking answers and for whom professional psychology should be providing effective services. (b) The current state of affairs in most residential services is woefully inadequate in fulfilling what should be their primary goal of providing effective and cost-efficient treatment to the most severely mentally disabled. (c) The current state of affairs need not remain that of the future, but a comprehensive, decision-focused, objective assessment technology is a prerequisite to bringing about positive and enduring change. (d) The operation of residential treatment facilities, although complex, can be understood within the framework of a relatively limited set of decision problems, which need trustworthy and comparable information for rational actions. (e) The classes of variables on which such information is needed fall within the client and staff domains and are the same for rational decisions at multiple levels of operation for clinical and management purposes and for scientific research. (f) The replicability, representativeness, relevance, and relative cost of obtained data provide a reasonable means for determining the potential utility of approaches to formal assessment, and the cost of *not* having data with maximum potential utility on which to base operations is much greater. (g) Nontraditional approaches to assessment in residential treatment settings—continuous direct observational coding (DOC) systems that target the ongoing actions and interactions of clients and staff in the treatment environment—are the best for providing the majority of the most important facts to support rational decision-making. (h) The Computerized TSBC/SRIC Planned-Access Observational Information System has sufficient promise as a core assessment system for supporting rational operations to seek out, study, and evaluate the more extensive materials detailing the nature and cost-effectiveness of the system, its components, and the related utility evidence.

I should also note in closing that the TSBC/SRIC system stands independently as a generalizable assessment system for the full range of adult populations in residential treatment facilities and is *not* tied to any particular treatment approach beyond the acceptance of empirical findings; however, the detailed information from that system is needed to properly implement a comprehensive social-learning program of treatment, which has been documented to be exceptionally effective and more than three times as cost efficient as traditional practices with the most severely disabled chronically institutionalized clientele (Paul & Lentz, 1977, in press). My colleagues and I obviously have considerable investment in the TSBC/SRIC system, having toiled on it for many years. Nevertheless, we are optimistic not only that it offers promise of placing decisions in and about residential treatment services on a rational, cost-effective basis, but that it provides a vehicle for service operations to approach the status of an applied science—an applied science in which effective treatment technologies become the rule for all populations rather than the exception.

NOTE

The work on the TSBC/SRIC system reported in this chapter was supported in part by Public Health Service grants MH-15553 and MH-25464 from the National Institute of Mental Health and by grants from the Illinois Department of Mental Health and Developmental Disabilities, the Joyce Foundation, the MacArthur Foundation, the Owsley Foundation, the Cullen Foundation, and the University of Houston, University Park, Center for Public Policy. The technology has been developed, tested, and implemented, and is being prepared for widespread dissemination, with the continuing collaboration of Mark H. Licht and Marco J. Mariotto and several years' work by Christopher T. Power, Ilena

Shelite, Kathryn L. Engel, and Joel P. Redfield. A host of observers, clinical staff, research assistants, and administrative decision makers from unit directors through the top levels of state mental health systems have contributed to the technology, helping to ensure its utility, practicality, and cost-effectiveness.

REFERENCES

Alkin, M. C., & Solomon, L. C. (Eds). (1983). *The costs of evaluation.* Beverly Hills, Calif.: Sage.

Cronbach, L. J., & Gleser, G. C. (1965). *Psychological tests and personnel decisions* (2nd ed.). Urbana: University of Illinois Press.

Cronbach, L. J., Gleser, G. C., Nanda, H., & Rajaratnam, N. (1972). *The dependability of behavioral measurements: Theory of generalizability for scores and profiles.* New York: Wiley.

Engel, K. L. & Paul, G. L. (1979). Systems use to objectivity program evaluation, clinical, and management decisions. *Journal of Behavioral Assessment, 1*, 221–238.

Engel, K. L., & Paul, G. L. (1981). Staff performance: Do attitudinal "effectiveness profiles" really assess it? *Journal of Nervous & Mental Disease, 169*, 529–540.

Errera, P. (1985). Personal communication. New Haven, Conn.: Veterans Administration Medical Center.

Fiske, D. W. (1978). *Strategies for personality research.* San Francisco: Jossey-Bass.

Fiske, D. W. (1979). A demonstration of the value of interchangeable observers. *Journal of Behavioral Assessment, 1*, 251–258.

Fiske, D. W. (1985). Personal communication. University of Chicago.

Glaser, E. M., Abelson, H. H., & Garrison, K. N. (1983). *Putting knowledge to use.* San Francisco: Jossey-Bass.

Hartmann, D. P. (Ed.). (1982). *New directions for methodology of social and behavioral science: Using observers to study behavior* (No. 14). San Francisco: Jossey-Bass.

Hedlund, J. L., Vieweg, B. W., & Cho, D. W. (1985). Mental health computing in the 1980s: I. General information systems and clinical documentation. *Computers in Human Services, 1*, 2–33.

HIRI/NIMH (Human Interaction Research Institute/National Institute of Mental Health). (1976). *Putting knowledge to use.* Rockville, Md.: NIMH.

Kohen, W., & Paul, G. L. (1976). Current trends and recommended changes in extended-care placement of mental patients: The Illinois system as a case in point. *Schizophrenia Bulletin, 2*, 575–594.

Liberman, R. P., & Phipps, C. C. (in press). Innovative treatment and rehabilitation techniques for the chronically mentally ill. In W. W. Menninger &

G. T. Hannah (Eds.), *The chronic mental patient II.* Washington, D.C.: American Psychiatric Press.

Licht, M. H. (1979). The Staff-Resident Interaction Chronograph: Observational assessment of staff performance. *Journal of Behavioral Assessment, 1,* 185–198.

Licht, M. H. (1984). Assessment of client functioning in residential settings. In M. Mirabi (Ed.), *The chronically mentally ill: Research and services.* New York: SP Medical & Scientific Books.

Licht, M. H., Paul, G. L., Power, C. T., & Engel, K. L. (1980). The comparative effectiveness of two modes of observer training on the Staff-Resident Interaction Chronograph. *Journal of Behavioral Assessment, 2,* 175–205.

Mariotto, M. J. (1979). Observational assessment systems use in basic and applied research. *Journal of Behavioral Assessment, 1,* 239–250.

Mariotto, M. J., & Paul, G. L. (1984). The utility of assessment for different purposes. In M. Mirabi (Ed.), *The chronically mentally ill: Research and services.* New York: SP Medical & Scientific Books.

Menninger, W. W., & Hannah, G. T. (Eds.). (in press). *The chronic mental patient II.* Washington, D.C.: American Psychiatric Press.

Paul, G. L. (1969). Behavior modification research: Design and tactics. In C. M. Franks (Ed.), *Behavior therapy: Appraisal and status.* New York: McGraw-Hill.

Paul, G. L. (1978). The implementation of effective treatment programs for chronic mental patients: Obstacles and recommendations. In J. H. Talbott (Ed.), *The chronic mental patient.* Washington, D.C.: American Psychiatric Association.

Paul, G. L. (Ed.). (1979). New assessment systems for residential treatment, management, research, and evaluation. *Journal of Behavioral Assessment, 1* (Whole No. 3).

Paul, G. L. (1980). Comprehensive psychosocial treatment: Beyond traditional psychotherapy. In J. S. Strauss, M. Bowers, T. W. Downey, S. Fleck, S. Jackson, & I. Levine (Eds.), *Psychotherapy of schizophrenia.* New York: Plenum.

Paul, G. L. (1981). Social competence and the institutionalized mental patient. In J. D. Wine & M. D. Smye (Eds.), *Social competence.* New York: Guilford.

Paul, G. L. (1984). Residential treatment programs and aftercare for the chronically institutionalized. In M. Mirabi (Ed.), *The chronically mentally ill: Research and services.* New York: SP Medical & Scientific Books.

Paul, G. L. (1985a). Can pregnancy be a placebo effect? Terminology, designs, and conclusions in the study of psychosocial and pharmacological treatments of behavioral disorders. In L. White, B. Tursky, & G. F. Schwartz (Eds.), *Placebo: Theory, research, and mechanisms.* New York: Guilford.

Paul, G. L. (1985b). The impact of public policy and decision making on the dissemination of science-based practices in mental institutions: Playing poker with everything wild. In R. A. Kasschau, L. Rehm, & L. P. Ullmann

(Eds.), *Psychological research, public policy and practice: Towards a productive partnership*. New York: Praeger.

Paul, G. L. (Ed.), (1986a). *Principles and methods to support cost-effective quality operations: Assessment in residential treatment settings*, (Part 1). Champaign, Ill.: Research Press.

Paul, G. L. (1986b). Net relative cost of the maximum potential utility paradigm. In G. L. Paul (Ed.), *Assessment in residential treatment settings* (Part 1). Champaign, Ill.: Research Press.

Paul, G. L. (1986c). The nature of DOC and QICS encoding devices. In G. L. Paul (Ed.), *Assessment in residential treatment settings* (Part 1). Champaign, Ill.: Research Press.

Paul, G. L. (Ed.). (in press a). *Observational assessment instrumentation for service and research: Assessment in residential treatment settings* (Parts 2–5). Champaign, Ill.: Research Press.

Paul, G. L. (Ed.). (in press b). *Observational assessment instrumentation for service and research—The Time-Sample Behavioral Checklist: Assessment in residential treatment settings* (Part 2). Champaign, Ill.: Research Press.

Paul, G. L. (Ed.). (in press c). *Observational assessment instrumentation for service and research—The Staff-Resident Interaction Chronograph: Assessment in residential treatment settings* (Part 3). Champaign, Ill.: Research Press.

Paul, G. L. (Ed.). (in press d). *Observational assessment instrumentation for service and research—The Computerized TSBC/SRIC Planned-Access Observational Information System: Assessment in residential treatment settings* (Part 4). Champaign, Ill.: Research Press.

Paul, G. L. (Ed.). (in press e). *Observational assessment instrumentation for service and research—The TSBC/SRIC System implementation package: Assessment in residential treatment settings* (Part 5). Champaign, Ill.: Research Press.

Paul, G. L., & Lentz, R. J. (1977). *Psychosocial treatment of chronic mental patients: Milieu versus social-learning programs*. Cambridge, Mass.: Harvard University Press.

Paul, G. L., & Lentz, R. J. (in press). *Psychosocial treatment of chronic mental patients* (2nd ed.). Champaign, Ill.: Research Press.

Paul, G. L., & Mariotto, M. J. (1986). Potential utility of the sources and methods: A comprehensive paradigm. In G. L. Paul (Ed.), *Assessment in residential treatment settings* (Part 1). Champaign, Ill.: Research Press.

Paul, G. L., Mariotto, M. J., & Redfield, J. P. (1986 a). Assessment purposes, domains, and utility for decision making. In G. L. Paul (Ed.), *Assessment in residential treatment settings* (Part 1). Champaign, Ill.: Research Press.

Paul, G. L., Mariotto, M. J., & Redfield, J. P. (1986b). Sources and methods for gathering information in formal assessment. In G. L. Paul (Ed.), *Assessment in residential treatment settings* (Part 1). Champaign, Ill.: Research Press.

Paul, G. L., & Shelite, I. (in press). The Clinical Frequency Recording System: Social-learning forms. Supplement to G. L. Paul & R. J. Lentz, *Psychosocial treatment of chronic mental patients* (2nd ed.). Champaign, Ill.: Research Press.

Peterson, D. R. (1968). *The clinical study of social behavior.* New York: Appleton-Century-Crofts.

Power, C. T. (1979). The Time-Sample Behavioral Checklist: Observational assessment of patient functioning. *Journal of Behavioral Assessment, 1,* 199–210.

Power, C. T. (1984). Assessment of staff and programs in residential treatment settings. In M. Mirabi (Ed.), *The chronically mentally ill: Research and services.* New York: SP Medical & Scientific Books.

Power, C. T., Paul, G. L., Licht, M. H., & Engel, K. L. (1982). Evaluation of self-contained training procedures for the Time-Sample Behavioral Checklist. *Journal of Behavioral Assessment, 4,* 223–261.

Redfield, J. P. (1979). Clinical Frequencies Recording Systems: Standardizing staff observations by event recording. *Journal of Behavioral Assessment, 1,* 211–219.

Rhoades, L. J. (1981). *Treating and assessing the chronically mentally ill: The pioneering research of Gordon L. Paul.* DHHS Publication No. (ADM) 81–1100. Rockville, Md.: NIMH.

Rogers, E. M. (1983). *The diffusion of innovations* (3rd ed.). New York: Free Press.

Saper, B. (1975). Requiescat for the state hospital? *Journal of Clinical Psychology, 31,* 223–235.

Stein, L. I., & Test, M. A. (Eds.). (1985). *New directions for mental health services: Training in the community living-model—a decade of experience* (No. 26). San Francisco: Jossey-Bass.

Stolz, S. B. (1981). Adoption of innovations from applied behavioral research: "Does anybody care?" *Journal of Applied Behavioral Analysis, 14,* 491–505.

Tornatzky, L. G., Fergus, E. O., Avellar, J. W., Fairweather, G. W., & Fleischer, M. (1980). *Innovation and social process.* New York: Pergamon.

Ullmann, L. P. (1967). *Institution and outcome: A comparative study of psychiatric hospitals.* New York: Pergamon.

Weinstein, A. S. (1975). Evaluation through medical records and related information systems. In E. L. Struening & M. Guttentag (Eds.), *Handbook of evaluation research.* Beverly Hills, Calif.: Sage.

Wiggins, J. S. (1973). *Personality and prediction: Principles of personality assessment.* Reading, Mass.: Addison-Wesley.

Winett, R. A. (1985). *Information and behavior: Systems of influence.* Hillsdale, N.J.: Erlbaum.

Assessment's Contribution to Social Revolution: Comments of a Consumer on the Residential Assessment Methodology of Gordon Paul and Colleagues

HARVEY J. LIEBERMAN

Psychological assessment techniques are among the most prominent products of psychology. As such, they must be judged in terms of their improved efficacy over previous assessment procedures, sophistication in comparison to other current technology, and marketability. The Time-Sample Behavioral Checklist/Staff-Resident Interaction Chronograph (TSBC/SRIC) system developed by Paul and his colleagues meets the technical requirements of these criteria head on. The documentation for the assessment package indicates that its methodology provides data so relevant and reliable that it can serve as an important element in high-risk decision-making. What is being offered to a consumer population of mental health professionals is a highly formatted system for assessing residential treatment environments. It is also a controversial work with broad social and political, as well as clinical and administrative, implications. With courage in his heart and revolution on his mind, Paul trailblazes the development of highly tailored, control-oriented psychological products that offer the potential for monitoring behavior in many settings. In their most limited interpretation, his methods are only designed to assess behavioral events in a specific class of environments. However, the methodology also provides general direction for weighing, selecting, and refining treatment milieu parameters in a manner that encourages application to other environmental settings. If there is any limit in Paul's approach to this project, it is that the necessary high technology is not yet available to achieve what must be the logical ultimate extension of a project of this type: complete, unobtrusive, automatic environmental monitoring. Only round-the-clock holographic scanning of all environmental events with direct data entry and analysis by computer could suffice for such a purpose.

Although the conceptual boldness and technical aesthetics of the TSBC/SRIC system are truly noteworthy, many issues about implementation remain open awaiting specific data. These issues concern user friendliness, organizational impact, and flexibility. Since Paul's presentation carries a promotional tone regarding system efficacy with high quality data, it must be treated in part as a sophisticated marketing prospectus as much as a scientific document. This requires a different attitude from a reviewer than that needed for the appraisal of typical psychological instruments. Some of my comments will therefore resemble test reviews in the *Mental Measurements Yearbook* (Buros, 1978), but others will resemble evaluative questions seen in popular consumers' electronic equipment magazines. My technical comments will be limited to a summary of the assessment package's potential benefits and to a guide for evaluating future information that will soon be made available. The overall intent of this review is to help mental health professionals engaged in some aspect of residential treatment operations determine if this potent new technology can be applied to their needs.

DOES THE TSBC/SRIC SYSTEM HERALD
A NEW ERA FOR PSYCHOLOGY?

When a psychologist of Gordon Paul's stature enters the market-place with bold claims, it signals an important event in the development of psychological products. Psychologists have provided assessment systems to commercial, industrial, educational, governmental, and clinical settings for many decades. Except for those few who have gone beyond the ethical boundaries of the profession, however, formal statements of efficacy for psychological techniques and products have been weak and filled with cautionary statements. For the first time, it appears that theoretically grounded psychological research may have led to the development of a sufficiently reliable and relevant technique to be respected by the public for its documented utility alone, without resorting to fakery or misleading sales techniques of any kind. This has been accomplished by bringing together concepts and approaches from many psychological specialties including the behavioral treatment, behavioral assessment, organizational, clinical, and quantitative methods sectors of the field. Along with Paul's talent and persistence, this combination is made possible by the data-processing capacities of computers with specially designed software.

If the TSBC/SRIC system lives up to its creators' expectations, it will mark an important new direction for reaffirming the role of psychology in our society. Few who follow the multidisciplinary scientific journals or federal funding allocations can fail to notice the relatively scant attention given to the psychological sciences. Despite widespread cultural and individual interest in psychology in terms of human self-understanding, it is generally regarded as yielding a low-potency technology that offers erratically delivered benefits with dubious effects compared to techniques derived from the biological and physical sciences.

The ability to control significant phenomena reliably in any technical area is closely tied to the availability of accurate and rapid assessment methodologies. The TSBC/SRIC system's power to analyze complex behavioral and interactive events, both microscopically and macroscopically, in a comparatively short time after they occur, permits the examination of data that exceed any individual's natural abilities of assimilation and organization. This development may be analogous to the galvanometer or cloud chamber in physics as methods for detecting hypothesized events beyond human sensory capacity. The technical gain may be a difference in kind, not merely a difference in degree. The hope for the TSBC/SRIC system is that it will permit a quantum improvement in assessment methodology, with the resulting capacity for dramatic progress in residential treatment.

GENERAL EVALUATION FRAMEWORK FOR RESIDENTIAL ASSESSMENT SYSTEMS

In order to discuss the features of the TSBC/SRIC system in an organized manner, a framework is needed in which to analyze its many facets. Below is a general evaluation format for investigating the organizational, clinical, administrative, and assessment tool test design characteristics relevant to any residential assessment methodology. Specific standards, methods, and further areas of exploration are delineated in question form for many of the factors. This model of analysis by inquiry is not exhaustive, but rather is heuristic in intent. As can be seen from the presentation below, administrative factors are strongly emphasized in the outline. This is appropriate, since most of the concerns about the package may be broadly construed as administrative in nature.

Clinical Factors

Adequacy of clinical content. Are relevant areas of concern assessed? Does the assessment tool consider verbal, behavioral, interactional, and environmental information from all patients and staff?

Adequacy of assessment frequency. Does assessment sampling take place frequently enough to give an accurate picture of all environmental events?

Presentation of data. Are data presented in a readily interpretable manner that allows focus on individual, group, and environmental activity in variable time sequences as well as for specific instances?

Meaningfulness of data. Do data make sense? Can data be used to differentiate clinical syndromes and identify subtle intervention effects? Can data predict future patterns of behavior?

Treatment effects. What effects does the assessment package have on treatment? Do the data stimulate new treatment approaches? Is clinical research facilitated by the assessment system?

Assessment Tool Factors

Validity and reliability of observations. Is it easy to obtain and maintain near-perfect rater agreement among trained raters? By traditional psychological test standards, how high are test validity indicators?

Usefulness of norms. Are the norms composed of sufficiently large and representative samples of patients and facilities?

Presence of observers. Do assessment procedures alter reported events?

Response sets. Are assessment procedures oriented to producing particular types of responses?

Recording observations. How quickly and accurately can data be processed and summarized in useful forms?

Administrative Factors

Assessment system implementation. In regard to system installation, how easy is it to purchase the assessment package and obtain timely delivery? Is necessary office space available? How much initial staff training is necessary? Must new staff be hired? How much lead time is required before operations can become routine? Are necessary new operational skills easily acquired?

In regard to system maintenance, how frequently do system break-downs occur? At what rate does system deterioration occur? Is there a routine maintenance schedule? What type of system monitoring is required and by whom? What are the consequences of system failure? Are system failures easily corrected? How frequently are outside consultants needed? Is it easy to maintain system supplies? Is ongoing staff training necessary?

In regard to cost, how expensive is system installation? How expensive is system maintenance? How easy is it to fund the system? How much does equipment cost? How much do maintenance supplies cost? Are there special training or consultant fees at different stages? What are installation and maintenance staff expenses? In what areas can money be saved as a result of operations, in regard to staff, patient, or administrative costs?

User friendliness. Is working with the assessment system considered a good job by employees? Are system procedures simple but interesting? Is it easy to put data in the system and take information out? Does system use involve any extraordinary environmental conditions or user characteristics?

Organizational impact. How threatened are staff by the use of the assessment package? Are union problems likely? Will staff reassignments or unemployment result as a consequence of the assessment system? Will the system make staff feel more effective? Will the system require staff to interact in different ways? Will the system require changes in organizational structure? How will patients react to use of the system? How much organizational energy is required to maintain the system? Will organizational attitudes change? Will organizational planning processes change? Within a state's system, how will different organizational factors be altered on a central, regional, and local administrative level? Within a facility, how will administrative, support, clinical, supervisory, and line staff perceive system implementation?

Goal Orientation. What are the administrative implications of the assessment package's effects on clinical treatment? What are the administrative consequences of potential new clinical interventions? What does it mean for management to monitor current clinical routines in a different fashion? From the administrative point of view, is it easier to promote good research with the TSBC/SRIC system? How does the system affect costs for staffing and other-than-personnel costs? With the system, does management have more accurate, meaningful knowledge of their programs? Can programs be better administered in specific areas? How are management goals altered by the assessment package at central, regional, and local levels within a state? Does the system help facilities meet accreditation standards more readily? Is paper work time decreased? Can patient flow through residential programs be more meaningfully integrated and monitored?

EVALUATION SUMMARY FOR THE TSBC/SRIC SYSTEM

An overview of Paul's material in light of the evaluation format indicates that there are many outstanding issues for which the wise consumer will seek answers before making any decisions regarding the utilization of the TSBC/SRIC system or any similar system. Some of the issues are addressed in the works Paul and his colleagues published in 1986. Other issues are likely to be addressed in forthcoming volumes. Until complete statements are available, however, it is important to emphasize that the assessment package requires a significant investment of organizational resources and is designed to alter standard organizational operating procedures in a manner that may have unforeseen consequences. For these reasons, care must be exercised before adopting the assessment system. Design excellence of the assessment package's clinical and assessment tool components is required for superior technical quality of the system. Success with administrative factor design elements is necessary for practical application.

Clinical Factor Evaluation

The TSBC/SRIC system appears to assess readily observable events of clinical concern with impressive thoroughness and frequency. The TSBC checklist allows designation of both healthy and "crazy" behaviors in most conceivable residential locations. Similarly, the SRIC offers a useful range of alternatives for classifying interactional possibilities. In the unlikely but possible circumstance that a facility has some idiosyncratic assessment need, customization of the TSBC/SRIC system appears limited. Extremely valuable data relevant to individual behaviors, behavior patterns, and behavior sequences can be clearly presented using the TSBC/SRIC system. Most clinicians, including Paul and his colleagues, would judge the TSBC/SRIC system data alone as lacking enough content detail to substitute wholly for clinically detailed chart progress notes or to lead to a definitive diagnostic statement. Paul's pre-

sentation notes that additional assessment strategies are explicitly recommended to cover such content as part of a comprehensive paradigm
employing the TSBC/SRIC system as the core strategy. Alternately, some
behaviorally oriented professionals who place little value on traditional diagnosis may find that the system produces most of the data
they consider meaningful.

Use of the TSBC/SRIC system can be justified solely by its prime
clinical strength, which lies in the area of clinical management and
monitoring. For the frequently encountered patient who is a poor verbal informant, the assessment system can provide the main source of
data for treatment planning. In other circumstances where reliable patient self-report information is available, the TSBC/SRIC system can
offer corroborative data.

Most important, it would be hard to imagine the smooth implementation of the assessment package as not having a strong, positive effect
on treatment outcome. For the first time, staff could routinely and accurately determine the effects of instituting a new treatment approach
for an individual patient or an environment-wide intervention. The assessment system may not only bring heightened staff confidence along
with improved treatment but also deepen staff humility as the limitations of their current therapeutic repertoire or the resistant nature of
certain patient clinical groups are pinpointed. Finally, clinical research
may become a more appealing endeavor as rapid and accurate TSBC/SRIC
information feedback is made available for experimental efforts.

Assessment Tool Factors Evaluation

This area is one of great strength for the TSBC/SRIC system. The impressive, almost astonishing interrater reliabilities, the face, content,
and concurrent validities, and the efficiency of data recording appear to
be outstanding for both the TSBC and SRIC components and far exceed
any other available instruments for their respective purposes. As to
effects of observer presence on residential events, Paul reports that assessors blend in smoothly with the milieu. It will be interesting to see
staff- and patient-attitude data available from actual operating assessment systems to corroborate this claim. Data summary reports are a
highlight of the TSBC/SRIC system. Special computer programs prepare
reports in a readily usable format. The possibility of interpreting data
in reference to norms based on other facilities offers a unique contribution, but benefits are moot at this time until the forthcoming volumes
allow direct evaluation. Unless a consumer, desiring to interpret data

from a local facility, is closely familiar with the operational parameters of the facilities on which norms were based, data interpretation may be risky. The recommended generation of regional norms and facility norms, which are easy to establish with the assessment package, would generally be a more useful approach for interpreting daily assessment operations.

Administrative Factors Evaluation

The TSBC/SRIC system's success in dealing with administrative factors is likely to be the crucial determinant of its acceptance by residential treatment providers. Although no one should expect Paul's relatively brief statement in this volume to answer all the administrative questions I have raised, his presentation should highlight the implications of these types of concerns. As he notes, implementing the system requires "fundamental changes in assessment and decision-making practices" for which "considerable time, effort, and preplanning should be expended" to minimize the "inevitable disruptions and concerns of staff occasioned by any major change." This is certainly the experience of many administrators (Duffy & Assad, 1980). Indeed, the organizational consequences of implementation of the assessment system must be viewed as having potentially strong enough consequences, positive or negative, to resonate through whole treatment systems rather than just the assessment process itself. That is its danger, but also its virtue.

Any attempt to install the assessment system in a facility must be considered a major institutional commitment requiring high energy persistently applied. The system offers valuable benefits at each hierarchical administrative and clinical level within facility or statewide treatment systems. However, the same procedure a regional administrator might regard highly may be perceived by a facility administrator or line staff clinician as a potential threat by way of reduced autonomy for local decision makers. More information does not always lead to more rational systems management. In some cases, a centrally initiated system may merely lead to stronger central control over local operations (Champion, 1975; Tricker & Boland, 1982).

Strong incentive for use of the TSBC/SRIC system may come from the favorable response it is likely to receive from residential accrediting agencies such as the Joint Commission on the Accreditation of Hospitals or the Health Care Finance Administration. The data produced by the assessment strategy allows for the formulation of the clearly stated clinical and administrative objectives and plans that are sought by these agencies but rarely found with the clarity and completeness offered by the TSBC/SRIC system. Similarly, hospitals will have at their disposal, for internal use, a quality assurance tool of unusual scope and relevance. A rare opportunity would be provided to study the relationships between a program's treatment effectiveness, discharge policies, and patient flow, all with minimal effort.

Regarding issues of system installation and ease of maintenance, the information Paul presents in this volume is an insufficient basis on which to draw firm conclusions. Initial monetary costs of system implementation are high but not prohibitive. Secondary costs may arise from staff inefficiency if the supporting computer system is improperly installed. In this regard, it would be helpful to have access to system breakdown rates and system repair costs. Finally, as with any new product, a warranty and strong service system offering close support in case of operations dysfunction would be a very valuable adjunct to the assessment package and would enhance consumer confidence in the product.

RECOMMENDATIONS FOR THE POTENTIAL CONSUMER

To sum up the possibilities for the TSBC/SRIC system based on the consumer-oriented analysis presented in this paper, it must be said that the assessment package is aimed at the highest abstract standards. By the ideal standards of modern electronic technology, it may fall short, but by any measure of practical expectation in human psychology, the work of Paul and his collaborators is extraordinary, revolutionary, and deserves great recognition. If the TSBC/SRIC system realizes its full potential, its impact on assessment and mental health services should be far greater than any single assessment procedure known so far.

The TSBC/SRIC system promises to bring the same excitement to residential operations that the newly invented electron microscope brought to the biology laboratory. As with the purchase of any radically different, complex new instrument, a cost/benefit analysis should be conducted before deciding to buy it. Any agency seriously considering implementation of the assessment package would be well served by the creation of a task force composed of staff from various levels within the organizational hierarchy. The task force's responsibilities should include:

1. Conducting a formal analysis of agency operations in relation to variables assessed by the TSBC/SRIC system
2. Becoming familiar with the forthcoming assessment volumes

3. Visiting at least two well-selected programs where the assessment package has been implemented

4. Customizing the list of evaluative questions presented in this commentary to the anticipated agency setting

5. Obtaining definitive answers for each evaluative question

6. Making recommendations to the agency's senior management with strong emphasis on administrative factors

As they process the task force's recommendations, agency decision makers should keep in mind the following sentiments. Overall, the TSBC/SRIC system is a significant step toward the ultimate development of an electronic behavioral monitoring and assessment system. It is a landmark innovation, which could yield many of the currently extrapolated social benefits and raise many of the social issues that have been speculatively linked to gains in behavioral monitoring and control. Within the next few years, I expect to see widespread experimental application of this technique in clinical settings. In fact, I look forward to initiating an implementation feasibility study for my own program.

REFERENCES

Buros, O. K. (1978). *The eighth mental measurements yearbook* (Vol. 2). Highland Park, N.J.: Gryphon Press.

Champion, D. J. (1975). *The sociology of organizations.* New York: McGraw-Hill.

Duffy, N. M., & Assad, M. G. (1980). *Information management: An executive approach.* Cape Town: Oxford University Press.

Tricker, R. I., & Boland, R. (1982). *Management information and control systems* (2nd ed.). New York: Wiley.

Chapter 6

Assessment for Decision in a Correctional Setting

RAYMOND D. FOWLER

Most states have prisons that are crowded, underfunded, poorly managed, and minimally staffed. Alabama prisons are only slightly worse than most.

In January, 1976, Judge Frank M. Johnson, Jr., Chief Judge of the U.S. Middle District Court of Alabama, declaring that the living conditions in Alabama prisons constitute cruel and unusual punishment in violation of the Eighth Amendment to the U.S. Constitution, ordered sweeping changes and reforms in Alabama's prisons. Judge Johnson based his decisions on several days of testimony and over 1,200 stipulations in which attorneys for the state acknowledgd improper treatment of inmates. He ruled that the prisons were characterized by rampant violence and a jungle atmosphere and by overcrowding, understaffing, and inadequate facilities. He further ruled that two of the four major institutions were wholly unfit for human habitation, that robbery, rape, extortion, theft, and assault were everyday occurrences, and that there were gross inadequacies in medical care.

From July to December, 1976, faculty members and students of the University of Alabama Department of Psychology were centrally involved in a massive federal-court-ordered program to evaluate and classify all of the inmates in the Alabama prison system. What was done and what was learned are the subjects of this paper.

THE CENTER FOR CORRECTIONAL PSYCHOLOGY

The involvement of the Department of Psychology in the Alabama prison litigation developed over a period of years. The department has had a long history of involvement in social change. This was partly because of the concerns and interests of faculty members as individuals and partly because Alabama, during the 1960s and 1970s, became virtually a national laboratory for changes in racial relations and social institutions. Established social patterns of the state were disrupted by federal court decisions that required desegregation of schools, public transportation, and changes in law enforcement, voting practices, and the institutionalization and treatment of mental patients. These court-ordered changes were met by active and passive resistance from state and local officials.

Faculty members and students in the psychology department were intensely interested in these developments and participated in related research, training, consultation, and social and personal action. In 1971, the psychology department was awarded a grant by the Law Enforcement Assistance Administration to develop, within the Department, a Center for Correctional Psychology. The center was organized to offer graduate and undergraduate education in correctional and forensic psychology, conduct research, and provide professional consultation on a regional and national basis.

In 1972, a center faculty member testified in *Newman* v. *Alabama,* one of the suits that were later combined to form a consolidated class-action suit, that health care was substandard and mental health care virtually nonexistent in the Alabama correctional system. With the agreement of the court, the Department of Corrections contracted with the center to develop a plan to provide mental health care in the state prisons (Gormally et al., 1972). Subsequently the center developed a four-volume master plan that recommended improved facilities and operations, appropriate medical, social, and psychological services, and a system to reduce the prison population by utilizing community alternatives to incarceration (Center for Correctional Psychology, 1973). Neither the mental health plan nor the master corrections plan was implemented by the Department of Corrections.

As conditions in the state prisons worsened, additional cases were filed against the state by inmates. Eventually, several were combined into a single comprehensive class suit against the Alabama Board of Corrections (*Pugh* v. *Locke,* 1976). Faculty members of the center were involved in the litigation at several stages: consulting with attorneys in the formulation of cases, inspecting the prisons, and giving expert testimony concerning prison conditions. A representative of the center who inspected the prisons testified that it was physically and psychologically hazardous to be imprisoned in Alabama prisons; that mental health, educational, vocational, and social programs were inadequate; and that no rational system of classification existed (Clements, 1975). In a preliminary order, Judge Johnson placed a moratorium on the admission of new prisoners and reserved ruling on other issues until January, 1976.

In April, 1976, the Board of Corrections submitted a plan for reclassification, which was essentially a restatement of the preexisting plan that had been ruled inadequate. Both the center and the attorneys for the plaintiffs recommended that the plan be rejected by the court. On June 28, 1976, the court rejected the state's plan and named the Director of the Center, Raymond D. Fowler, to be chairman of a panel of experts to carry out the reclassification. In effect, this order assigned to the center the responsibility for planning and directing the classification program of the state prison system. This was a marked change from the earlier order in which the center was to aid the Board of Corrections in implementing the Board's own classification plan.

THE PRISON CLASSIFICATION PROJECT (PCP)

With the assignment of principal responsibility for the classification effort, the staff of the center moved rapidly to organize the resources necessary to carry out the project. The center's reclassification plan, approved on June 28, called for a four-week pilot phase (Phase I) to begin July 6. In less than a week, a staff of 20 was recruited and oriented, and all of the other preliminary tasks completed. This included selecting assessment instruments, designing forms and having them printed, purchasing supplies, arranging for living quarters and support staff, selecting a site to begin the classification project and carrying out the routine logistics of packing and arranging for transportation for the group.

The core planning group consisted of four faculty members from the Center for Correctional Psychology: Raymond Fowler, Stanley Brodsky, Carl Clements, and Charles Owens. The planning group was responsible for the development of the procedures and the selection and training of staff. Fowler assumed general administrative responsibility including coordination with the Department of Corrections, the court, and the court-appointed Citizens Advisory Committee. Brodsky assumed primary responsibility for staff training.

The initial PCP staff was made up of faculty members, graduate students, and recent graduates of the University of Alabama Department of Psychology. Others, including recent law and social work graduates, were recruited for the project later. A common thread of motivation among the initial recruits seemed to be the feeling that the project would be a challenging learning experience with significant implications for professional psychology and important humanitarian aspects as well. The group was suffused with a "Peace Corps" idealism, and the students seemed to relish the idea of leaving the ivory tower for an experience that would be grueling but stimulating.

The staff included people with various levels of experience, from beginning graduate students to postinternship students and recent graduates. The operation of the group reflected these levels of competence; more experienced members of the staff became the teachers and advisors to those with less experience. Even first-year graduate students, who initially were closely supervised in their work, had an opportunity to teach and supervise as new staff joined the project. Most staff members were in their early to mid-twenties; about half were women. None of the students had much prison experience, and most had none at all.

Communication within the PCP group was facilitated by already established relationships. Faculty members were long-time colleagues and friends, and many students were friends. The faculty, who had taught and supervised all of the students at the university, extended the mentor role to the prison setting. In both locations, the relationship was cordial and informal. Group cohesiveness was enhanced by makeshift living arrangements, with PCP staff members crowded into rented houses located near the prison. Cooking and clean-up duties were shared, as were the project duties.

THE PRISON SYSTEM

At the time of the court order, the Alabama prison system had most of the problems of other state correctional systems, compounded by the relative poverty and low tax base of the state. The prison facilities were old, dilapidated, and burdened with twice as many inmates as they were designed to house. Most of the prisons were located in the impoverished and sparsely populated rural areas of southern Alabama, although the homes of most of the prisoners were in the population centers of the more industrialized northern part of the state. Visits from relatives, who might live as much as 250 miles away, were made even more difficult by the lack of public transportation and sometimes rude and inconsiderate treatment by prison staff.

The prisoners, like the prisoners in other states, tended to be young, urban, poor, uneducated and, in disproportionate numbers, black. Most had a history of previous arrests and many had served time in juvenile facilities or jails. Their crimes tended to be the crimes of the poor and the young: robbery, burglary, and larceny. Those who had committed crimes of violence had usually chosen as victims their friends, relatives, or lovers.

Most of the inmates had experienced little success in school. Although generally of normal or near-normal intelligence, they had neither the patience nor the motivation to submit to classroom routine and consequently had few basic skills. Although not happy to be in prison, they were not very surprised. Most had friends, relatives, and siblings who had "done time" and they had expected that they would do likewise.

Within the prison, the men lived under circumstances that were degrading, humiliating, dangerous, and often painful. The popular conception of a prison with single- and double-occupancy cells comes from Hollywood's portrayal of the "big house." Alabama prisoners, like the prisoners in many other states, slept and spent most of their time in large barracklike rooms. These dorms or cell blocks contained 50 or more double-decker beds crowded a few inches apart and covering most of the floor space. They were occupied by prisoners assigned almost randomly: Hardened, aggressive prisoners slept next to young and vulnerable inmates. Extortion, beatings, and gang rape were commonplace.

Most prisoners, except those who had become passive sexual partners to stronger protectors, were armed with knives made from pieces of metal taken from beds or other prison equipment. Because of this, guards did not enter the sleeping areas after dark. The inmates, locked inside for the night without protection, had to fend for themselves. Judge Johnson's use of the term "jungle atmosphere" was particularly apt. As in the jungle, the predators prowled at night with little fear of detection or retaliation.

Despite the meanness of their circumstances, prisoners do not welcome surprises. They live in a world in which unexpected events tend to be unpleasant ones. They carefully scrutinize each new event in terms of its potential for making their lives worse. In such an atmosphere, the invasion of the prison by a large group of strangers caused considerable activity on the prison grapevine. The fearful speculations of the prisoners were reinforced by distorted information and rumors spread by the guards and other prison employees. Prisoners came to believe that the consequence of the forthcoming classification might be transfer to a harsher prison or, worse, to one of the notoriously bad state institutions for the mentally ill and mentally retarded. Talks between PCP staff members and prison leaders helped to counter some of the misinformation and to inject new, more favorable information into the grapevine. From that point forward, the Prison Classification Project received an extraordinary level of cooperation from the inmates.

THE DEPARTMENT OF CORRECTIONS

The Commissioner, who, like most of his central office staff, had come up through the Alabama correctional system, defended the system against the changes mandated by the court. Since the Prison Classification Project represented the first tangible step in the change process, it was the target of resistance and resentment.

The professional staff of the Department of Corrections included psychologists, social workers, and classification specialists. The court order required that most of the professional staff be assigned to the PCP to assist in its activities. Some of the professional staff, particularly those at the administrative level, were resentful of the intruders. Strongly committed to the status quo, they resisted every change in classification, although they were aware that changes were required by the court order. Some of the staff members who were assigned to PCP shifted loyalties and became enthusiastic members of the project.

The individuals who had most contact with the prisoners were the guards. Although the prisoners tended to be young urban blacks and whites, the guards were mostly middle-aged rural whites. The two groups were similar in intelligence and educational achievement, and both were overwhelmingly from the lower socioeconomic levels. The guards seemed to have little interest in, or involvement with, the prisoners. Since they were unarmed and heavily outnumbered by the prisoners and not in a position to conrol them, they were more a symbol of authority than a significant controlling force within the institution.

THE JUDGE AND THE GOVERNOR

Two individuals played essential behind-the-scenes roles in the state prison litigation. Most important was Judge Johnson, a distant, Olympian figure whose orders and whose continuing authority deeply affected the lives of all of the other participants. For 20 years Judge Johnson had issued orders that deeply affected the state of Alabama, including the integration of the Montgomery bus system, the desegregation of over 100 Alabama school districts, and the protection of Martin Luther King's civil rights march from Selma to Montgomery. Depending upon one's perspective, Judge Johnson was feared, hated, or respected, but his power and influence in the state were generally conceded.

The other important person, although playing an unusually subdued role, was Governor George C. Wallace. A controversial political figure, Wallace had gained much of his state and national visibility through his steadfast and futile opposition to the orders of Judge Johnson over the past two decades. Charging that the prison reform would create a "hotel atmosphere" in Alabama's prisons, the governor ordered state officials to appeal the court's decision. The Commissioner of Corrections and his staff took their cue from the governor and cooperated with the Prison Classification Project only to the extent that the court specifically required.

THE PILOT PROJECT

The classification plan submitted by the center and approved by the court called for a four-week pilot phase (Phase I). Its goals were:

1. To employ, orient, and train the classification staff
2. To develop procedures of classification based on inmate behavior, characteristics, and needs
3. To achieve and maintain a rate of classification of 100 inmates per week
4. To complete the classification of approximately 10% of the inmates in the system
5. To identify any problems the prison system might have in adapting to an intensive program of classification for all inmates
6. To propose to the court any modifications or additions to the plan that might be needed to successfully carry out the remaining phases of the classification project

The project of 24 work days was divided as follows: 2 days for train-ing, task familiarization, and staff orientation; 2 days to develop teams, synthesize materials, and test the reporting guidelines and format; 5 days for pilot-testing the classification procedures, with emphasis on quality control, reliability of judgments, and collaborative relation-ships; 15 days for trial implementation of classification procedures, meeting quality and quantity goals. At a rate of 100 inmate classifica-tions per week, a period of 10 months was projected for completion of the entire classification project.

DESIGNING A SYSTEM

The development of a comprehensive, actuarially based and empirically valid classification plan is a process that might reasonably take from 2 to 10 years or even more, depending upon the amount of resources one is able to develop. The systems developed by Quay (Cf. Quay & Par-sons, 1970) and Warren (1971) took 20 years, and the system developed by Megargee (1977), based on MMPI typologies, about 7 years.

The emergency nature of the Prison Classification Project precluded the development of an elegant system. Efforts were made to adapt an existing system to the purposes of the project, but none fit the require-ments of the court order or the resources available. Most of the classifi-cation systems required information not readily available from existing files or other prison records. Our classification system, although influ-enced by other systems, was designed to address the provisions of the court order and our particular circumstances.

GOALS OF THE PROJECT

As Clements (1984) observed, "Classification decisions must result in: meaningful distinctions among groups; reasonably accurate predic-tions about behavior; and implications for differential management and treatment" (p. 52). The goals of the Prison Classification Project were, quite literally, determined by the January 13 court order. In order to as-sure compliance with the court order, the relevant sections were exam-ined sentence by sentence and methods were devised to achieve each of the objectives.

Operationally, the plan required the accomplishment of three major tasks:

1. Assign an appropriate custody level to each inmate with special attention to:
   a. Determining least restrictive level of custody for each inmate inside the prison
   b. Identifying those prisoners able to function outside of the prison in community-based facilities
2. Screen for inmates who require transfer for specialized treatment because of:
   a. Psychological disturbance
   b. Mental retardation
   c. Reduced mental functioning due to age or physical condition
3. Identify inmates who need:
   a. Educational or vocational programs
   b. Job assignments
   c. Health care
   d. Mental health care

CUSTODY ASSIGNMENTS

The heart of any prison classification system is the establishment of the level of surveillance required for each inmate. As the court observed, this aspect of classification clearly was not working in the Alabama system. Far too many inmates were classified as maximum security, and those appropriate for community placement were not being identified. The criteria for placement in each of the custody grades were ill-defined, and grades could be changed by prison personnel because of minor disciplinary infractions unrelated to custody requirements.

In developing a system of custody grades, the project staff was guided by a strong mandate to determine the least restrictive custody for each inmate while identifying those inmates who were likely to endanger other inmates. Judge Johnson, in specifying that the custody be "the least restrictive possible" noted: "The Supreme Court recently identified three legitimate functions of a correctional system: deterrence, both specific and general; rehabilitation; and institutional security. . . . When an inmate is restricted in a manner which supports no such valid purpose, that restriction cannot stand" (*Pugh* v. *Locke*). The system developed to assign custody level was influenced by a substantial literature on the subject. Works by Chappell and Monahan (1973), Monahan (1976), and Wenk et al. (1972) were particularly useful, as were publications by the Federal Bureau of Prisons (1973) and the American Correctional Association (1966). Particular attention was directed toward the issue of dangerousness. The research of Monahan (1975), Megargee (1975), Kozol et al., (1972), and Wenk et al. (1972) indicated that predictions of dangerousness and violence based on clinical impressions are virtually useless. Clinical judgments greatly overpredict the probability of violent behavior, in part, as Megargee (1976) observed, because they attribute it to a trait rather than a state variable.

The PCP accepted three variables in predicting dangerousness: frequency, recency, and severity of explicit, verified, harmful acts against others. A form called the "violent behavior checklist" was developed to elicit, from the inmate and from institutional records, information relative to past dangerous behavior. The operating procedure was to classify individuals to the less restrictive levels of custody in the absence of explicit evidence to the contrary. Unless there was evidence from past behavior that individuals had been dangerous to others, it was assumed that they were not dangerous. The nature of the crime for which the individual was convicted was only considered a factor if it was judged likely to influence prison behavior. Individuals convicted of violent crimes were not necessarily considered dangerous in the prison, nor were individuals convicted of nonviolent crimes considered safe. We were aware that as a result of plea bargaining there may be little relationship between the crime committed and the crime of record.

LEVELS OF CUSTODY

Prior to the court order, the Department of Corrections used the classifications of maximum, medium, and minimum. It was the policy of the department that all inmates were assigned initially to maximum custody, often for a period of six months or more. Maximum custody also was assigned to inmates who had committed crimes judged to be particularly offensive to the community, who had "detainers" (criminal charges in other jurisdiction, which might require that the individual be turned over to other justice authorities after completing their sentence), or who had been returned to prison as a result of parole violations (even if these were minor or technical). The major problem, however, was disciplinaries. Classification was used as a principal form of punishment in the system, rather than as a diagnostic and predictive procedure. An inmate who was insolent to a correctional officer, who wore his clothing incorrectly, who combed his hair wrong, or who committed a variety of minor offenses could be reclassified maximum. This meant that the maximum category was made up, to unknown degrees, of violent and nonviolent inmates. Medium custody was a transitional category between maximum and minimum. Minimum, which might be achieved by an inmate who remained free of disciplinary actions for a long period of time, was necessary for passes, home visits, and trusty status. (Just prior to the Prison Classification Project, the department split maximum into two groups of those most dangerous and violent and those less dangerous.)

The PCP adopted the nomenclature used by the Federal Bureau of Prisons and many state systems: maximum, close, medium, minimum, and community. Each was defined in terms of the requisite behavior and the level of security required.

Maximum. This category was reserved for inmates who posed an extreme threat of violence to others. Assignment was made if reliable evidence showed recent episodes of extreme violence toward others, accompanied by reliable evidence sufficient to justify a reasonable belief that the inmate would engage in extreme violence again if not closely supervised.

Individuals assigned to maximum custody required a high level of surveillance to protect other inmates, prison staff, and the general public. Restriction to designated areas in the institution, single-occupancy cells, and secure facilities were prescribed. Inmates were not allowed to leave the institution unaccompanied by a correctional officer.

Close. This category was reserved for individuals whose recent dangerous behavior was less severe than those in maximum, but serious enough to justify strict supervision. The category also included individuals viewed as dangerous to themselves as evidenced by recent suicidal behavior.

Individuals assigned to close custody required single-cell housing and direct sight supervision within the institution. They were not allowed to leave the institution unaccompanied by a correctional officer.

Medium. This category was reserved for inmates who posed an extreme risk of nonviolent criminal offenses or serious rule infractions and/or escape. Nonrecent episodes of violence toward others or suicide attempts also justified this assignment. Many of the inmates in medium were escape risks who were not judged to pose a risk of violence. The PCP system differentiated between them and escape risks who might be expected to be violent, whereas in the old system all escape risks were considered maximum. The level of surveillance for medium inmates was similar to those in close.

Minimum. This category was reserved for individuals who did not pose the risks associated with the preceding custody levels, but who were not judged ready for immediate community custody because of evidence to justify a reasonable belief that they might commit a criminal offense or otherwise be unable to meet the responsibilities associated with community placement.

Community. This category was reserved for individuals who did not pose the risks associated with other custody grades. Inmates assigned to community custody were eligible for immediate housing in prerelease, study release, work release in other community facilities or, if appropriate, in a hospital, nursing home, or private residence. Assignment to community custody was done with greatest care, since this custody level resulted in the greatest change in the inmate's status and had, should an error be made, the greatest potential for danger to the public.

THE DUE PROCESS MODEL

To assure that inmates received fair and consistent treatment, detailed rules of procedure were prepared. A law professor, who was a voluntary consultant to the project, reviewed and modified the rules to assure that the procedures were necessary and sufficient to meet the requirements of the court order and that the legal rights of inmates were protected. Each inmate had access to a copy of the rules and to a handout that explained the procedures in clear and simple language.

The PCP system was constructed on a due process model. Simply stated, it was assumed that the individual was innocent until found guilty; that is, the individual was assumed not to be dangerous unless evidence existed to show that he was dangerous.

In the previous classification system, an individual automatically began at the most extreme security level and gradually moved toward less and less secure facilities as he or she "deserved" it. The PCP system required that evidence be present to justify extreme security measures.

Other aspects of the due process model for classification included:

1. *The opportunity to be confronted with material used against or about oneself in the decision.* Every offender attended a meeting in which the information upon which the classification decision was made was discussed with the inmate, who was then allowed an opportunity to provide additional information.

2. *The opportunity for appellate review.* The classifications by the

primary board were reviewed at sequential levels by more senior individuals.

3. *The use of explicit written procedures.* The steps in classification were described in detail, and the inmates were told what to expect. Each classification category was defined and made available in written form to the inmate.

4. *Every action had a specific set of objectives against which it could be measured.* The court order required that several issues be considered for each individual. Thus, every assessment action, procedure, and decision followed this problem-oriented, explicitly defined, court-mandated charge.

The due process model affected other aspects of the classification procedure. For example, it was assumed that an individual could make use of educational and vocational opportunities and other services until he or she proved to be unwilling to accept them or failed to make use of them.

CLASSIFICATION PROCEDURES

A standard classification procedure was followed with each inmate in accordance with the rules of procedure. When an inmate's name came up to be classified, he was put on the "stop up" list for the next morning. This meant he would not be sent out of the prison on work detail and would be available for the classification interview.

Each inmate was assigned to a monitor, that is, one staff member who assumed responsibility for bringing the inmate through the entire classification procedure. Prior to seeing the inmate, the monitor reviewed the inmate's file for completeness and then prepared a recommendation summary that included the inmate's crime history; any information related to violence and/or escape; and issues related to custody, appropriateness for community placement, educational and vocational history, intellectual, psychological, and health status, and special needs. The sources of information included the central files of the Department of Corrections, which contained the inmate's history in the Alabama system and his crime record; the institutional record, which included information about recent behavior such as disciplinaries, escape attempts, work record, and services received; and the psychological files, which contained the results of psychological tests administered to the inmate. Most inmates had received a brief intelligence test and an MMPI with a computer interpretation. Other tests were administered as needed.

After reviewing and summarizing the records, the monitor conducted an individual interview with the inmate in which the inmate's interests, perspectives, skills, and impairments were explored and defined. The topics to be covered were specified in a suggested guide. The rules of procedure called for the monitor to do the following in the individual interview:

1. Review the classification process and the inmate's files with the inmate

2. Refer the inmate to a medical examiner if the inmate requests it or if the monitor has reason to believe that attention is needed

3. Permit the inmate to state what classification assignments the inmate believes are appropriate and support the request with information and reasonable argument

4. Discuss the inmate's future plans

5. Afford the inmate an opportunity to fully discuss any matters relevant to classification

At the conclusion of the interview, the monitor prepared a summary of the information obtained, made specific recommendations for the inmate in each of the areas of classification, and outlined plans to accomplish those recommendations.

The completed forms in Table 6.1 illustrate the kinds of information obtained on a sample inmate. The inmate was a 38-year-old black male serving a 15-year sentence for the theft of a truck from a lumber yard. Information from the presentence investigation indicated that he was intoxicated at the time of the crime.

In the interview, the inmate seemed relaxed, polite, and interested. He discussed most aspects of his life comfortably except his school experiences, which he described as very painful. Although he felt that he was as intelligent as his peers, he could not learn to read. He spent most of his time in special classes for slow learners, but received no special treatment for his learning disability.

He began drinking secretly when he was first placed in a special class at the age of 10, and acknowledged that he has had problems with drinking since the late teens. His drinking pattern consists of several months of sobriety followed by binges, usually triggered by some disappointment or humiliation, of several days duration and loss of memory for what took place during the binge.

He stated that his health is excellent, and he has no physical prob-

TABLE 6.1
Prison Classification Project Recommendation Summary

NAME   Alfred J. Sample   SEX   M   RACE   B   AGE   38

PAROLE DATE   9/4/77   SENTENCE   15 yrs.   PRISON #   234268

CURRENT CONVICTION   Grand Larceny: Stole truck from lumber yard; apparently intoxicated at the time.

MONITOR SUMMARY AND PLAN

1. CURRENT CUSTODY: Medium

  DETAINERS   None

  VIOLENT HISTORY   None in prison. Suspended sentence, age 20, assault with deadly weapon (fight with cousin who was also convicted and served time—both drunk.)

  ESCAPE   No attempts.

  DISCIPLINARIES   Two, late for work. One, drinking with a visitor, two years ago.

2. COMMUNITY PLANS   Consider for community placement in 6 months. Primary reservation is past drinking problem. Permit passes and home visits to monitor ability to maintain sobriety. Refer to AA immediately.

3. VOCATIONAL ABILITIES AND INTERESTS   Normal intelligence, but poor reading skills. Successful employment in heavy construction for five years prior to conviction.

  PLAN   1. Refer Adult Basic Education program for basic reading.
       2. Refer to Vocational Rehab. for training as heavy equipment operator (this training can continue while he is on community placement).

4. EDUCATIONAL INTERESTS AND ABILITIES   Agrees to Adult Basic Education to improve his reading. No interest in further school work. Primary interest is in vocational training.

  PLAN   Arrange Adult Basic Education.

  CURRENT WORK ASSIGNMENT   Kitchen

  PLAN   Move to outside construction work contingent upon treatment of leg pain.

6. SPECIAL CARE NEEDS
  PHYSICAL   Pain in right leg, especially in winter, since injury on construction. No medical treatment.

  PLAN   Refer to medical examiner.

7. PSYCHOLOGICAL

INTELLECTUAL   IQ = 103. Possible learning disability—reverses d & g, d & b, and m & w. Arithmetic and information good, reading very poor (2nd grade). Good visual motor coordination.

EMOTIONAL   History negative. No evidence of problems in interview. MMPI normal for prison—impulsive, energetic. Evidence of mild periodic drinking problem of "youthful binge drinker" type.

PLAN   No referral necessary.

8. OTHER CONSIDERATIONS FROM MONITOR, INMATE, OR BOARD:
   1. Inmate hesitant about Basic Education program—bad past experiences here and in school. Needs support.
   2. Inmate enthusiastic about transfer from kitchen to outside construction.

BOARD ACTION

The Board supported all of the monitor's recommendations, with proviso that heavy equipment training contingent upon participation in basic education program and AA.

Classify MINIMUM, consider COMMUNITY in six months. Refer to medical examiner.

MONITOR   William J. Staff   Signature _____

BOARD MEMBERS' SIGNATURES:

APPROVE: DISSENT:

_____   _____

_____   _____

_____   _____

lems except for leg pains, which have troubled him periodically since an injury on a construction job.

He was married at age 23 and divorced after two years. He has been successfully employed in the construction business for most of his adult life. His work mainly involved heavy manual labor, and he has always hoped to be trained as a heavy equipment operator.

He has been on medium security because of his drinking problem. His classification officer felt that if he were placed in minimum and thus allowed passes, he might drink and get into trouble.

The following is a summary of the recommendations made by the monitor:

This inmate's custody classification should be changed from medium to minimum security. He should be enrolled in Adult Basic Education to give him reading skills and should receive vocational training as a heavy equipment operator. He should be medically examined for periodic pain in his right leg, and he should attend AA to help him deal with a drinking problem which has caused vocational instability and other difficulties. He should be granted day passes immediately and weekend leaves as he becomes more confident of his ability to maintain sobriety. He should be considered for placement in a community facility in six months.

After this information was obtained and the monitor's summary and recommendations completed, the inmate was brought before a classification board consisting of a senior PCP staff member, a Department of Corrections staff member, and the monitor. The monitor acted as "host" to the inmate, introducing him to the board members and summarizing his files and the interview in the inmate's presence. The inmate was given an opportunity to state his own position and, at the conclusion of the meeting, was informed of the board's decisions. In short, the inmate was treated as an intelligent participant in the classification procedure. Approximately 80% of all reports were unanimous. Virtually all of the dissents came from Department of Corrections employees, and most came from one classification specialist who consistently voted for higher degrees of control. After the meeting of the classification board, the monitor prepared minutes of the meeting and summarized the recommendations in each area on the classification assignments form.

In order to make the classification procedure as accurate as possible, several levels of approval were required for each classification. After the board meeting, the forms went through a quality control procedure to prevent errors and to supply missing information. A PCP staff member who had not participated in the decisions examined the report to ensure that each item specified in the court order had been addressed, and that the recommendations were consistent and appropriate. Unsatisfactory reports were returned for additional work. Next, the forms went to a PCP supervisor who reviewed and signed the recommendations, or referred them back if he disagreed with any part of the classification recommendations.

The approved recommendations were forwarded to the Classification Review Committee of the Department of Corrections for review and comments. The final decision on each classification, made by the PCP director, was transmitted back to the Department of Corrections for implementation. The court ruled that the decisions of the Prison Classification Project were to be implemented within 15 days unless the Department of Corrections registered further objections. Disagreements were reconciled in face-to-face meetings between the PCP director and designees of the commissioner. In cases in which no agreement was possible, the Department of Corrections had the option of implementing the PCP classification or appealing it to the court. Only 136 cases were eventually appealed.

COMPLETING THE PROJECT

During the initial four-week period, the staff of the Prison Classification Project developed forms and procedures for rapid classification, recruited and trained staff members, and achieved a rate of classification that somewhat exceeded the projected 100 cases per week. Rules of procedure were formally established to govern the process of classification, review, and appeal, and new custody categories were adopted.

The second phase (August 6 to September 24) was a transitional period. The original full-time staff, mostly faculty members and students of the Center for Correctional Psychology, became part-time staff. New full-time employees were recruited and trained during this period, and some of the original staff remained to assume full-time leadership positions.

As a result of staff expansion and more efficient procedures, the classification rate increased from 100 per week to 350 per week with no reduction in quality. On September 23, the Court, ordering still another acceleration, approved a modified plan submitted by the Center for Correctional Psychology that called for:

1. Assigning all qualified prison system employees to the Prison Classification Project

2. Recruiting additional PCP personnel

3. Scheduling the project for completion in a total of 18 weeks as opposed to the 43 weeks originally projected

This required increasing the rate of classification from the initial rate of 100 a week to 100 a day. A total of 78 staff members were involved in the classification project at various times, with an average staff of about 30.

At the end of the 18-week period, all of the inmates in the prisons and work release facilities at that time had been classified.

The following months were spent reviewing the files, negotiating disagreements, and appearing in court to defend PCP decisions when they were challenged by the Board of Corrections. Of the 136 classification decisions appealed to the court by the Board of Corrections, all but 6 were decided in favor of the PCP.

RESULTS OF THE RECLASSIFICATION

This project represents the only complete reclassification of a state prison system by an outside group. As it became apparent that the classifications assigned by the PCP were less restrictive than the ones assigned by the prison staff, considerable resistance began to emerge. In the first group of 100 classifications, the prison authorities disagreed with almost every changed classification. Without the pressure of the court to force compliance with the new classifications, there would have been little change in the custody distributions.

At the time of the court order, 4,422 inmates who had been classified under the previously existing classifications system were incarcerated in Alabama prisons. Because of the moratorium on new prison admissions and the early release of some prisoners to reduce overcrowding, the number of inmates reclassified by the PCP was 3,192. Although the definitions of the custody grades were not remarkably different under the two classification systems, the results of the two procedures differed considerably.

The major custody changes that took place under the PCP system were at either end of the custody range. Under the Department of Corrections classification system, 1,504 inmates (34%) were identified as requiring maximum custody, the most restrictive category. Under the PCP procedures, only 104 (3%) were found to require that level of supervision. The principal difference in the two systems was the requirement in the PCP system that "reliable evidence shows recent episodes of extreme violence toward others accompanied by reliable evidence sufficient to justify a belief that the inmate will engage in extreme violence toward others if he or she is not strictly supervised." There were no such behavioral criteria under the old system. The old and new systems placed similar percentages in medium custody (17% and 22%) and in minimum custody (40% and 43%). The general trend was for inmates in maximum to be reclassified as medium and minimum.

The resistance to the PCP classifications was particularly strong with respect to community placement. Prior to the court order, the Department of Corrections did not use the community custody category, although some minimum security prisoners were allowed to live in community work release centers. Having prisoners in community facilities had some obvious advantages. The cost of maintaining the prisoners was less, and the prisoners gained an opportunity to learn work skills while making a gradual transition into community life. Balanced against these advantages was the fear on the part of correctional officials that escapes or violent behavior on the part of work release inmates would create strongly negative community reactions. Some officials believed that no more than 10% of the inmates could safely be housed in community facilities, and indeed the number so placed at the time the project began was 9%. As the number of inmates classified by the PCP for community placement exceeded the 10% rate, the objections grew stronger. Of the 136 disagreements finally referred to the court, nearly all were issues of community custody.

The PCP defined "least restrictive custody" as including community placement. Particular care was exercised to select only inmates who had exhibited no violent behavior. After reclassification, 1,025 inmates (32%) had been judged ready to live in community settings, an increase of 3½ times the number thus classified by the Department of Corrections.

The Prison Classification Project resulted in a major redefinition of the inmate population. The decrease in those requiring the closest supervision, from more than ⅓ of the population to only 3%, might suggest that the PCP staff was advocating much looser supervision within the institutions, thereby putting inmates at more risk. In fact, most of the inmates previously classified as maximum were treated the same as medium and minimum prisoners within the institution. The PCP identified a relatively small number of prisoners as extremely dangerous, making it possible to supervise them more closely and restrict their access to more vulnerable inmates by housing them in single-occupancy cells as required by the court order.

With respect to community custody, the PCP classifications had the effect of removing from the prison environment a large number of individuals judged not likely to harm others and in many cases especially vulnerable to the conditions that Judge Johnson ruled ". . . create an environment in which it is impossible for inmates to rehabilitate themselves—or to preserve skills and constructive attitudes already possessed—even for those inclined to do so."

ASSESSING THE PRISON SYSTEM

The system-wide reclassification necessitated a survey of available services and their quality. Although few services were provided for inmates, it had been the position of the prison system that the services available were all that were needed or wanted by the inmates. It was the conclusion of the PCP staff that the failure of inmates to use existing services resulted from the kind and quality of services being provided. For example, in the area of education, only the most rudimentary Adult Basic Education course existed. These classes often were taught by bored, poorly qualified instructors who exhibited contempt for the inmates. Not surprisingly, the few available classes were often unfilled. The Prison Classification Project made educational recommendations for 1,255 inmates, all of whom needed educational assistance and indicated their willingness to accept it.

Vocational training in the prison system was better organized, but inmates were often denied these opportunities because they were in maximum security. The PCP identified over 1,000 inmates for whom vocational training was indicated. Many who had been ineligible because of maximum security became eligible as a result of reclassification.

With respect to health care, several hundred inmates were found to have untreated medical problems. The facilities for medical care were even more primitive and lacking in respect for the inmates than the educational facilities. A number of inmates asserted that they would not accept medical care except in dire emergencies, and there was considerable evidence of medical incompetence.

The PCP made over 1,000 referrals for counseling of various types. This was done with little confidence that counseling would occur or that the staff available would be appropriate to provide it. The area of personal counseling was approached with some ambivalence, as psychological treatment per se was not viewed as an effective method of rehabilitating inmates. However, hundreds of inmates were found to be desperate for someone willing to listen to and respond to their concern and distress. It was concluded that the availability of short-term crisis counseling was necessary to prevent further deterioration in an environment of high stress.

One important result of the classification was the identification of prison services that required expansion. The court's orders required the state to develop program capacity to provide the needed services.

FOLLOW-UP

The circumstances that led to the classification project and the adversarial situation that existed then and continued to exist for some time after the completion of the project made systematic follow-up impractical. It would be useful to know whether prisoners recommended for remedial programs received them and if they profited from them. It would also be useful to know whether the changes in custody status had any effect on the number of disciplinary incidents or escapes, or whether the inmates assigned to community custody were more or less able to adjust to that status than were those previously so assigned. Even if the data to answer these questions had been obtained, their quality and accuracy would have been very difficult to judge.

In an effort to obtain indirect evidence concerning the appropriateness of classifications, Brodsky (1982) followed a sample of 149 prisoners who had been classified by the Prison Classification Project and subsequently released from prison. The purpose was to determine if there was a relationship between recidivism and the custody category into which the inmate had been assigned. It was assumed that prisoners who received the more severe custody grades while inmates would be more likely to commit additional crimes and be returned to prison after they had completed their sentences and been released. The criterion data for recidivism were gathered by local law enforcement agencies and supplied to the Alabama Criminal Justice Information Center. The sample was selected by drawing every tenth name from the list of inmates classified by PCP, and eliminating those who had not yet been released and those for whom data were unavailable.

The results showed that recidivism and assigned custody grades were positively related. The recidivism rate was 30% for the inmates who had been assigned to community custody compared with 41% for minimum custody, 55% for medium security, and 63% for the maximum security offenders. Only about 10% of the group had committed violent offenses. Although this small number makes it more difficult to detect a trend if one exists, it appeared that violent crime was related to custody assignment. Violent crimes were committed by 6% of the inmates who had been in community custody, compared with 7% of minimum security and 16% medium security inmates. Brodsky noted that the community custody inmates had been released earlier and therefore had more time at risk. He observed that, considering the dismal record of social scientists in predicting violence, the present outcome appeared noteworthy.

LATER DEVELOPMENTS

As the conclusion of the Prison Classification Project approached at the end of 1976, the staff and the attorneys for the inmates began to be concerned about the need for some means of assuring that the new classification system would be continued. Both the staff and the attorneys were concerned that without supervision the behavioral criteria would be abandoned, and the system might revert to what existed prior to the reclassification. A proposal that the Center for Correctional Psychology oversee the classification activities of the Department of Corrections was rejected by the court in favor of having all aspects of compliance with the court order monitored by a court-appointed Human Rights Committee.

The PCP staff and the attorneys for the inmates worried that the committee would not have the time or the expertise to monitor classification closely, and that the system might well deteriorate. In fact, there is evidence that it did so over the next two years. By 1978, the court heard testimony that the behavioral criteria for classification had been largely abandoned, and that the department had reinstituted various restrictions and time criteria for movement through the custody levels. The court ruled that the classification system had deteriorated and no longer functioned in accordance with the court order.

Changes in personnel and leadership in the Department of Corrections since 1979 have resulted in steady progress in the classification program and in the services available to inmates. The Professional Services Division has been divided into mental health services and classification services, both headed by psychologists. At the present time, inmates have access to a broad range of mental health services that were not available at the time of the PCP. The mental health staff is now developing a prisoner incentive program to provide positive reinforcement for constructive behavior and a staff incentive program to reward staff for identifying eligible inmates.

The current classification program is generally similar to the program developed during the Prison Classification Project. The classification staff, under new leadership, has resumed the use of behavioral criteria for classification, including the use of rating scales to assess escape risk and potential for violence. The current system uses the five levels initiated by PCP. The following is a comparison of the percentage of inmates at each level before the PCP, after reclassification, and at the present time: maximum and close (34%, 3%, 1.5%); medium (17%, 22%, 43%); minimum (40%, 43%, 29.2%); and community (9%, 32%, 17.7%). There has been a drift toward the more restrictive medium and maximum categories (51%, 25%, 44.5%), but the increases are in the medium category; there are actually fewer in maximum and close. There are fewer inmates in community custody (17.7%) than after PCP (32%), but almost twice as many as before PCP (9%). The currrent community program includes a supervised inmate restitution program, which allows 700 inmates, under supervision, to live at home and work while paying restitution to crime victims and contributing to the cost of their supervision.

OBSERVATIONS AND CONCLUSIONS

In biology, classification is the systematic grouping of organisms into categories based on shared characteristics or traits. In the field of corrections, classification is the process by which prisoners are subdivided into groups on the basis of behavioral, demographic, and other characteristics. Judge Johnson, in his January 13, 1976, opinion in *Pugh* v. *Locke*, observed, "There is no working classification system in the Alabama penal system and the degree to which this impedes the attainment of any proper objectives of a penal system cannot be overstated." The lack of a functioning classification system in the Alabama prisons intensified the problems of a system already troubled by overcrowding, underfunding, and inadequate facilities. The epidemic levels of violence, especially toward vulnerable, nonviolent inmates, could have been controlled by proper identification of those prone to violence and segregated living facilities for them. The overcrowding could have been alleviated by the identification of inmates who could function in alternative community facilities. The staff of the Center for Correctional

Psychology accepted the responsibility assigned by the court with confidence that the application of skills common to behavioral scientists would yield a rational, functioning system of classification. The uniqueness of our task—the classification of an entire prison system in 18 weeks—required us to build our own system. We used techniques that were familiar: careful observation and systematic collection of the observations of others; collecting information relevant to the behavior to be predicted; predicting future behavior on the basis of past behavior; validating data from one source with data from another. Our project was developed within the natural science paradigm with a strong technological/managerial orientation. Within psychology, our project probably fits best in a community psychology model, but we used clinical techniques such as interviewing, behavioral observation, and psychological assessment to achieve our goals.

What was accomplished by the Prison Classification Project? From a practical point of view, the most significant accomplishment was the removal of one-third of the population from prison to community facilities. We can only speculate about the effects that being out of the institution and employed in the community may have had on the recidivism rate, but we know that a thousand inmates were removed from a dangerous and inhuman environment into a situation that at least made it possible for them to rehabilitate themselves. The fears of the prison officials that release of so many prisoners would result in a wave of violence, escapes, and community indignation were never realized. Now the use of community facilities is commonplace in the Alabama prison system, and new programs are being developed.

Additionally, some of the techniques, procedures, and other aspects of the classification project have been adopted by the Alabama prison system, and seem to be having a long-term effect on the classification project. Members of the project staff have drawn upon their experience and the procedures developed to provide consultation to the National Institute of Corrections and to a large number of prisons and jails throughout the country.

REFERENCES

American Correctional Association. (1966). *Manual of correctional standards.* College Park, Md.

Brodsky, S. L. (1982). Prison class action suits: The aftermaths. In Gunn, J. &

Farrington, D. P. (Eds.), *Abnormal offenders and deliquency, and the criminal justice system*. London: Wiley.

Center for Correctional Psychology. (1973). *A state plan for the Alabama correctional system*. University, Ala.: Alabama Law Enforcement Planning Agency.

Chappell, D., & Monahan, J. (Eds.). (1973). *Violence and criminal justice*. Lexington, Mass.: Lexington Books.

Clements, C. B. (1975). *A report on the Alabama prison system*. University, Ala.: Center for Correctional Psychology.

Clements, C. B. (1984). Toward an objective approach to offender classification. *Law and Psychology Review, 10*, 45–55.

Federal Bureau of Prisons. (1973). *Differential treatment: A way to begin*. Washington, D.C.: U.S. Government Printing Office.

Gormally, J., Brodsky, S. L., Clements, C. B., Fowler, R. D. (1972). *Minimum mental health standards for the Alabama correctional system*. University, Ala.: Center for Correctional Psychology.

Hippchen, L. (1975). *Correctional classification and treatment*. Cincinnati: W. H. Anderson.

Kozol, H., Boucher, R., & Garofalo, R. (1972). The diagnosis and treatment of dangerousness. *Crime and Deliquency, 18*, 371–392.

Megargee, E. I. (1976). The prediction of dangerousness. *Criminal Justice and Behavior, 3*, 1–21.

Megargee, E. I. (Ed.). (1977). A new classification system for criminal offenders. *Criminal Justice and Behavior, 4*, 107–216.

Monahan, J. (1975). The prediction of violence. In Chappell, D., & Monahan, J. (Eds.), *Violence and criminal justice*. Lexington, Mass.: Lexington Books.

Monahan, J. (Ed.). (1976). *Community mental health and the criminal justice system*. New York: Pergamon.

Newman v. *Alabama* (1974). 503 D. 2nd 1320 (5th Circuit).

Pugh v. *Locke* (1976). F. Supp. 313 (M.D. Ala.)

Quay, H. C., & Parsons, L. B. (1970). *The differential behavioral classification of the juvenile offender*. Morgantown, W.Va.: Robert F. Kennedy Youth Center.

Warren, M. Q. (1971). Classification of offenders as an aid to efficient management and effective treatment. *Journal of Criminal Law, Criminology, and Police Science, 62*, 239–258.

Wenk, E., Robinson, J. O., & Smith, G. W. (1972). Can violence be predicted? *Crime and Delinquency, 18*, 393–402.

Correctional Classification:
A Tool for Rehabilitation
or a Response
to Public Pressure?

FREDERICK ROTGERS

In reviewing Fowler's chapter I was struck by the similarity between the Alabama prison system's classification procedures prior to the Prison Classification Project and the classification system currently in use in the state prison system in which I worked for more than 11 years. In most areas, the impact of psychological knowledge on the practice of corrections has been minimal. Where psychological knowledge has been used, it has usually been restricted to the provision of counseling or individual evaluation services with little influence on actual system practices. There are many reasons for this state of affairs, some of which I will mention in my comments.

Fowler's accomplishment should be seen in perspective. What he did may seem relatively simple and commonsensical to practitioners who have never worked in correctional institutions. Of course one should classify inmates on the basis of behavior. What other rational approach is there? However simple and sensible Fowler's approach was, it was clearly not accepted with open arms by the system it was designed to aid. The resistance that the PCP encountered is characteristic of the resistance shown by many correctional administrators toward the practical utilization of psychological knowledge, particularly if they believe such practices might lead to public outcry.

The PCP system of classification represents a monumental effort. Although relatively unsophisticated in its use of psychological assessment technologies (compared, for example, with Megargee and Bohn's

240

complex MMPI-based system), it did use established psychological concepts (e.g., past behavior is the single best predictor of future behavior) to construct a rational, behaviorally based classification system that resulted in a significant improvement of conditions for many inmates in the Alabama prison system. The PCP classification system had the further advantages that it was based on data that are relatively easy to obtain, and that it was linked with a contingency management system that was based on inmate behavior, not on an externally applied label (e.g., murderer serving 25 years). The tie between classification and performance offered the inmates an opportunity to change their status within the system in a positive way simply by changing their behavior. This opportunity must certainly have provided a greater sense of self-efficacy and personal control over their destinies to prisoners who previously were at the mercy of unchanging and unchangeable labels.

The simplicity of Fowler's system needs to be emphasized, particularly in light of the apparent recent failures of much more complex and sophisticated systems to provide accurate predictions of institutional adjustment of inmates in a variety of settings (Carbonell et al., 1984; Hanson et al., 1983; Louscher et al., 1983). The procedure of assuming an inmate was dangerous only if he had recently behaved in an assaultive manner makes great intuitive sense. Unfortunately, the tensions that had developed during the classification project made systematic follow-up impossible, a major flaw in the project from a scientific standpoint. Fowler provides indirect evidence that the use of the simple predictive rule works well (cf. Brodsky's study of recidivism). Nonetheless, this indirect evidence cannot substitute for systematic follow-up research.

If it is so simple to implement, is based on solid psychological data, and has some indirect follow-up support, why has the PCP's classification system not been more widely adopted? One reason may be lack of dissemination. Although I heard of Fowler's efforts several years ago, this was my first opportunity to review the procedures in writing and in detail. However, the lack of publicity is only a minor impediment to the implementation of such a system. I suspect most psychologists are very familiar with the basic principle that past behavior is the most reliable predictor of future behavior. Yet it took a severe order from a federal judge, who took oversight of the whole Alabama correctional system as his responsibility, to enable the implementation of a rational, behaviorally based classification system.

In my view, there are several reasons why correctional systems are so resistant to outside influence, particularly from noncorrectional professionals such as psychologists. These reasons form the basis for criticism of Fowler's system from the standpoint of a practicing correctional professional. The first is revealed in Fowler's first sentence. Most prison systems are "crowded, underfunded . . . and minimally staffed." Particularly in urban areas such as the northeastern United States correctional managers are faced with a political climate that favors segregation and punishment rather than more creative and rehabilitative approaches to altering criminal behavior. Funds are readily and easily obtainable for construction of new prison facilities and for staffing these facilities with appropriate numbers of correction officers to provide adequate security. Unfortunately, the funds often get sparse when the needs of prisoners beyond the basics of food, shelter, and security must be addressed. Thus, funding for the staff to run a system like that of the PCP (monitors, classification officials, etc.), as well as provision of services to meet inmate needs that were identified by the process, is very difficult to obtain.

Prisons have multiple and often conflicting roles in our society. These roles, in order of priority as indicated by the proportions of correctional budgets spent on them, are to segregate, incapacitate, punish, and rehabilitate. Politically, the climate in this country favors the direction of attention toward the first three goals, with little funding or attention directed to the last. For this reason, any system like Fowler's becomes difficult to implement without, as the PCP had, a strong external force requiring implementation. When a prison is located in a populated area, the surrounding communities are often reluctant to allow inmates with particular offenses or sentences (labels) into their areas. It is difficult to persuade people whose view of personality and behavior is based on trait, rather than state, conceptualizations that recent behavior can and should be a major criterion in classification of inmates into less restrictive settings. Most people believe, "Once a murderer, always a murderer," or at least that the risks of random murder are vastly higher for one-time murderers than for people in general. The attitudes are similar to those that inhibit the establishment of community residential facilities for developmentally and psychiatrically disabled people. The perception of risk, based on trait-thinking and uninformed stereotypes, is simply too strong to be politically acceptable. This means that correctional administrators, having the continuation of their programs uppermost in mind, are very likely to yield to political pressures to classify on the basis of offense and length of sentence, thus reducing the numbers of inmates likely to be placed in community or less restrictive settings. It is only when politically independent pressure is brought to bear that correctional systems begin, with great resistance and reluctance, to look beyond political criteria for community placement. Without the lawsuit initiated on behalf of Alabama prisoners, and Judge Johnson's sweeping mandate in response, it is unlikely that any change would have occurred in the Alabama prisons.

Prisoners are social pariahs in our society. They have only a small constituency arguing in their behalf. The social attitude toward prisoners is that they have hurt others so badly that they don't deserve any leniency. The "lock them up and throw away the key" approach is a popular one at the present time, making it difficult to promote significant changes in correctional philosophy, particularly if these changes can be construed as reducing the security limitations on prisoners' behavior and moving them into community settings. Thus, even though a classification system such as that developed by the PCP would have clearly salutary effects on prisons themselves (e.g., by reducing crowding and providing more internal security and safety for inmates and staff), as well as significant rehabilitative effects (e.g., by providing easier transition back into the community for prisoners), correctional officials are loath to adopt them for fear of political opposition that might jeopardize funding. They must walk a fine line between providing the best possible rehabilitative services, satisfying community demands, and maintaining institutional security. In view of the very poor record corrections has in convincing communities that they should be allowed more leeway in their placement of inmates, it seems unlikely that the PCP classification system would be warmly received in most correctional agencies, unless some hard, clearcut, follow-up data were available showing that the system is largely failure free. Unfortunately, freedom from failure is unlikely because of the limited predictability of human behavior.

Thus, although the PCP system makes perfect sense from an intuitive, psychological, and humanitarian perspective, the political realities of correctional practice make it very unlikely that similar systems will be adopted by correctional systems without considerable external pressure.

REFERENCES

Brodsky, S. L. (1982). Prison class action suits: The aftermaths. In J. Gunn & D. P. Farrington (Eds.), *Abnormal offenders, delinquency and the criminal justice system*. London: Wiley.

Carbonell, J. L., Megargee, E. I., & Moorhead, K. M. (1984). Predicting prison adjustment with structured personality inventories. *Journal of Consulting and Clinical Psychology, 52,* 280–294.

Hanson, R. W., Moss, C. S., Hosford, R. E., & Johnson, M. E. (1983). Predicting inmate penitentiary adjustment: An assessment of four classificatory methods. *Criminal Justice and Behavior, 10,* 293–309.

Louscher, P. K., Hosford, R. E., & Moss, C. S. (1983). Predicting dangerous behavior in a penitentiary using the Megargee typology. *Criminal Justice and Behavior, 10,* 269–284.

Megargee, E. I., & Bohn, M. J., Jr. (1979). *Classifying criminal offenders.* Beverly Hills, Calif.: Sage.

ASSESSING INTERPERSONAL BEHAVIOR AND GROUP PERFORMANCE

The next two chapters are concerned with the study of interpersonal behavior in small groups. Instead of examining antisocial behavior as individual action, Patterson and his colleagues study the social interactions that encourage and maintain antisocial behavior. They center on the family as an arena in which hitting, fighting, and other forms of aggression are learned, and in which efforts to control antisocial behavior are exercised. Instead of examining the functioning of air crews as aggregates of individual behavior, Hackman and Helmreich study air crews as work teams. They show that many air crashes are consequences neither of mechanical failure nor of pilot error, but of failures in communication and control among the members of the crew. In both chapters, conceptualization and assessment methodology go beyond the person to the group.

For over 20 years, Patterson has worked to construct a performance theory of children's antisocial behavior. From clinical experience and prior research, preliminary definitions of theoretical constructs are attempted. Antisocial behavior and such factors in parental skill as discipline are conceptually outlined. Then the long process of developing measures is undertaken. Information is sought from many agents by many methods. The psychometric properties of the measures are examined and relationships among indicators are determined. The relationships form a network that defines the theoretical construct with which the various measures are linked. From the redefined construct, additional measures may be generated and examined in further investigations. The cyclical process of theoretical formulation, measurement, redefinition of constructs, and refinement of measures can be conceived as a "bootstrapping" operation. In the chapter by Patterson and Bank, the process is illustrated by a detailed account of the development of two constructs of parental action, Monitoring and Discipline, which are shown to be distinct though correlated, and related in carefully defined ways to antisocial behavior among children.

The fundamental aim of Patterson's work is the systematic study of social behavior through research. Assessing operations are developed less to guide practical decisions than to define theoretical concepts. Yet it seems likely that this research program, like that of Gordon Paul, may yield an extraordinarily robust and useful assessment technology. The chapter by Patterson and Bank is discussed by Jeanne Wurmser, executive director of a community mental health center that focuses on family services. Wurmser notes that preventive efforts aimed at such complex forms of behavior as aggression have not been very successful to date, but sees Patterson's work as a promising basis for effective prevention programs to be developed in the future. The interplay of extensive clinical experience, rigorous theoretical definition, and painstaking empirical investigation that marks Patterson's work is considered especially likely to produce a useful technology. Suggestions are offered for extending Patterson's bootstrapping methodology to other clinically important aspects of social behavior.

Patterson's work bridges the gap between individual and social behavior. Hackman and Helmreich move to a different position in the systemic spectrum and emphasize the relations between group performance and organizational context. Their research program is designed to suit a general class of work groups in organizational settings. They have begun their investigations by studying air crews in commercial airlines, where effective team performance is of life-and-death importance and where the issues that arise in assessing team performance stand out with special clarity. Current regulations and practices for maintaining air safety are almost entirely restricted to mechanical surveillance and evaluations of individual competence. Yet Hackman and Helmreich show that many, if not most, air crashes are caused by failures in team performance. Essential information may not be transmitted from flight engineer to pilot. Leadership skills may fail in a crisis. An effective methodology for assessing team performance does not exist, and the authors devote considerable attention to reasons for the lack. They do so by thoughtful, knowing analysis of the historical, political, and organizational context in which air crews function and within which any efforts to construct useful assessment methods are constrained. Economic incentives that govern airline management, opposition from pilots' unions, and legal vulnerability are among the conditions that discourage accurate assessment of crew behavior. For all these limits, Hackman and Helmreich see promising challenges in the field they have chosen to investigate, and are combining their research programs to develop more effective methods for studying team performance in complex organizations.

Their chapter is discussed by Nathaniel Pallone, Academic Vice President and University Professor of Psychology at Rutgers University. In his administrative position, Pallone is responsible for evaluating the performance of academic groups, such as departments and research institutes, in the organizational context of a state university. He draws some interesting parallels and contrasts between the kinds of problems Hackman and Helmreich face, and those that confront university administrators who must evaluate individual performance in units where research is done cooperatively, and evaluate units in which independent contribution is prized. Pallone is impressed above all with the axiological issues implicit in enterprises of the kind Hackman and Helmreich have undertaken. Our society values independent performance, yet the well-being of society depends on effective organization and group performance. In their assumption of interdependence, as much as in new technique or novel theory, Hackman and Helmreich may offer their most fundamental contribution.

Chapter 7

When Is a Nomological Network
A Construct?

GERALD R. PATTERSON and
LEW BANK

The social learning perspective presented the developmental and clinical psychologist with a set of appealing metaphors that seemed directly related to issues surrounding the socialization of the child. It seemed, in principle at least, that some combination of reinforcement contingencies and imitative learning could be used to explain almost any kind of normal or deviant child behavior (Bandura & Walters, 1963; Skinner, 1953). Well-controlled laboratory studies demonstrated that both reinforcement and modeling mechanisms could be used to alter aggressive behaviors of children (e.g., hitting a rubber clown). These studies were carefully reviewed by Bandura (1973). However, as both he and others have pointed out, the laboratory analogue studies serve merely as promising indications. It remains for field studies to demonstrate whether these or other mechanisms such as social cognition actually determine individual differences in children's aggression, achievement, and other patterns of behavior in natural settings. It could be the case, for example, that the peer group never provides social reinforcers for aggression. It may also be the case that a child seated next to a diligent peer in the classroom learns nothing from that experience, and that the negative attributions entertained by the aggressive child do not precede his or her acquisition of deviant behavior, but are rather a concomitant.

This chapter is part of a programmatic effort to construct a performance theory of children's antisocial behavior. The objective is to

249

translate hypotheses from analogue studies or from clinical experience into measurement operations that can be used to account for major portions of the variance in criterion measures of antisocial behavior. We detail some of the decision process that is involved in moving from clinical experience and laboratory analogue concepts to an effective performance model. In this context, the "bootstrapping" metaphor is a useful one. The idea is to start with some sort of model that identifies the determinants for children's antisocial behavior. The next step is to translate the ideas into a measurement model and then use that model to estimate variance accounted for in the criterion measure. The empirical findings are used as a means of evaluating the methods of assessment and improving some of them; at the same time, additional variables might be added to increase the explanatory power of the model. The particular theory one entertains in beginning the bootstrapping operation is of little moment. The demands of constructing a performance theory are such that it becomes obvious that no existing theory, by itself, can account for a majority of the variance. The only constraint in building a performance theory is that one's favored variables must be accompanied by a specifiable means of measurement. This chapter describes the bootstrapping process involved in building two constructs, Monitoring and Discipline. These are multilevel assessment measures of parenting skill thought to be primary determinants for children's antisocial behavior. The two constructs are part of a larger performance model designed to account for the variance in children's prosocial and antisocial behavior (Patterson, 1982; Patterson et al., in press).

The senior author of this paper became convinced some 20 years ago that parents' global reports of their children's aggressive behavior were inadequate, if not totally misleading, as a dependent variable. A series of studies suggested that, in a majority of families having difficulties with an aggressive child, the parents' report of improvement was uncorrelated with assessments by spouses, teachers, and trained observers (see Patterson, 1982, Chapter 3, for a review of this literature).

It became apparent that actual observation of children and their parents in their own homes was necessary to measure aggressive behaviors reliably, as well as to understand the family interactional sequences that are predictive of these aversive encounters. To do this, an observation code had to be devised. The Family Interaction Coding System (FICS) was developed, revised, and deemed reasonably complete by the late 1960s (Patterson et al., 1969; Reid, 1967).

At this point, some new questions were formulated. Why do some children aggress at rates very much higher than other children? Why does the same child demonstrate widely different rates of aggressive behavior in different contexts? Why does a child use a particular aggressive response more often than other ones? This focus replaced the earlier emphasis on the acquisition of aggressive behaviors. There remained little doubt that, as Bandura and Walters (1963) had observed, most children by a very early age had learned a variety of aggressive behaviors modeled by their parents and friends.

Performance theory was created in an attempt to account for these differential rates of aggressive behavior across children and contexts. New variables, such as parental monitoring, setting consequences, and sidetracking were suggested by clinical experience and behavioral observation. If such variables accounted for significant portions of variance in rates or probabilities of child aggression, then they were incorporated into the performance theory; otherwise, they were dropped.

The general model for antisocial behavior emerged in part as the result of clinical experience gained in treating several hundred families of antisocial children (Patterson et al., 1982). The general model, particularly the Monitoring and Discipline constructs, reflects both this clinical experience as well as the information gleaned from the field observation studies in the homes of several hundred normal families. The general model is currently being tested in a longitudinal design (Patterson & Dishion, 1985).

Before this general model can serve a useful purpose, a series of problems must be solved. The first concerns the means by which one measures any one of the 11 key dimensions in the model. How does one assess the extent to which parents are knowledgeable about their child's whereabouts? How does one measure parental discipline? What is the best measure of a child's antisocial behavior? The structured interview or parent questionnaire typically used to assess such matters seldom produces correlations with antisocial child behavior that account for more than 10% of the variance. Even when they do occur, they often cannot be replicated. For these reasons, we decided to aggregate across modes and across agents in tailoring the assessment for each of the constructs in the model. Although the details of how to assess the Monitoring and Discipline constructs will be discussed later, it should be said here that this first, and most critical, stage in bootstrapping required three years of NIMH-supported effort. In summary, then, it required several decades of clinical experience and three years of psychometric labors before we were in a position to initiate this intricate dance between clinical hypotheses on the one hand, and means of measurement on the other.

Given a concept such as Monitoring or Discipline and the availability of the newly constructed multilevel assessment procedures, the next question was, "Does the set of measures for the construct relate in a meaningful way to the other constructs in the model?" The report by Patterson, Reid, and Dishion (in press) specified a fit among the key constructs; in keeping with the requirements of a performance model, the constructs in the model also accounted for the majority of the variance in a Fighting construct, which was measured by peer, teacher, and parent reports (Patterson, Dishion, & Bank, 1984). From this same NIMH-sponsored planning study, it was possible to demonstrate with the adolescent subsample that the relevant constructs in the model accounted for the majority of the variance in a composite (self-report, official records) measure of delinquency (Patterson & Dishion, 1985; Patterson & Southamer-Loeber, 1984). For these adolescents, the model also accounted for significant portions (but not a majority) of the variance in measures of academic success (Patterson, 1984b). Finally, it was shown in two different studies that the relevant aspects of the model accounted for the majority of the variance in measures of relationships with both normal (Patterson et al., 1984) and deviant peers (Patterson et al., in press).

These findings suggest that the first round of bootstrapping produced a set of constructs and their means of measurement that were modestly successful. However, several of the constructs were measured by only one variable. It also seemed possible to improve the power of even some of the better constructs. Several months were then spent developing additional methods for assessing each of the constructs; those variables that seemed effective were, of course, retained. It is also the assumption that constructs based on aggregations across methods and across agents constitute a highly generalized measure that is more likely to stand up under efforts to replicate. All of these assumptions point to the need to introduce a replication sample as the basis for the next round of bootstrapping. This chapter describes the outcome of this second round with the Discipline and Monitoring constructs.

ASSUMPTIONS ABOUT CONSTRUCTS

Before beginning any empirical studies, it was necessary to make some tactical decisions with far-reaching implications. Our general approach was to adopt the perspective presented in the seminal paper by Mac-Corquodale and Meehl (1948) and elaborated in Cronbach and Meehl (1955). This perspective took a major step away from the earlier, narrowly defined, radical operationalism of Bridgman (1927); it was in keeping with the development of Feigl's (1956) logical empiricism and directly reflected the influence of Carnap's (1956) ideas about theoretical constructs.

According to Carnap (1956), a theoretical construct is one that cannot be completely defined, not even by extended observation language. This is analagous to the term *hypothetical construct* and the idea of construct validity developed in the MacCorquodale and Meehl (1948) and Cronbach and Meehl (1955) papers. Given that no single measurement operation defines the meaning of a construct, then one perforce becomes interested in the network of operations by which one does define it. For a construct to be scientifically admissible, at least some of the statements (or laws) must involve observables; and there may be several steps between one and the other. As pointed out by Kagan (1984), this general formulation initially won widespread acceptance, but was then followed by two or three decades of silence. The present writers believe it may be time to return to the task of defining the meaning of constructs and exploring empirically the means by which this might be done. The critical problems involve decisions about what kinds of measures to include in the nomological network and how to integrate this information once it is obtained.

ASSUMPTIONS ABOUT HOW TO MEASURE

As a working heuristic, it was decided that each assessment device has its own built-in bias in measuring a given construct. If we ask children to rate their perception of how well parents track their whereabouts, their ratings may reflect many conditions, including their own views of what would be a reasonable amount of tracking. Similarly, the parents would have their own set of standards against which they anchor their ratings. These are not really errors of measurement in the ordinary sense of the word, since the internal consistency in the item pool could be high for each agent reporting. Also, it is possible to obtain good test-retest reliability for such ratings. It is not error in the traditional sense that concerns us here, but rather distortions in the definition of what the construct means. Presumably, aggregating across modes of assessment will partially control for the biases/distortions inherent in each measurement device. Obviously, the strategy of choice would be based on prior knowledge of the exact nature of the distortions as well as the unique contributions of each measure. Given such information, it would be possible to specify which indicators are required and, perhaps, how each is to be weighted. For the present, we proceed blindly in constructing as many indicators as time and budget allow and hope that at least three or four will survive the confirmatory factor analysis. This is hardly a satisfactory state of affairs. It seems that even bootstrapping itself is a bootstrapping operation. For the present, the distribution of scores is standardized for each indicator prior to the confirmatory factor analysis. The constellation of each set of indicators surviving the confirmatory factor analysis defines the respective construct.

The next, and last (unanswerable), question concerns the matter of when one has completed the definition of the construct. How is the decision to be made to stop adding new indicators? There is no method for addressing the question directly, but structural equation modeling provides an interesting indirect approach. It is possible to estimate residual terms for both the independent and dependent variables with this method; these residuals define the magnitude of unexplained variance in the measure of each construct. Each residual term is determined by the set of indicators used to define that construct as well as the hypothesized process depicted by the model. For example, a residual value of .440 specifies that 56% of the variance in the latent variable is accounted for by the model given that specific set of indicators. Again, note that error in this context refers to that which is unknown plus unreliability of measurement. The residual specifies that some measures of the construct may have been omitted and/or that the model itself may be incomplete in its specification of determinants for that construct. The residual term can be thought of as an estimate of incomplete knowledge or ignorance. One does not know whether the error lies in the weakness of the model or in the weakness of the indicators defining the construct itself.

In most cases, there will only be one or two "criterion" constructs within a model that one could expect to be completely specified. For example, in the general model discussed here, it may be the case that the criterion construct Antisocial will reach some lower residual term such as .300. This would mean that 70% of the variance for the criterion construct is explained by the preceding constructs in the model. If adding further potential determinants for antisocial behavior does nothing to reduce this residual term, and if adding indicators for the criterion or other latent variables in the model does nothing to improve the situation, what is one to conclude about how well the construct Antisocial is being measured? In terms of a performance thory, the residual term suggests that 70% of the variance is accounted for. That is very good indeed. In fact, for the present stage of development in social science, it probably represents an upper limit of what can be achieved. If it were also the case that the construct was a valid measure (it related to other measures that should be affected by the antisocial status of the child, such as achievement, poor prognosis for adult adjustment, and other variables), then the writers would conclude that the bootstrapping process had reached a successful conclusion.

We assume that each agent, as well as each mode of assessment, carries its own unique distortions, plus both an overlapping and a unique contribution to the definition of a latent construct. To define Monitoring, we might query the mother, father, and child about the matter. Each agent might be asked to stipulate his or her overall impression of the adequacy with which the parents track the whereabouts of the child. In doing so, we introduce some errors in memory as well as differences in interpretation of what was meant by the question itself. We then must ask, "What are some alternative modes of assessment that do not share these distortions?" For example, are there some methods that rely less on long-term memory and thus generate fewer distortions arising from global judgments of tracking adequacy? A brief daily telephone interview has been developed as an assessment device that we believe diminishes distortion and has established reliability and validity (Chamberlain, 1980). For the behavior in question, the parent and the child are asked to summarize experiences over the past 16 hours, or the past 3 days (Jones, 1974; Patterson et al., 1973). This assessment mode is used as an indicator for several of the constructs in the general model, including Monitoring (see Methods section).

It is assumed that making provisions for defining constructs by networks including multiple agents and multiple modes of assessment will give a more generalizable estimate of any particular construct. Aggregating across modes and agents would presumably give an estimate with two important characteristics: First, it would relate to the widest possible network of relations among constructs in the model (stipulated in advance by the theory), and second, the more generalizable estimates should provide more replicable results than scores based on just one or two indicators. Neither of these assumptions has been tested, nor are they the focus for the present report. Both of them will be tested within the confines of the replication study currently under way.

The building of assessment devices to measure constructs was heavily influenced by the generalizability hypothesis. For both the pilot study and the current longitudinal study, strenuous efforts were made to design assessment procedures sampling multiple agents and modes. Needless to say, we were not always successful. Some constructs are better defined than others. The two constructs that serve as the focus for this discussion, Discipline and Monitoring, are central to the general model. Each also provided rather special problems in its construction, which will be discussed in detail.

INTEGRATING NETWORKS

In the Cronbach and Meehl (1955) publication, no effort was made to specify how information in the nomological network would be coordinated to define the meaning of the hypothetical construct. The problem was stated in the most general terms, "The laws in a nomological network may relate (a) observable properties or quantities to each other; or (b) theoretical constructs to observables; or (c) different theoretical constructs to one another. These laws may be statistical or deterministic" (p. 187). However, one might interpret this statement, and one that follows in another section of the same paper, as being directly related to the last decade's work on structural modeling: "The system involves propositions relating test to construct, construct to other constructs, and finally relating some of these constructs to observables" (p. 193).

The recent developments in structural equation modeling (Bentler, 1980), with their specific emphasis on the necessity of multiple indicators in the definition of constructs (Sullivan, 1974), have important implications for these issues. Developments in maximum likelihood estimation in the 1940s, and computer technology in the 1950s, paved the way for Jöreskog and Sörbom's (1978) introduction of structural modeling in the early 1970s. This work makes it possible to directly address three of the questions raised several decades earlier in the work of the logical empiricists.

The structural modeling approach has systematically emphasized the need for multiple indicators in the definition of latent variables (Bentler, 1980; Sullivan, 1974). Our own use of multiple mode, multiple agent assessment is directly an outgrowth of this earlier point of view. The second structural modeling perspective that relates to the questions raised in the MacCorquodale and Meehl (1948) publication concerns the requirement that the investigator specify, a priori, the relation among the constructs that define a model. As a rough metaphor, one might think of structural modeling as combining two forms of statistical analyses, factor analyses and multiple regression analyses. Confirmatory factor analysis requires that the investigator stipulate which indicators will load on each construct (i.e., how is the nomological network to be defined and how will it be integrated?). It may also require that the investigator identify which indicator is the exemplar for the latent factor.

One may accept factor loadings as a reasonable means for specifying which indicators define which construct. It is still not clear, however, that these operations totally satisfy the question of what it is that a construct means. Part of what a construct means is defined by the methods of measurement, but part of the meaning is also a function of how this latent variable fits into the larger picture, the model. Within the model, what is it that the construct does? Specifically, how is it related to the other constructs? How does it relate to the criteria that set the objectives for the performance theory? Certainly, one could apply multiple regression techniques to this set of questions. It is also the case, as pointed out by Bentler (1980) and others, that structural equations may serve the same function even better. The assumption is that the structural equations provide the most precise statement of the relation of one construct to another.

We will use confirmatory factor analysis to define the nomological networks for two constructs, Monitoring and Discipline. We next raise the question whether these two measures of parenting skill are really one and the same thing, or represent different influences. Are inept Monitoring and Discipline simply an iteration of a single theme, bad parenting? One model would have it that the two constructs are defined by different indicators and constitute two separate measures of parent skills. The alternative hypothesis is that a single factor would subsume both sets of indicators (i.e., the correlation between the constructs is greater than the covariation among the indicators within constructs).

Data will also be represented that evaluate the differences in contribution made to the model itself. Do the two constructs have different validities and different functions? To evaluate this, the scores for Monitoring and Discipline will be related to the criterion variable for the model itself; this variable is defined by the Antisocial construct. Presumably, Monitoring relates directly to this criterion, whereas the effect of poor Discipline is mediated by yet another construct, Microsocial. The relationships of the two constructs to the larger model are briefly discussed in the following section.

THE GENERAL MODEL

Clinical experience in treating several hundred families of antisocial children suggests that these referrals were characterized not only by high rates of observable deviant behavior, but by socially unskilled behaviors as well (Patterson, 1982). The dual nature of this problem has also been noted by others (e.g., Rutter & Garmezy, 1983). It is believed that the determinants for the skill deficits are different from those for the antisocial behaviors. Figure 7.1 summarizes the constructs thought to serve as the main determinants for antisocial behavior. This general model was tested against the same sample used in this chapter in the study by Patterson and Bank (1986). As shown there, the effects of disruptions in parental discipline are not thought to have a direct effect on the child's antisocial behavior. The effect is indirect and through two different paths. On the one hand, the disruptions in discipline are thought to increase parental difficulties in monitoring the child. For example, the child may refuse to give the necessary information as to his or her whereabouts. As shown in Figure 7.1, disruptions in parental monitoring are thought to directly increase the likelihood that the child will engage in both overt and clandestine antisocial behaviors within and outside the home.

Disruptions in discipline also have an indirect effect on antisocial behavior as mediated by a second path through the Coercion and Microsocial constructs. The failure of the parents to discipline increases rates of coercive exchanges among the siblings and between the target child and the parents. The disruption is assumed to be quickly followed by increases in the length of the coercive exchanges and concomitant increases in high amplitude responses such as hitting. Extended coercive chains have been shown to characterize both the antisocial target

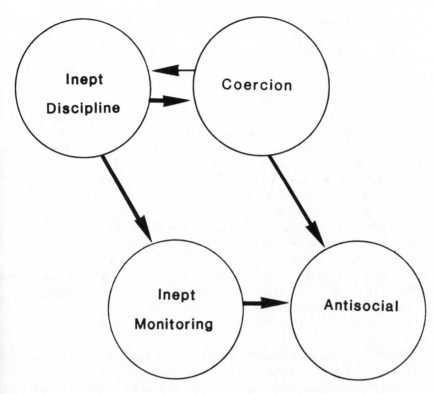

FIGURE 7.1. A Process Model Illustrating Indirect Effects of Discipline on Antisocial

child (Patterson, 1980) and the siblings (Patterson, 1984a). The analyses by Reid (1986) showed that extended coercive chains (over 23 seconds in length) were accompanied by significantly greater likelihood for hitting. The Microsocial construct (not shown in Figure 7.1 for the sake of simplicity) is based on variables from observations made in the home that describe the likelihood of the target child starting up conflicts with parents and siblings plus the mean duration of his coercive exchanges with family members (see Methods). Thus, it appears that disrupted discipline provides the occasion for increased training in the basic fundamentals of the coercion process, which leads, in turn, to increased antisocial behavior in the home and the school.

The Antisocial construct is based on the summary of standardized scores from four agents—peers, teachers, parents, and child self-report—and from three modes of assessment—questionnaires, peer nomination, and telephone interview (see Methods). It is thought to be a highly generalized measure of both overt (e.g., fighting) and clandestine (e.g. stealing) behaviors that occur within both the home and the school.

It is assumed, then, that Monitoring and Discipline scores would correlate differently with the Microsocial and Antisocial scores. These differences would, in turn, define their differential functions in the overall model. Presumably, the Discipline scores would correlate significantly with the Monitoring and the Microsocial scores, but with Monitoring and Microsocial partialled out of Discipline, a statistically nonsignificant relationship with Antisocial should obtain. On the other hand, the Monitoring score should correlate significantly and directly with the Antisocial score but not with the Microsocial score. These issues will be explored in the following section.

It will also be of some interest to explore the validity of the individual indicators that define the two constructs. For example, would it be feasible to employ only one or two indicators for the Monitoring construct and yet account for substantial amounts of variance in the Antisocial scores? This issue will be explored in the discussion of cost utilities below.

Using the same four constructs, alternative models to that depicted in Figure 7.1 have been tested, and at least one yields an acceptable fit. In this competing model, a direct path from Discipline to Antisocial is hypothesized and the path from Coercion to Antisocial Behavior is constrained to zero. It is hypothesized that this second model, with a direct path from Discipline to Antisocial Behavior, is more likely to characterize the process with younger boys (perhaps up to age 9 or 10), whereas the indirect effects model in Figure 7.1 might be more appropriate for preadolescent and adolescent boys.

INDICATORS FOR MONITORING AND DISCIPLINE

As noted earlier, an NIMH-supported planning study made it possible to tailor an initial battery of assessment procedures to the Monitoring, Discipline, and other nine constructs that defined the model. Following this, a second phase in the construction of assessment procedures, summarized in Figure 7.2, resulted in four indicators for the Monitoring and four for the Discipline construct. Generally, each indicator included two or more variables that had been selected, a priori, as de-

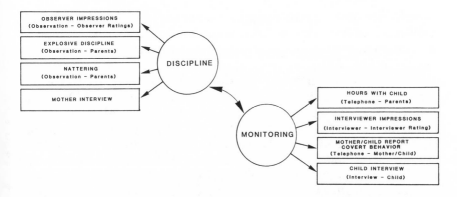

FIGURE 7.2. Specifying Nomological Networks

fining that construct. It was also required that internal consistency analyses (Cronbach's alpha) be equal to or greater than .60 (see Methods for details). It should be kept in mind that, for both constructs, several indicators were constructed but failed to meet the requirements. For example, interview scales for mothers, fathers, and target children were designed to assess both discipline and tracking practices. The only successfully formed indicator from these data was mother interview on discipline.

A great deal is still to be learned about building constructs. Some constructs are defined in a molar fashion by indicators that are entirely based on self-report data (e.g., the Antisocial construct), and some constructs based on estimates of action-reaction sequences are poorly served by self-report data (e.g., sections of the Monitoring and the majority of the Discipline construct). The self-report indicators, although internally consistent (reliable), rarely load on the same factor or correlate in the expected fashion with other constructs in the model. At this point, we know only that there are molar and microsocial variables in the model, which serve very different functions and require different construction techniques.

As shown in Figure 7.2, the second phase of assessment resulted in the two constructs being defined by a number of indicators (shown as boxes in the Figure). Part of the task was then to specify the relation between each indicator, or measure, and its construct. A confirmatory factor analysis was used to test the hypothesized networks of indicators. Note that the Discipline construct was defined by three modes, sequential observation data collected in the home, and global ratings

made by the same observers after their sessions, as well as mother interview on discipline. The Monitoring construct is based on two modes,
interviews and telephone interviews, and reports from two agents,
mother and child.

The third requirement in the Cronbach and Meehl (1955) specification of the nomological network concerns the laws relating the
constructs to one another. The line connecting the Monitoring and
Discipline constructs in Figure 7.2 is defined by a simple bivariate correlation. The hypothesis to be tested is that, for a given construct, the
convergence among the indicators is greater than the correlation between the two measures of parenting skill, resulting in two correlated,
yet distinct, features of parenting ability. The present analyses clarify
the fit between the experimenters' a priori decisions about the constructs and their indicators on the one hand, and the actual data on the
other. Do the indicators define one parent skill—bad parenting—or are
there, as the investigators would have it, two? Do the dimensions reflect anything more than method variance? These questions are addressed by a set of confirmatory factor analyses.

The pragmatics of construct building also requires an empirically
oriented study. What are the relative costs for collecting the data for
each of the eight indicators on the present study, and what are the relevant utilities accruing from the use of just one, two, or three of the indicators to account for criterion variance? Presumably, this kind of
cost/utilities analysis will provide a data base for the investigators'
decision-making process in using these measures and constructs to test
hypotheses.

METHODS

Three major school districts in the Eugene, Oregon, area agreed to participate in the study. Using juvenile court data for the frequency of
delinquent episodes reported by the police, the incidence of police
offenses was calculated for each of the 15 schools in the districts. Of
the 15 targeted high-risk schools, 14 agreed to participate. The 10 highest risk schools were randomly ordered, and the first 6 schools were
recruited.

Each school provided a list of families of fourth-grade boys. Of these
154 families, 21 were declared ineligible: 6 were foreign speaking, 5
moved out of state, 3 moved before contact, 7 for other reasons. Of the
133 eligible families, 103 (77%) agreed to participate in the study. Of

TABLE 7.1
Demographics on Longitudinal Sample: Cohort 1 (1984)

	National probability sample—1974		Planning study (Eugene)	Longitudinal study (Eugene)
Family structure				
2 biological parents	72%		57%	46.2%
Single parent	18%		35%	25%
1 biological, 1 stepparent	09%		07%	28.7%
Social class (Hollingshead, 1975)				
Lower	41.9%		29.8%	52.4%
Working	29.5%		25.7%	14.6%
Middle	22.7%		41.9%	08.5%
No employed parent	(6% other)		02.7%	24.4%

Parental drug use	Mothers	Fathers	Mothers	Fathers
Tried marijuana			22%	66%
Used marijuana in the last year	21%	23%	22%	19%
Tried hard drugs (cocaine, speed, etc.)	41%	44%		
Used hard drugs in the last year	02.8%	02.1%	19%	25%

the 30 families (23%) who refused, most said they were too busy or not interested. Each family was paid up to $300 for participating in the full assessment battery.

Table 7.1 gives a profile of these families in terms of family structure, social class, and parental drug use.

The assessment modes that provided the data base for the four constructs consisted of highly structured interviews with the parents and the child; six brief, telephone interviews with the parents and child, which focused on the occurrence of deviant behavior; three observations in the home; observers' global ratings following each session;

peer nomination data; and data from a child-behavior checklist filled
out by the parents and teachers.

The first step in building each of the constructs consisted of listing
each variate thought to define a latent variable. This was done separately for each of the modes. Next, each listing for an assessment mode
was examined to determine the internal consistency (Cronbach's alpha) for that set. Those variables that did not meet the requirement
were dropped. A set was generally dropped if the alpha value did not
exceed .60. Given that the potential indicator was accepted, then each
variate was standardized so that all the items in a scale made commen-
surate contributions to the total score. The third step was to demonstrate that each of the a priori aggregates correlated significantly with
all other aggregates in that set. Intercorrelated composite scores were
retained; those aggregates that did not correlate .30 or better with the
other members were dropped. The variates and aggregates described below have survived this three-step process.

Although the Monitoring and Discipline constructs are the focus of
this chapter, indicators for those constructs used in the discussion of
validities are also described here.

The Monitoring Construct

This construct is defined by the following four indicators.

Child interview. A structured interview was developed for use with
the target children (Patterson, Dishion, Reid, Capaldi, & Forgatch,
1984). Six items from the child interview that related to the latent variable survived the screening process. They were: (1) How often do you
tell parents when you'll be home? (2) How often do you leave a note
about where you are going? (3) How often do you check in after school?
(4) How often is someone home within one hour after school? (5) How
often do you know how to reach parents if they are out? (6) How often
do you talk to parents about daily plans?

All six variates achieved an item total correlation greater than .20.
The Cronbach's alpha equalled .5926. The items were standardized, and
each child's score is the mean of these six standardized scores.

Interviewer impressions. A questionnaire developed by the staff at
the Oregon Social Learning Center (OSLC) was filled out by each interviewer directly after the interview was finished. Those who interviewed the parents were asked to give their impressions of how carefully the parents monitor the target children; those who interviewed

the child were asked their impressions of how well supervised the children were by their parents.

The interviewer impressions indicator is the mean of these three standard scores (or two scores in the case of single-parent families).

Hours spent with child. A telephone interview questionnaire was developed by the staff at OSLC to track behavior in the family (Dishion, et al., 1984a, 1984b). The data base consisted of six telephone interviews with the parent and with the child. Among other things, the parent was asked how many waking hours he/she spent with his/her son yesterday. The score is the total hours divided by the number of calls. These scores are standardized over the sample.

Family agreement on child behavior. In an attempt to measure how much of the children's antisocial behavior the parents actually monitor, scores were developed based on the difference, or agreement, between the parents' report of the children's behavior over a specific period, and the children's report of the same behaviors over the same period. Both the parents and children were asked if the children engaged in any of the following clandestine behaviors within the last three days: told a lie, trouble at school, took money from family, broke things on purpose, smoked cigarettes, drank alcohol, or smoked marijuana.

If both parents and child answered yes, then that item was scored as a 3; if parent and child both answered no, then that item was scored 2; if parents answered yes, and the child no, that item was scored as 1; if parent answered no, and the child yes, the score was 0. Final scores were calculated by summing the assigned scores over the items for all six calls, and dividing by the number of calls made to that family.

The Discipline Construct

The observations in the home formed a data base for deriving three composite scores: parent nattering, parent explosive punishment, and observer global impressions. The mother's structured interview provided information for the fourth indicator.

Parent nattering. A conditional probability was calculated separately for each parent reacting negatively if interacting with the child. Given time spent interacting with the target child, what is the proportion of the parent-child interaction characterized by nonexplosive negative responses of the parent? This score is a composite of two types of parental reactions, starting up conflict and reacting aversively to coercive child behavior, which have been shown in a series of studies to characterize clinic-sample families (Patterson, 1982, 1984b; Reid, in press). The test-retest reliability for this nattering score was .41 (N = 16 families) for an interval of 8 to 12 weeks. The observer reliability with 99 sessions was r = .66. The composite score is the mean of the two standardized scores for the parents.

Parent explosive punishment. This score is based on the studies of abused children by Reid (in press). His investigations showed that, compared to parents or normals, child abusive parents tended to use more yelling, threatening, hitting, and humiliation. The score for each parent is the likelihood the parent will use one of these extreme forms of punishment given an interaction with the child.

The composite score is the mean of the two conditional probabilities. Interrater reliability was r = .79 with N = 99 observation sessions; the test-retest stability was r = .52 for an interval of 8 to 12 weeks for 16 families.

Observer impressions. The observer impression checklist is a revised version of the assessment device described by Reid (1978). After each observation session, the observer responds to 46 items. From the a priori set of 22 discipline items, the following survived the item analysis for both the mother and father: (1) Parent gave rationales, (2) parent overly strict, (3) parent erratic, inconsistent, haphazard, (4) parent consistent, even-handed, firm, and (5) parent used nagging to get compliance. An additional item, parent teased out of sour mood, formed a significant part of the composite for mothers. The alpha coefficient for mothers was .78. For fathers, the following items were included in addition to those for both parents: clearly pinpointed behavior, used time out, used points, was overly permissive, was in good control of child, and had little control of child. The alpha for the set of 11 items for the fathers was .83. The observer agreement for 99 sessions was r = .57. The composite scores for mothers and fathers were significantly intercorrelated, r = .73. The scores for the two parents were each standardized and combined to form the composite.

Mother interview. Part of the structured interview that mothers and fathers did separately was a set of questions concerning their discipline practices and perceived effectiveness. Six questions from mothers survived item analysis with Cronbach's alpha = .67: (1) Do you follow through with threatened punishment if the misbehavior doesn't stop? (2) Does your son get away with things? (3) Do you get angry when you punish your son? (4) How often does your punishment depend on your mood? (5) Are you confident you can change your child's misbehaviors? (6) Do you feel you are having problems generally managing your son? The alpha for fathers was not sufficient to form a composite.

The Antisocial Construct

Item analyses were conducted to develop composites with acceptable item-total consistency. These composite scores were used as indicators of antisocial behavior. Scales were developed separately for overt and clandestine behaviors, as well as for mothers and fathers. The score used for each indicator was the mean of the remaining items in each composite. Three of the five composites as indicators of antisocial behavior are from various forms of parent report; two are from data collected at the schools.

Parents' child-behavior checklist. Both parents completed the Achenbach and Edelbrock (1979) checklist of child behaviors. This composite contained 12 items reflecting aggressive or clandestine behaviors (Patterson & Skinner, 1984). Cronbach's alpha for mothers and fathers were .79 and .80, respectively.

Parents' report of overt and covert behaviors. An OSLC-developed questionnaire surveyed parents' perceptions of their children's antisocial inclinations. Parents indicated how frequently their sons talked back to adults, screamed or shouted, lost tempers, teased brothers or sisters, threw things, and hurt animals. In addition, parents rated 20 items as often true, sometimes true, or not true, most of which referred to stealing or fire setting (Patterson & Skinner, 1984). Cronbach's alpha for both parents was .83 for mothers and .81 for fathers.

Parent telephone interview. As part of the interview described previously, parents were asked if, within the last 24 hours, their child had talked back or sassed an adult, screamed or shouted, swore, fought, teased, disobeyed parents, hit siblings, or thrown things. The standard score is actually averaged over six phone calls made three days apart. Cronbach's alpha = .77.

Teachers' child-behavioral checklist. Child behavior-checklists were completed by the teacher for each boy in the sample. The resulting 18-item scale included questions concerning both overt and covert behavior problems in the school.

Peer nominations. Each of the boys in the sample was asked to nominate three boys in his school, who were also in the study, for each of nine items: play rough, fight a lot, get in trouble, push and shove, talk back to teachers, have hot tempers, are honest, take others' things, and skip school. Cronbach's alpha = .80.

Child telephone interview. The telephone interview was administered to each of the boys as described (see parent telephone interview). They were asked if they had committed a variety of antisocial behaviors of both an overt and covert nature (Patterson & Skinner, 1984). Their average endorsement rate for each behavior over the six calls was standardized and then averaged across behaviors. Cronbach's alpha = .83.

The Microsocial Construct

Three variables reflecting the child's irritable behavior in the home were derived from observational data. Two conditional probabilities—the probability that the child will start conflict with his parents and the probability the child will start conflict with his siblings—were used, and the average length of the child's negative interactions with other family members was the third indicator.

The conditional probability was calculated for each child's onset of conflict given that the parent had acted in a positive or neutral mode within 16 seconds prior to the child's negative behavior. Another conditional probability was developed for the child's onset of conflict with siblings. This variable was calculated in the same manner as child onset of conflict with parents.

The average length, in real time, of the child's coercive chains was calculated separately for interactions with the mother, the father, and with siblings. In all cases, a chain consisted of at least two consecutive negative codes between the two agents. The total duration of these chains was divided by the number of chains identified in the observation data resulting in the average length of coercive chains.

Early difficulties: Son's early history. Parents completed a questionnaire on their child's early history. The first composite score was made up of how easy the child was to care for in the first five years, as well as 8 items from a list of 11 problems parents may have encountered in this time. These problems included colic, tantrums, disobedience, sleeping problems, and hyperactivity. This score reflects the extent of management problems the child presented in early childhood.

Early difficulties: Parental concern. This score reflects the extent to which the parents were preoccupied with their child's development. The parents reported how often they worried about their child's physical and mental development, and whether they thought their child had behavior or emotional problems when growing up. The average standard score was used for each child.

RESULTS

Three different questions are to be considered. First is the matter of integrating the nomological networks for the two constructs. Related to this is the issue of whether these constructs are really two different aspects of parent skills or simply redundant of the *bad parent* theme. The second question concerns the validity of the constructs, and the third, the cost utilities that accrue from using single indicators to perform the same functions for which the more generalized construct scores were designed.

Integrating the Nomological Networks
for the Two Constructs

Intercorrelations for the eight indicators expected to define Monitoring and Discipline are presented in Table 7.2, where it can be seen that the Discipline indicators covary with each other (median .40), while the indicators for the Monitoring construct also tend to covary with each other (median .30). The vast majority of the cross-construct indicator correlations are of lower magnitude (median .08) than are the within-cluster correlations. The most notable deviations from low-magnitude cross-construct correlations are those between the Monitoring indicator *interviewer impressions* and all of the Discipline indicators with the single exception of *mother interview*.

A more precise view of these relationships within their hypothesized nomological networks is provided by confirmatory factor analysis. The spss-x (1983), lisrel VI (Jöreskog & Sörbom, 1983) option was used to evaluate the adequacy of the two-factor (Monitoring and Discipline), theoretically driven model depicted in Figure 7.2. It was also used to compare the efficacy of that model to the more parsimonious single-factor model (Poor Parenting).

Confirmatory factor analyses following the lisrel framework re-

TABLE 7.2

Correlation Matrices for Monitoring and Discipline

	Observ. impress.	Parent nattering	Explosive discipline	Mother int.	Int. impress.	Hours with child	Child int.	Teleph. diff.
Observer impressions	1.0							
Parent nattering	-.592	1.0						
Explosive discipline	-.392	.417	1.0					
Mother interview	-.289	.317	.218	1.0				
Interviewer impressions	.361	-.486	-.291	-.092	1.0			
Hours with child	-.020	-.105	.012	.047	.282	1.0		
Child interview	.180	-.266	-.055	-.068	.388	.110	1.0	
Telephone difference	.182	-.252	-.010	-.014	.370	.314	.177	1.0

quire the estimation of factor loadings, errors of measurement, and latent variable variances and covariances. One loading on each factor, however, is set equal to 1 so that it may serve as a reference indicator.

The two-factor confirmatory analysis resulted in statistically significant factor loadings beyond the .01 level for all eight indicators. As can be seen in Table 7.3 the parent nattering indicator had the highest loading on the Discipline construct, and the interviewers' global impression had the highest loading on the Monitoring construct.

The Discipline-Monitoring correlation showed that indeed parents who were inept at Discipline also tended to be less effective in their Monitoring scores. The correlation was .57 (p less than .01).

The confirmatory analysis also showed that the measurement model fit the a priori specification that Monitoring and Discipline were two separate, though correlated, parenting skills, chi square(18) = 13.63, p greater than .75, indicating a nonsignificant difference between the sample covariance matrix and the covariance matrix reproduced by the specified model.

The second confirmatory factor analysis tested the alternate model depicting inept Discipline and Monitoring as a single dimension, bad parenting. The fit for this model was unsatisfactory, chi square(19) =

TABLE 7.3
Two-Factor Solution for Monitoring and Discipline

	Factor loadings		Standard	Errors of
Indicators	Discipline	Monitoring	errors	measurement
Observer impressions	.781		(ref. ind.)	.389
Parent nattering	−.941		.209	.115
Explosive discipline	−.461		.207	.787
Mother interview	−.345		.179	.881
Interviewer impressions		.872	(ref. ind.)	.239
Hours with child		.320	.143	.897
Child interview		.442	.152	.805
Telephone difference		.442	.152	.805

31.98, p less than .05, although, once again, all factor loadings were statistically significant. The solutions to the two models were compared
to determine whether they were indeed significantly different from one
another. They were; chi square(1) = 28.35, p less than .001. Clearly, the
two-factor solution is an adequate representation of the data and offers
a significantly better solution than observed in the single-factor confirmatory analysis.

Validity of the Constructs

Within the larger model, the Monitoring and Discipline constructs are
thought to play quite different roles (Patterson et al., in press). As noted
earlier, Monitoring relates directly to antisocial child behavior, whereas
the effects of Discipline are thought to be mediated by both Microsocial and Monitoring constructs (see Figure 7.1). It was also thought
useful to explore differences in relations within a list of 10 variables
expected to relate differentially to the 2 latent variables.

For example, it seemed reasonable to suppose that Discipline might
relate more to rejection by normal peers (because of the coercive interpersonal style), whereas Monitoring would relate more to a drift toward
membership in a deviant peer group, as shown in the earlier findings
from the planning study (Patterson et al., in press). A child's abrasive
style and inability to accept negative feedback might also relate to difficulties in academic achievement. This being the case, the Discipline
scores would covary with achievement, though Monitoring scores
might not. There is some evidence that child temperament might play
a role, interacting with a lack of parent skill in determining antisocial
child behavior (Olweus, 1984; Parke & Slaby, 1983; Werner & Smith,
1977). To test this possibility, a composite was formed based on parent
retrospective reports of difficulties with the child during the first five
years of life (see Methods).

It was also thought that parents with a history of criminal activity
might be prone to monitor their boys less effectively; perhaps socioeconomic status would play a similar role. Finally, it was assumed that
extrafamilial stressors and measures of conflict within families would
correlate with both measures of parent skills. Findings from earlier
studies had shown that outside stressors tended to disrupt parenting
skills and to be related to increased antisocial behavior (Patterson,
1982).

As shown in Table 7.4, the retrospective measure of child tempera-

TABLE 7.4
Different Constructs, Different Functions

| | Correlations with: | |
Variables	Monitoring	Discipline
Early difficulty with child	−.073	−.138
Child's reading level	.195*	.429***
Child rejected by peers	.175*	.246**
Child committed to deviant peer group	−.361***	.253**
Socioeconomic status	.204*	.319*
Parents' frequency of arrests	.064	−.068
Extrafamilial stressors		
Mothers	−.248*	−.085
Fathers	−.251*	−.164
Within-family hassles		
Mothers	−.299***	−.067
Fathers	−.156	−.118

NOTE: Ns vary from 69 to 103.
*p less than .05.
**p less than .01.
***p less than .001.

ment showed nonsignificant correlations with both measures of parent skill, which fails to replicate the findings in an earlier study by Olweus (1984). Both measures showed low-level but significant correlations with the composite measure of rejection by normal peers. The more difficulties the parents had with tracking and disciplining the child, the more likely the child was to be perceived as being rejected by the normal peer group. The findings from the present sample of fourth-grade boys replicated the earlier findings from adolescent samples: Parental failure to monitor correlated significantly with an involvement with deviant peers.

Although the measure of parental arrests did not covary significantly with either measure of parenting skill, higher levels of socioeconomic status significantly predicted better monitoring and discipline practices. Notice, also, that three of the four measures of extrafamilial and intrafamilial measures of stress correlated significantly with the Monitoring score, whereas there was no significant covariation with disruptions in discipline. These findings provide some support for the hypotheses (1) that stressors are related to disruptions in parenting skills, and (2) that Monitoring and Discipline scores may be differentially sensitive to such disruptions.

The idea of a generalized estimate of a latent dimension has several implications. One of the key ideas is that the overall construct, defined via its nomological net, relate to other constructs with minimal distortions. Presumably, if one used the most generalized estimates, there would be minimal shrinkage during replication. This procedure should also allow a better fit of theoretical model to data. To obtain a generalized estimate, we averaged the weighted, standardized indicator scores for each construct. It is important to remember that a latent dimension is indeed latent. These scores are only approximations to theoretical constructs.

The luxury of multiple-mode, multiple-agent data sets appears to us to be a necessity in the development of reliable factor structures and valid process models. Given an already demonstrated, adequate process model, some investigators might wish to use only one or two of the indicators. This practicality raises the question of cost and utility (i.e., benefit, efficiency, usefulness).

Patterson and Bank (1986) tested the model and found it to be adequate, thus replicating the Patterson, Dishion, and Bank (1984) structural equation analyses using pilot-study data and a smaller number of indicators. Thus far, then, there are two studies using independent datasets with outcomes that are consistent with the process model depicted in Figure 7.1. To choose the best one or two indicators to represent Monitoring and Discipline, it is important to note that in the process model analyses (Patterson & Bank, 1986) nattering and observer impressions loaded highest on Discipline, whereas interviewer impressions and number of hours with child loaded highest on Monitoring. Interview and questionnaire data are certainly the least expensive type to collect, but it appears likely that the usefulness of the model will be vitiated without some indicators based on observational data.

The cost estimates in Table 7.5 are based on per family varying costs such as staff time and supplies. No estimates of start-up costs are given since expenses associated with office space, telephones, computer services, and so on vary greatly around the country. The equipment and

TABLE 7.5
Cost per Family of Discipline and Monitoring Indicators

Indicators	Administering measure	Data analysis management	Total
Observations:[a]			
Nattering			
Explosive discipline	45.00[a]	160.00	205.00
	Plus equipment and software $7,000.00		
Observer impressions	7.00	10.50	17.70
Mother interview	4.00	7.50	11.50
Child interview on monitoring	3.10	7.20	10.30
Interviewer impressions on monitoring	1.50	7.50	9.00
Telephone interview[a]	12.00	25.00	37.00

[a]Estimates for three observations and six telephone interviews

software referred to for observations include the cost of one OS-3 event recorder, one computer terminal, and programs for entry and formatting OS-3 data. OSLC incurred further expense performing reliabilities on 20% and retest on 10% of all observations, observer impressions, interviews, and interviewer impressions. About 25% of the observations and interviews required rescheduling due to dry runs (no shows) or cancellation.

DISCUSSION

In this chapter we have attempted to describe a method for the measurement of theoretical constructs and to document an effort at developing measures for Monitoring and Discipline, two constructs of parental skills believed to be central to the prediction of antisocial behavior of boys in a variety of contexts (Patterson, 1982; Patterson & Bank, 1986; Patterson et al., in press).

Following the psychometric contributions of Carnap (1956), Cronbach and Meehl (1955), MacCorquodale and Meehl (1948), and others, it was assumed that the optimal approach to defining hypothetical constructs was by a *network* of theoretically determined indicators, preferably indicators representing multiple agents and methods. These indicators must be quantifiable and form distinct and predictable clusters. These clusters (i.e., factors or latent dimensions) must, in turn, prove adequate in process model validity tests (for example, see Figure 7.1). The collection of multimode and multiagent data for each network of indicators minimizes distortions in our estimates of theoretical constructs, and therefore reduces biases in estimating the relation between two (or more) theoretical constructs (Dwyer, 1983).

The confirmatory factor analyses were consistent with the hypotheses that (1) the eight theoretically driven indicators would form two distinct, though correlated, factors identifiable as Monitoring and Discipline, and that this measurement model would provide a satisfactory fit to the data; (2) a single-factor solution, dubbed *poor parenting*, would not provide a satisfactory fit to the data; and (3) the initial two-factor—as compared to the single-factor—solution would provide a statistically significant better fit.

Thus, the development of indicators for the Monitoring and Discipline constructs has passed the first hurdles. It appears likely, then, that parental skills must be divided into at least these two categories. It should be remembered, however, that the Monitoring and Discipline constructs emerged from clinical experience and theory in the prediction and treatment of antisocial behaviors; therefore, it is possible that the prediction of criterion constructs other than Antisocial Behavior will suggest additional and distinct parent skills constructs.

The apparent adequacy of the nomological networks defining Monitoring and Discipline is further buttressed by Patterson and Bank's (1986) finding of a satisfactory fit of the process model depicted in Figure 7.1. In addition, that model accounted for approximately 40% of the variance in the criterion construct, Antisocial Behavior. These results lend strong support to the notion that Monitoring and Discipline are indeed valid theoretical constructs. One caution in interpreting these findings is that several of the indicators derived from the observation data showed relatively low test-retest reliabilities. With the nattering indicator, for example, the test-retest reliability is only .41. Clearly, this coefficient is limited by an interrater reliability of .66, and no doubt further limited because the nattering variable uses only a small subset of all the codes used by observers. (That is, reliabilities for the entire coding system are higher: .75 to .85.) In addition, it is possible that the 8–12 week retest interval used in this study produces reliabilities far weaker than might result from, for example, a 1-week retest interval. Despite these difficulties, it is noteworthy that the validities for nattering are as hypothesized and account for considerable variance in the antisocial criterion variable.

We continue to use the bootstrapping approach to construct development for other constructs and their indicators. As an approach to complex questions concerning the measurement of theoretical constructs, the methods explored in this paper appear quite promising, but the need for further replication remains. In addition, tests of generalizability of these constructs across a variety of criterion constructs, differing ages, and subject populations are crucial.

NOTES

This investigation was supported by funds from the NIMH section on violence and antisocial behavior (MH37940-03). The writers gratefully acknowledge the contributions of Martie Skinner in programming the analyses and preparing working drafts of some sections of the manuscript. The collection of the data that served as the data base was supervised by Deborah Capaldi and her lieutenants S. Thibodeaux and K. Gardner. The writers owe a debt of gratitude to them for the privilege of working with a high quality set of data.

REFERENCES

Achenbach, T. M., & Edelbrock, C. S. (1979). The child behavior profile: Boys aged 12 to 16 and girls aged 6 to 11 and 12 to 16 (Vol. 2). *Journal of Consulting and Clinical Psychology, 41*(2), 223–233.

Bandura, A. (1973). *Aggression: A social learning analysis.* Englewood Cliffs, N.J.: Prentice-Hall.

Bandura, A., & Walters, R. H. (1963). *Social learning and personality development.* New York: Holt, Rinehart & Winston.

Bentler, P. M. (1980). Multivariate analysis with latent variables: Causal modeling. *Annual Review in Psychology, 31,* 419–455.

Bridgman, P. W. (1927). *The logic of modern physics.* New York: Macmillan.

Carnap, R. (1956). The methodological character of theoretical concepts. In H. Feigl & M. Scriven (Eds.), *Minnesota studies in the philosophy of science: The foundations of science and concepts of psychology and psychoanalysis* (Vol. 1). Minneapolis: University of Minnesota Press.

Chamberlain, P. (1980). *Standardization of a parent report measure.* Unpublished doctoral dissertation, University of Oregon, Eugene, Oreg.

Cronbach, L. J., & Meehl, P. E. (1955). Construct validity in psychological tests. In H. Feigl & M. Scriven (Eds.), *Minnesota studies in the philosophy of science: The foundations of science and concepts of psychology and psychoanalysis* (Vol. 1). Minneapolis: University of Minnesota Press.

Dishion, T. J., Patterson, G. R., Reid, J. B., Capaldi, D., Forgatch, M. S., & McCarthy, S. (1984a). *Longitudinal documentation: Child telephone interview.* OSLC Working Paper (Oregon Social Learning Center, 207 E. 5th, Eugene, Oreg. 97401).

Dishion, T. J., Patterson, G. R., Reid, J. B., Capaldi, D., Forgatch, M. S., & McCarthy, S. (1984b). *Longitudinal documentation: Parent telephone interview.* OSLC Working Paper (Oregon Social Learning Center, 207 E. 5th, Eugene, Oreg. 97401).

Dwyer, J. H. (1983). *Statistical models for the social and behavioral sciences.* New York: Oxford University Press.

Feigl, H. (1956). Some major issues and developments in the philosophy of science of logical empiricism. In H. Feigl & M. Scriven (Eds.), *Minnesota studies in the philosophy of science: The foundations of science and concepts of psychology and psychoanalysis* (Vol. 1). Minneapolis: University of Minnesota Press.

Hollingshead, A. B. (1975). *Four factor index of social status.* Unpublished manuscript. Department of Sociology, Yale University.

Jones, R. R. (1974). "Observation" by telephone: An economical behavior sampling technique. *Oregon Research Institute Technical Report, 4* (No. 1).

Jöreskog, K. G., & Sörbom, D. (1978). *LISREL IV.* Chicago: Natural Education Resources.

Jöreskog, K. G., & Sörbom, D. (1983). *LISREL VI.* Chicago: Natural Education Resources.

Kagan, J. (1984). Meaning and procedure. Unpublished paper. Harvard University.

MacCorquodale, K., & Meehl, P. E. (1948). On a distinction between hypothetical constructs and intervening variables. *Psychological Bulletin, 55,* 95–107.

Olweus, D. (1984). Development of stable aggressive reaction patterns in males. In R. Blanchard & D. C. Blanchard (Eds.), *Advances in the study of aggression.* New York: Academic Press.

Parke, R. D., & Slaby, R. G. (1983). The development of aggression. In R. M. Hetherington (Ed.), *Handbook of child psychology* (Vol. 4) *Socialization, personality, and social development.* New York: Wiley.

Patterson, G. R. (1980). Mothers: The unacknowledged victims. *Monographs of the Society for Research in Child Development, 45* (5, Serial No. 186), 1–64.

Patterson, G. R. (1982). *Coercive family process.* Eugene, Oreg.: Castalia.

Patterson, G. R. (1984a). Siblings: fellow travelers in coercive family process. In R. J. Blanchard & D. C. Blanchard (Eds.), *Advances in the study of aggression.* New York: Academic Press.

Patterson, G. R. (1984b). Stress: a change agent for family process. In N. Garmezy & M. Rutter (Eds.), *Stress, coping and development in children.* New York: McGraw-Hill.

Patterson, G. R., & Bank, L. (1986). Bootstrapping your way in the nomological thicket. *Behavioral Assessment, 8,* 49–73.

Patterson, G. R., Chamberlain, P., & Reid, J. B. (1982). A comparative evaluation of parent training procedures. *Behavior Therapy, 13,* 638–650.

Patterson, G. R., Cobb, J. A., & Ray, R. S. (1973). A social engineering technology for retraining the families of aggressive boys. In H. E. Adams & I. P. Unikel (Eds.), *Issues and trends in behavior therapy.* Springfield, Ill.: Charles C. Thomas. (Also in S. Steinmetz & M. Straus [Eds.], *Violence in the family.* New York: Dodd, Mead.

Patterson, G. R., & Dishion, T. J. (1985). Contributions of families and peers to delinquency. *Research in Criminology, 23*(1), 63–79.

Patterson, G. R., Dishion, T. J., & Bank, L. (1984). Family interaction: A process model of deviancy training. In L. Eron (Ed.), *Aggressive Behavior* (Special ed.), *10,* 253–267.

Patterson, G. R., Dishion, T. J., Reid, J. B., Capaldi, D., & Forgatch, M. S. (1984). *Longitudinal documentation: Child interview.* OSLC Working Paper (Oregon Social Learning Center, 207 E. 5th, Eugene, Oreg. 97401).

Patterson, G. R., Ray, R. S., Shaw, D. A., & Cobb, J. A. (1969). *Manual for coding of family interactions* (revised). Unpublished manuscript.

Patterson, G. R., Reid, J. B., & Dishion, T. (in press). *A social learning approach: 4. Antisocial boys.* Eugene, Oreg.: Castalia.

Patterson, G. R., & Skinner, M. L. (1984). *Antisocial construct.* Oregon Social Learning Center Technical Report No. L01.

Patterson, G. R., & Southamer-Loeber, M. (1984). The correlation of family management practices and delinquency. *Child Development, 55*(4), 1299–1308.

Reid, J. B. (1967). *Reciprocity in family interaction.* Unpublished doctoral dissertation, University of Oregon, Eugene, Oreg.

Reid, J. B. (1978). *A social learning approach to family intervention. II: Observation in home settings.* Eugene, Oreg.: Castalia.

Reid, J. B. (1986). Social-interactional patterns in families of abused and non-abused children. In C. Zahn Waxler, M. Cummings, & M. Radke-Yarrow (Eds.), *Social and biological origins of altruism and aggression.* New York: Cambridge University Press.

Rutter, M., & Garmezy, N. (1983). Developmental psychopathology. In E. M. Hetherington (Ed.), *Handbook of child psychology.* Vol. 4 *Socialization, personality, and social development.* New York: Wiley.

Skinner, B. F. (1953). *Science and human behavior.* New York: Macmillan.

Sullivan, J. L. (1974). Multiple indicators: Some criteria of selection. In H. M. Blalock (Ed.), *Measurement in the social sciences.* Chicago: Aldine.

Werner, E. E., & Smith, R. S. (1977). *Kauai's children come of age.* Honolulu: University Press of Hawaii.

From Explanation to Prediction and Prevention: Future Implications of a Performance Theory for Antisocial Behavior

JEANNE WURMSER

Mental health professionals working in various health, mental health, education, or other community-based settings constitute a group of consumers who are eager to take sound, replicable research findings and apply them in programs that target a wide range of distressing outcomes for prevention.

In community mental health centers, efforts are constantly being made to allocate attention and resources toward groups in the community who are seen as experiencing serious problems or causing problems for others. Among those groups toward which planning agencies have mandated special efforts are battered women, abused children, delinquent adolescents, and dysfunctional young adults who are characterized as "young chronics" because they appear recurrently in large numbers in multiple sections of the health, mental health, social service, and corrections systems. Abuse of drugs and alcohol appear to be present in the multiproblem families from which many of these "target groups" are identified. In many cases, similar family patterns seem to recur in generation after generation. The costs to society in treating these troubled individuals and their victims are high. Those who have tried to design treatment systems for persons with long histories of aggressive and antisocial behavior are all too aware of the inadequacies of our current technologies. Although advances in treatment and rehabilitation efficacy are needed, many who design programs at the community level feel that greater returns may come from efforts at early identification and prevention. Without careful design and evaluation, however, prevention efforts can salve our consciences but have little demonstrable impact. The field of public health has provided many examples of prevention efforts that have been successful. Understanding the etiology and relationships among factors contributing to physical disease syndromes has allowed identification of those at risk and design of interventions that can be monitored to prove effectiveness. In preventive efforts to manage complex patterns of human behavior, however, clear demonstrations of effectiveness are rare. The painstaking work of Gerald Patterson and his colleagues at the Oregon Social Learning Center may constitute the beginnings of an exception.

Patterson's efforts to design treatment programs for antisocial children and to develop and test a theoretical model that explains to some degree the development and maintenance of antisocial behaviors provide a rare prototype of the scientist-practitioner at work. Patterson has chosen an area of human behavior with broad implications for the larger society. He has engaged in a program of research and practice that has the potential not only to help us understand the development of antisocial behavior patterns but to develop our capacity for early identification and successful intervention. Throughout descriptions of his "bootstrapping" strategy for developing constructs, and in his choice of variables and creation of multiagent and multimode assessment devices, his base of experience in field research and in clinical treatment of families is clearly communicated. Patterson's ability to move back and forth between two roles with related but different goals—the scientist and the practitioner—favors the likelihood that his research findings will ultimately have a real impact on practice. The potential for using these findings, not only in therapy with individuals and families but in the development of policies and programs in which behavior-disordered youngsters are placed for the purpose of education, rehabilitation, or treatment is of great importance. Patterson communicates an appreciation for the complexity of dealing with children with true, full-blown behavior disorders, not laboratory analogues in which one or two relatively simple variables are manipulated to control relatively simple aspects of behavior.

Patterson's report that a recent study showed his model to account for approximately 30% of the variance in the criterion construct of Antisocial Behavior and also supported the adequacy of his "nomological networks" design for assessing the parent behaviors of Monitoring and Discipline, indicates that his work could lead to successful and cost-efficient prevention projects. His research has also resulted in the development of tested assessment procedures for key variables.

Some of the assessment techniques developed by Patterson and his colleagues remain quite costly for routine application in most community program settings. Although the technology of his system is well developed, maintaining teams of trained observers and analyzing extensive amounts of data would be difficult outside a university setting with specifically allocated research funding. In a systematic evaluation of a prevention demonstration project, however, such resources could be justified and generated. The work presented in this chapter whets the appetite of practitioners for similar development of the other constructs in the general model. As the constructs are refined through further research and the assessment technology is developed to measure each construct, the ability of practitioners to design interventions for families in therapy and programs for high-risk groups will be enhanced. The frustration is that so much more effort is needed before the potential of Patterson's work can be realized on a broad-scale basis.

In addition to assessing the contribution of the other constructs in the general model to the "other 70%" of the variance in the construct of Antisocial Behavior, clinical experience with children suggests that other potential contributors must be examined to extend our ability to predict and prevent antisocial behavior. For example, physiological contributors such as genetic abnormalities may affect certain forms of aggressive behavior. In a clinical population, a diagnosis of attention-deficit disorder is often a concomitant of aggressive and antisocial behavior patterns. The interactions among learning disabilities, peer perceptions, peer relationships, and antisocial behavior are discussed clinically in individual evaluations and should be considered in comprehensive research. Clinical experience suggests that parent behavior in families with antisocial children is often related to parental drug or alcohol abuse. These among other factors appear to be worthy of study in the attempt to account for variance in children's prosocial and antisocial behavior.

Patterson's research raises the expectations of a large community of research consumers who are attempting to cope with antisocial behavior and its effects in our society. His considered thoughts and further efforts to define the linkages between explanation, prediction, and prevention will be most welcome. Widespread dissemination of his technology and effective application in preventive intervention, however, remain as tasks for the future.

Chapter 8

Assessing the Behavior and Performance of Teams in Organizations: The Case of Air Transport Crews

J. RICHARD HACKMAN and
ROBERT L. HELMREICH

About 1815 PST, Flight 173 crashed into a wooded, populated area killing 8 passengers and 2 crewmembers, and seriously injuring 21 passengers and 2 other crewmembers. The National Transportation Safety Board determined that the probable cause of the accident was the failure of the captain to monitor properly the aircraft's fuel state and to properly respond to the low fuel state and the crewmember's advisories regarding fuel state. This resulted in fuel exhaustion to all engines. Contributing to the accident was the failure of the other two flight crewmembers to fully comprehend the criticality of the fuel state or to successfully communicate their concern to the captain.

The Safety Board believes that this accident exemplifies a recurring problem—a breakdown in cockpit management and teamwork during a situation involving malfunctions of aircraft systems in flight. (Excerpts from Aircraft Accident Report NTSB-AAR-79-7)

This is one example from a growing body of accident and incident reports indicating that the functioning of cockpit crews as *teams* merits further study. In this accident, and indeed in most commercial accidents, the first finding reported from the investigation is that "the flightcrew was properly certified and qualified for the flight." However, as noted by Helmreich (1984), recent data from NASA aviation research suggests strongly that the assumption that technically proficient individuals will form effective working teams is incorrect. Analyses of safety-related accidents and incidents show that approximately two-thirds of them result from failures in crew coordination (Cooper et al., 1979). Despite increasing awareness of the significance of crew coordination deficiencies in aircraft accidents and incidents, little research has been devoted to the problem. Why is this the case?

First, there is little public pressure for learning more about crew functioning because of the outstanding safety record of commercial aviation. Flying an air carrier is, without question, the safest way to get from one place to another if one examines the number of deaths and injuries per passenger mile traveled. Moreover, even though substandard performance by flight crews can result in increased costs (such as fuel and maintenance expenses) and greater-than-necessary risks to safety, poor crew performance usually is invisible to the flying public. Individuals outside the aviation community have little reason to call for additional studies of crew behavior and performance.

Another reason for the paucity of research on cockpit crews, one particularly germane to the present topic, is the absence of appropriate *methodologies* for describing, analyzing, and evaluating cockpit crews. Consider, for example, the accident report just cited. Several pages of that report are devoted to analyzing a minor mechanical problem, which initially distracted the crew's attention. Yet despite the ultimate finding that the crash was due *not* to the mechanical defect but instead to ineffective crew performance, the analysis of the interaction among members of the crew of Flight 173 is primarily speculative and described in terms of what "could have" or "should have" been done to avoid the crash. There are no generally accepted methodological tools or procedures available for assessing how effectively members of a cockpit crew work together.

OBJECTIVES AND PLAN

This chapter examines methodological and conceptual issues that arise when one attempts to measure the behavior and performance effectiveness of work groups that operate in organizational settings. We propose some ideas that promise general applicability to team assessment by focusing in detail on one kind of team—crews that fly jet transports for scheduled airlines. We have chosen to focus on such teams for three reasons. First, as will be seen below, challenging issues in assembling team behavior and performance are present with special clarity and vividness in aircraft crews. Second, the stakes are high. Assessment outcomes are potentially of life-and-death significance, and both pilots and those who assess them care a great deal about how, and how well, performance assessments are done. And third, we have considerable direct experience with these teams, and believe we can use that experience to frame and discuss some issues that will be of general interest to people who study and manage groups in organizations.

Our aspiration to develop conclusions of general applicability is not without limits, and we begin the chapter by conceptually delineating our domain of interest. Then we show how airline crews fit within that domain, and describe how crews function as they go about their work.

We then turn to a discussion of the context within which assessment of airline crews takes place. This is done in considerable detail, because a major point of our chapter is that team assessment cannot be accomplished without accommodating substantially to the historical, political, and organizational contexts within which the teams (and their would-be assessors) function.

Then we identify and discuss several special challenges that must be met by those who would conduct assessments of crew behavior and performance, and we draw on our current research to illustrate some alternative ways to deal with these challenges. Although our chapter focuses exclusively on cockpit crews in airlines, we hope that readers will find in it some ideas and perspectives that are useful in considering assessment models and practices for a variety of other kinds of teams in other types of organizations.

DOMAIN

Work Teams in Organizations

Our concern in this chapter is with the assessment of work teams in organizations. By this we mean teams that are: (a) *real* groups (that is, intact social systems complete with boundaries and differentiated roles among members), (b) groups that have one or more *tasks* to perform, resulting in discernible and potentially measurable outcomes of members' collective work, and (c) groups that operate within an *organizational context* (for more detail regarding specification of the domain, see Hackman, 1983, 1986).

This turns out to be a fairly inclusive statement. The domain would include, for example, a group of executives charged with deciding where to locate a new plant, a team of rank-and-file workers assembling a product, a health care team tending to the needs of a group of patients, and a group of economists analyzing the budgetary implications of a proposed new public policy. Nonetheless, many sets of people commonly referred to as "groups" are excluded. Social groups are out (no task), as are reference groups (not an intact social system), coacting groups, that is, people who may report to the same manager but who have their own, individual tasks to perform (no *group* task), and freestanding groups (no organizational context).

Cockpit Crews as Work Groups

Do cockpit crews fall within our domain? Are they real groups, with a real piece of work to accomplish? Or are they, perhaps, mere aggregations of individuals who have their own more-or-less independent work to do in the cockpit, appearing to be a group only because crew members occupy the same small space for a period of time?

Even to raise this question may seem silly: Of course cockpit crews are real groups with interdependent work to accomplish. We address the matter explicitly because, as will be seen later, the great majority of existing assessment methods are designed and administered as if success in flying a multiengine aircraft involves little more than the prechoreographed execution of individual performances.

Our approach, by contrast, addresses in detail the *interactive* feature of cockpit work. So we begin by describing the make-up of cockpit crews and the kind of work they do, to make sure that these groups do fall within our domain of interest.

Crew composition. Although the exact composition of cockpit crews varies across airlines and aircraft types, there are enough commonalities among them to permit description of a "typical" airline crew.

There are three roles in the cockpit: captain, first officer (sometimes called "copilot"), and second officer (sometimes called "flight engineer"). Pilots move through these roles in a planned, orderly fashion in the course of their careers. A newly hired pilot begins cockpit work as a second officer. When a vacancy occurs for a first officer position on an appropriate aircraft, the most senior second officer has the opportunity (and, in virtually all airlines, the obligation) to enter a program of training and testing that, if successfully completed, would qualify the individual as a first officer. The pilot serves in that role until reaching the top of the first officer seniority list, at which time he or she begins another program of training and testing to qualify for a captaincy.

Duties are clearly defined for each role. The captain has overall responsibility for the flight and for management of the cockpit crew. The captain cannot be ordered to undertake a flight by airline management (or by anyone else) if in his or her judgment the flight would be unsafe (e.g., because of mechanical or weather problems). The first officer shares flying duties with the captain, and normally flies every other leg of a trip. The captain can take control of the aircraft at any time, for example, in particularly challenging circumstances. If the captain is flying, federal aviation regulations allow the first officer to take control only when he or she observes that the captain is incapacitated (e.g., ill or severely emotionally distraught). But it is professionally risky for a first officer to do this, and it happens very rarely. The second officer controls the mechanical systems of the aircraft (the engines, fuel, the electrical and hydraulic systems, and so on). He or she conducts the external walk-around inspection of the aircraft before each departure, and is the primary point of interface with the cabin crew (for example, adjusting the air conditioning or attempting to repair cabin equipment that malfunctions in flight).

Individual crew members bid for sets of flights (called "trips"), and in most airlines requests are honored in order of seniority. The composition of a given crew, then, depends both on the bids submitted by its members and the assignment rules used by the airline's crew scheduling system. Crew members typically are rostered together for one month (the usual airline bid cycle), but it is not uncommon for their time together to be shortened or interrupted because of vacations, training schedules, or personal matters. Some pilots bid for, or may be assigned, "reserve" duty, filling in for absent crew members as needed.

Work activities. Crew members meet for the first time in the airline's flight operations office (or, occasionally, in the cockpit). They may or may not have a structured briefing about the trip to be flown, depending on the airline's policies and the captain's proclivities. A day's flying may involve a single long flight (e.g., transcontinental) or as many as half a dozen short segments. At day's end, the crew may wind up at members' home base (in which case individuals are likely to head for their personal homes as soon as possible) or at a distant airport (in which case crew members are likely to spend considerable time together in social or recreational activities).

The actual tasks performed are of five general types: (a) planning and decision-making, including reviewing flight plans, making operational decisions in flight, and dealing with abnormal circumstances; (b) manipulating the flight controls (i.e., actually flying the airplane), (c) monitoring and adjusting various mechanical and electrical systems, such as navigational equipment and the aircraft's engines; (d) completing paperwork, such as computing the "weight and balance" form prior to departure, and entering various data in logbooks, and (e) communicating with other individuals and groups who are involved in the flight (specifically, air traffic controllers, the airline's flight operations and maintenance staffs, and the cabin crew on board the aircraft).

The crew's workload is very uneven, and typically is bimodal—with substantial work on all five types of tasks occurring near the beginning of a flight (preparing for departure, takeoff, and climb) and then again near the end (planning the approach to the destination airport, executing the approach and landing, and "closing the books" upon arrival at the gate). During these two periods, all three crew members are quite busy, and a great deal of communication and coordination among them is required. If an unusual situation develops during one of these periods, the capacity of the crew can be pushed to its practical limit, posing a considerable challenge to the captain's leadership skills and the capability of members to function as a team. During the time that the aircraft is cruising at its assigned altitude, on the other hand, performance demands are minimal. Indeed, on long and uneventful trips, crews often have to work hard to fend off boredom during the cruise portion of the flight.

Summary. Do cockpit crews fall within our domain? Are they intact social systems, even though they are small in size and have a relatively short life-span? Yes. Do they have a set of tasks to be performed whose outcomes can be discerned and, potentially, assessed? Yes. And do they operate in an organizational context? Yes—many contexts. Cockpit crews, for all their unique features, clearly qualify as organizational work teams.

Yet the uniqueness of these teams must not be overlooked, because the special features of cockpit crews pose some major challenges for those who would assess them. The teams are, for example, both temporary and composed of individuals who typically did not choose to work together (assignments having been made by a computer in response to *individual* bids and seniority). Moreover, team members usually have little time to get to know one another before their first period of demanding collaborative work begins. Also noteworthy is the variance in workload: long periods of routine activity, punctuated by demands for intense and highly interdependent teamwork, some of which are predictable ahead of time (such as landing in marginal weather), but some of which are not (such as an extended and unexpected hold or wind shift that raises questions about the sufficiency of the fuel on board).

THE CONTEXT OF COCKPIT CREW ASSESSMENT

Let us now turn to an examination of the context within which the assessment of cockpit crews takes place, for it is this context that shapes both what is appropriate and what is feasible in designing, conducting, and using the results of a team assessment program.

Current Practice

Federal aviation regulations require pilots to be assessed on a regular basis. These assessments include a "proficiency check" and/or a "line check." The line check consists of observations of the pilot's performance on a regularly scheduled flight. The proficiency check involves flying a series of required maneuvers in an aircraft simulator. These maneuvers address both technical skills and emergency procedures, such as steep turns, loss of an engine, aborted takeoffs, landings with an engine out, missed approaches, and precision and nonprecision approaches.

The frequency of checks required varies as a function of position (captains are evaluated more frequently than first officers or second officers). The evaluation may legally be conducted either by a Federal Aviation Administration (FAA) inspector or by a check airman, a pilot designated by the air carrier and approved as an evaluator by the FAA. Whether the evaluator is from the FAA or is a check airman, the only possible outcomes of a check are "pass" or "fail." A pilot who fails is reexamined after additional training. Failing the reexamination results in loss of license and hence, loss of the right to function as a crew member in commercial airline operations.

Anecdotal reports from FAA officials, check airmen, and other airline officials, as well as the personal observations of the authors, support a view that this dichotomous classification of acceptability as a flight-crew member masks a wide range of performance variability. Moreover, the focus of evaluation in the proficiency check is a pilot's ability to demonstrate *individual* technical proficiency in the control of the aircraft under a standardized set of conditions. What is distinctly not measured in this evaluation is the pilot's ability to evaluate alternatives and make decisions in a complex, stressful environment, to draw appropri-

ately on the knowledge and perspectives of co-workers, and to coordi-
nate one's own work activities with those being performed by other
crew members.

These omissions are particularly worrisome for captains, whose role
requires them to manage a complex array of technical and human resources, and to employ those resources effectively in nonstandard situations. A significant proportion of accident analyses implicate poor
leadership and management as causal factors. Typical is a case in which
a captain fails to respond to input from crew members indicating that
the captain's behavior is endangering the flight. Recall, for example, the
incident referred to in the opening paragraph of this paper. The captain
disregarded repeated warnings that the fuel state was dangerously low
while preoccupied with the possibility that the landing gear was not
locked in the down position. The aircraft eventually ran completely
out of fuel and crashed.

In general, only pilots who are obviously and dangerously incompetent fail checks, and even they have a high likelihood of passing upon
reexamination. It is not possible (because of the simple pass-fail criterion used) to estimate how much variation there is among those who
pass their checks. Nor is it possible to determine with existing data
whether or not existing check procedures address those aspects of performance that are most critical to flying as a member of a two- or three-
person cockpit crew.

Historical Context

Psychologists interested in assessment have been involved with aircraft
crews for several decades. During World War II, for example, American psychologists were mobilized to help solve the practical problems
surrounding the selection and training of large numbers of military pilots. Throughout the war, the criterion used in selection research was
completion of (vs. elimination from) pilot training. The investigators
were plagued by the fact that this criterion was largely subjective. Although attempts were made to standardize grading and to obtain ratings
from multiple instructors, subjectivity in evaluator judgment was not
eliminated.

Forty years later, subjectivity remains a disconcerting issue for both
pilots and their evaluators. Although criteria for standard evaluations
have improved and computers allow the precise measurement of how
flight controls are manipulated in aircraft and simulators, the critical
areas of judgment, leadership, and decision-making are still rated sub-

jectively. There have been few attempts to train evaluators in how to assess these "soft" aspects of pilot competence, or to develop standardized ways of measuring them.

In one of the major studies of training success conducted in 1942, the relative importance of four major categories of performance was tabulated by computing the percentages of pilots eliminated from training who had been cited as deficient in each (Melton, 1947). The categories were: (a) coordination and technique, (b) alertness and observation, (c) intelligence and judgment, and (d) personality and temperament. Results showed that 81% of the failures had to do with poor coordination and technique, with the consequence that subsequent training and evaluation programs placed by far the greatest emphasis on the technical, "stick and rudder" aspects of flying. Although intelligence testing was (and is) included in most pilot selection programs, personality factors have received relatively little attention. When personality assessment is employed, its use has been primarily to *screen out* individuals on the basis of actual or potential psychopathology. Few efforts have been devoted to *selecting in* individuals on the basis of personality attributes associated with particularly effective performance, for example, by identifying characteristics associated with pilot effectiveness and using these characteristics to select individuals from a pool of technically qualified applicants.

The concentration on individual proficiency rather than crew effectiveness, a hallmark of current assessment practice, also has its roots in history. The tradition in the military has been to give individuals at the top of their classes first choice of aircraft type. Most choose single-pilot, fighter aircraft, leaving multipilot bombers and transports to their less proficient colleagues. Given the coordination and agility required for single-engine combat in World War I, and the "white scarf" tradition of the Red Baron and Captain Eddie Rickenbacker, this philosophy was probably justified. Today, given the different skills and aptitudes required to fly a complex multiengine jet aircraft in a crowded and demanding air traffic environment, it probably is not. Yet, as seen in the previous section, airline pilots continue to be evaluated as individuals and to be assigned grades of "pass" or "fail" based mainly on their skill in manipulating flight controls.

Perspectives and Stake of the Airlines

It is clearly in the interest of airlines for cockpit crews to perform as competently as possible. A crash, for example, has severe financial consequences for the company, beyond the incalculable personal costs to those involved. Revenue is lost because potential passengers avoid the carrier, insurance rates (a major cost item for the airlines) rise, and investors may develop second thoughts about the wisdom of owning the airline's stock. Good performance in the cockpit also contributes directly to an airline's financial well-being. On-time performance may be improved (which can result in a reputation for reliability that attracts passengers), the amount of fuel burned on a flight (another major expense) can be significantly reduced, and maintenance delays and costs can be minimized.

Yet despite the demonstrable benefits of improving flight crew performance, U.S. airlines have been notably nonaggressive in seeking more comprehensive evaluation of flight behavior and in striving for higher levels of crew performance. Many airline executives may feel that the economic challenges they face (which are of obvious relevance to long-term corporate survival) take precedence over the pursuit of improved crew effectiveness, a not unreasonable position, given the overall safety record of the industry. There are, moreover, some seemingly good reasons for executives *not* to push for broader and more intensive assessment of cockpit crews. One has to do with the impact of deregulation on corporate priorities, one with the state of labor relations in the industry, and one with the legal risks of maintaining records that document variations in pilot competence and performance.

The impact of regulation and deregulation. Until 1978, both the routes flown by individual carriers and the fares charged were controlled by the Civil Aeronautics Board. During this period, carriers were given generally noncompetitive assignment of routes, and passenger fares were federally controlled to provide a "reasonable rate of return" to the airlines, even including subsidies for carriers flying to certain destinations where traffic was light. There was little incentive to contain costs since they could be passed on to passengers with federal blessing.

After deregulation of the industry in 1978, airlines found themselves in a fully competitive environment where routes were freely available and where fares and profits would be determined by the free play of the marketplace. Predictably, this resulted in greater attention to costs, and programs that could not be shown to contribute directly to an airline's ability to compete often were eliminated or reduced in size.

Investments in research and development for pilot training and evaluation were substantially reduced by many airlines, just at a time when flight training staffs were beginning to recognize that crew dynamics were critical to the safety of flight. Moreover, the increased competitiveness of the airline industry appears to have lessened the sharing that traditionally had characterized relations among flight training groups in different companies. The net result was that individual airlines had less material relevant to crew training and assessment to share *and* less incentive to share it than they had prior to deregulation. The FAA, which might have picked up the research and development activities being curtailed by the airlines, did not do so.

Performance evaluation and labor relations. U.S. pilots and their professional (union) organizations generally have opposed increases in formal pilot evaluation, for reasons to be explored below. In recent years, the airlines have had little incentive to press the issue. In the early 1980s, established carriers felt the double jeopardy of an economic downturn (which reduced loads and revenues) and intense competition from new, low-cost carriers with nonunion workforces. In response, a number of airlines asked for significant concessions in wages and work rules from pilots. These negotiations have been delicate and important, and most airlines have avoided or deferred any issue that might turn them sour. It is, then, not surprising that there has been little pressure from the established airlines to increase the scope or intensity of pilot evaluation.

The newer, low-cost airlines, on the other hand, having already obtained a pilot force willing to work longer hours and undertake more varied responsibilities for *less* pay, were not motivated to upset this profitable and productive state by imposing performance evaluation standards more rigorous than those of the established carriers. As a consequence, virtually all carriers have stayed clear of evaluation issues and have simply complied with federally mandated standards.

Potential for liability. An airline that collected and maintained assessment data documenting differences in pilot competence and performance could be especially vulnerable to litigation in the event of an accident. If, for example, an accident were found to be caused by "pilot error" and if it were further determined that assessment data for crew members on that flight placed them below the carrier's average, then litigants could argue that the airline had callously endangered passengers' lives by boarding them on a flight staffed by substandard personnel. A case in point is the Air Florida jet that crashed into a bridge shortly after takeoff from Washington National Airport (NTSB, 1982). Pilot judgment and performance were determined to have been causal factors in that crash, and it happened that the captain had failed a proficiency check prior to the accident, although he had passed the examination after retraining. It is not possible to determine the precise effect this disclosure had on the outcomes of lawsuits and the subsequent failure of the airline, but its impact was clearly negative.

Perspective and Stake of Pilots

U.S. pilots have generally opposed changes of current performance evaluation practices. Moreover, they have resisted proposals to increase the quality and scope of data obtained from cockpit voice recorders and to make data from flight data recorders accessible to aviation researchers. Organized opposition has been spearheaded by the Air Line Pilots Association, the largest and most powerful union representing airline flight crews.

There are conflicting interests for both pilots and their representative organizations. Obviously, it is in pilots' personal and professional interest to achieve a high degree of safety and to promote the financial health of their employers by enhancing operational efficiency. On the other hand, negative performance evaluations can result in loss of license and professional livelihood.

At first glance, it might appear that pilot opposition to comprehensive performance assessment represents a triumph of narrow self-interest over a collective good. Many of pilots' concerns about how assessment data are collected and used are, however, well founded. Subjectivity in evaluations, for example, has been and continues to be a real problem. The recent emphasis on assessing the decision-making and managerial skills of captains, and the capability of the crew as a whole to work together effectively, has increased the salience of concerns about subjectivity. To date, the technology of evaluation and the training of assessors have not advanced far enough to reassure pilots that evaluations of the nontechnical aspects of their performance will be accomplished reliably, validly, and impartially.

Adding to the evaluation anxieties of pilots is the fact that labor-management relations between pilots and airlines have been more adversarial than collegial in recent years. Part of this conflict grew from the fact that pilots typically earned significantly more money for significantly less time at work than nonflying middle and upper managers. Although this situation has been changing dramatically since deregulation, there is still a perception among pilots that management would like to use evaluation as a club to bring pilots into line. It would be possible, for example, to use subjective evaluations to terminate individuals who are particularly effective spokesmen for pilot concerns;

or, perhaps, cockpit voice recordings of flights flown by these individuals could be subjected to special scrutiny as a means of discouraging dissent.

Finally, pilots, like their managements and federal regulators, tend to perceive the crew as an aggregate of individuals rather than as a team with the captain as manager/leader. Helmreich (in press) found that 66% of captains agree with a statement that command performance is not adversely affected by having an inexperienced or less capable crew member in the cockpit; 92% believe that they should take control and physically fly the aircraft during nonstandard or emergency situations. Many first officers' attitudes fit well with this view, and 29% of those surveyed state that they should not question the decisions or actions of the captain except when there is a *direct* threat to the safety of flight.

In sum, the reluctance of pilots to endorse changes that would expand the scope or intensity of performance assessment is quite understandable, for reasons of self-interest, certainly, but also because of problems with the quality of the tools available for collecting data about the nontechnical aspects of pilot and crew performance.

Perspective and Stake of Federal Agencies

The FAA is charged with mandating practices that will ensure the highest level of safety in commercial aviation.[1] However, the FAA must also respond to a number of conflicting pressures. Although safety is presumably paramount to the FAA, the agency also recognizes the need to promote civil air transport and is sensitive to pleas from carriers regarding the financial consequences of proposed regulations. Moreover, the FAA is subject to direct lobbying activity, both from representatives of pilots' organizations (who may argue that their constituents would be harmed by certain regulations) and from passenger and public interest groups (who often seek more stringent controls on pilot behavior and more thorough evaluations of crew competence and performance).

The strongest advocate of improved performance measurement and evaluation is the National Transportation Safety Board (NTSB), a federal agency charged with determining the causes of accidents and recommending procedures to avoid their recurrence. Based on its analyses of data from a number of airline crashes, the NTSB has repeatedly recommended that the FAA increase requirements for data capture by flight data recorders and cockpit voice recorders, and that greater emphasis be placed on training in assertiveness for junior crew members and in crew coordination for all pilots. Despite the weight of the NTSB data and recommendations, the FAA has been slow to change regulations governing pilot training and assessment. Given the political forces to which the FAA is subjected, it is doubtful that the organization will become significantly more aggressive in these areas in the foreseeable future.

Summary

This section has laid out some of the factors that impede innovation in the assessment of flight crews as task-performing teams. The list is long: a strong historical emphasis on assessing pilots as *individuals* on a pass-fail basis, cost considerations that are increasingly important to airlines in a deregulated competitive environment, the felt need by pilots and their unions for protection from biased evaluations and disciplinary actions, the deteriorating labor relations climate in the airline industry, airlines' concerns about their liability for the results of accidents, and even the uncertain relationship between the two major federal bodies concerned with aviation (the FAA and the NTSB).

Even if one had a superb, validated method for assessing the behavior and effectiveness of crews qua crews, one could not simply present it to the airline community and expect it to be adopted. There are, for example, technologies already available that could be used to improve crew assessment and training, such as multichannel digital flight data recorders used for operational analysis in Europe and found valuable there. Yet these devices are found only on wide-body aircraft in the U.S., and then only because they were installed by the manufacturer when the planes were built.

Whatever new procedures or devices are devised for assessing cockpit crews, they must be adopted and used within the relatively constraining historical, political, and organizational context described above. Contextual factors, too often overlooked by psychologists charged with the design of psychometrically sound assessment devices and procedures, strongly condition what one can do, and what one can reasonably expect to accomplish, in assessing cockpit crews in U.S. air carriers.

CHALLENGES IN ASSESSING COCKPIT TEAMS

Having explored the context within which assessment of cockpit crews takes place, we now identify and discuss several challenges in the actual conduct of such assessments. As will be seen, a number of opportunities to obtain particularly informative data lurk just behind the challenges described below.

1. A great deal of assessment and regulation of flying performance does occur in airline organizations but the form of those activities makes it of limited use to organizational representatives responsible for proficient safe flying operations.

Pilots constantly assess one another, although they would not use that word. Airline flight operations departments buzz with conversation about flying and about pilots. This is understandable, given that people generally like to talk about their work. Pilots seem especially fond of talking about who is a great pilot, who is shaky, and who is and is not a good team player in the cockpit. Although these conversations are, in some ways, like the gossip one hears in the coffee rooms of any organization, they are more than that: Pilots are talking about things that are potentially life- or license-threatening. For all the humor that characterizes such discussions, pilots *care* about what is being said, and they store much of it away for future reference.

The focus of the informal assessments pilots do is on individuals, not crews. Although many stories are exchanged of the type "So there *we* were at 35,000 feet. . . ," the assessments and attributions that are made are almost invariably about individual crew members. One might, for example, hear something like this:

. . . so there was this flock of geese having a tea party right over 22 Left [a runway designation], and the tower switched them to 29 just when Charlie was getting lined up on the ils [instrument landing system]. Well, the weather was a mess, they were vectoring old Charlie all over the place, and he got confused and got behind. Three times Phil had to remind him about something, and eventually Phil just took it and landed the damn thing.

One would be far less likely to hear an account of the same set of events that went like this:

. . . so after they got atis [a recorded radio transmission giving weather and runway information] they just assumed it would be a routine ils approach to 22 Left and they started chewing the fat. They didn't hear the talk on the radio about the geese over the runway, so when the tower switched runways at the last minute it was scramble time. Charlie was flying, and he had his hands full because of weather and the new vectors he was getting. Phil started changing the radios to set up for the new approach, but didn't tell Charlie what he was doing, and Charlie couldn't figure out what the hell was going on. Nobody really got things organized, everybody got confused, and eventually Phil got so frustrated that he took the airplane and landed the damn thing himself.

In the first account, the one most likely to be heard, Charlie has a problem. He let a situation that was not that demanding get the better of him, and he had to be bailed out by Phil, his captain. The attributions made are all to individuals. The second account invites a group-level interpretation: The *crew* got itself into trouble, by not paying attention to changing situational demands, by not planning and organizing the work (either contingently beforehand, or in real time after the runway change was announced), and by poor between-member communication and coordination. Indeed, if someone is to be blamed in this situation, it might most appropriately be Phil for not managing his cockpit well, an interpretation unlikely to be made based on the first account, in which Phil is implicitly viewed as the savior.

This illustration is not meant to imply that most attributions of responsibility for negative events are made to junior crew members. Indeed, the opposite is more often the case: There is rich lore in every airline we know specifying which captains have what quirks. People talk incessantly about the personality and behaviors of their leaders, and captains are not exempt from such talk. The point, instead, is the individualistic orientation of the informal assessments made by airline pilots. This is not surprising, given the focus of airline selection, training, and evaluation programs. But it does suggest that most pilots may be neither experienced nor comfortable making group-level assessments and interpretations about what happens in a cockpit, even though, as in the example given above, it often is the crew, as a crew, that gets itself into trouble.

The informal assessments pilots make of one another do result in some informal regulation and pilot-to-pilot coaching and counseling. At the extreme, certain captains are known to "run a bad cockpit," and are not to be flown with if at all possible (even, in some cases, to the extent of calling in sick if one is rostered with that captain). Less extreme are data about how a crew member needs to behave with some captain (e.g., "don't make any suggestions; he bristles if you do"), or advice about help a given crew member needs (e.g., one captain telling another about the particular flying foibles of a first officer). These data are in the system, but they are not available *to* the system, and certainly not to the regulatory aspects of the system (i.e., the FAA, check airmen, or airline managers). Pilots, for all their concern with safety, are also members of a fraternity: One protects another from potential disciplinary action, with the confident expectation that the reverse will be true should the tables someday be turned.

In sum, there are rich assessment data already available in every airline, and those data are used to some extent for self-regulation by the pilot community. But the data are kept strictly within that community, and they mainly have to do with the behavior and skills of individuals. The potential of informal assessment data for pilots' learning (about themselves as individuals and about their functioning as teams) is considerable, for example, through a systematic program of peer feedback and group self-assessment. Given the political and organizational realities discussed earlier, however, it will not be easy to find ways of using these data systematically to foster pilot and crew effectiveness.

2. *Objective indicators of crew performance are incomplete and inadequate, perhaps inherently so.*

It is common when discussing strategies for assessing task-performing teams to call for collection of "objective" performance measures. There are three reasons why we do not join in that call.

First, truly significant hard data (i.e., the occurrence of a crash or serious incident) become available very infrequently. Therefore, these events are useful mainly in retrospective analyses of the technical and human factors that may have contributed to them. The NTSB conducts these investigations, drawing on a variety of data (including those from cockpit voice recorders and flight data recorders), and much is learned from them. But, fortunately, there are few occasions to conduct them and for that reason they do not play a major role in the day-to-day assessment of airline pilots and crews.

Second, the completeness and quality of available hard data are quite limited. Flight data recorders on the majority of aircraft in service in the U.S. provide only analog recording of limited data on metal foil, and cockpit voice recorders yield low-quality recordings (from a single cockpit microphone) on a continuous-loop 30-minute tape. Even these relatively primitive data cannot be used except by the NTSB in the case of a reportable accident or incident, in contrast with practice in Britain, where multi-channel digital data are collected for every scheduled flight and used both to develop statistical summaries and to counsel individual pilots. (For a more complete description of British practices, see Helmreich and Hackman, 1984, and Mearns, 1983). Again, political realities make it doubtful that more sophisticated and complete "hard" data will be available for use in crew assessment in the near future. Even in Britain, labor-management agreements require that pilots' identities be kept confidential (except in the case of serious or repeated lapses from safe practice), which limits the usefulness of the data for assessment purposes.

Finally, even if data from flight data recorders were more complete, of higher quality, and more readily accessible to assessors (whether airline personnel concerned with flight standards or researchers) they would be of limited use for *crew* assessment. For one thing, these data address only technical, "stick and rudder" issues. Moreover, they serve mainly to identify *bad* performance, such as control manipulations that lie outside acceptable parameters, or deviations from correct procedures or flight paths. More importantly, hard data provide no clues about how well the crew, as a task-performing team, has functioned. Even the British measures, which are probably the best presently available, are not analyzed (and, by their nature, probably cannot be) in a way that would allow assessment of cockpit resource management and crew coordination issues.

The problem with objective performance measures is, at root, conceptual rather than technical or methodological. Just as there are multiple routes one can fly and still get from New York to Chicago, so are there multiple ways that a crew can operate and still achieve essentially the same performance outcome. Systems theorists (e.g., Katz & Kahn, 1978) call this property of social systems "equifinality," and it is one reason why simply looking at a given outcome (e.g., arriving safely in Chicago) may not tell one much about how well the cockpit crew functioned. The phenomenon of equifinality obviously complicates the assessment task, as does Tyler's (1983) notion of "multiple possibilities." Tyler asserts that there are *many* possible outcomes that can emerge in any given situation, and the particular one actualized is not completely determined by the causal factors that precede it. Multiple possibility theory envisions a world with some "play" in the system, and it encourages attention to human and social choice as a factor that transforms multiple possibilities into single courses of action.

So where equifinality alerts us to the fact that the same outcome can occur in response to many different causes, multiple possibility theory posits that the same cause can generate a variety of different outcomes. Taken together, the two notions call into question assessment methods that assume that single causes (e.g., certain behaviors in the cockpit) are tightly linked to specific performance outcomes (e.g., optimally efficient fuel burn—one of the measures that could be obtained from a sophisticated flight data recorder).

In sum, though it would be good if more and better hard data were available, the likelihood of that happening in the existing organizational and political context is low. Moreover, even if such data were available they would be of limited use in crew assessment because the link between how members of a team behave and eventual group performance outcomes is not a tightly coupled, deterministic relationship in which specific behaviors always lead to a given performance outcome. Objective performance data simply do not provide a sturdy or complete enough base on which to build a robust cockpit crew assessment program.

3. *"Process criteria" of performance provide an alternative to objective measures, one fraught with both risk and opportunity.*

If hard outcome measures are not obtainable (or fully appropriate) for use in assessing cockpit crew performance, can observations of the performance *process* of crews as they work be used instead? In fact, this is already being done, and with success, for certain kinds of performance situations, which we will call, for want of a better term, "acute" situations.

Since crews are rostered temporarily, and therefore do not have time to develop their own strategies for handling all situations they might encounter, airlines have developed highly standardized procedures to be followed in unusual or particularly demanding circumstances. One example is a "Category II approach," in which the crew lands an appropriately instrumented airplane on instruments in low visibility conditions. A Category II approach requires extremely close coordination among crew members at a critical time (i.e., the instant when a decision must be made either to land or to execute a missed approach). Other acute situations include an engine fire warning, instructions from air traffic control to change course immediately to avoid a collision, and so on. In each of these cases, all crew members are trained beyond proficiency in their specific duties, and when the triggering event occurs, the prescribed processes are executed precisely as previously choreographed and practiced. A crew of well-trained strangers should be able to handle an acute situation just as competently as a crew that has flown together for many weeks.

Because there is only one right way to behave in most acute situations, it is reasonably straightforward for an assessor (one who is expert in the procedure, of course) to determine how well the team handled it and, if mistakes were made, to specify exactly what they were and who made them. Process criteria provide an appropriate way to assess crews in acute situations, and check airmen routinely use them in simulator exercises to help crew members become proficient in performing their parts of overall team tasks.

The use of process criteria to assess cockpit crews is a very different undertaking when the situation is not acute. In these circumstances, which we will call "continuing situations," conditions require a decision-making process involving consideration of alternative courses of action and the development of a shared strategy for action. These are situations that are *not* overlearned and in which only general training and experience are relevant. Examples include mechanical malfunctions that do not pose an instantaneous threat but place in jeopardy the safe continuation or completion of a flight (e.g., landing gear problems, or engine, hydraulic, or electrical difficulties). These problems require the coordinated action of the full crew and, not surprisingly, are the kinds of situations frequently encountered in incidents and accidents where conclusions of "pilot error" are reached.

It is more difficult to use process criteria of effectiveness in continuing situations. There are, to be sure, better and worse ways to handle them, and how a given problem is dealt with can significantly affect both the likelihood that new problems will develop later, and the capability of crew members to work together competently later in the flight. Yet these "better and worse ways" cannot be specified in advance the way one can for an acute problem, and that makes the assessment task considerably more challenging.

Competent check airmen report that they are able to *sense* how well a crew handles continuing problems. And, after a period of time observing a crew, they may confidently conclude that Captain X is a "poor leader" or that members of a given crew "have real problems working together," although they often are unable to articulate the precise reasons for these judgments. When pressed for evidence, check airmen tend to talk about poor decision-making processes, slippage in coordination among crew members, and incomplete or inadequate communication, rather than about the technical aspects of flying.

Such talk makes them uncomfortable, even though they invariably discover, when they check with their colleagues, that others have very similar assessments of a given pilot or crew. The discomfort is strong enough that a number of check airmen have expressed to us doubts about whether such "soft and groupy" matters are legitimate for them to address at all. These items, they say, are wholly ignored by the FAA in its requirements for pilot assessment, so why should we take them so seriously? But they take them seriously nonetheless, partly because the FAA does focus so exclusively on individual technical proficiency. Assessments of leadership and team processes in the cockpit, for all their subjectivity, fill an important void.

If check airmen are to become more comfortable, and more competent, in assessing cockpit crews as teams, they will need both (a) tools for doing so and (b) training in the appropriate use of those tools, neither of which is presently available. Development of such materials is, in our view, well worth doing, and we will have more to say about it below, including discussion of a technology that may facilitate that work.

4. Many events important to competent crew functioning occur outside the cockpit.

It is natural to look where the key team behaviors are actually occurring if one is interested in assessing how well a team is functioning. In our case, that obviously is the cockpit. But there are problems with focusing exclusively on what happens in the cockpit.

First, although the cockpit is where the team does its work, the crew typically is formed and disbands, for the day or permanently, elsewhere. What happens in the flight operations office—where crews check in, get their dispatch releases, and perhaps have a cup of coffee—can be critical to team functioning, especially at the moment when crew members meet and form their first impression of the captain. Similarly, what happens at the end of a day's flight, perhaps on the crew bus or over dinner, can have a profound influence on subsequent crew performance. At one extreme, dinner can serve as an extended debriefing session that strengthens the team as a performing unit; at the other, it can strain relationships among members in a way that damages their ability to work together subsequently. We know from group research (e.g., Gersick, 1983, 1984) that the beginnings of groups, their midpoints, such as the evening at an outstation on a two-day trip, and their endings are especially critical in understanding a team. It would seem advantageous, therefore, to address these noncockpit times in assessment methodologies.[2]

Second, there is increasing recognition of the importance of the organizational context in determining how groups function. Organizational features such as information systems, reward practices, control procedures, available communication channels, and even the way physical space is designed have significant effects on crew behavior and performance (Hackman, 1983).

Consider, for example, an airline that had a driving commitment to on-time performance, with bonuses for crews that consistently achieved company targets. Such a reward system surely would alter crew dynamics, and might even tempt crews to take shortcuts that could waste fuel and/or compromise safety.[3] Or consider what can happen to a crew in an airline where there are too few operations personnel available to handle all the radio requests received from cockpits on bad weather days. A crew observed by one of us discovered, in flight and in rapid succession, that (a) the airport from which it had just departed had closed, (b) its destination airport had closed, (c) weather at its alternate airport was deteriorating fast and that airport was expected to close, *and* (d) it was not possible to get the attention of a dispatcher, because all dispatchers were already fully occupied with other urgent business. At that point, the captain became extremely autocratic and evaluative in his dealings with other crew members (behaviors he had not exhibited previously in the flight), and the climate in the cockpit became tense and sullen, a climate unlikely to foster effective team problem-solving and decision-making. Finally, consider something as mundane as the existence of a quiet briefing room, where pilots can get psychologically prepared for their flight. The simple presence or absence of such a facility can have strong effects on how crew members relate to one another when they first start their work together. And those first encounters, in turn, can establish a style of interaction that may be difficult to change for the rest of the day—or the rest of the month.

If it is true that structural and contextual factors condition crew interaction, and we believe the evidence is clear that they do, then any robust assessment methodology should include measurement of such features. Without such data, it may not be possible to interpret correctly what is observed in the cockpit. Moreover, it may be that interventions intended to correct poor team behavior should focus on the larger organization in which the crew operates rather than on specific exchanges that take place among crew members. Assessors of cockpit crews must be alert to organizational influences, and not fall into the trap (a trap already well-populated with disheartened small group researchers) of acting as if member interaction is all that needs to be examined if one wishes to understand and evaluate a task-performing team.

5. An assessment system that is appropriate for determining train-
ing needs can be inappropriate for the evaluation of crew members—
and vice versa.

A classic issue in organizational performance appraisal is the tension between using assessments for training and development purposes versus for evaluation and control (see, for example, Porter et al., 1975, chapter 11). Training-oriented assessments, though they may be anxiety-arousing for the assessee, are consequential mainly for his or her own learning and development. Evaluation-oriented assessments, on the other hand, are more broadly consequential and may, for example, affect the size of one's raise, the probability of a promotion, or even the security of one's job.

Organizations, understandably, want to use appraisals for *both* purposes, and many managers have sought assessment techniques that can be used simultaneously for training and for evaluation—procedures that provide incentives for people to learn while discouraging them from "gaming" the process to secure a favorable outcome. Such procedures are hard to find. Even to search for them can be risky, in that attempting to achieve both objectives can sometimes result in achieving neither.

Although the trade-off between training and evaluation is relevant to all aspects of crew assessment, the tensions are especially vivid in Line Oriented Flight Training (LOFT), a program that is arguably the most significant development in air crew training in recent years. In a LOFT exercise, a complete two- or three-person crew undergoes the simulation of an entire line flight between cities. The goal of the simulation is to reproduce the complete flight environment including dispatch releases, weight and balance computations, en route weather, and communications with the cabin crew, air traffic control, and company operations. Typically, one or more abnormal or emergency situations are introduced during the flight. Aviation psychologists, especially those associated with NASA, have been heavily involved in the development of LOFT and have developed guidelines for maximizing the training benefits of the experience (Lauber & Foushee, 1981).

Even highly experienced crews report that LOFT is a powerful training tool that allows them to test all their skills, both technical and managerial, under extraordinarily realistic conditions. Crews can gain many valuable insights from the experience itself, especially when the simulation is videotaped and can be reviewed by the full crew, and when the debriefing is conducted by a competent and credible trainer.

When meaningful measures of team processes and outcomes become available (a matter for which we intend our own research to be helpful) the power of LOFT technology for individual and team training should increase even more.

Although originally conceptualized as a training tool, LOFT also is useful for formal evaluations of pilot competence. It is relatively straightforward, for example, to construct scenarios that allow observation of performance on complex but standardized flying tasks; in addition, special scenarios can be developed that allow observation and assessment of behaviors that may be of concern for a certain pilot. The FAA has recognized the usefulness of LOFT for evaluation and has approved the substitution of a LOFT exercise for one of the annual checks required of all pilots. In doing so, the FAA also instituted a requirement that performance must be "satisfactory," that is, it must meet the general standards applied in evaluating individual pilots in a simulator or line check.

This requirement poses great difficulties for the check airman conducting a LOFT exercise. On the one hand, he or she must contend with the fact that there are neither validated measures available to use in assessing crew process and performance, other than measures of technical flying skill, nor any single best way to conduct a flight safely and competently—matters we have discussed previously. But beyond those problems, check airmen experience great difficulty in balancing the training and evaluation components of LOFT exercises. They are, for example, extremely reluctant to give "unsatisfactory" ratings for LOFT, using the argument that "if the crew found it a significant learning experience, it was a satisfactory session regardless of the performance exhibited." On the other hand, check airmen are deeply troubled by the prospect of releasing for continued line flying pilots whose behavior in the exercise revealed serious safety-related problems.

In our view, the LOFT technology provides an opportunity to provide air transport with an excellent means of pursuing *both* training and performance evaluation objectives. But this opportunity will be realized only if several developments occur. First, as noted earlier, is the development of an assessment technology that is accepted by operational personnel as being reliable, valid, and objective. Second is achievement of a reduction in the pressures against evaluation operating on both airline management and pilot groups. And third is the development of a means of using LOFT that threads a course between the two horns of the training-evaluation dilemma.

RESEARCH APPROACHES

The objective of our research is to generate means of understanding, measuring, and constructively influencing team performance[4] and to do so in ways that promote both improved organizational practice and the accumulation of scholarly knowledge about groups and group effectiveness. Although this chapter is the first joint research or writing we have done, our interests have been converging in recent years as both of us have experienced the engagement and the frustration of trying to make sense of groups and to figure out what might be done to help them perform more effectively.

Helmreich has been mainly concerned with the isolation of personality and motivational factors relevant to individual and group performance, especially as they relate to flight crews (Helmreich, 1982, 1983; Helmreich & Spence, 1978). He also has examined the effects on performance of composing crews with differing personality constellations and the ability of various training procedures to counter or enhance the behavioral effects of personality. Hackman (e.g., 1982, 1983) has focused his recent research on task and organizational factors that affect group processes and group task effectiveness. He has developed a normative model that specifies aspects of teams and situations that may be particularly potent in promoting excellent performance, and that organizes those factors in a way that invites their use in the design and management of task-performing teams. In collaboration with Robert Ginnett, he is currently in the process of revising the normative model for specific application to cockpit crews.

In the sections that follow, we sketch some of the major features of these two research programs. As will be seen, both programs seek better ways of conceptualizing and assessing cockpit crew processes, with Helmreich approaching the problem from his research on individual differences, and Hackman from his research on task and organizational variables. Both programs are committed to the development of a descriptive empirical data base against which theoretical constructs can be tested and the impact of interventions assessed.

The Helmreich Project

This approach to the assessment of team processes and performance is explicitly multidimensional, including observations and ratings both in unconstrained line operations and in controlled flight simulations that present the same operational problems to a number of crews. In addition to observer judgments, self-assessments by crew members following simulator flights are collected to understand participants' perspectives on the processes and outcomes of flight segments.

An important element of the approach involves the development of multiple coding schemata designed to capture the molecular aspects of performance enactment. Coding categories are evaluated using time-lined videotapes of a LOFT scenario flown by line crews. Three broad areas are specified: information transfer, control, and group climate. Information transfer components include both operational and social-emotional communications, as well as breakdowns of the relative contributions (initiated and reactive) of team members, and the qualitative aspects of the interaction (i.e., the forms of communication). Control factors consist of direct and indirect attempts to influence and "manage" the ongoing situation. Climate refers to indicators of the affective tone of group interactions and the inferred states of individual team members. No attempt has been made to impose independence on the behavioral categories; they are related cuts of the same phenomena.

Process variables such as those just described are difficult to interpret except within the context of the task situation. For this reason, several different frames of reference are being explored. The most basic consists of examining each phase of flight (preflight, takeoff, climb, cruise, descent, approach, and landing) discretely and, within each phase, classifying the situation as normal, acute nonstandard, or continuing nonstandard. Another approach involves classifying activities in terms of their relationship to necessary actions during each phase of flight. That is, actions may be directed toward coping with the immediate situation, may be attempts to complete activities that should have been accomplished earlier but were deferred, or may be focused on future actions and the development of action strategies. A final approach consists of utilizing captain behavior as a benchmark against which to measure the behaviors of the other team members. At this stage in the research, it is impossible to tell how useful each of these approaches may be, or if some combination of measures and referents will prove most informative.

After preliminary evaluation of alternative behavioral coding strategies, other phases of the research will involve composing crews on the basis of personality and demographic characteristics and exposing them to the same LOFT scenario. Additional research questions involve assessment of the effects on group process and performance outcomes of different training techniques, especially training in crew coordination and cockpit resource management. A particularly important applied objective of the research is the development of relatively simple evaluation categories that can be used by operational personnel to expand and improve the formal evaluation process.

The Hackman-Ginnett Project

The normative model on which this project is based posits that the overall effectiveness of a work team is a joint function of three factors: the level of *effort* group members collectively expend carrying out task work; the amount of *knowledge and skill* members bring to bear on the group task; and the appropriateness to the task of the *performance strategies* used by the group in its work.

We refer to effort, knowledge and skill, and performance strategies as *process criteria of effectiveness*. They are the hurdles a group must surmount to be effective. To assess the adequacy of a group's task processes, then, we might ask: Is the group alert enough and working hard enough to get the task done well and on time? Do members have the expertise required to accomplish the task, and are they using their collective knowledge and skill efficiently? Has the group developed an approach to the work that is fully appropriate for the task being performed, and are members implementing that strategy well? Answers to these questions provide useful diagnostic data about a group's strengths and weaknesses as a performing unit, and they are the conceptual hook on which the rest of the research hangs.

Three classes of variables are specified as particularly good points of leverage for creating conditions that foster achievement of the process criteria: (a) how the group is designed (including properties of the team task, the composition of the team, and the core norms that regulate member behavior); (b) the level of support it receives from the organization (with special attention to the adequacy of material resources needed by the team, and to organizational reward, education, and information systems); and (c) how the role of the group leader, or manager, is structured and the behavior of the person who occupies that role (with special attention to condition creating, team building, and process management activities).

A set of instruments is under development to assess both the criterion measures and each of the condition-setting variables as they apply specifically to cockpit teams. These measures will involve the use of multiple methodologies whenever possible to triangulate on the concepts being assessed. Survey and interview methods will be used to assess the chronic state of variables that are not expected to vary substantially in the short term (e.g., aspects of the organizational context), and to obtain crew members' perceptions of their team and its work. Intense, detailed observations and descriptions of crew behavior will be collected at "task critical" and "group critical" times in the life of the group. (These are specifiable occasions when what happens next is likely to significantly affect the group's performance or its viability as a performing unit, respectively.) Critical incident techniques will be used to capture significant events that occur at unpredictable times.

Based on what is learned from data collection activities, including both cockpit observations and studies done in simulators, the measures will be revised and retested until (a) they are usable by a trained observer/interviewer without excessive difficulty, and (b) they can be shown to capture gross differences on variables of research interest. At that point, a more systematic set of research activities will be instituted, to validate the instruments and to assess their usefulness in training and evaluating cockpit crew members.

The findings from the Helmreich and Hackman-Ginnett research programs will be integrated and evaluated using specially designed LOFT scenarios. Data from these exercises will be used to develop a parsimonious hybrid assessment system that builds on the common and unique features of the two research programs. The hope is that the hybrid system will prove useful both as a research tool and, in abbreviated form, as a reliable technology for assessment in both operational and crew training environments.

CONCLUSION

We began this writing project in hopes of surfacing some general issues and insights about the assessment of teams that do work in organizations. Yet virtually the entire chapter has been devoted to exploration of the special challenges faced in attempting to assess the behavior and performance of crews that fly aircraft for commercial airlines. Have we slipped off the mark, so that our work will claim the attention of only a small group of researchers with special interest in cockpit crews?

That is, of course, for the reader to decide. Our belief, and certainly our hope, is that even readers with no interest in cockpit crews will find here some issues that also are salient in assessing other kinds of task-performing groups and teams. Are there teams for which historical, political, and organizational contexts do not significantly constrain and direct assessment activities? Does any team generate objective performance outcomes that everyone agrees capture precisely how well the team has functioned? Are there any managers who are untroubled about their need to rely on subjective judgments about group processes, or any team members who do not worry about those judgments being used capriciously or unfairly? Are the internal processes of any team unaffected by organizational structures and systems, matters over which team members may have little control but that can strongly affect how, and how well, members work together? Do we know of any team for which the tension between training/development and assessment/control is not a serious problem, or any organization that does not have difficulty using constructively the rich informal assessments that exist about teams and the contributions of their members?

The challenges in assessing task-performing teams, we believe, are as pervasive as they are difficult. We hope that by writing about how those challenges are manifested in cockpit crews we may have provided at least a few ideas or leads that will be useful to other researchers concerned with the assessment of other teams in other contexts.

NOTES

Preparation of this chapter was supported in part by NASA Grant NAG 2-137 and Cooperative Agreement NCC 2-286 from the Ames Research Center (Robert L. Helmreich, principal investigator), and by Office of Naval Research Contract N00014-80C-0555 to Yale University (J. Richard Hackman, principal investigator). We are indebted to Valerie Edwards, Connie Gersick, Robert Ginnett, Daniel O'Leary, and John A. Wilhelm for their help and comments. Special thanks go to Clayton Foushee of NASA who, in generously sharing with us his thinking about cockpit crews, has made invaluable contributions to our conceptions and research.

1. We discuss here only the FAA and the National Transportation Safety Board (NTSB). Although these are the primary agencies directly involved with crew performance and flight safety, it should be noted that NASA also contributes to these issues by conducting research on aeronautical topics and by advising both the airlines and the FAA.

2. The NTSB has begun to collect and analyze data of this kind in its investigations of accidents. In analyzing the 1981 crash of a Cascade Airways Beach 99A, for example, the NTSB explored in detail both how the crew functioned on previous legs of the fatal flight and recent events in the personal lives of crew members (NTSB, 1981).

3. The "fast buck" program initiated by Braniff International in 1968 re-

quired the airline to pay each passenger a dollar if a flight did not arrive at its destination within 15 minutes of schedule. This program may have contributed to the crash of a Braniff Electra turboprop in May of that year. The flight had been delayed on departure and was pushing the 15-minute limit as it neared the destination airport. The crew attempted to penetrate a line of thunderstorms rather than navigate around them, and lost control of the aircraft in turbulence (Nance, 1984, chapter 6).

4. Our ideas about how this might be done, which are still under development, are described in a companion paper (Helmreich & Hackman, 1984). In brief, we propose a means of partitioning analyses of individual and crew performance in LOFT exercises, and we suggest development of a second version of the technology (called LOCK, for Line Oriented Check) intended explicitly for use in formal assessments.

REFERENCES

Cooper, G. E., White, M. D., & Lauber, J. K. (Eds.). (1979). *Resource management on the flight deck* (NASA Report No. CP-2120). Moffett Field, Calif.: NASA Ames Research Center (NTIS N80-22283).

Gersick, C. J. G. (1983). *The life cycles of ad hoc task groups* (T.R. No. 4). New Haven, Conn.: Research Program on Group Effectiveness, Yale School of Organization and Management.

Gersick, C. J. G. (1984). *The life cycles of ad hoc task groups: Time, transitions, and learning in teams.* Unpublished doctoral dissertation, Yale University.

Hackman, J. R. (1982). *A set of methods for research on teams* (T.R. No. 1). New Haven, Conn.: Research Program on Group Effectiveness, Yale School of Organization and Management.

Hackman, J. R. (1983). *A normative model of work team effectiveness* (T.R. No. 2). New Haven, Conn.: Research Program on Group Effectiveness, Yale School of Organization and Management.

Hackman, J. R. (1986). The design of work teams. In J. W. Lorsch (Ed.), *Handbook of organizational behavior.* Englewood Cliffs, N.J.: Prentice-Hall.

Helmreich, R. L. (1982). Pilot selection and training. Paper presented at the American Psychological Association annual meeting, Washington, D.C.

Helmreich, R. L. (1983). What changes and what endures: The capabilities and limitations of training and selection. In N. Johnston (Ed.), *Proceedings of the Aer Lingus/Irish Airline Pilots Association Flight Symposium,* Dublin, Ireland.

Helmreich, R. L. (1984). Psychological issues in space station planning and design. Unpublished manuscript. Austin, Tex.: University of Texas.

Helmreich, R. L. (in press). Cockpit management attitudes. *Human Factors.*

Helmreich, R. L., & Hackman, J. R. (1984). Evaluating flightcrew performance:

Policy pressures, pitfalls, and promise. Unpublished manuscript. Austin, Tex.: University of Texas.

Helmreich, R. L., & Spence, J. T. (1978). The Work and Family Orientation Questionnaire: An objective instrument to assess components of achievement motivation and attitudes toward family and career. JSAS *Catalog of Selected Documents in Psychology, 8*(35), Ms. 1677.

Katz, D., & Kahn, R. L. (1978). *The social psychology of organizations* (2nd ed.). New York: Wiley.

Lauber, J. K., & Foushee, H. C. (1981). *Guidelines for line oriented flight training* (Vol. 1) (NASA Report No. CP-2184). Moffett Field, Calif.: NASA Ames Research Center.

Mearns, D. J. (1983). FDR—The pilot's friend: BA/BALPA co-operation in action. In N. Johnston (Ed.), *Proceedings of the Aer Lingus/Irish Airline Pilots Association Flight Symposium*, Dublin, Ireland.

Melton, A. W. (1947). *Army air forces* (Aviation Psychology Program Report No. 4). Washington, D.C.: Defense Documentation Center.

Nance, J. J. (1984). *Splash of colors: The self-destruction of Braniff International.* New York: Morrow.

National Transportation Safety Board. (1979). *Aircraft accident report* (NTSB Report No. AAR-79-7). Washington, D.C.: NTSB Bureau of Accident Investigation.

National Transportation Safety Board. (1981). *Aircraft accident report* (NTSB Report No. AAR-81-11). Washington, D.C.: NTSB Bureau of Accident Investigation.

National Transportation Safety Board. (1982). *Aircraft accident report* (NTSB Report No. AAR-82-8). Washington, D.C.: NTSB Bureau of Accident Investigation.

Porter, L. W., Lawler, E. E., & Hackman, J. R. (1975). *Behavior in organizations.* New York: McGraw-Hill.

Tyler, L. E. (1983). *Thinking creatively.* San Francisco: Jossey-Bass.

The Implicit Axiology of Hackman and Helmreich

NATHANIEL J. PALLONE

In their call to this conference, Peterson and Fishman asked that the researchers who would present major papers be particularly attentive to the explication of the epistemological paradigm upon which their work rests. With due respect to our hosts and without minimizing the conceptual significance of the work of Hackman and Helmreich, what strikes one with the greatest force in their work is neither the substantive findings, important as they are in real-world terms, nor the epistemological paradigm upon which their investigations are founded, as spare as that is in social/industrial psychological studies; rather, what strikes one with the greatest force is the axiological paradigm implicit in their work. Not facts, not methods, but the fundamental values that guide human action in the world Hackman and Helmreich are exploring, and that guide their quest, raise questions of the most profound importance.

Hackman and Helmreich make it clear that the focus of their study is not a collection of individual actors engaged in a prechoreographed execution of individual performances, but rather the members of a genuine group, each performing a determinate but mutually interdependent role in a task group in a situation in which specific roles are differentiated, reciprocal, and hierarchical (though, one observes, differentially rewarded) and in which the success or failure of the group depends on effective team interaction. Such a configuration, often encountered but not often studied in a society that still preaches indepen-

314

dence at the expense of interdependence and universally bases its formal reward systems on the implicit assumption that both adequacy and excellence are the products of independent individual effort, cannot help but raise fundamental axiological, as well as conceptual and empirical, issues. Hackman and Helmreich have succeeded in operationalizing a paradigm for assessment of the effectiveness of a mutually interdependent group in such a way as to underscore the too-often neglected axiological dimension.

This commentator starts from a perspective that holds that every truth he knows, whether philosophic or scientific, points to the interdependence of being. Whatever their personal proclivities, Hackman and Helmreich start from a similar position empirically. In the narrative that describes the complex legal-economic-personal-social context in which their studies are undertaken, they examine with pungent clarity the forces that support assumptions and methods utilized in the evaluation and reward of air crew members, which are clearly inadequate against the criteria of crew performance and passenger safety. To paraphrase: Corporate survival may depend upon explicating and operationalizing an axiological paradigm that proceeds from the fundamental assumption of interdependence.

The spare and striking contribution to the methodology of assessment made by Hackman and Helmreich occurs precisely here, in their operationalization of a paradigm of interdependence, not in some trivial exemplar (such as an athletic team whose efforts at achievement are tempered by efforts at individual stardom), but in an important sphere of human activity that affects both human life and safety and the economic fortunes of major corporations. No less important is their discussion of the inelasticity of formal reward systems employed by the airlines, indeed in common with other large corporations. Promotion pathways lead from one hierarchical position as a member of an air crew to another clearly conceived as superior and therefore to be compensated more handsomely, so that formal judgments of worth continue to pivot on assessment of individual characteristics and performances, which can be distinguished from group performance only at the gravest expense to conceptual clarity, no less, in entirely practical terms, than to corporate well-being.

In their instructions to me, Peterson and Fishman suggested that I consider the applicability of the Hackman/Helmreich work to the arena of higher education, presumably because I spend a good deal of my time in assessing the performance not only of faculty and students but of "teams" of faculty and students, such as departments and colleges. From time to time, I am also called upon to assess methods for such assessment.

Few experiences in my rather traditional academic past in the social and behavioral sciences had prepared me, when I joined the administration of a major university, to evaluate the readiness for promotion to higher academic rank among our physicists. Psychology has its clear canons concerning multiple authorship. These are implicitly based, I think, on a nineteenth-century model of the lone Teutonic scientist in his laboratory. Modern physics is quite another matter. In that discipline, frontier-extending research frequently requires the use of singular equipment valued in the tens of millions of dollars and sometimes available in only one site in the hemisphere, along with the active collaboration of a cadre of other scientists. Moreover, the canons of the discipline stipulate that multiple authors be listed alphabetically in journal publication rather than, as in our discipline, in accordance with some prejudgment of the relative contribution of each to the design and execution of the study. Imagine my horror, then, when first I found myself called upon to assess the individual accomplishments of members of a discipline that had clearly already operationalized a paradigm of interdependence, issuing perhaps not from personal philosophic conviction but from the inherent necessities of their scientific enterprise, but who nonetheless sought individual rather than group academic promotion! I cannot claim to have solved the problem. From an academic administrator's standpoint, I can only note that evaluation of individual performance and of group performance are both required for the decisions that have to be made, and that the distinction of one from the other is a difficult problem indeed.

Beyond these practical matters stands a still more important issue, that is, the question of how we go about teaching our students and ourselves to abandon constructs like individuality and independence, which no longer mirror the realities of life in a global village, in favor of constructs like group effort and mutual interdependence, while we continue to insist (as do the airline companies of the Hackman/Helmreich study) that we employ evaluation methods at variance with those realities.

ASSESSING PERFORMANCE
IN ORGANIZATIONS

Finally, we consider issues in assessment at the highest level of complexity with which this book is concerned, that is, the organization. The issues are illustrated in two settings in which psychologists are often engaged: mental health agencies and business organizations. How can we evaluate and improve the effectiveness of a mental health center? How can we evaluate and improve the productivity of a corporation? Broskowski's chapter offers some answers to the first question. Gilbert's chapter offers some answers to the second. Both chapters show the importance of extending inquiries beyond the particular level with which assessment is primarily concerned. The survival of a community mental health center may depend as much on the support of the surrounding community as on the efficiency of internal operation. The productivity of a business firm depends ultimately on the performance of the individuals who work in it.

Broskowski has worked both as a designer and as a consumer of methodologies for evaluating mental health programs. In his current role as director of a community mental health center, he is as much concerned with conditions that inhibit the use of formal data systems as with conditions that encourage their use. From long experience in systematic program evaluation and from a review of pertinent research, he discusses the kinds of information administrators actually use to guide important decisions. Unlike business organizations, where financial profits offer a relatively clear "bottom line," mental health agencies serve mixed aims of multiple constituencies whose demands often conflict, and determination of goals and values can be extremely difficult. Broskowski reviews the key performance indicators that, in his view, offer reasonable promise of useful information about the effectiveness of not-for-profit human service organization. He shows, however, that data of these kinds will be used or ignored according to the interests of the "winning coalition" among the competing groups who control the organization.

Edna Kamis-Gould is Chief of Research and Evaluation in the Division of Mental Health and Hospitals of the New Jersey Department of Human Services. Among her recent activities has been development of

317

a formal performance assessment system for human service organizations throughout the state. She agrees with Broskowski about the political complexities of nonprofit mental health systems, but believes the main problems can be overcome if people with stakes in operating and using the agencies are given active roles in developing and implementing assessment programs. To Kamis-Gould, "laundry lists" of performance indicators are useless. Before any formal assessment begins, the basic values and priorities of the organization must be articulated. Those values and priorities define the meaning of any measures that are developed, and allow judicious interpretation of data when evaluations are conducted. The Performance Management System now in operation in New Jersey exemplifies the kind of organizational assessment that Kamis-Gould considers feasible and useful.

Gilbert began his career in psychology in a university, but soon left the academy to attempt applications of psychology in business organizations and governmental agencies. The ensuing 25 years of experience as a performance engineer have provided a well-illuminated picture of the way human behavior is commonly appraised in work settings. In Gilbert's view, managers rarely have a clear idea of the economics of key jobs in their organizations, measures of performance are rarely relevant to economic outcomes, and the environmental supports required for optimal performance are seldom to be seen. Over the years, Gilbert has developed a strategy for assessing performance in the workplace that is designed to remedy these defects. The system is composed of three large, interdependent components. First is a program for developing economically relevant measures and standards. The trait ratings commonly used to evaluate performance Gilbert considers useless. In their place, he installs measures of attainable performance and standards of exemplary performance that are directly linked to economic outcomes of importance to the organization. The second component of the system is concerned with job design. Models of performance are defined by stipulating the leading accomplishments required for productive work, and the criteria of an effective model are specified. The third component of the system is concerned with profiling behavior. Gilbert argues that assessing the environmental supports needed for effective performance are as important as evaluating the performance itself. Drawing on basic concepts originally set forth by Skinner and Lewin, he defines a method for profiling performance in any job that can be extended to specific criteria by which performance can be appraised.

Gilbert's methodology is discussed by Victor Kline, whose job is the management of organization development and training programs in a large corporation. In a time of fierce economic competition from foreign companies, the survival of American business depends above all on effective performance of workers at all levels. Kline's own experience in the corporate world leads him to agree with most of Gilbert's descriptions of common practice in performance evaluation. He considers Gilbert's basic strategies intrinsically sound and highly promising for improving both productivity and morale, but notes that acceptance of the model will require persuasion of top managers that the model itself cannot bring about. For those who are persuaded, Gilbert's methods provide the tools needed to link the performance of employees with the dominant objectives of the organization.

Chapter 9

Assessment and Decision-Making in Community Mental Health Centers

ANTHONY BROSKOWSKI

This chapter explores the role of formal assessment methodologies in the management of community mental health centers and other not-for-profit human service organizations (NPHSOS). I bring two perspectives to bear on this topic. First, until 1977, a major part of my professional life was devoted to the development of program evaluation methodologies and management information systems for NPHSOS. I strongly advocated such systems for helping managers to improve the management and planning of their operations. In 1977 I became the executive director of a community mental health center (CMHC), and thus a critical consumer as well as creator of such formalized, quantitative evaluation and management systems. Consequently, this chapter reflects my experiences with such systems from both perspectives, with elements of enthusiasm and cynicism blended throughout. On balance, however, I have chosen to present more concerns with the feasibility of immediate and widespread application of formalized decision support systems than I have in extolling their potential benefits.

Since I was trained as a scientist, and enjoyed a reputation for doing applied evaluation research, I naturally gravitated to management information systems (MIS) and program evaluation studies as sources of assistance in making decisions when I became a CMHC director. Generally, I was familiar with a number of analytical methodologies that could be applied in my efforts to make "good" decisions. On more than one occasion I have used each of the following methods in my role as a CMHC director:

Applying research designs and standard statistical analyses to such data as client outcome measures

Analyzing financing data, such as detailed reviews of separate cost and revenue centers, and comparing budgeted with actual cost and revenue information

Developing quantitative performance indicators based on client data, measures of staff performance, and accounting information, and using these indicators to set goals and monitor progress

Forecasting the future through the analyses of past trends in statistical and financial indicators

Develpoing quantitative "models" of organizational units to carry out "what-if" simulations (what if a certain decision was made, or what if the environment changed in certain ways)

I also understood that these methodologies would require the CMHC to have a well-developed information system, one that could provide the necessary client, staff, and financial data to put the methods into effective use. Furthermore, the information system would have to have the capability of providing these data in a timely fashion, allowing linkages across time and among the various data elements within the data base. In my case, the story of the evolution of MIS design and implementation is long and boring. Suffice it to say that I managed to install a system capable of supporting my efforts in short-range planning, daily management, and a few efforts at program evaluation.

Despite my comfort with formalized management information systems, and the availability of rudimentary client, staff, and fiscal information, I cannot remember many instances of turning to my MIS or program evaluation staff whenever I was faced with major decisions. This begs the question, What is a "major decision"? I will discuss that point later. First I want to consider the role of information in the decision-making process and begin to identify the circumstances that determine when formalized assessment systems will be useful and used, and when they are likely to be ignored.

Intuitively, we all understand that information is needed at all stages of the decision-making process, in making initial decisions as well as reviewing the impact of earlier decisions in order to adjust administrative processes. It just sounds right when someone says decisions should be based on reliable and valid information. But any person directly responsible for that decision, when time and money are real-world constraints, will begin to ask a number of questions: What do we mean by the term "information," the simple compilation of facts or numerical indicators within formalized data collection systems? What is the most relevant information I need for this particular decision, and where can I get it quickly and cheaply? How do I know this "formal" information is any more reliable than my personal hunches or the "informal" information I receive through other channels? Are the rumors I hear or the staff advice I receive (two types of informal information) any less compelling than the formal analyses derived from MIS data?

Line administrators may conclude, as I did after several years of introspection, that formal information systems and program evaluation studies are not a *sufficient* solution to the problem of making decisions on the basis of information. In part, this conclusion derives from some further questions: Are my decisions getting better because I installed and used a management information system (MIS)? Can my MIS indicators validate other, informal indicators of my own performance as an organizational leader? Do the MIS reports substantiate my own suspicions or staff suggestions that I have serious problems in parts of the organization?

Assuming a good decision is one that will contribute to a more effective organization, the organization's effectiveness becomes a criterion for validating decisions. Conversely, the study of organizational decision-making and the types of information systems needed to improve it depends on understanding the characteristics of an effective organization.

MODELS OF ORGANIZATIONAL EFFECTIVENESS

The literature on organizational effectiveness has been thoroughly reviewed by Goodman et al. (1977), Miles (1980), and Kanter and Brinkerhoff (1981). Many audiences are vitally interested in how well any given organization, or set of organizations, is operating. However, there is little agreement on the definition of organizational effectiveness or on the validity of the myriad indicators proposed to measure it. Although management information systems and decision-support systems are increasingly present in all types of organizations, we need to know more about the underlying factors that may determine an organization's effectiveness as measured by the MIS variables, that is, the *how* and *why* of organizational effectiveness (Van de Ven & Ferry, 1980).

The literature on organizational effectiveness does not offer a single, coherent model that one can readily use under all circumstances. Rather, any review of this literature will impress upon the reader that what is deemed to count for organizational performance is largely contingent upon one's perspective. For example, the definitions of an organization's effectiveness range from "the ability to achieve its goals" (Etzioni, 1960), the ability to "acquire scarce and valued resources" (Yuchtman & Seashore, 1967), the ability to "satisfy the needs of its members" (Cummings, 1977), to "the maximization of return . . . by economic and technical means (efficiency), and by political means" (Katz & Kahn, 1966). This is only a sampling of the wide variety of definitions offered by different theorists.

Most theorists and practitioners agree that an organization's performance is to some degree contingent upon its environment. Therefore, any assessment of performance must include an assessment of the environment and the organization-environment interactions. The complexities become quickly apparent. Most MISS limit themselves to measuring *internal* activities, although some go beyond that to look at "market conditions" or other *external* factors.

There are also different *levels of analysis* to consider, both internally and externally. One can examine the performance (still undefined) of the overall organization, units within the organization, staff members within the unit, or tasks within the staff member's job description. Interaction effects, within and across these internal levels and with the external environment, must be further differentiated.

As with any complex subject, one must be guided by a theory or model. Here, as in most fields of inquiry and action, there are various models from which to choose. Generally, theories of organizational effectiveness fall within two broad categories: goal attainment models and general systems models.

The goal attainment theories stress that organizations are goal-seeking systems, motivated by a future purpose. Here the emphasis is on the organizational ends, as opposed to means. Designers of these models must struggle with several problems. How are goals to be identified? Are there differences between "public" goals and "operative" goals (Perrow, 1961)? Not uncommonly, one can identify competitive subunit goals within the same organization. Under these circumstances one must be able to order the priority of different goals.

Another popular set of models can be classified as systems models.

Here the emphasis is on means rather than ends. These models also stress intraorganizational and environmental interdependencies. For example, although a goal attainment model will stress "profit maximization," or how much can we extract from our environment, a systems model will stress long-term survival by maintaining a balance of exchanges with the environment. Flexibility, adaptation, and self-correction (i.e., feedback) are common systems model criteria.

Like the goal attainment approach, the systems approach has some problems. Critics point out that vague constructs like "balance" or "survival" defy precise measurement. Furthermore, an organization may survive even though most persons agree that it is no longer serving a useful purpose or attaining a specific goal. The goal of survival does not define immediate operational goals required for survival. Although systems models have helped to highlight the weaknesses of the goal attainment approach, they simply postpone, but do not solve, the problems of identifying and measuring organizational goals (Miles, 1980). Clearly, neither the goal attainment model nor the systems approach is adequate by itself.

The range of theories within these two categories has produced an extensive list of criteria or operational indices of organizational performance. John Campbell's (1977) review of the research yielded no less than 30 constructs (e.g., productivity, efficiency, profit, growth, turnover, accident rates, morale, control, readiness, stability, etc.). In turn, each of these constructs could be operationally defined in numerous ways and for various levels within the organization. Although needs for multiple measures and replication may appear obvious, Campbell found few examples of research that used multiple measures in a single study or the same measure across multiple studies. In my own review of the literature on factors affecting the development, maintenance, and effectiveness of interorganizational linkages, I found no fewer than 32 constructs (Broskowski, 1982a, Broskowski et al., 1982, Marks & Broskowski, 1981).

Recent reviews have begun to stress the contingent nature of defining organizational effectiveness. What is deemed to be effective depends on the perspective one adopts (Attkisson & Broskowski, 1978; Connolly & Deutsch, 1980; Kanter & Brinkerhoff, 1981). Not only do different constituencies have different perspectives, they have different preferences they actively seek to promote. Therefore, we must introduce the notion of power in understanding the definition and the measurement of organizational or system effectiveness (Perrow, 1977). Often the "agreement" one sees in the definition of an organization's criteria for effectiveness is a reflection of the preferences of the "dominant coalition" (Yuchtman & Seashore, 1967). By this reasoning, certain measures of effectiveness that are highly valued and consistently used, such as profit maximization or market share, reflect the consensus of a coalition within the organization, such as shareholders and chief executives. In essence, the organization's operative goals reflect the end product of a conflict and bargaining process, whereby different groups had some access to the specification of the goals, and some coalition of interests won out over others. By this standard the effective organization is the one that attains the goals set forth by the winning coalition (Elmore, 1978).

MEASURING PERFORMANCE IN THE NOT-FOR-PROFIT HUMAN SERVICE ORGANIZATION

The measurement of organizational performance varies considerably with the nature of the organization, its primary mission, its ownership, the complexity of its technology, and a multitude of additional factors. It is a particularly difficult task in NPHSOS, where there is a high level of disagreement on such issues as the appropriate definition of services (i.e., outputs) or the appropriate "bottom line": quantity or quality, effectiveness or efficiency, responsiveness to all or focus on a few priority populations. Difficulties notwithstanding, we find an increasing number of proposals to use financial and statistical indicators for planning, management, and resource allocation decisions (Drtina, 1982; Hadley et al., 1983; Hall, 1981).

One system proposed for mental health service organizations, the Key Performance Indicator (KPI) system, is the latest in a series of performance monitoring systems that have grown out of efforts by the National Institute of Mental Health to develop measures of the relative performance of federally funded CMHCs. The KPI project, however, is sponsored by the National Council of Community Mental Health Centers and funded by a grant from the Pew Foundation (Sorensen et al., 1984). The KPI system is placed as a voluntary system, whose costs will be borne by the CMHCs that use it.

The KPI system acknowledges the need of managers for reliable and valid information about clients, staff, financial resources, services provided, and the costs and outcomes of these services. It is an attempt to accomplish several objectives. First, boards and managers could evaluate performance and improve cost efficiency, thereby improving their

TABLE 9.1
Key Performance Indicators for
Community Mental Health Organizations

=====

A. *Revenue mix indicators:*
   1. Dollars of revenue for unduplicated count of clients served
   2. Percentage distribution of revenue by source of revenue
   3. Amount billed before adjustment as a percentage of total billable charges
   4. Amount billed after adjustment as a percentage of total billable charges
   5. Collections as a percentage of amount billed after adjustment
   6. Expense convergence rate for each type of clinical service
   7. Current ratio
   8. Net cash flow to total debt
   9. Unfunded expense recovery rate

B. *Client mix indicators:*
   10. Minority caseload indicator for each type of minority
   11. Percentage of clients of each primary diagnostic group
   12. Percentage of severely mentally disabled for each major age group

C. *Staff mix indicators:*
   13. Percentage of distribution of clinical staff effort for each clinical service
   14. Median and mean salaries and benefits for each major discipline
   15. Proportion of compensation expenses to total expenses

D. *Service mix indicators:*
   16. Average number of service units per FTE day for each major clinical service
   17. Average caseload of service for each major clinical service
   18. Percentage of time devoted to consultation and education
   19. Ambulatory program productivity percentage
   20. Inpatient/residential program productivity ratio
   21. Staff cost per client for each major clinical service
   22. Staff cost per direct hour of care or effort for each major clinical service
   23. Total cost per unit for each major service
   24. Average client utilization of each major service
   25. Total client turnover

=====

Source: Adapted from James E. Sorensen, William Zelman, Glyn W. Hanbury, and A. Ronald Kucic, *Key performance indicators for community mental health organizations: A conceptual framework*, National Council of Community Mental Health Centers, Rockville, Md., 1984.

ability to compete in the marketplace and justify programs and budgets to funding sources. Second, government agencies could evaluate the use of their funds by comparing various providers. Finally, managers (presumably state and local level) could be provided with improved information to educate legislators and other decision makers about the efficacy and viability of mental health programs.

The KPI system establishes four sets of indicators: revenues, clients, staff, and services. Additional sets are generated by the interaction among these primary sets. For example, the intersection of client indicators and revenue indicators would generate such indices as the "average cost per client served" or the "average revenue collected per client." Of the over 50 indicators thus generated, 25 are considered to be *key* performance indicators. A summary of the key indicators is presented in Table 9.1.

Managers who make operational decisions can use these indicators to compare a center's program with a "standard," with trends over time (i.e., with one's own past performance), or with the performance of one or more comparison programs (within or outside the center). The KPI system allows comparison of a program with other programs, along several dimensions: location or level, such as national, state, or local; size, as measured by budget, staff, or clients served; type, such as "outpatient only," "general hospital with inpatient," "freestanding"; and community characteristics, such as urban-rural or socioeconomic mix of clients.

Recently the KPI system was being pilot-tested in two states, Colorado and Ohio (Sorensen et al., 1984). In addition to the reliability, validity, and utility of the actual indicators, the system's designers are concerned with its operating characteristics. To qualify for general use, it must be acceptably inexpensive to operate, accessible to centers who wish to join, accommodating to a wide variety of users (by type of center and level within the center), adaptable over time as centers change, nonintrusive and minimally demanding upon a center's current internal MIS, and capable of providing quick turnaround of reports that are easily interpretable (e.g., bar graphs, trend lines, simple tables).

FACTORS FACILITATING OR INHIBITING THE USE OF FORMAL ASSESSMENT SYSTEMS

In my opinion, the KPI system represents the best effort to date to design and implement a useful decision-support tool that goes beyond the internal statistical and financial functions that must be performed by each CMHC's own internal MIS, such as billing and staff service reporting. Whether or not it succeeds will depend in part on its intrinsic value to the end user, the CMHC decision makers, and whether or not it is abused or misused by those responsible for state or local funding.

Although performance indicator systems such as the KPI hold promise for advancing our understanding of NPHSOS, they are being proposed and tested in a very turbulent and reactive environment, where cost cutting and "cutback management" are the most salient concerns (Broskowski, 1982b). At the same time new cost reimbursement systems are expected, such as the payment for health services based on "diagnostic-related groups" (DRGS), prepaid capita contracts, and discounted contracts between insurors, employers, and "preferred providers." Consequently, efforts to validate key indicators could easily become bogged down in a morass of political and economic agendas. For example, the Health Care Financing Administration is reporting signs of "DRG creep," caused by hospitals reporting those diagnoses that have the highest profit margins. The tendency for such incentive or regulatory systems to produce countermoves on the part of the regulated agency is so pervasive that it has earned a name unto itself in contemporary management: "gaming." Every NPHSO seeking to survive can develop a rationale for discrediting any measure that makes its own performance questionable. If the measure cannot be discredited, then the organization may attempt to discount its value or manipulate the data collection system used to measure it.

Despite organizational efforts at gaming any system, funding and regulatory agencies are moving forward under pressure of limited tax funds and continuing demands for more accountability. Because of these pressures, it is expected that the state of the art in measuring performance of NPHSOS will advance more rapidly than in previous years. But in place of needs assessments and client outcome studies, we will witness a return to measuring basic financial and staff/client statistical criteria. These are presumably indicators of the *process* of delivering mental health services, but measures that have a direct bearing on service costs and organizational viability.

The forces inhibiting and/or promoting the application of KPI systems are instances of the more general forces that will affect the use of formalized data collection systems within a complex organization and a complex interorganizational field. Table 9.2 summarizes 12 factors that I believe are instrumental in determining whether or not formalized data collection and analyses will be used.

TABLE 9.2
Factors That Facilitate or Inhibit the Use of Formalized Data
in the Decision-Making Process

Factor	Facilitative	Inhibitory
Identical decision made very frequently	×	
Data system inexpensive relative to mission costs	×	
Small number of clear options	×	
High consensus on the system's goals/values	×	
Availability of time and resources for analyses	×	
Simple cause-effect linearity assumed	×	
Complex but unknown system assumed		×
External interdependencies, reactivity, and turbulence		×
Proactivity effect on outcomes or their probabilities		×
Outcome important to multiple groups		×
Action implemented incrementally		×
Problem experientially familiar but not frequent		×

At least with reference to making organizational decisions, the choice is seldom between using data and not using data. In reality, we are likely to observe a continuum, ranging from complete dependency on formalized data (in which case we will probably automate the decision process), through the blending of formal and informal information, to the complete disdain for any formalized data analysis whatsoever.

Table 9.2 represents a modest effort to organize my current understanding of the circumstances or conditions that facilitate or inhibit the use of formalized data systems, including the use of ongoing monitoring systems or special research studies, within the decision-making process. For example, when an identical decision must be made frequently, such as "Does this person have what it takes to succeed in college?" then it is more likely that decision makers will attempt to use some formalized data collection and analyses in reaching a decision.

In thinking about these variables, I explicitly assumed that I could ignore individual differences among decision makers. I further assumed that the decision maker has a choice with respect to the use of discretionary time, money, and other human resources at his/her command. In one sense, Table 9.2 represents my guesses as to how most organizational leaders would prefer to use time, money, and staff in the process of making decisions: to collect and analyze data or to take incremental action steps toward an uncertain future without benefit of formal data.

What follows is a review of some of the conditions that have led me to predicate the 12 factors in Table 9.2. Although many of the other chapters in this book provide clear examples of the practical application of formalized assessment systems, I have chosen to emphasize those factors that inhibit the widespread use of such models within complex organizations embedded within a turbulent and ambiguous environment. That is not to say that formalized systems cannot be used under such conditions. Their application, however, is seldom a straightforward matter.

Although formalized planning and evaluation methods have been commonly available for use in CMHCs since the early 1970s, critics have frequently noted that such systems were seldom used appropriately by CMHC leaders or their governmental funding sources (Attkisson & Broskowski, 1984, Kepper-Seid et al., 1980). At worst, such systems have been indicted for creating a host of unintended, dysfunctional side effects, such as encouraging insurance claims, defining target populations, developing quotas, meeting demands from accrediting agencies, and measuring treatment outcomes (Ginsberg, 1984). Campbell (1979) has succinctly stated the following observation: "The more any quantitative social indicator is used for decision making, the more subject it will be to corruption pressure and the more apt it will be to distort and corrupt the social processes it is intended to monitor" (p. 85).

An understanding of the potential uses, misuses, and abuses of formalized organizational assessment systems within the CMHC setting requires an analysis of the contemporary CMHC as an organization and of the context in which members of its governance and management domains make decisions.

Specifically, the concept of the dominant coalition (Elmore, 1978), used by theorists of organizational effectiveness, can shed considerable light on the difficulties of using such information systems within the

TABLE 9.3
Domains of Human Service Organizations

	Policy domain
Members	Board of Directors
Principle	Ownership, final responsibility, mutual consent
Success measure	Equity in the distribution of resources
Structure	Representative government, equality in participation, one person/one vote
Work modes	Voting, bargaining, negotiating
	Management domain
Members	Top and middle managers
Principle	Control through hierarchical authority, chain of command, and coordination
Success measures	Efficiency and effectiveness
Structure	Bureaucratic, differentiated, standardized
Work modes	Management controls and coordinative devices
	Service domain
Members	Professional service staff
Principle	Autonomy and self-regulation
Success measures	Quality of service, professional standards
Structure	Collegial, based on credentials and privileges
Work modes	Client-specific or problem-specific techniques

SOURCE: Adapted from Kouzes and Mico (1979).

NPHSO. Kouzes and Mico (1979) have pointed out that within the typical NPHSO there are three domains: the policy domain, the management domain, and the service domain. Each has its own membership, structure, operating principles, work modes, and measures of success, as outlined in Table 9.3.

Naturally, under these circumstances there will be a considerable potential for internal discord and conflict in the selection of effectiveness criteria. Although a board of directors may stress indicators reflecting equity in the distribution of resources, such as measures of services being provided to minorities, managers will be concerned with measures of the potential to recover costs through billing the middle class and to reduce the "cost per unit of service" by increasing the volume of care and/or reducing the length of treatment per client. Meanwhile, a professional staff in the service domain are interested in reducing management controls, increasing staff salaries and privileges, and providing long-term psychotherapy to a selected subpopulation capable of benefiting from such interventions.

Why should any of these domains resist the use of information systems? Information conveys power, and those in each domain may feel that there is little enough to go around internally, much less to share with external sources.

Most NPHSOs are intrinsically vulnerable to the misinterpretation of information. This condition arises from the fact that the governance and management structures of public service organizations, governmental or not-for-profit, are designed to be extremely "permeable," or open to multiple external influences. Any citizen, elected official, advocacy group, or tax-paying corporation has a legitimate right to "evaluate" the effectiveness of such organizations. This right is usually justified on two grounds: the concept of the citizen's right to the service and the fact that it is being paid for in whole or in part by government funds. Therefore, it is argued, almost everyone has a right to evaluate the organization, if they want to take the time and energy to do it. Conversely, the organization must be accountable, and accountable to multiple sources of potential control or harrassment. Thus, proposals for the collection of numerous indicators, particularly those with norm-based standards of comparison, are realistically viewed with caution and concern.

Although consumerism and civil rights movements institutionalized one rationale for accountability, stressing such criteria as accessibility and responsiveness to needs, supply-side economics and government cost cutting have stimulated more recent interest in assessing the performance of public services, stressing such criteria as costs, efficiency, and "real demand."

Now we have two institutionalized pressures demanding accountability, and the NPHSO cannot afford to ignore either one. Consider what can happen over the long haul. Assume that the results of an evaluation, based of course on the criteria and perspective of the coalition that conducted it, suggest that programs are ineffective, particularly because of poor governance or inefficient management. Consequently, suggestions are made to have the service performed by a profit-making organization, one presumably managed more efficiently. However, when a profit-making organization operates the service, its efficiency and effectiveness are contingent upon its ability to control its boundary. To exercise this control, it may become more selective in its choice of clientele, less concerned with its choice of means, and generally less open and willing to be evaluated by multiple constituencies (Broskowski, 1984). The cycle comes full circle when another coalition gains enough power to insist that this "uncaring and closed" organization have its responsibilities transferred to a public, or not-for-profit, organization, one that will be open to all who need it. I offer current trends in health care, particularly the growth of profit-making hospital chains and the increasing limits on health care for the indigent, as evidence for this process (Lewin & Lewin, 1984).

Thus, because of its boundary permeability within a pluralistic society, the typical NPHSO is vulnerable. Consequently, its managers may be reluctant to set clearly measureable (i.e., public) goals, particularly when the technology exists to measure them. It is bad enough that the process of setting organizational goals can readily create internal tensions. The leader must also consider the increased probability that a misinterpretation of key indicators could lead to a consensus decision that the organization failed to achieve its public goals, leading to an early demise.

Further aggravating the situation, the typical NPHSO is mandated to achieve a large number and variety of goals by the wide variety of its external funding, regulatory, or accrediting agencies. These goals may be mutually exclusive, and in some cases contradictory to one another (e.g., to serve the poor but at the same time attract the middle-class to subsidize less-than-adequate government funding). What set of books does one show to which regulatory or funding agency? Which set of indicators does the organization try to maximize?

Parenthetically, the reluctance to set clearly measureable goals is not limited to the not-for-profit sector. A wisdom commonly shared by many chief executives of large corporations is that to maintain their corporation's options and responsiveness to opportunities they should avoid a declaration of highly specific goals and objectives (Broskowski, 1982b; Kotter, 1982; Mintzberg, 1975; Wrapp, 1984). Although the chief executive may have a "vision" of the future and an "agenda" of long-range issues and goals, he or she may not share them with all interested parties, and will resist reducing them to highly specific and measurable objectives.

EMPIRICAL STUDIES OF NPHSO DECISION-MAKING

Some insights into the possible uses, misuses, and nonuses of formalized information systems and key performance indicators can be gained by reviewing the theory and research on utilization of evaluative research and the decision-making process (Rich, 1977; Weiss, 1981; Windle & Volkman, 1973). These and other studies suggest that the uses of evaluation and formalized information systems in the process of decision-making is fairly constrained and sensitively dependent upon such factors as the characteristics of the organization, of the persons inside and outside the organization, and of the research study or the information system being used. Within these three broad categories are a host of more specific limiting factors (Patton et al., 1977).

Mintzberg's (1973) empirical observations of managers revealed several discrepancies between the "facts" and the "folklore" of effective management. Similarly, systematic observation of the way decisions are made in a typical CMHC is enlightening and surprising. The best illustration I can offer is provided by Cox and Osborne (1980) in their study of the ways four CMHC executive directors did or did not use formalized evaluation data in the process of making some important decisions.

Cox and Osborne followed four CMHC directors over a span of several months to determine the characteristics of the problems that influenced their choice of different problem-solving strategies. Two sets of variables were examined: (1) characteristics of the problem, such as its unfamiliarity, ambiguity, complexity, and instability, and (2) the characteristics of the "decision environment," such as the risks involved, the irreversibility of the decision, the accountability of the decision maker, and the time and resource constraints. Using a decision-making contingency model proposed by Beach and Mitchell (1978), they expected that as the problems became increasingly difficult or important, and as the risks and/or the accountability increased the decision makers would demonstrate an increasing use of analytical and quantitative decision-making strategies. In other words, they would more likely turn to formalized information systems and program evaluation methods.

Cox and Osborne found little evidence to support their expectations, but their observations provide valuable insights into why that was the case. The directors rated their familiarity with the problems they were facing as "high," and they generally felt comfortable in moving forward to solve them. Ambiguity was rated low, and the directors reported that they were fairly clear about their objectives and their choice of the criteria to use in choosing an acceptable solution. Although the details of the alternative options were not always clear to them, especially in the early stages, the directors could readily identify the general categories of alternative, acceptable solutions.

"Key beliefs," based upon personal or organizational values and the director's cumulative experiences, were used to make some critical simplifying assumptions. These assumptions were used to rule out alternatives, guide the search for more specific information, and guide in the selection of subsequent problem-solving activities.

Problem complexity was rated as only moderate. Although the problems involved multiple interest groups and required consideration of multiple cost/benefit trade-offs to consider, the directors accepted this as an integral aspect of their job responsibilities. Problem instability, the degree to which the goals, criteria, or constraints on the solution shifted over time, was not considered to be a major concern. Instability was accepted as a given and *exploited* by the directors. The instability allowed the director to become proactive in a turbulent environment and to increase the probabilities that a given solution would have greater acceptability or payoff.

Few problems were seen as requiring irreversible decisions, and the directors expressed confidence in their ability to solve the problem in an acceptable manner regardless of the reversibility issue. Accountability for the decision was also not a major concern, but considered as part of the job's responsibilities. Nor did time and resource constraints appear to be a major concern. Cox and Osborne report that the problem-solving activities proceeded at a "somewhat leisurely pace" over six to nine months, culminating in a brief but intense period of activity.

Essentially, these authors describe the process as an interactive one, in which the decision maker is proactive or manipulative, rather than simply passive or analytical. The directors tried to create opportunities, not just study them as problems. Environmental instability was not a source of "error variance" but a condition to be exploited. In fact, some of the directors' initiatives were often designed to increase such instability. Such problem characteristics as complexity and instability appeared to have their strongest impact on the decision-making process by requiring the involvement of more people and elevating the level of authority at which a final decision could be made.

The chosen solutions for each problem were characterized by a few *critical tasks*. The information the directors found most useful was that which facilitated these critical tasks. In only one of the four cases was that information derived from a formalized information system.

Of course, it is possible to raise the question of these decision makers' effectiveness. Would they have made better decisions if they had used evaluation research and analytical methods? But that question also begs the question of what constitutes a "good" or "better" decision in an environment of rapid change, uncertainty, and vulnerability to shifting coalitions, each with its own definition of effectiveness. It is also clear that these directors were not motivated to ignore or avoid formal evaluation methods by fear of losing power or control. They appeared to "own up" to their responsibility and would have used other types of information had it been available and appropriate to the problem.

Following up on the work of Cox and Osborne (1980), DiNitto et al., (1984) surveyed the directors of 42 CMHCS in Florida and North Carolina (64.5% response rate). Information was collected concerning the size, structure, financing, and decision-making processes of each center, as well as the education and experiences of the directors. According to DiNitto et al., 83% of the centers reported doing an evaluation of a program's effectiveness or impact within the previous 12 months. Respondents indicated that there was a strong relationship among perceptions of the need for change, the influence of the research on the decision to make a change, and the amount of change actually implemented. However, among the eight factors from which directors could choose as important in the decision-making process, 93% believed that the "availability of funds" was the most important. The other factors and corresponding percentages which rated the factors as "very important or important," were client demand (78%), data on client need (78%), data on effectiveness (66%), community pressures (56%), data on efficiency (44%), staff opinion on effectiveness (36%), and staff desires to provide a service (15%). "In actual decision-making situations reported by the CMHC directors, evaluative data was mentioned as a reason for change only 16 times out of a total of 140 programmatic changes" (p. 179).

One lingering concern I have had with the kinds of findings reported by Cox and Osborne stems from my knowledge of the education and training of my fellow directors. Many of them may not realize how formal information and evaluation technologies can be helpful to them, so they fail to seek systems that might be useful. Their evaluators and financial support staff do not fully understand the complex nature of the problem the director is facing, and fail to suggest creative uses of their technical methodologies. In essence, the problem is one of wedding the appropriate methodology to the particular problem at hand. To do so, the technician/methodologist and the person responsible for solving the problem must have enough in common to enable them to communicate with one another.

One method for teaching managers the value of analytic methods, while showing the methodologists the value and domain complexities of the decision process, involves the computer simulation of a complex system. A computer model can allow a team to try different strategies, basing decisions on data or hunches, and observing the effects within a sufficient time frame to allow learning and improvement in performance.

Quarton and Cross (Cross, 1984) have developed such a system model to teach psychiatric residents the complexity of administrative decision-making. Their model assumes a community of 100,000 and a budget of $10,754,500, to be allocated between six types of direct service programs, a category of "no treatment," and three types of preventive intervention. the funds can be invested in "capacity," such as beds or therapy slots, or "quality." There are two types of patients to be served in the system: "alphas," with acute and/or less serious disorders, and "betas," with serious and chronic conditions. Patients move through the "system" and get better or worse along an eight-point scale of severity, depending upon their initial condition and the type, amount, and quality of the service they receive. In addition to making allocation decisions affecting system capacity and quality, one can vary the admission criteria or the discharge conditions, thereby affecting patient flow through the system. In a simplified version, the decision maker can attempt to achieve, (maximize? optimize?) one or more of eight objectives, covering prevention, treatment, equity, and efficiency concerns. Each objective can be measured by one or more system measures, including a comprehensive index called SWAPP (severity weighted average point prevalence). Other measures reflect the perspective of different constituencies, such as "civil restraint" scores to reflect living in the least restrictive environment for patients, and measures of "bizarre encounters," "assaults on the public," "homicide," and "suicide" rates.

During the decision-making process, it becomes clear that decisions to allocate funds or alter patient flows have many unanticipated side effects. Making decisions to maximize patients' rights may increase patient suicides. Allocating too much money for the betas may increase the rate at which the alphas go untreated and gradually become betas. Investments in "quality" increase the rate of flow from more to less severe levels of pathology, but putting too much into quality reduces the capacity of certain types of services within the continuum, inhibiting the efficient flow of patients through the system. Although funding one type of preventive intervention has no effect, dollars invested in another has the effect of reducing the dependency of the betas on the more expensive levels of service.

The beauty of the model is that it makes the issues of value preferences and resource trade-offs explicit, and it highlights the ambiguity inherent in defining the qualities of a "good" decision. The judgment that one's decisions have improved the system depends on the choice of alternative criteria, which depends, in turn, on the values and superordinate goals of the decision makers.

The model can also illustrate critical interdependencies among programs. If different decision makers, in charge of separate service programs, begin making independent (and probably secret) decisions with respect to the investment of funds or the criteria for service admissions and/or discharges, the overall effects of any one person's decisions become far less predictable and the effectiveness of the overall system of patient care is more difficult to control, no matter what criteria or value systems are used.

Despite its surface complexity, this model is a relatively simplified one in comparison with the real world. Considerable research will be required to validate its equations. However, it "behaves" in many ways as experienced administrators would expect, and it forces them to face the complexity of decisions and the trade-offs implicit in the social values and government policies that guide their decisions. Even though the computer provides much of the necessary "data," and the outcomes are more or less predictable once we learn the equations linking the various measures, the decision maker is still faced with the uncomfortable dilemma of choosing among multiple costs and benefits.

FUTURE RESEARCH AND PRACTICE

My recommendations for further research and practice are organized according to the framework suggested by Fishman and Neigher in the second chapter of this volume. My first recommendation is that such models as theirs continue to be described, and whenever possible, tested under "real-world" conditions. Certainly, the complexities of *organizational* decision-making suggest the need to develop a sufficiently complex and coherent strategy for designing, pilot-testing, and institutionalizing formalized assessment systems for such settings.

The first steps within the Fishman and Neigher model are concerned with conceptualizing the decision process that will apply in a given setting or field. This in itself will prove to be a very difficult task within most organizational settings. I would begin by recommending that a typology, or classification, system be developed that could be used to reliably classify the various types of decisions that are made in an organization. Such a typology could be based on the various "attributes" of a decision, such as its frequency, and whether or not it is forced on the organization by an external crisis or developed out of a careful plan for the long-range future. Such a typology would allow researchers to begin the process of counting decisions and identifying the points in time when they are initially identified and finally made.

The rate at which certain types of decisions are made will offer a valuable clue to the feasibility of formalizing any data collection systems to enhance such decisions. For example, certain decisions are confronted routinely and are commonly called "operational" or "tactical." Less frequently, one can identify more important, strategic decisions. Furthermore, some strategic decisions are encountered unwillingly, often confronted as a crisis but seldom embraced as an opportunity. Although routine tactical decision-making may lend itself to formalized assessment procedures, the rare but strategic decision is likely to be, at best, only influenced by formalized data.

Another important dimension centers on the notion of development, or evolution. The initial decision or issue can readily change and evolve with time. Sometimes the decision evolves gradually, as more information is gathered; sometimes it changes dramatically, as might occur when a leader deliberately reinterprets what appears to be a crisis as an opportunity. This reinterpretation will often broaden the scope of problem-solving behaviors, including the search for relevant information, and avoid fixation on a single decision.

The level of risks inherent in a decision is still another factor that any typology could consider. As indicated earlier, there is some intuitive reason to suppose that formalized data collection efforts will increase with increasing levels of risk. But risk level may also interact with the factor of timing. A leader may come to the conclusion that the time and cost of data collection only increase the risks by delaying the decision. A leader may also use other risk-buffering mechanisms to forgo the need for extensive and highly reliable data collection. The importance of a decision is not always related to its obvious risk levels. Although it makes dramatic history to focus on Eisenhower's decision to proceed with the invasion of Normandy in the face of changing weather, that decision, though important, was trivial in comparison to numerous other tactical and strategic decisions that were made to ensure a successful invasion. Most importantly, there was a commonly understood mission and an incredible devotion at all levels to its accomplishment. If Vietnam was a war managed by measurable goals and objectives (and supported by computerized decision models), World War II was an example of management by mission.

Fishman and Neigher correctly identify the importance of understanding the "context and culture" of the decision-making environment. This can be an exceedingly important factor in determining how decisions are made. Therefore, decision research at the organizational level will have to be based on a clear classification of organizational subtypes. This will not be easy. Organizations, as much as, if not more than, individuals, exhibit tremendous variations from one another and over time in their structures and environments, and thus vary widely in the culture and context surrounding their decisions. Therefore, more attention must be given to the problem of classifying and measuring organizational environments and interorganizational relationships (Broskowski, 1982a), and then studying the effects of variations in these on the organization's selection of criteria for effectiveness and the selection of decision models.

Also, the question of context and culture must address the importance of values. Values may or may not be explicit but they are always present. They may or may not be negotiable, but they inevitably determine the selection of measurement criteria. Values may also provide a clue regarding the best typology of organizations. We can certainly see the relative importance given to the "bottom line" in comparing profit and nonprofit health delivery systems.

As an example of the importance of the context and culture issues, consider CMHCs as a whole. Their environment has always been extremely complex and turbulent, and more so in recent years. The instability and high rate of change precludes any deliberate "choice" of a decision-making model, other than the interactive, proactive, and manipulative model described by Cox and Osborne (1980). Undoubtedly, there have been and will continue to be times when analytic models can be applied within the CMHC context. But contrary to Beach and Mitchell's (1978) model for the selection of decision-making approaches, I believe such scientific-analytic models are currently *less likely* to be used within CMHCs, particularly as the importance of the decision increases. It is people, not models, who are held responsible for making decisions and carrying out the actions necessary to implement them. The wise CMHC leader realizes that he/she needs committed followers, and that decisions are made in the context of multiple domains and a turbulent and watchful environment. Consequently, strategic decisions will be made on the basis of a consensus model, which may give little weight to any formalized analytic methods that would suggest a different course of action. Somehow we have to take such "implementation factors" into consideration in studying the selection of a model.

As suggested above, the organizational and interorganizational context of CMHCs has been characterized by complexity, instability, and conflict. The decision makers within this context have to consider several dimensions of the decision being faced before deciding how much energy and time the organization should expend in conducting any formalized data collection and analysis. Such factors as the decision's irreversibility and importance (i.e., risks/benefits), as well as the decision maker's personal accountability for the results, are generally taken into account. Time and money constraints are always present. Undoubtedly, the cognitive style of the decision maker is also critical. Since CMHCs are organizations with multiple constituencies and shifting coalitions (including internal professional staff and existing clients), the CMHC leader and governing board are seldom faced with opportunities to use scientific methodologies. At best, they are pleased when there are some historical data and a reasonable vision of the future.

The design of prototype data systems is the next major set of steps proposed by Fishman and Neigher. In my opinion, more work has already been done on this phase than on the above set of issues. Furthermore, I see fewer obstacles here than in the conceptual phases above. Admittedly there are some serious technical problems associated with the measurement of variables and their efficient collection, storage, and retrieval. But I consider these to be technical problems that are highly overrated by the technicians. I will say more on that later, in discussing interpretation problems. These technical measurement and collection problems are also the most frequently discussed and studied in academic settings because they offer the illusion of a problem with a simple solution, one requiring precision and control. Our fascination with computers, including my own obsession, makes it comfortable for us to talk about the technical problems and solutions associated with complex and massive data collection efforts, while at the same time we gloss over the complexity of the "culture and context" of the organization.

Major challenges are encountered in the area of data interpretation. Consider the KPI system. The biggest potential barrier limiting its widespread implementation is the potential for misinterpretation of the indicators. Most persons can be taught that the indicators being reported are only a *symbolic* representation of real-world clients, staff, and services. These real persons, events, and objects are simply being "encoded" in the form of letters, codes, numbers, or other symbols for easy manipulation. These symbolic data elements are collected, edited, stored, and retrieved using a wide variety of manual and electronic methods. Eventually the data elements take on the quality of "information" through the process of aggregation, analysis, and synthesis—and thereby the quality of "reality" for some interpreters.

Distortions and unreliabilities leak into a system at many points along the way (Attkisson & Broskowski, 1984). However, we tolerate these errors within our systems because we find that the aggregated and analyzed symbols are a sufficiently accurate reflection of real-world relationships for certain, but limited, purposes. Depending upon the importance of the decisions to be made, we may choose to invest more time, energy, and money into making the system a more valid and precise reflection of reality. But it is never more than a reflection. Reliability, validity, and precision are all relative to the purposes for which the data were collected and analyzed. In my view, we have put too much emphasis on "technologies" for collecting and analyzing data, and have paid insufficient attention to teaching end users how to interpret the meaning of the analyses in light of internal and external circumstances. This is particularly critical if the end users are to include those outside the operating system who will be expected to make resource allocation decisions on the basis of formalized information systems.

Suppose I design a formalized data collection system for my mental health center. Although I may understand the limits of my system, and hence the quality of my "information," outsiders may not. I also have access to "informal information systems" (Broskowski et al., in preparation) that help me to understand the "meaning" of the formal indicators within the context of the center's past and current circumstances, as well as its immediate environment and all the resources and constraints that the environment provides. But can I trust some distant regulatory bureaucrat to understand this phenomenon? Will the typical county commissioner or state legislator take the time to appropriately interpret the results of a KPI system when making budget decisions? The vital issue is: Who sees the information and who interprets it for purposes of making an important decision?

Another critical interpretation problem arises from the linear nature of most indicators. Despite the interactive and systemic features of such simulation models as the one designed by Quarton and Cross (Cross, 1984), most of the systems in which we operate are not well understood in terms of second-, third-, or fourth-order interactions. Computer simulation models offer us only a dim glimpse of systemic complexity, and it will require years of systematic research to validate their underlying relationships. At best we can currently examine the relationships among one or two ratios, involving three or four key indicators. But anyone who has managed a complex system understands that there are second-and third-order relationships, nonlinear relationships, and relationships of a reciprocal nature, so that as one index increases, forces come into play to suppress it and reestablish an equilibrium.

These primary and secondary feedback cycles require more complex mathematics and models than we are currently capable of using on a routine basis. Such "system dynamic" modeling, however, is being done and some basic simulations of mental health programs are in the process of design and testing. Although such models may not provide substantive clues as to what decisions to make, they can be a very useful tool for teaching the complexity of the data interpretation and decision-making process to all those who must participate.

Setting aside the political and economic pressures for accountability, the current and widespread interest in "key" performance indicator approaches reflects our best efforts to overcome the overwhelming complexity and diversity within and between individual CMHCs by using the time-honored scientific strategy of collecting "normative" data on multiple members of the species. It is probably a necessary step in the evolution of our understanding of organizational performance. The next generation of researchers can begin to examine the relationships among the minimum set of key indicators of internal performance and the characteristics of the environments in which the organization operates.

Fishman and Neigher propose that any data system be pilot-tested before being implemented on a full-scale basis. Certainly I would not disagree. At the same time we are all familiar with full-scale systems that have been implemented with only the most cursory field testing. I believe this phenomena must be related to the same human ambition and self-confidence that makes many decision makers act as if formal information systems were not necessary in any case. I would also stress that adequate field testing means testing a system under a range of conditions. A formalized method that works in one organization may not work in another. Robustness and adaptability are desirable features.

Quite aside from the future of research efforts, and despite the limitations and dangers of misinterpretation by "hostile forces," the prudent center executive will continue to seek out indicators of organizational effort, effectiveness, adequacy, and efficiency (Broskowski, 1977).

The wise leader will be the one who knows when the time, energy, and risks are likely to be worth the benefits. By definition, the effective leader is one who understands the difference between doing things right and doing the right things.

REFERENCES

Attkisson, C., & Broskowski, A. (1978). Evaluation and the emerging human service concept. In C. Attkisson, W. Hargreaves, M. Horowitz, & J. Sorenson (Eds.), *Evaluation of human service programs*. New York: Academic Press.

Attkisson, C., & Broskowski, A. (1984). Human service information systems. In C. Windle (Ed.), *Program performance measurement: Demands, technology, and dangers* (NIMH Series BN No. 5, DHHS Pub. No. ADM 84-1357). Washington, D.C.: U.S. Government Printing Office.

Beach, L., & Mitchell, T. (1978). A contingency model for the selection of decision strategies. *Academy of Management Review, 3,* 439–449.

Broskowski, A. (1977). Management information systems for planning and evaluation in human services. In I. Davidoff, M. Guttentag, & J. Offutt (Eds.), *Evaluating community mental health services: Principles and practice* (NIMH, DHEW Pub. No. (ADM) 77-465. Washington, D.C.: U.S. Government Printing Office.

Broskowski, A. (1982a). Linking mental health and health care systems. In H. C. Schulberg & M. Killilea (Eds.), *The modern practice of community mental health*. San Francisco: Jossey-Bass.

Broskowski, A. (1982b). Leading and managing mental health centers. In H. C. Schulberg & M. Killilea (Eds.), *The modern practice of community mental tal health*. San Francisco: Jossey-Bass.

Broskowski, A. (1984). Organizational controls and leadership. *Professional psychology: Research and practice* (Special Issue), 5, 645–663.

Broskowski, A., Attkisson, C., & Alberts, F. (in preparation). *Information systems: A primer for managers and staff of health and human service agencies.*

Broskowski, A., O'Brien, G., & Prevost, J. (1982). Interorganizational strategies for survival: Looking ahead to 1990. *Administration in Mental Health, 9,* 198–210.

Campbell, D. T. (1979). Assessing the impact of planned social change. *Evaluation and Program Planning, 2,* 67–90.

Campbell, J. (1977). On the nature of organizational effectiveness. In P. Goodman, J. Pennings, & Associates (Eds.), *New perspectives on organization effectiveness*. San Francisco: Jossey-Bass.

Connolly, T., & Deutsch, S. (1980). Performance measurement: Some conceptual issues. *Evaluation and Program Planning, 3,* 35–44.

Cox, G., & Osborne, P. (1980). Problem characteristics, decision processes and evaluation activity: A preliminary study of mental health center directors. *Evaluation and Program Planning, 3,* 175–183.

Cross, J. (1984). An interactive simulation model of community mental health delivery systems. Unpublished manuscript, Mental Health Research Institute, University of Michigan.

Cummings, N. (1977). The anatomy of psychotherapy under national health insurance. *American Psychologist, 32,* 711–718.

DiNitto, D., McNeece, A., & Johnson, P. (1984). Receptivity to the use of evaluation in community mental health centers. *Administration in Mental Health, 11,* 170–183.

Drtina, R. (1982). Financial indicators as a measure of nonprofit human service organization performance: The underlying issues. *New England Journal of Human Services, 2,* 35–41.

Elmore, R. (1978). Organizational models of social program implementation. *Public Policy, 26,* 185–228.

Etzioni, A. (1960). Two approaches to organizational analysis. *Administrative Science Quarterly, 5,* 258–278.

Ginsberg, P. (1984). The dysfunctional side effects of quantitative indicator production: Illustrations from mental health care (a message from Chicken Little). *Evaluation and Program Planning, 7,* 1–12.

Goodman, P., Pennings, J., & Associates (Eds.). (1977). *New perspectives on organizational effectiveness.* San Francisco: Jossey-Bass.

Hadley, T., Wilcox, J., Rossman, G., & Nazar, K. (1983). Performance standards and allocation of funds in community mental health programs. *Administration in Mental Health, 10,* 155–161.

Hall, M. (1981). Financial condition: A measure of human service organization performance. *New England Journal of Human Services, 2,* 25–35.

Kanter, R., & Brinkerhoff, D. (1981). Organizational performance: Recent developments in measurement. *Annual Review of Sociology, 7,* 321–349.

Katz, D., & Kahn, R. (1966). *The social psychology of organizations.* New York: Wiley.

Keppler-Seid, H., Windle, C., & Woy, R. (1980). Performance measures for mental health programs: Something better, something worse, or more of the same? *Community Mental Health Journal, 16,* 217–234.

Kotter, J. (1982) *The general managers.* New York: Free Press.

Kouzes, J., & Mico, P. (1979). Domain theory: An introduction to organizational behavior in human service organizations. *Journal of Applied Behavioral Science, 15,* 449–469.

Lewin, M., & Lewin, L. (1984). Health care for the uninsured. *Business and Health, 1,* 9–14.

Marks, E., & Broskowski, A. (1981). Community mental health and organized heath care linkages. In A. Broskowski, E. Marks, & S. Budman (Eds.), *Linking health and mental health*. Beverly Hills, Calif.: Sage.

Miles, R. H. (1980). Organizational effectiveness. In R. H. Miles (Ed.), *Macro organizational behavior*. Santa Monica, Calif.: Goodyear Publishing.

Mintzberg, H. (1973). *The nature of managerial work*. New York: Harper & Row.

Mintzberg, H. (1975). The manager's job: Folklore and fact. *Harvard Business Review, 53,* 49–61.

Patton, M., Grimes, P., Guthrie, K., French, B., & Blyth, D. (1977). In search of impact: An analysis of the utilization of federal health evaluation research. In C. H. Weiss (Ed.), *Using social research in public policy making*. Lexington, Mass.: D. C. Heath.

Perrow, C. (1961). The analysis of goals in complex organizations. *American Sociological Review, 26,* 854–866.

Perrow, C. (1977). Three types of effectiveness studies. In P. Goodman, J. Penning, & Associates (Eds.), *New perspectives on organizational effectiveness*. San Francisco: Jossey-Bass.

Rich, R. (1977). Uses of social science information by federal bureaucrats: Knowledge for action versus knowledge for understanding. In C. H. Weiss (Ed.), *Using social research in public policy making*. Lexington, Mass.: D. C. Heath.

Sorensen, J., Zelman, W., Hanbury, G., & Kucic, A. (1984). *Key performance indicators for community mental health organizations: A conceptual framework*. Rockville, Md.: National Council of Community Mental Health Centers.

Van de Ven, A., & Ferry, D. (1980). *Measuring and assessing organizations*. New York: Wiley.

Weiss, C. (1981). Measuring the use of evaluation. In J. A. Ciarlo (Ed.), *Utilizing evaluation: Concepts and measurement techniques*. Beverly Hills, Calif.: Sage.

Windle, C., & Volkman, E. (1973). Evaluation in the Center's program. *Evaluation, 1,* 69–70.

Wrapp, H. E. (1984). Good managers don't make policy decisions. *Harvard Business Review, 62,* 8–21.

Yuchtman, E., & Seashore, S. (1967). A systems resource approach to organizational effectiveness, *American Sociological Review, 32,* 891–903.

Successful Formal Performance Assessment: The Bottom Line Is Meaning

EDNA KAMIS-GOULD

Anthony Broskowski's "Assessment and Decision-Making in Community Mental Health Centers" offers to explore the role of formal assessment methodologies in the management of community mental health centers. Instead, it provides an interesting background and a contextual description of favorable and unfavorable conditions for management utilization of formal assessment methodologies. Doubts about the feasibility and utility of formal performance assessment for decision-making provide another theme for the chapter.

The author capitalizes on his impressive credentials, knowledge, and experience in describing the management of mental health centers. He accurately identified the complex nature of not-for-profit human service organizations (NPHSOs), the multifaceted nature of performance, the difficulties inherent in the conflicting agendas of NPHSO stake holders, and the dangers of corruption of data as described by Campbell (1979) and Ginsberg (1984). Broskowski's description of selected empirical studies of NPHSO decision-making provides a sample that ranges from interesting (e.g., studies by Cox and Osborne and by DiNitto et al.) to exciting (Quarton and Cross's stimulations). The chapter provides a broadstroke description and a rough sketch of issues in the assessment and management of mental health centers.

The author raises questions about the merits of formal versus informal information, which he does not pretend to answer, and seems to regret discovering that decision-making cannot be abdicated to information systems and performance indicators. He describes managers of NPHSO as not analytical, given their backgrounds, but as functioning at acceptable levels. This is not a very flattering description, but is probably an accurate one.

Broskowski's delineation of factors that facilitate the use of formal assessment is not comprehensive, and it is unclear why he chose to exclude some. One might add technological advances, managers' sophistication, accountability requirements, economic competition, or numerous other factors listed by Love (1983). I would add historical pattern and prevailing political context (e.g., the conditions that exerted massive force in the rise and decline of the Prison Classification Project described by Fowler in Chapter 6) as equally important in inhibiting formal assessment systems in mental health centers. Overall, the chapter is informative, but no synthesis is provided to guide readers toward more useful assessment operations. Our experience with formal performance assessment in New Jersey, particularly the development of the Performance Management System (PMS), will illustrate several conceptual and practical points that need to be considered in a positive approach to the assessment of organizational functions.

Most attempts at developing sets of performance indicators, including the Key Performance Indicators (KPI) of Sorenson et al. (1984) have produced something akin to a laundry list of items, either continuous or divided into subsets. Such lists are characterized by their content (clinic characteristics, financial variables, etc.) and tend to be long. In our experience, sound and useful sets of indicators must be derived from gradual detailing and operationalizing of significant and meaningful management questions. The resulting indicators should reflect the meanings of what they are to measure. Rather than appearing as isolated bits of data, performance indicators need to reflect agreed-upon content and meaning for (1) composite descriptions of NPHSOS, (2) comparisons among organizations, and (3) predictions of performance levels.

Systems of performance indicators are designed to introduce explicit and systematic approaches to assessment of the degree to which contractual agreements have been met and to the examination of management issues (Caro, 1980; Clifford & Sherman, 1983; Gooding, 1980). It is important to keep in mind that performance assessment via indicators does not create management decisions. Decisions are made with or without formal assessment. At issue is whether performance assessment improves decisions.

I agree with Broskowski that of the three levels of management decisions, technical/operational, tactical, and strategic, formal assessment is most suitable for the middle one, that is, the tactical level, especially since strategic decisions are highly determined by philosophical framework and value systems. In New Jersey, a clear philosophical intent has been articulated for the mental health system. It includes basic principles, values, and priorities. Throughout, assessments were to reflect whether performance was congruent with mandate and whether it produced intended results; whether programs were doing what they were supposed to do and how well they were doing it. To correspond with the philosophical framework, four dimensions of management concerns and of performance were identified: (1) *appropriateness,* mostly correspondence to management priorities of serving high-risk target groups, (2) *adequacy,* mainly efforts to assure quality, (3) *efficiency,* as expressed in productivity and cost containment, and (4) *effectiveness,* including both client and system outcomes.

The four dimensions were gradually translated into operationally defined performance indicators available from routine reports. Major components of the dimensions and the roles they play in performance monitoring are shown in Figure 9.1. Delineation of items for one of the dimensions, *appropriateness,* is shown in Table 9.4. Data from which performance indicators are derived are maintained in client, staff, service program, and budgetary files. The variables are produced by program elements (inpatient, outpatient, partial, residential, etc.), the building blocks of the system, and units of analysis. This is to assure that only comparable programs are compared. The conceptual model of PMS can be viewed as a cube, the cells of which are defined by: (1) building blocks of the system, that is, the program elements, (2) content files, and (3) dimensions of performance. Findings can then be employed to monitor performance in any element of any program in the system, as well as composites of those elements. PMS is a system of indicators designed to provide needed information. The meaning and interpretation of the indicators were spelled out in advance and provided the structure for the system.

Broskowski raises the issues of defining organizational effectiveness, distinctions between process and outcome assessment, and the multifaceted nature of performance. Formal assessment can and should consist of a consensus about the purpose of intended evaluation and all the constructs to be included (Love, 1983). PMS is an example of such an approach. Recognition of potential trade-offs among the facets of performance is built into the system, its dimensions, and the statistical decision model employed in its use. Low performance in the New Jer-

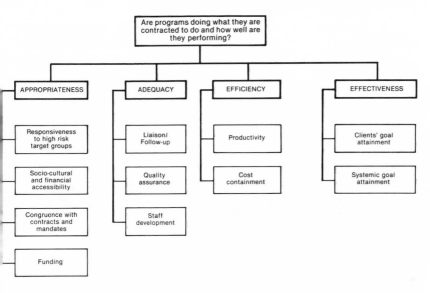

FIGURE 9.1. Relationships among Basic Objectives, Dimensions of Performance, and Performance Indicators

sey system is defined as two standard deviations below the mean of at least two indicators, within at least two dimensions, for at least two consecutive quarters. Similarly, high performance is defined as two standard deviations above the mean of at least two indicators in two dimensions and for two quarters with no indications of low performance. Thus a program that "excels" in efficiency at the expense of other aspects of performance could be very high in that dimension only and therefore not considered a high performer.

In the evolution of PMS, we encountered many of the issues raised by Broskowski. We acknowledged that existing standards of performance lacked empirical bases. We therefore decided to develop empirically based norms and standards and to suspend any consequence of performance, be it reward or punishment, until norms could be developed. The final design and implementation of the system could best be described as development and management by task forces. Work groups composed of central office personnel, service agency staff, and academicians were the developers and owners of the system. PMS stimulated requests for automation and technical assistance and fostered both intraorganization and interorganization communication. It also required

TABLE 9.4
Taxonomy of Performance Indicators for Appropriateness of Programs

I. Client and staff composition

  A. *Responsiveness to high-risk groups*

      1. Admissions from state and county hospitals[a]
      2. Admissions of former patients[a]
      3. Admissions with "Level of Functioning" scores[a]
      4. Admissions of children[a]
      5. Admissions of elderly[a]
      6. Clients residing in boarding homes

  B. *Accessibility*

      1. Sociocultural
         a. Clients
            (1) Black clients/black population
            (2) Hispanic clients/Hispanic population[a]
         b. Staff
            (1) Minority staff/minority population
            (2) Minority staff/minority clients
      2. Financial
         a. Clients in poverty[a]
         b. Indigent clients
         c. Social Security insurance/Social Security Disability insurance clients

II. Congruence

  A. With mandate
  B. With contract commitments

III. Funding

  A. Budget per population
  B. Need-based allocations

[a] Key indicators.

us to develop a dictionary of terms and statistical and accounting standards.

Broskowski expressed concerns about immediate and widespread applications of formalized assessment for decision support. Our experience suggests that emphasis on meaningful indicators fosters utilization, but that all sound developments are slow. Fishman and Neigher had major input into the development of PMS. Not surprisingly, they promoted an implementation process consistent with the framework of the decision-focused assessment described in Chapter 2 of this volume. A clear conceptual framework, improved accuracy of data, a pilot test prior to implementation, and intended ongoing monitoring of operations and utilization have been built into the step-wise implementation. Safeguards were delineated prior to implementation. The slow pace of the development and implementation suggest that formal assessment transcends short-range planning and management and requires a long-term view.

PMS was designed to promote sound management via explicit performance expectations and the offering of incentives. As noted by Broskowski, organizations respond to all monitoring and management systems by attempts to maximize their benefits. At times such behavior takes on the form of "gaming." However, if attempts to maximize one's own benefit are recognized and approached constructively, then behavior can be modified and improved via offered incentives. The best means of assuring high-quality services is to reward quality assurance. Systems of performance indicators should represent an optimal balance of comprehensiveness versus simplicity, regulation versus promotion of competition, predictability versus responsiveness to change, and cost containment versus quality assurance. The balance of these characteristics and trade-offs must be carefully reviewed in the design of each system. Its execution can be managed by incentives. In the New Jersey system, performance data are being used in a wide range of applications, from performance contracting and allocation of resources to experimental econometric analysis. Desired performance in areas that traditionally have not been rewarded, such as clinical supervision, research, and evaluation, is built into the incentive system.

Broskowski only touched briefly upon the risks associated with formal assessment. Although formal assessment provides an important management tool, it also introduces risks of which managers should be aware. These include distortions of data resulting from different procedures and derivations (Zelman et al., 1982), misinterpretation of reports (Smith, 1984), and issues of trust. Distrust of and biases toward formal assessment are often reflected in the choice of words describing it. Negatively, the use of indicators can be described as bureaucratic (Ginsberg, 1984); positively, as managerial. Similarly, monitoring and control can be referred to as harassment.

These views represent my perspective as a manager and evaluator in the New Jersey statewide mental health system and as an instrumental person in the development of the Performance Management System. I found Broskowski's chapter most interesting as a cautionary statement, but lacking the detail and synthesis required for positive design and implementation of formal assessment systems. My suggestions to those contemplating performance indicators are: (1) Consider intent, before content; and (2) hang the laundry lists.

REFERENCES

Campbell, D. T. (1979). Assessing the impact of planned social change. *Evaluation and Program Planning, 2,* 67–90.

Caro, F. G. (1980). Leverage and evaluation effectiveness. *Evaluation and Program Planning, 3,* 5–22.

Clifford, D. L., & Sherman, P. (1983). Internal evaluation: Integrating program evaluation and management. *New Directions for Program Evaluation, 20,* 23–46.

Ginsberg, P. E. (1984). The dysfunctional side effects of quantitative indicator production: Illustrations from mental health care (a message from Chicken Little). Evaluation and Program Planning, 7, 1–12.

Gooding, R. Z. (1980). Systems engineering: A problem-solving approach to improving program performance. *Evaluation and Program Planning, 3,* 95–103.

Love, A. J. (1983). The organizational context and the development of internal evaluation. *New Directions for Program Evaluation, 20,* 5–22.

Smith, M. L. (1984). Distorted indicators in special education: A response to Ginsberg. *Evaluation and Program Planning, 7,* 13–14.

Sorenson, J. E., Zelman, W. N., Hanbury, G. W., & Kucic, A. R. (1984). *Key performance indicators for community mental health organizations: A conceptual framework.* Rockville, Md.: National Council of Community Mental Health Centers.

Zelman, W. N., Stone, A. V. W., & Davenport, B. A. (1982). Factors contributing to artificial differences in reporting mental health costs. *Administration in Mental Health, 10,* 40–51.

Chapter 10

Measuring Performance at Work

THOMAS F. GILBERT

Some 23 years ago, I left university teaching to apply principles of learning to the training of people in the world of work. I had grown weary of psychological evaluation and its depressingly low correlations with what people actually did. I felt that if I could not predict human behavior with much accuracy, I might as well try to control it. Heavily influenced by both B. F. Skinner and the more eclectic laboratories of learning, I had developed the beginnings of a system for applying what we know about learning to the design of teaching methods. Selling and applying this system was the start of my career as an engineer. (I consider the term "engineer" appropriate, since the focus of most engineering is control, not prediction.) When I began my career as a performance engineer, considerations of assessment were the least of my concerns.

I made certain assumptions about the behavior of managers that seemed to put to rest the issues of assessment. The assumptions were dead wrong, but I had no way of knowing so at the time. My only previous experience in business had been in a mom-and-pop shop, or rather in a mom shop, my mother's cleaning and tailoring business. I reasoned that if my assumptions held true under her management, they would hold for my clients. Apart from my personal experience, the assumptions seemed rational. They did not appear to differ from the assumptions most sensible people would make under similar conditions.

WHAT WERE MY ASSUMPTIONS?

Almost immediately, I found many and varied opportunities to apply my craft. And over the past 20 years, I have been asked to train laboratory technicians and design engineers, telephone company repair clerks and high-technology sales representatives, strategic analysts and financial planners, factory supervisors and meat inspectors, packaging-machine operators and insurance salespeople, not to mention managers of almost every kind and level. By now, I have served more than 300 large organizations, both huge corporations and the federal government. Through this experience, I have found at least some of my assumptions about managerial behavior to be wrong nearly all of the time. The assumptions cover five areas of concern.

Economic models. I started with the naive belief that my client managers would have a relatively precise and no-nonsense picture of the economics of the key jobs, if not all the jobs, in an organization. Management would know, I assumed, how each job and its major components were reflected in measures such as return on investment (ROI) and other indices of productivity. For example, I thought that *Yellow Pages* advertising sales managers would know better than to deploy their expensive, highly skilled sales representatives in unprofitable segments of their market, such as those segments better served by mail. They would certainly know when it was unprofitable to require the representatives to do paper work that a clerk could do. I assumed, too, that automobile-manufacturing production managers would surely know how many labor hours could be profitably invested in salvaging, not scrapping, a part that had failed to pass quality control. And naturally I believed that the managers of high-technology, process-design engineers would know how any of the details in the preliminary designs would affect the variable costs of manufacturing.

Why did I care? I cared because I didn't want to waste my time training people in activities having little to do with productivity. I didn't want to train sales representatives to do paper work, for example, if paper work could be done equally well at less expense by others.

Job designs. I assumed that people in the world of work would have well-designed jobs and that they would be able to say what these jobs were. Even if they could not accurately describe the processes of their jobs (top tennis players do not often watch their feet), they would surely be able to describe the important results they should accomplish, results closely related to the economic leverage of their jobs.

Why did I care? I cared because I didn't want to train people to do the wrong job well.

Performance measures. I assumed that people at work were measured accurately, frequently, and most important, relevantly. I also assumed that these measures would reflect the economic models that applied to their jobs. For example, management would know the quality and costs of the efforts of government meat inspectors, people selling parts for large earth-moving equipment could be held accountable for the profitability of their sales efforts, and supervisors on an auto assembly line would be measured by their contribution to profits.

Why did I care? I cared because I wanted to be able to show how effective my training efforts were in improving relevantly measured human performance.

Behavioral supports. I assumed that at least in competitive business, if not in government, behavioral environments would be excellent. I thought that workers could count on having adequate, timely, unconfusing data pertaining to their work. I assumed that frequent and early feedback would be routinely given. Information would be related to results, it would be selective and specific, and it would be positive and educational. I expected incentives in business to be powerful in their effects and closely linked with performance. I anticipated that the tools, procedures, and resources needed to do a job would be uniformly available and efficiently supplied.

How mistaken I was. I did not imagine that product packers would have to wait a year to discover how productive or unproductive they had been. I never suspected that few managers, except at the highest levels, actually participate in the profits of an organization to the extent that they contribute to them. Indeed, I was astounded to learn how few managers even know how much or how little their efforts contributed to profitability. I would not have guessed that archaic, misleading, and confusing data systems were the bane of a typical production manager's job. I certainly did not expect most managers to blame their problems on the capacity and motives of wage workers rather than on the environments over which they had significant control. And I never could have suspected that "performance" appraisals would focus far more on traits such as "attitude," "flexibility," and "loyalty" than on job accomplishments.

Why did I care? I cared because I didn't want to waste time trying to improve performance through training if much more productivity could be gained by improving the way behavioral supports were provided through environmental change.

Assessment of training. When I entered the world of work, I already knew that improvement was needed in instructional technology. After all, that improvement was my main challenge. I took for granted, however, that the economics of training were well understood. I assumed that training was monitored as an investment, that the returns on that investment were tracked, and that the effects of training on performance were measured.

I could not have dreamed that most major corporations accounted for only 5% or 10% of their true training costs, and that almost none of them measured the effectiveness of training on job performance. Nor could I have imagined that if organizations measured the training effort at all, they also rewarded training directors for keeping as many people in training as possible, thus rewarding training as an activity rather than as an accomplishment. And I had not yet conducted my study of the cost of training, which revealed that the training of people at work annually equaled or exceeded the defense budget, and that the federal government's "sophisticated" annual training-cost report uncovered only a nickel on every dollar spent (Gilbert, 1976a, 1976b).

It should be obvious why I cared. If the accountants were to count training costs as only what they spent on me, and not count the true training costs and the effectiveness that I might improve, I would find it hard to sell my craft.

WHY WERE MY ASSUMPTIONS SO POOR?

When I first learned how faulty my assumptions were, I wanted to don the robes of a prosecutor. Understandably but wrongly, I felt superior. Slowly I came to realize how young the modern organization is and how complex. The modern business organization was born only 75 to 100 years ago (Gilbert, 1982a). Human resource and development departments have emerged within my lifespan. Industrial engineering, "sophisticated" accounting and financial analysis, statistical quality control, modern production control and distribution systems are all barely older than I. The computer is younger than I am. Training departments emerged from apprenticeship programs almost within my recall. Psychological assessment is equally immature, and only a few of its advanced students, unfortunately not always the best ones, have entered the world of work. Those who entered the workplace did so mostly to sell predictive testing. Great wonder that the modern organization is as productive as it is.

The rapid appearance of the modern organization was the result of the confluence of a number of developments. These include explosions of knowledge in physical science and engineering, innovations in financial institutions, great improvements in the productivity of natural resources in such areas as farming and mining, and revolutions in transportation and communication. Major developments do not include significant growth of a science or technology of human behavior in the workplace. The work of human factors people, industrial engineers, and efficiency experts is not to be disparaged. Their efforts, however, have been rather narrowly focused and limited in application.

In the main, psychology has focused on the activity of human individuals. Presumably, the ultimate benefit of such a science will derive from its use in engineering greater productivity in people. We will not be able to do that engineering well without relatively accurate and precise, that is, valid and reliable, means of assessment. In the world of work, assessment procedures should be organized in a coherent system of procedures for collecting, interpreting, and applying information. From my dual vantage points as a scholar of learning and as an applied psychologist concerned with human performance in a wide range of settings, I offer the following system for assessment in the workplace.

AN ASSESSMENT SYSTEM IN THE WORLD OF WORK

In designing a system, engineers must draw from many disciplines. Chemical engineers, for example, are fundamentally chemical scientists, and they must know that science well in order to design a chemical manufacturing process. But they must also understand physics, financial modeling, and human factors. They must even know something about such apparently peripheral fields as real estate in order to use most wisely the land on which a factory is to be located. In a sense, nothing is new or unique about what chemical engineers do. They seldom create new knowledge. Their contributions are seen in the systems they design, as well as the systems they use in creating those designs.

The same is true for "psychological engineers," or "performance engineers," the people who apply science to the design of improved systems for managing the performance of people in jobs. To design these systems, the performance engineers draw freely on whatever disciplines offer relevant knowledge. Their charter is not to create new knowledge, but to create new or better job performance systems. Assessment, which consists of both measurement and evaluation, is at the heart of engineering. Without it, decisions about change cannot be rationally derived, and the effects of change cannot be documented in any reliable way. In the following section, the three large and independent components of performance assessment, as applied in the world of work, are summarized. After that, each component is discussed in detail.

Summary of Components of Performance Assessment

One component of assessment is *accomplishment-based job designs.* Even if excellent job conditions are created, the efforts may be counterproductive if the job itself is ill-conceived and poorly designed. It is foolish to train and reward people for doing the wrong things. Yet in thousands of interviews and in working with and observing countless job incumbents, my colleagues and I have found that relatively few employees or their managers have a clear picture of the most valuable accomplishments of their jobs. To assess performance, we must know what should be accomplished. Later, I will describe an approach that I have found useful for developing job models.

Another key component of assessment is *economically relevant measures and standards.* We have great quantities of data in industry and government purporting to be measures of job performance. Even so, many jobs simply are not measured at all. When job accomplishments are measured, many times the measures are not the most economically relevant ones. Managers measured principally by budget compliance are unwittingly encouraged to pinch pennies at the sacrifice of larger revenues in the long term. The economics of many other jobs are also poorly understood.

Even if performance measures were excellent, the setting of performance standards would need a drastic overhaul. When standards are set at all, they are typically set according to historically average performance. Or they are established intuitively—derived by the "finger-in-the-wind" method. Shortly, I will describe an approach that I have found helpful in selecting economically relevant measures and setting sensible standards of exemplary performance.

The third component of assessment I call *profiles of behavior.* This is probably the kind of assessment most familiar to psychologists. Certainly professional psychologists have contributed usefully to assessing behavior on the job, with applications for behavior modification, training, human factors, and selection. However, behavioral supports and other conditions affecting performance must also be considered. These include *data* required for performing the job that are adequate, parsimonious, timely, and not confusing; *feedback* that is work-related, frequent, selective, and educational; *tools, procedures,* and *other resources* that are efficient; *incentives* that are effective and provide a good balance of consequences for performing well; *training* that is efficient and effective; and the *capacity* and *motives* sufficient to do the job. Each of these aspects of behavior must be assured to determine where the most effective changes can be made. Application of a new feedback system on a job for which poor data or inadequate training are the major barriers to performance, for example, will not improve performance.

In practice, performance engineers look at all three components simultaneously, and at several stages, from assessing how a job is performed now, to designing a model for ideal performance of the job, to designing and developing a system for realistic improvement in job performance given constraints in the present environment. In discussing these components, however, I will start with measurements first, continue to accomplishments, and end with behavioral supports. Job accomplishments cannot be set in the absence of an understanding of the economics of the environment, and consideration of behavioral supports is meaningless in the absence of an understanding of what the job is and how it is measured. In discussing each component, I will also describe the tools that I use to measure performance, to set standards, to draw up reasonable job models, and to assess the behavioral supports needed in order for good performance to occur.

Measures of Attainable Performance (MAP)

When one examines a job as a performance system, the first challenge is to make sure that economically relevant measures are obtained and that standards are set at high but attainable levels. Each of the following three examples illustrates a common problem in measurements of performance in the workplace. Some solutions to the problems are also recommended.

Punishing the exemplary performer. The client was a large automobile manufacturer. The organizations of particular concern were metal-stamping plants, where workers stamped out and assembled the parts of doors, fenders, and other auto components. The client requested that I study the training needs of the first- and second-line supervisors. The first steps were to study the economics of these jobs, how they were measured, and what constituted exemplary performance. I found that the supervisors were measured carefully and accurately by the labor dollars spent to stamp out and assemble the automobile parts. The standard was based on averages in the company.

But how should they be measured? To answer that question, I imagined that I had purchased a stamping and assembly line and sold its product to the company. I then set up an economic model for the line, nothing complicated, just a simple sort of balance sheet that showed costs and profits as clearly as possible. Company financial analysts were of no help in this task, although they had developed intricately complex models dealing with many aspects of the business. While looking at the line as a profit center, I discovered that it could be quite unprofitable if large numbers of doors with minor defects were scrapped rather than worked on so that they could be salvaged. Salvaging a door required extra labor hours, of course. But the cost of those extra labor hours did not nearly equal the cost of the lost labor and metal when the door was scrapped.

With this information, I was able to develop a new performance measure that combined labor dollars and the cost of scrap. I called the new measure "line profitability" (LP). Then, with the LP measure in hand, I searched for the exemplary performer in the interest of setting some standards.

The top performer, according to the LP measure, was a supervisor who hated to scrap good doors with easily correctable defects. Measured by labor dollars alone, he was the worst performer in the plant. Indeed, he was often called to account for his poor labor-dollar performance. At the other end of the scale, the top performer by the labor-dollar measure turned out to be the poorest by our new LP measure.

The conclusion of this study was that the only training the supervisors needed was in the use of a job aid to help them judge when to salvage a door. Middle management approved the LP measure and the training proposal, but, unfortunately, top management rejected the new measure for reasons unknown. Further training obviously would be useless, since supervisors would continue to be punished for salvaging doors. The moral of the story? Think twice before blaming problems of productivity in the auto industry on the assembly-line workers or their supervisors.

Failing to obtain data on economically relevant variables, or the only perfect correlation I have ever seen. The Winkle Company, as I shall call it, is one of the world's largest corporations. It manufactures chemicals and employs over 100 process-design (PD) engineers. The PD engineers are "smart" engineers. Some have PhDs from MIT. When a new chemical is invented by the Winkle Research and Development Department, the PD engineers design the complex manufacturing processes required to produce the chemical.

My assignment at the corporation was not to train anyone, but to design a system for improving PD engineering productivity by performance engineering. The president of the company had told his managers that they must improve productivity by some method, or else reduce the number of employees by 10%.

Again, I began looking at the economics of the job. The company's economic analysts were able to help in this case, since they had a lot of relevant data on the economic leverage of its factories. However, they thought in more global terms than process design, and as far as I could tell none of them had ever met a PD engineer.

After analyzing a great amount of data, I concluded that the economic leverage of the performance of PD engineers was enormous. Here were some mere hundred people who probably had more effect on the economics of the multibillion-dollar organization than anyone else, except for the researchers who invented the chemicals. Any variance in the performance of these PD engineers could have many millions of dollars of effect on the company's profits each year. And no amount of marketing and sales effort or care in manufacturing could make up for the costs of a defective process.

In order of importance, here are the economic variables that PD engineering variances could effect:

1. *Variable costs of manufacturing.* These are the costs that vary with the quantities manufactured, such as energy and catalysts. The principal features of the performance of the PD engineers that could affect variable costs are:

   a. Quality of the process designs.

   b. Economic optimization, or getting the most value for the cost.

2. *Fixed costs.* These are the costs incurred whether a little is produced or a lot. Examples are the costs of owning equipment and the space required for manufacturing operations. The principal features of the performance of PD engineers that could affect the fixed costs are:

   a. Maintainability: How well did the designs avoid unnecessary maintenance costs?

   b. Constructability: How well did the designs avoid unnecessary problems in construction?

3. *Safety and environmental impact.* How could improvements in design avoid unnecessary problems of safety and environmental effluents?

4. *Unexpected investment costs.* These are costs incurred beyond initial projections about the return on the original investment. Such costs, of course, also contribute to fixed costs. Chief among these are:

a. Timeliness of the design: Were the designs completed in time to meet the schedule of construction?

b. Construction labor and material costs: Did the designs require exceptional costs in construction of the factory?

5. PD *engineering costs.* These are the costs of the process-design engineering itself in engineering salaries and overhead.

The order of importance is critical and was established after a review of the past history of designs. I found that improvements in past designs could have improved variable manufacturing costs far more than any other economic factor. On the other hand, reducing PD engineering costs would have saved very little, and might even have increased total costs of production.

Having established the economic variables of design performance, I next asked whether management knew how well their design engineers were performing against these economic criteria. To answer the question, I used a well-anchored rating scale from "1" to "5." A "1" meant that management had precise and accurate monthly data on the performance of the economic variable. A "5" meant that management had practically no information at all, and some of the little information they had was misleading. Intermediate points on the scale were also defined.

Next I compared what management knew about the economics of design quality with what was important to know. Table 10.1 summarizes these findings. As a statistically trained psychologist, I had never before seen a perfect correlation in the natural world. As shown in Table 10.1, the importance of what management knew was correlated perfectly and inversely with the content of what it actually knew. Accurate monthly reports were available on the cost of engineering, for example, and the Vice President for Technological Services managed the PD Engineering Department mainly by those measures.

How were these PD engineers assessed? You might suppose their supervisors kept close tabs on the quality of the designs, but you would be wrong. The supervisors were technically sophisticated people who spent most of their time engineering and doing paper work. The social culture in the company was such that it was considered almost insulting to question the competence of a PD engineer. Without a system for evaluating the designs, which did not exist until my clients and I con-

TABLE 10.1
The Relationship between What Process-Design Engineering
Management Knew about Engineering Performance and What Was
Important to Know

Economic factors	What was known	Importance
Variable-cost factors (economically optimal design quality)	5[a]	1
Fixed-cost factors (maintainability and constructability)	4	2
Safety and environmental impact	3	3
Investment-cost factors (timeliness and construction costs)	2	4
Engineering salaries and overhead	1	5

[a] 1 = a lot; 5 = a little.

structed one, supervisors would practically have had to redesign poorly
engineered manufacturing systems to assure quality.

The major assessment instrument they had used to evaluate PD engineers was the company's annual performance-appraisal form. Over the
years, my colleagues and I have collected hundreds of such appraisals
from hundreds of organizations. The form used at Winkle was typical.
An unanchored rating scale from "1" to "5" asked for an "overall" performance proficiency, based on the supervisor's personal criteria. The
other ratings were judgments of such presumed but untested correlates
of performance as "initiative," "flexibility," "loyalty," and "punctual-
ity." The terms meant whatever the supervisors wanted them to mean.
One engineer put it quite well: "Productivity of PD engineers is measured by the formula $P = f(A \& T)$, where A is attitude and T is the
display of technical impressiveness. It should be measured by $P = f(Q
\& E)$, where Q is design quality and E is the efficiency of creating the
designs."

Having had several clients in the design-engineering business, I did
not find the situation at Winkle exceptional. Armed with economics, I
was eventually able to design a system for assessing the quality of PD

engineering. The details of the system are too complex to describe here but an essential requirement was periodic review of the most critical factors in each design of new processes, aimed principally toward correcting design defects rather than deriving numbers to rate the engineers.

Failure to construct adequate financial models, or don't ask accountants about profits. Woerm Industries, as I shall call it, is a large, successful manufacturer of industrial machinery, so successful that a prestigious business school uses it as a case example in management information systems. The company asked me to examine the training needs of its unprofitable fork-lift truck subsidiary. Woerm has a hundred dealerships selling these trucks, as well as more profitable lines of equipment.

At Woerm's insistence, I started my analysis with the sales function. Woerm Trucks sells new, used, and rental trucks, as well as parts and service. Although we studied many dealers, I will describe WNJ, Inc. (Woerm of New Jersey). This is a $100 million dealership, with $12 million in its lift-truck subsidiary.

As always, I began by studying the economics of the business. As so frequently happens, I found large amounts of data, but scarce information about the economics of the several kinds of jobs in sales. Most misleading and almost useless for management purposes was the monthly financial statement. No one could doubt its bottom line—WNJ Trucks was consistently losing money—but the financial statement alone gave no clue to reasons for the loss. According to the financial statement, gross profit (revenue less the cost of goods) on new trucks was 6%. For used trucks it was 14%. The statement did not specify the *net* profits on these two lines of trucks, however, although it seemed to confirm management's firm belief that used trucks were more profitable than new ones. Other vital data were also hidden in the summaries of the financial statement.

With the help of management, I then constructed a financial model of sales on the lines of management accounting. In this new financial model, I tried to isolate the various lines of business as profit centers. For example, I broke out the revenues and expenses of new trucks in several categories (i.e., sold singly, sold as fleets, sold to key users, and sold under closed bid). Similarly, I broke out used trucks in categories such as the way they were acquired (from rental-fleet retirement, trade-ins, wholesale, etc.) and the way they were sold (with warranty and without, to wholesalers, etc.). In doing this job, we asked for help from the financial officers at Woerm's national headquarters and also from

WNJ's accountants. They could not help us. So, to fill in our financial worksheets, the president of WNJ Trucks and his principal managers had to sort through raw data (invoices, warranty notes, etc.). This was an arduous task for the managers but it was not one that could be assigned to clerks, since clerks could not interpret the data.

When we finished, two different financial models had emerged. The first reflected WNJ Trucks' actual performance for the past two years of business. The second model, which I call a "performance inventory" (PI), showed what the subsidiary might look like if two things were done: (1) if business were practiced differently and (2) if people performed the key jobs in an exemplary manner.

The results were astonishing but pleasing. The PI showed that WNJ Trucks had the potential for a 24% return on investment. For example, new trucks turned out to be very profitable in most cases. However, new trucks that were sold under closed bid to large organizations ate up most of the profits. The WNJ used trucks, on the other hand, were extremely unprofitable after we factored in all the expenses. They were unprofitable for four principal reasons, given here in order of importance:

1. Used trucks acquired as trade-ins were purchased at much too high a price.

2. Warranties were given too freely on poor equipment.

3. Too many odd models sat in inventory too long.

4. Trucks not promoted sat in inventory too long.

Since the business of selling and trading trucks requires a used-truck component, we could not simply eliminate the used-truck division on grounds of low profit. Instead, we examined all of the jobs at WNJ, with the aim of finding ways to improve performances and profits. I will focus here on the job of used-truck management and the recommendations we made to increase profits on used trucks.

A typical used-truck manager was evaluated solely by the amount of used-truck sales revenue generated. We can ignore the inevitable annual performance appraisal that Woerm supplied its dealers. It was a standard form calling for summary judgments of "initiative," "flexibility," and other personality characteristics. By the measure considered most important by management, namely revenue, one of the managers (let us call him Al) was considered an exemplary performer among the hundred dealers. However, the more revenue his department generated, the more money WNJ lost. The PI showed that the expenses accrued by his department were very high, for all the reasons shown above. In effect, Al was giving away the store.

I therefore decided to modify the way Al's overall job was measured. The first step was to set a somewhat lower revenue standard, on the theory that salesmen who do not give away the store might not sell as much as those who do. The principal measure applied to his performance was the return on assets (ROA) under his control. Return on assets was calculated by dividing profits by assets. Since WNJ had a large inventory, these assets were considerable. The standard applied was an ROA of 25%, which was obtained from the PI.

Other measures were also applied to Al. For example, to measure effective performance in acquiring used trucks, we analyzed the decisions to be made when used trucks were acquired. The acquisition price (AP), we reasoned, should be a function of five factors. The first factor should be the price objective (PO) when the company sold the used truck. Next would be the gross profit objective for the sale. Third would be the estimated repair cost (R). The more repairs that had to be done, the lower the price paid to acquire the truck. Fourth would be the estimated time (T) a model would remain in inventory before being sold (WNJ Trucks had good data on this). And the fifth factor would be the cost of money (m), the interest charge on the inventory. Putting all these factors together, I developed the formula:

$$AP = \frac{.80\,(PO - R)}{1 + mT}$$

The ".80" is the number needed to obtain a 25% gross profit (or a 20% gross margin).

Notice that this formula was developed by a psychologist, not by an economist or an accountant. When financial experts cannot provide useful formulas for assessing jobs, the formulas must be developed ad hoc. I also developed measures for assessing other components of Al's job. Moreover, for each measure I established a standard of exemplary performance, which was evident from our PI.

Standards of Exemplary Performance (the PIP)

In assessing people at work, two kinds of accomplishment measures are needed—measures of proficiency in using capital (ROI, costs, revenues, parts per hour, etc.) and measures of the relative competence of people. The latter are especially important in establishing standards of performance. Measures of capital and measures of people are logically independent. One organization may have an excellent ROI, even though its people are working far below their potential. The competition may be weak, or the demand for its product and services might be exceptional. Another organization, with strong competition and low demand, may have a weak ROI but still be able to get the best out of its people under the circumstances.

Over the years, I have found a simple ratio to be the most useful single measure of competence of people. The ratio shows how well people are living up to their potential. I call this ratio the PIP, for *potential for improving performance*:

$$\text{PIP} = \frac{\text{Exemplary performance}}{\text{Typical performance}}$$

I have measured the performance of many different people in many different jobs according to this ratio, and found some surprising results. For example, the best long-distance telephone operators are about 25% more productive than the average, since the operator productivity PIP is 1.25. This figure represents an exceptionally high degree of competence in a complex clerical operation. In fact, it is the lowest productivity PIP I have ever seen among clerks and shows that telephone operators are unusually well trained and managed. Most clerical operations have PIPS ranging from 1.5 to 1.75. Sales functions have considerably higher PIPS, usually ranging from 3.00 to 10.00 or more. In my own experience, the management and training of sales representatives are of a surprisingly low order of quality.

The PIP is a variance measure, but is far superior to the standard deviation for the task of assessing performance. The standard deviation of the revenues in insurance sales representatives may be quite low, whereas the PIP can easily reach 5.00 or more. The PIP also seems to unveil a paradox. It says, "The more incompetent people are, the easier it is to improve their performance." Or, the larger the PIP, the greater the opportunity for improving performance. My colleagues and I look for big PIPS; they are a joy to the performance engineer.

The reason the "paradox" is not mystifying is twofold. First, the units of the PIP are always measures of accomplishment, not measures of behavior. With behavior measures, such as IQ tests, the greater the distance a group of people are from the top, the harder it supposedly is to improve their performance. Yet it is difficult to find decent correlations between IQ or other behavior measures and accomplishment.

Poor accomplishment, represented by high PIPS, is more the result of poor management and poor training than of the genius of top performers. In real life, many top performers appear to have serious "behavioral" handicaps. One exemplary sales representative we traveled with, for example, was a short, plump black woman with a pronounced lisp. Yet she was tops in selling *Yellow Pages* advertising, principally to white men in southern towns. Her self-management, determination to train herself, and shrewd concept of what she should accomplish in her job made her outstanding. She displayed a kind of genius, but in a form that would not have shown up on the usual kind of psychological tests. Having administered hundreds of IQ tests in my career, I do not believe that she would have scored much higher than 110. But she did for herself what others could be managed and trained to do, maybe not quite as well, but far better than a third as well. The opportunity to improve the performance of these representatives was considerable. Their key PIP was over 3.00. The typical representative in her area didn't bother to make appointments, for example. Our exemplary performer assiduously did so. Others seldom "cased" customers to find out what they sold and what their economic tender spots were. Our exemplar never failed to do this. She also applied smart tricks to help her position, like locking her handbag in the car when making a sales call, so that she would be as unencumbered as a male doing the same job.

The PIP is not as simple as it may appear. Specifying exemplary performance is half measurement and half the art of estimating. The best single indicator of exemplary performance is the top performer. At least that is where I start. But as the analysis continues, I usually find that the exemplary performer is handicapped by management, and that even his or her performance can be improved. For example, our black woman selling to white southern businessmen was required to spend a third of her time selling to extremely poor prospects. That was management's constraint. Let loose, her achievement might have been even farther ahead of the pack. Therefore, I sometimes advise setting an even higher standard of performance than that of the exemplar.

On the other hand, the exemplary performer occasionally sets a standard better than we can expect others to approach. My colleagues and I have found a few geniuses whose performance is far in front of the next best performers for reasons we cannot discover. We then take, as our tentative standards, people who are more representative of the human race and whose performance others may reasonably hope to emulate.

Also, perhaps more frequently than we find geniuses, we find top performers who play by unorthodox rules. Unfortunately, the most "productive" long-distance operators cheat by hanging up on customers with complicated call requests. In this way, they increase the number of calls they handle per hour but may leave alienated customers fuming at the other end of the line. Some "top" sales representatives bribe customers. Some "key" performers work extra long hours. In these and other ways, figures can deceive, and copying the behavior of top performers is not always desirable. Finally, good performance engineering usually improves the performance of the exemplars, though the performance of the typical person is ordinarily improved to a greater extent.

What are the limits to which we can reduce the PIP? There is no precise answer, but I doubt that it can ever be reduced to 1.00. Intelligence, motivation, and insight still produce effects that performance engineering may not affect. In professional sports, where training and management are often unusually good, PIPs are very low but never reach 1.00. Jack Nicklaus, probably the greatest golfer the game has ever known, was only about 5% better than the average pro on tour (in strokes, not money). Unlike people in most places of work, professional golfers have "perfect" tools, high incentives, excellent feedback, fine data, closely prescribed procedures, all the resources they need, fine training, excellent accomplishment-based selection, and driving motives. If I had to give personal estimates for jobs in the usual world of work, I would set standards of the PIP at about 1.15 for clerical jobs (even telephone operators can improve), at about 1.3 for managers, and around 1.5 for sales representatives.

The PIP is not arithmetically as simple as my description of the ratio suggests. To make the ratio understandable, brief digression into some simple theory is needed.

The PIP is a measure of performance (P), which can be defined as a transaction between costly behavior (B) and valuable accomplishments (A).

$$P = B \rightarrow A$$

But we are not interested in performance for its own sake. Our concern is with *worthy* performance (W). The task of the manager or performance engineer is to make sure that the values of accomplishment exceed the costs of behavior. Behavior is costly because we must pay for knowledge, motivation, effort, and so on. Therefore, the true performance function to look for is:

$$W = f\left(\frac{A}{B}\right)$$

This ratio is an analogue of the most fundamental economic expression, that is, worth as the ratio of value to cost, or:

$$W = \left(\frac{V}{C}\right) = f\left(\frac{A}{B}\right)$$

When we compare exemplary performance with typical performance, we take a ratio of exemplary worth (W_e) to typical worth (W_t). The PIP becomes:

$$\text{PIP} = \frac{W_e}{W_t}$$

The PIP, then, is the ratio of two ratios:

$$\text{PIP} = V_e/C_e \div V_t/C_t$$

Simplified algebraically, the ratio becomes:

$$\text{PIP} = \frac{V_e C_t}{V_t C_e}$$

The PIP always shows the larger number in the numerator. When value units are compared, exemplary performance is in the numerator. When cost units are compared, typical performance is in the numerator. If costs is constant but value varies (for example, two sales representatives spend about as much gas and time in selling, but one sells more than the other), the PIP is V_e/V_t. If value is constant but costs vary (for example, two production supervisors produce about as many car doors, but one produces far more scrap), the PIP is C_t/C_e.

The PIP is only useful when the units that compose it are economically relevant. In the previous example of auto line supervisors, the least profitable supervisor was the exemplary performer in labor dollars per part produced. This matter is most important, because if ROI-related measures are not economically relevant, the PIP can encourage setting standards for unproductive performance.

Nothing is quite so enlightening in performance engineering as actually working with and observing the exemplars; traveling with exemplary sales reps, sitting with excellent managers, working on the assembly line managed by superior supervisors, observing over many days the best design engineers. Exemplars are smart about their jobs, and they offer many insights that are often unknown to their managers. But even with exemplary performers, it is essential to listen critically. Without meaning to mislead, they may offer descriptions of what they do that do not match reality. As mentioned above, top tennis players rarely watch their feet. Similarly, the verbalizations of exemplars about what they do must be verified either by observation or critical logic, or by both.

Leading-Accomplishment Models of Performance (LAMP)

As we begin to identify the relevant economic variables of performance, we also begin to model the jobs we hope to engineer. When we do this, we often find it useful to redesign the jobs to meet economic realities. This is comparable to the kind of bootstrapping operation G. R. Patterson describes in Chapter 7. As we learn more about the economics of the job, we begin to see what its true accomplishments should be; as we learn more about the accomplishments, we revise our economic models. This job-modeling component of the assessment and engineering system is not quite as simple as it may sound here. Interested readers can find more detail elsewhere (Gilbert, 1978, chap. 1, 4, and 5).

To model a job, three actions are required. First, we need to identify the mission, the ultimate accomplishment of a job. Second, we need to identify its major component accomplishments. Finally, we need to find the relevant "dimensions" of the mission and each major accomplishment. I call these dimensions the *requirements* of the job. Requirements are such measurable characteristics as quality, productivity, timeliness, and costs. I shall describe the first two of these components of a job model through example. For a more thorough discussion of requirements, see Gilbert (1978).

The importance of appropriate mission statements, or how to fire an exemplary manager. The client was a large manufacturer of one kind of auto part (I will call this client Multicommon), and it sold the parts to dealers across the country. Throughout the nation it had a number of area sales offices reporting to corporate sales management, and an equal number of area credit offices reporting to corporate credit management. The credit officer arranged for dealers to buy the Multicommon parts on credit.

Ms. Good, I will call her, was an area credit manager who was about to be fired. She objected. She thought she should be promoted, and was about to file a lawsuit against Multicommon. The exemplary performer in her job was considered to be Mr. Poore. He was about to be promoted. Just because I was there and was a consultant to Multicommon on other matters, a vice president asked me to look into Ms. Good's case to see if she actually had an argument. Over her lawyer's protests, I managed to gain her confidence and tried to learn something about the economics of what she was doing. Her case did not look good on the surface. The mission of her job was clearly stated. In brief, it was to collect money. It was also rather precisely measured by dollars and days in past-due accounts. By these measures, she had the worst record of some 150 area credit offices. Mr. Poore, the "exemplar" by company standards, had the best record.

Ms. Good's case began to look even worse as I delved deeper. I carefully studied her huge personnel dossier of memos, performance appraisals, letters, and tests. The evidence I found there would persuade very few judges to favor her. Table 10.2 summarizes the contents in the dossier about Ms. Good and also Mr. Poore.

When I confronted Ms. Good with this "evidence," she seemed undisturbed and suggested that I consider how well her credit work actually helped the company make sales. She ventured the opinion that her job mission should be seen as "lending money," not collecting it. Collecting, she said, was a lesser responsibility. Taking her cue, I then visited the sales offices in both Good's and Poore's areas. What I found in those offices made it clear that Ms. Good was actually an exemplary performer, whereas Mr. Poore was in reality losing money for the company.

Ms. Good's area sales managers were also her strong fans. Even more significant, their area was one of the top five in sales performance in the company. When we created a financial model that included sales and credit as one operation, Ms. Good's area was shown to be extremely profitable. Superior sales offset past-due payment costs many times. Sales management attributed much of their success to Ms. Good's smart methods of granting credit to sluggish dealers, since sales were permitted that otherwise would not have been made. Furthermore, despite her high past-due record, she accumulated no more bad debts to be written off than Mr. Poore.

In Mr. Poore's area, the opposite story was revealed. His area sales managers were extremely resentful of Mr. Poore, who, they said, hounded their customers and blocked many sales with his unusually tight credit policies. Sales in his area were among the worst in the company.

When I presented this picture to Multicommon's management, they took swift action. They promoted Ms. Good, and they reorganized the

TABLE 10.2
Comparison of Ms. Good's and Mr. Poore's Personnel Folders

Factor	Mr. Poore's ratings	Ms. Good's ratings
Assessment center evaluation	Very high	Dropped out
IQ	125	110
Hard work	Very high	Low
Motivation	Very high	Low
Attitude	Very good	Poor
Education	MBA (A's & B's)	BS (average)
Punctuality	Excellent	Poor
Appearance	Excellent	Poor
Job knowledge test	Very high	Low

credit department to become an integral part of sales. They also changed the description of the credit manager's mission from collecting money to "financing sales."

The original mission of the credit manager's job was not tied to the economic realities of parts sales. It also did not pass the ACORN test (Gilbert, 1978). ACORN is an acronym and a memory aid for the five criteria that I have found useful in assessing descriptions of job missions:
   A. Does the mission statement describe a clear accomplishment, not activity?
   C. Does the incumbent have significant, if not major, control over the accomplishment of the mission?
   O. Does the mission statement describe the overall objective of the job rather than a subsidiary accomplishment?
   R. Is excellent performance of the mission reconcilable with other missions in the organization? If the mission is fulfilled to high standards, will it hurt the organization?
   N. Can a number be put on it—can it be measured?

Ms. Good's original mission statement, "collecting money," failed the O and R parts of the ACORN test. Collecting money should not have been the overall objective of the job. Our economic model told us that. And Mr. Poore proved that high standards of his kind of performance actually hurt company sales.

Many other mission statements for other jobs fail to pass the other

ACORN criteria. The impact of not meeting these criteria is that people are not likely to perform in an exemplary fashion. In examining large numbers of job descriptions, I have found it is the rule, not the exception, that mission statements fail at least some part of the ACORN test.

Keeping job models simple but complete. Al, our used-truck manager, had a long, detailed job description, which was written by the personnel people in the national organization. As is typical of such descriptions, however, most of the language was that of trait psychology, describing such unmeasurable characteristics as "taking initiative" and "being creative." Minor duties were described, along with major accomplishments, in long strings of descriptors set off by commas. If all of his job descriptors were separately listed, there would be some 50 of them, with no distinction made between important and minor characteristics. Furthermore, most of the descriptions were vague. For example, Al was said to be responsible for "acquiring used trucks." This descriptor also appeared in three other job descriptions, that of the sales representative, that of a clerk who wrote up the contracts to acquire trucks, and that of the service representative who had to get the contracts signed and the trucks delivered. All three were involved in acquiring trucks, but in different ways that the job description failed to distinguish.

Here is an excerpt from Al's job description:

> The incumbent will be responsible for all aspects of used-truck inventory, including taking initiative in acquiring used trucks, judging their quality, protecting the inventory from damage and neglect, reporting monthly on the status of the inventory, informing the sales department of opportunities to sell used trucks, minimizing space requirements for inventory, being creative in finding ways to reduce inventory, assisting in the management of the Inventory Manager, displaying inventory in an attractive way, responding to inquiries about inventory status, resolving questions about acquisition contracts, reporting on problems in delivering inventory to or from the customer's premises, providing judgments about parts and labor needed to maintain the inventory. . . .

Yet missing from this description is the economically most important act of acquiring a used truck, especially on a trade-in—establishing a price for it. Al's management had assumed that he was chiefly responsible for doing this. Although he had tried, he had largely given up. In actuality, the sales representatives were setting the prices, and they had every incentive to set them too high, because a good purchase price for a trade-in helped make a sale for which they earned a commission. Our financial model helped us identify Al's major accomplishments and responsibilities. There were four accomplishments whose principal effects would make his operation profitable. We wanted to highlight those accomplishments, not give him a list of 50 descriptors. In order of their economic importance, the accomplishments were:

1. Setting an acquisition price on each used truck
2. Deciding whether to sell each used truck with warranty, as is, wholesale, or junk
3. Controlling inventory turnover
4. Promoting sales of used trucks

Those four accomplishments constituted Al's job model. To complete it, we needed to add the measures and exemplary standards, as well as the behavioral supports the company had to provide Al to help him meet those standards. Al did not need a list of 50 descriptors, even if the descriptors had been accurate. He already knew how to do his job; management simply had not told him what it was. A complete leading-accomplishment model of performance (LAMP) for Al's job will be shown at the end of this chapter.

For another example of the need to identify leading-accomplishment models of performance, consider again the process-design (PD) engineers at Winkle. The considerable economic leverage of their jobs on Winkle's overall economic health has already been discussed, as has the design of a system to assess the quality of the designs. While performing this analysis, we began to examine the PD engineering job model. Our findings had strong implications for making the economic leverage of the PD engineers felt.

When Winkle's research and development department invented a new chemical product, a product and market-planning group assumed control of the new invention. These, too, were smart engineers, with considerable training in marketing. First, they decided whether there was a market for the new chemical, and then they developed a set of specifications for manufacturing the product. The specifications stated such standards as the desired purity of the product, the desirable side products to be created in manufacturing, and the annual production quotas needed. But, in point of fact, specifications were a "hope" list, written in the belief that PD engineers would be clever enough to meet them.

Each set of business specifications arrived on the desks of the PD engineers in the form of a letter. Although some were fairly clear, most of them left a good deal to the imagination. In several meetings, the business-planning engineers explained their letters to PD engineering management, but never to the PD engineers themselves. The explanations were considered unnecessary for the engineers, and the engineers were regarded as too busy to attend the meetings.

As one PD engineer said, "It is as if some people had asked you to design a rocket to fly to Aquarius. They hoped you could give them assurance of 99% probability of getting there, and that the vehicle could carry a hundred people. The cost would be under $10 million, and it would be absolutely free of pollution. It would be white, so that it photographed well. You would have six months to do this. But you would not be allowed to ask questions of those who made the request. You would not even know why they want to go to Aquarius. You would just have to get them there."

Here is what typically happened when the PD engineers set out to design a process. The specifications might call for a process to make a chemical that was 98% pure. After a week or so, the engineers knew that attaining quality at this level would cost countless dollars. However, a process to achieve 95% purity was economically feasible. Still, they stuck to their original charge, knowing it would be a wasted effort. Through six months of expensive work, they would design the countless-dollar process, and then present it to management. Of course it would be turned down. At this point, and through several indirect lines of communication, a 95% purity would be suggested. The PD engineers would then complete the design. They would be judged on their performance appraisals as "slow" but "cooperative."

The mission statement of the PD engineers passed the ACORN test: "Create process designs." But some of the major accomplishments required to meet this mission, the ones with the greatest economic leverage, were not identified. In developing the job model, the client and I redesigned the PD engineer's job. At least two new accomplishments were added: (1) clarification of the business-plan specifications and (2) preliminary designs showing process alternatives.

The first of these accomplishments required the PD engineers to attend the meetings at which the specifications were set forth, and they were given a list of questions that had to be answered in order to make the specifications clear. The second required the engineers to develop rough designs of alternative processes, so that decisions could be made early about the feasibility of a chosen process.

Profiling Behavior (PROBE)

Once we have established the economic context of a job and defined it so that it matches that context, we can turn our attention to psychologists' favorite subject: behavior. Behavior must be assessed in order to learn what the behavioral barriers are to reaching exemplary standards of performance. To do this, we must have a model of behavior, and one specially tailored to our engineering aims. Because I have been unable to find an academic model suitable to these purposes, I have made my own and I call it PROBE (Gilbert, 1978, chap. 3, 1982a, 1982b). Despite common meanings of its terms, PROBE is not designed to yield an in-depth analysis of an individual person's emotions, motives, capacity, or thought processes. Rather, it has the practical assessment purpose of helping to identify major barriers to performance that tend to affect almost every incumbent in a particular job.

Two ideas well known in general psychology are basic to PROBE. First is the descriptive behaviorist's linkage of stimulus-response-reinforcement ($S^D — R \cdot S_r$ in B. F. Skinner's notation) as a fundamental unit of action. This description of behavior identifies three ways in which behavior can be modified: (1) by changing incoming information, or S^D, (2) by modifying the response, or "instrumentation," or (3) by changing the conditions of reinforcement.

A second concept of behavior is taken from "transactionalists," especially Kurt Lewin. According to this concept, behavior (B) is a transaction between people and their repertories (P) and the environment (E). Or: $B = f(P \cdot E)$. This is an important concept, although it is ignored by many psychologists. We often fail to recognize the environment as an integral part of behavior, and instead posit behavior within the confines of the skin. As I write this, I am looking out the window, watching my son chop wood. To engage in this behavior, he must have a repertory of skills, the capacity to handle an ax, and the motive to work for available incentives. But external to his skin, in the environment, he must also have information about what wood to cut, an ax, and some incentives to do the job. His behavior can be greatly modified by dulling the ax, say, or by providing misleading data. If a rat does not work, the reason may just as likely be that it is not fed (external incentive) as that it is not hungry (internal motive). The letters P and E identify the two aspects of behavior toward which behavioral engineers can direct their efforts.

These two basic concepts of behavior can then generate a two-dimen-

TABLE 10.3
The PROBE Model for Profiling Behavior

	Information (S^D)	Instrumentation (R)	Motivation (S_r)
E	Data	Implements	Incentives
P	Knowledge & skill	Capacity	Motives

sional model (see Table 10.3), giving us the six cells of PROBE (Gilbert, 1978, chap. 3).

These six cells draw our attention to six important ways to modify behavior, and also to six possible barriers to the behavior desired on a job. They represent six ways of looking at the single unitary event we call behavior; they are not six disjointed "pieces" of behavior. The model needs to be viewed as fully "transactional." For example, it says that information is not data, but a transaction between data and the skill to process it. Similarly, motivation requires both incentives and motives (food and hunger).

For the model to become a useful assessment and engineering tool, it must be expanded and the element in it must be specified. In the first step of expansion, we describe the major components of each cell. For example, data can be both directional (it tells people what to do) and confirmational (it provides people with "feedback" about how well they did). Implements can be tools (such as axes and typewriters), procedures, and resources. Incentives can be monetary or nonmonetary. People may bring intrinsic motives to the job, or something may induce those motives. Capacity can be mental, physical, or emotional. Knowledge may occur as an inductive (overview), as a concept (generalization), or as a discrimination skill. An expanded PROBE model, reflecting more specific ways to modify behavior, is shown in Table 10.4.

Still the model is too general to be a useful assessment and engineering tool. Needed next are some criteria for, say, excellent directional data, good tools, and excellent feedback. I have described these criteria elsewhere (Gilbert, 1982a). Here, I can only suggest this step, and then move to the next. For example, directional data should be adequate and accurate, parsimonious (free of "data glut"), timely, and unconfusing.

TABLE 10.4
An Expanded PROBE Model

Information (S^D)	Instrumentation (R)	Motivation (S_r)
Data:	**Implements:**	**Incentives:**
1. Directional	1. Tools	1. Monetary
E 2. Confirmational	2. Procedures	2. Nonmonetary
(feedback)	3. Resources	
Knowledge:	**Capacity:**	**Motives:**
1. Inductive	1. Mental	1. Intrinsic
P 2. Concept	2. Physical	2. Induced
3. Skill	3. Emotional	

Feedback ("confirmation" is a better word) should be work-related, immediate and frequent, selective and specific, and educational. It is now fairly easy to move from such criteria to a useful assessment tool. To do this, the criteria are converted into specific questions, which we can ask about the behavioral conditions on any job, for any accomplishment. Table 10.5 illustrates a detailed PROBE.

Other questions might be added, but Table 10.5 includes most that I have found useful. They are designed so that if the answers to the questions are no it indicates that behavioral conditions are inadequate to support exemplary performance. The questions should not be asked or answered mechanically, since some care and experience are required to make best use of the tool. A detailed example of asking questions and assessing answers is given elsewhere (Gilbert, 1982b). The procedure can be illustrated here with a few examples.

Turning a bright loser into an exemplary performer. We saw that Al, our used-truck manager, was not setting acquisition prices well. He was not even setting good prices on trade-ins, although the assumption was that he would. It was, in fact, one of his responsibilities, and he had the authority to carry it out. So, we can ask what behavioral barriers might prevent him from reaching the exemplary standards we have set for him. To find these answers, we turn to the PROBE questions.

The standard Al is supposed to reach is to keep within a plus-or-minus percentage of the acquisition price formula. Remember:

TABLE 10.5
PROBE Questions

Questions about the behavioral environment (E)

A. *Directional data*
   1. Are there sufficient, readily accessible data (or signals) to direct an experienced person to perform well?
   2. Are they accurate?
   3. Are they free of confusion—"stimulus competition"—that slows performance and invites errors?
   4. Are they free of "data glut"—stripped down to simple forms and not buried in a lot of extraneous data?
   5. Are they up-to-date and timely?
   6. Are good models of behavior available?
   7. Are clear and measurable performance standards communicated so that people know how well they are supposed to perform?
   8. Do they accept the standards as reasonable?

B. *Confirmation*
   1. Is feedback provided that is "work-related"—describing results consistent with the standards and not just behavior?
   2. Is it immediate and frequent enough to help people remember what they did?
   3. Is it selective and specific—limited to a few matters of importance and free of data glut and vague generalities?
   4. Is it educational—positive and constructive so that people learn something from it?

C. *Tools and equipment*
   1. Are the necessary implements usually on hand for doing the job?
   2. Are they reliable and efficient?
   3. Are they safe?

D. *Procedures*
   1. Are the procedures efficient and designed to avoid unnecessary steps and wasted motion?
   2. Are they based on sound methods rather than historical happenstance?
   3. Are they appropriate to the job and the skill level?
   4. Are they free of boring and tiresome repetition?

E. *Resources*
   1. Are adequate materials, supplies, assistance, etc., usually available to do the job well?
   2. Are they efficiently tailored to the job?
   3. Do ambient conditions provide comfort and prevent unnecessary interference?

F. *Incentives*
   1. Is pay for the job competitive?
   2. Are there significant bonuses or raises based on good performance?
   3. Does good performance have any relationship to career advancement?
   4. Are there meaningful nonpay incentives (recognition, etc.) for good performance (based on results and not behavior)?
   5. Are they scheduled well, or so frequently as to lose meaning or so infrequently as to be useless?
   6. Is there an absence of punishment for performing well?
   7. Is there an absence of hidden incentives to perform poorly?
   8. Is the balance of positive and negative incentive in favor of good performance?

Questions about behavioral repertories (P)

G. *Knowledge and training*
   1. Do people understand the consequence of both good and poor performance?
   2. Do they grasp the essentials of performance—do they get the "big picture"?
   3. Do they have the technical concepts to perform well?
   4. Do they have sufficient basic skills—reading, etc.?
   5. Do they have sufficient specialized skills?
   6. Do they always have the skills after initial training?
   7. Are good job aids available?

H. *Capacity*
   1. Do the incumbents have the basic capacity to learn the necessary perceptual discriminations with accuracy and speed?
   2. Are they free of emotional limitations that would interfere with performance?
   3. Do they have sufficient strength and dexterity to learn to do the job well?

I. *Motives*
   1. Do incumbents seem to have the desire to perform when they enter the job?
   2. Do their motives endure—e.g., is the turnover high?

$$AP = \frac{.80\,(PO - R)}{1 + mT}$$

Imbedded in this formula are all the decisions that Al must make. We can begin, then, by asking the PROBE questions about each of these decisions, starting with "directional data." Did Al have adequate, accurate, timely, parsimonious, and unconfusing data to make decisions about (1) a price objective, (2) the length of time a model is expected to sit in inventory, and (3) the cost of money? In Al's case, the answers to these questions were all yes. Did he have such data about the estimated repair costs of the used truck? To the question about the accuracy and adequacy of these data, the answer was a resounding no. The estimates he got were from sales representatives who were anxious to buy the used trucks at any price so they could sell new ones and get their commissions. They were swayed by special interest. Apart from personal motives, the sales representatives were rarely well qualified to judge the repair costs of a used truck. Answers to most other questions were yes, except that Al had no feedback about how profitably WNJ Trucks was acquiring trucks, nor did he have any monetary incentives for acquiring trucks profitably.

John Dewey once said that if you asked the right questions, the answers would follow. People in management are not always trained in this concept. Too frequently, managers are judged by their ability to produce answers, whether or not the questions are relevant. Al's managers knew lots of answers; they just hadn't asked the right questions. As they worked through PROBE, useful answers came easily. To help Al become an exemplary performer, they immediately saw that four things needed to be done:

1. A field-inspection system needed to be set up so that service representatives could judge the repair conditions on critical truck trade-ins, such as especially expensive trucks or fleets. This would give Al much of the data needed.

2. An anchored rating system with a job aid was needed to help those who judged a truck's repair condition reach a more precise standard of accuracy.

3. A cumulative record was needed to help Al know whether he was keeping close to the standard set for him.

4. A monetary incentive was needed to reward Al for keeping close to the standards.

The same PROBE was conducted for Al's performance in warranty, inventory control, and promotional efforts. An interesting observation is that Al's managers had thought about all these "answers" before. But they had considered so many answers that they had no systematic way to assess them. As the president of Al's company remarked, "PROBE gave me the sense that I had covered the waterfront and had asked all of the important questions." He also remarked that the entire "behavioral" exercise would have been unconvincing if he had not first engaged in the economic and job models (MAP and LAMP).

Comments on PROBE. Any manager can ask the PROBE questions without the PROBE model. Often they do, but more often they do not. The heart of successful engineering is to ask these questions systematically. However, PROBE does not delve deeply, for two reasons. First, people familiar with a job have much of the knowledge and experience to delve deeply if they confront the right questions. PROBE is a psychologist's tool that poses useful questions. Job incumbents and their managers are better qualified to suggest productive answers than any outsider can be. The second reason PROBE does not delve deeply into behavior is that it is a strategic tool, not a tactical one. PROBE is an acronym for "profiling behavior," not for digging deeply. It is designed to uncover large barriers to performance that affect all or most incumbents in a job, not for discovering peculiarities of individuals. This is not to disparage in-depth analysis of individuals, but to underline the condition that I have found in the world of work. The greatest leverage in improving productivity in the workplace lies in improving the behavioral conditions that affect most people in a job. The most urgent problems faced by performance engineers are those of groups of quite normal people with poor training who work in inefficient environments. One day, when poor information, primitive training, weak incentives, and other massively influential conditions are routinely corrected at work, we can afford to spend more of our efforts on the particular difficulties of individuals.

There is little new about PROBE except that it is a coherent system, designed for use in a strategic way. It can help psychologists, industrial engineers, and especially managers to focus on the best use of their tactical skills. If the answer is no to the question "Are data unconfusing?" one can begin to use human factors skills. If the answer is no to the question "Are incentives out of balance in favor of punishment?" one can use behavior modification skills to adjust incentives. The main use of PROBE is to focus systematically on the few behavioral conditions that commonly impede exemplary performance.

Among the six cells of PROBE, the last two cells have to do with capacity and motives. These are interesting aspects of psychology and they fascinate managers as much as they intrigue psychologists. Indeed, my colleagues and I have asked thousands of managers who have attended our workshops what they thought were the biggest barriers to performance. Most line managers identified the capacity and motive cells (people are too dumb or don't care) as most influential. The problems of productivity are attributed to deficiencies in people's repertories, not to the environment over which managers have greater control. In effect, managers have shifted responsibility away from themselves and have given it to the people they manage.

That is a mistake. Although capacity and motives are critical for doing a job, most people at work have capacities and motives in adequate quantities, until the environment defeats their motives. Even if they did not have the required abilities and drive, managers could do little about it. Psychologists, of all people, should know how difficult it is to change those two aspects of behavior.

The greatest leverage in improving job performance lies in changing the environment. Among many possible environmental changes, improving directional data outranks all others in leverage. Next comes improving incentives and feedback. After these come ways to improve procedures, then resources, and sometimes the tools to work with. Training is very important. But too often training is applied as a sole solution when other aspects of performance need to be changed first. Once these other aspects of performance are improved, training can be applied to great advantage.

Can the performance engineer do anything about capacity and motives? I think so. Selection and placement of people in jobs are directed especially to these aspects of behavior. So far, results have not been encouraging although some models are interesting and show promise. Elsewhere I have described one such model, a self-selecting, self-motivating training program (Gilbert, 1978, pp. 325–330). The area is wide open for fresh research and new approaches.

A SUMMARY ASSESSMENT GUIDE

The three-component system I have described, MAP, LAMP, and PROBE (the tools needed to seek gold in dark caves), represents a multifaceted assessment program. Many assessment artifacts are generated by the performance analysis. One artifact is particularly useful for summarizing the results of the performance analysis. Table 10.6 is an example of such a document. My clients persist in calling it a LAMP, although it summarizes all three components of the analysis.

This table is a LAMP for Al. First, it shows his mission, and how he will be measured and to what standards. The left-hand column identifies the leading accomplishments of his job, those with significant eco-

TABLE 10.6

A LAMP for a Used-Truck Manager

(Mission: disposal of used trucks; gross revenues, $2.5 million; return on assets, 25%)

Accomplishments	Measures and standards	Behavioral conditions
Sets acquisition price of used trucks	Average price will not deviate more than 2% from acquisition formula	1. Field-inspection system to be installed (N)[a] 2. New inspection rating system (R) 3. Feedback on cumulative acquisition formula (N)
Determines if trucks sold as is, with warranty, scrap, or wholesale	No more than 10% deviation from classification system	1. Installation of classification system (K) 2. Classification feedback program (N)
Controls inventory turnover	Average turnover of 45 days; no unit in stock more than 6 months	1. Turnover reporting system begun (N) 2. Exception report on unit turnover begun (N) 3. Turnover feedback program (N)
Conducts promotion and advertising	Budget: .5% of sales; response standards to be set	1. Advertising log set up to track response (K) 2. Acquisition of memorex typewriter (L) 3. Practices set up for direct mail (N)

[a] Initial of manager committed to seeing that condition was met.

nomic leverage. It changes the language of his personnel job description, which listed the acquisition of trucks along with 49 other items. Al, this LAMP says, does not acquire trucks, but he is responsible for the most important aspect of the acquisitions, that is, setting the acquisition price. Another LAMP, for sales representatives, shows them responsible for getting an agreement to acquire the trucks. Another person's

LAMP, for a clerk, indicates responsibility for creating an acquisition contract. A service representative's LAMP shows a responsibility for getting the trucks delivered. The old personnel job description made no such distinctions, and implicitly claimed that all of these people "acquire" used trucks. Now, with LAMP, these four employees can be assessed only for accomplishments that are peculiar to their jobs, rather than for a general accomplishment that they cannot produce alone.

The middle column describes the measures and standards of attainable performance. All of these are derived from the earlier economic analysis, and they are exemplary standards. If Al meets these standards, he will satisfy his mission. In the year following this performance analysis, Al met all the standards but one. He exceeded his revenue standard by 20%. Besides, he no longer had to fight with the sales representatives, since everyone in the dealership had a copy of everyone else's LAMP and knew the standards of each job.

The third column describes the results of PROBE, the behavioral conditions that Al's management promised to arrange for him. Without these behavior modifications, Al could not be expected to be an exemplary performer. Notice the initial after each item. In each case, it is the initial of the manager who took responsibility for creating these conditions. Since WNJ used a management-by-objectives (MBO) program, these items became objectives in the MBO file for the appropriate manager.

Most of my clients now use LAMPs like this one as ongoing management tools. Many incumbents post their LAMPs on their walls or desks rather than hide them away in a file. Incuments are given any training they need in order to thoroughly understand the document. This is made easier because nothing is arbitrary or superfluous about the LAMPs. Everything listed is vital to the health of the organization.

Performance assessment and engineering are not easy work, but they are rewarding in that the measures of the results are built into the system. They are hard to sell because the effort required is considerable and the linkage of concepts is complex. It is far easier to sell a prepackaged "solution" to behavior problems. For all its difficulty, performance engineering offers a challenging opportunity for professional psychologists, one that I hope more of them will seize.

REFERENCES

Gilbert, T. F. (1976a). The high cost of knowledge. *Personnel, 35,* 116–122.

Gilbert, T. F. (1976b). Training: The $100 billion opportunity. *Training and Development Journal, 35,* 181–203.

Gilbert, T. F. (1978). *Human competence: Engineering worthy performance.* New York: McGraw-Hill.

Gilbert, T. F. (1982a). A question of performance: I. The PROBE model. *Training and Development Journal, 32,* 21–25.

Gilbert, T. F. (1982b). A question of performance: II. Applying the PROBE model. *Training and Development Journal, 32,* 101–118.

Performance, Performance Evaluation, and Survival in Business

VICTOR M. KLINE

"Productivity improvement" is more than a catchword. It is a matter of survival for a major segment of work organizations in America in the 1980s. Threatened by significant incursions into our markets by foreign competitors, both large and small organizations have been forced to reexamine and reconceptualize the ways they have been running their businesses. Ripple effects from the commercial sector have been felt in nonprofit and public organizations as well. For all of us, the need to "run leaner" and more efficiently has become a necessary condition for continued existence.

Central to this productivity challenge is the need to ensure that we are getting maximum utilization from our human resources. Organizations should be able to adapt their structures and the systems of roles they require to the demands of the changing environments in which they operate. They must also channel the efforts of their people more precisely toward the target outcomes the organization has chosen to attain. It is to these ends that Gilbert has dedicated his efforts, and through his work provided a well-instrumented model that can be of value for both human resource professionals and line managers.

Gilbert's three interdependent components of performance assessment—accomplishment-based job designs, economically relevant measures and standards, and profiles of behavior—can all contribute to better employee performance. Taxonomically, I would not place his profiles of behavior (PROBE) in the same category as the other two. PROBE might more appropriately be considered a behavior management tool. However, all three elements appear essential to useful performance appraisal. Gilbert's model requires that managers define the relevant measures upon which the value of the job and the assessment of any individual's performance will be based. In far too many organizations, people are measured on factors not directly linked to the achievement of business or organizational objectives. The significance of this, as Gilbert clearly illustrates in his examples, goes beyond the risk of limited efficiency. It introduces the possibility that people might be working at cross-purposes with each other and contrary to the aims of the organization.

This is certainly not a new notion. The rationale and technique of management by objective have been available for several decades. What Gilbert offers that is new is a guide to a definition of relevance that is grounded directly in the achievement of organizational objectives. It is this dimension of relevance that has been entirely lacking or inadequately addressed in other models, and provides the needed link between the individual's performance and the achievement of the goals of the work group and organization.

The underpinning of Gilbert's model is the notion of the "economic leverage" of a given job. We are asked to look at the impact a job has on the organization's most critical business objectives. In the example of the process-design engineer, the importance of accurate determination of economic leverage is vividly illustrated. It is ironic that many organizations devote countless hours and large sums of money to using intricate formulas and carefully validated "Hay systems" to define precisely the values of jobs for pay purposes, and then give little or no attention to measuring the actual performances of job holders against relevant standards. Were they to use Gilbert's measures of attainable performance (MAP), standards of exemplary performance (the PIP), and leading-accomplishment models of performance (LAMP), they would be able to link both job designs and standards of performance to the organization's objectives.

I take issue with Gilbert's insistence that all measures be "economically relevant." Many organizations do not have financial profits as their primary reasons for existence. Universities and social service agencies, for example, are directed toward other aims. Gilbert's model would have broader applicability if he used a term such as "organizational relevance" to replace the narrower, specifically financial term.

Besides its direct use in performance evaluation, Gilbert's system should be useful for supervisory counseling to improve performance. If we are really interested in improving performance, we need something more than the trait appraisals most commonly used in the past. These provide neither supervisors nor employees the relevant and useful information upon which productive performance discussions can be based. Whether in chemical manufacturing, banking, or retailing, we have tended to equate working hard with worker effectiveness. But have we been measuring the right behaviors? LAMPS, MAPS, and PIPS give us an opportunity to find out. More than just assessment tools, they provide a framework within which supervisors can work with employees to identify ways to improve performance. They serve both as a guide to the establishment of standards, that is, a definition of what fully competent performance should look like, and as a focus for performance improvement discussions. And they can offer equally valuable self-assessment tools to the employees themselves.

Although not based on traditional scientific research, the insights Gilbert has derived from years of practical performance engineering in the workplace seem authentic and powerful to those of us who have also spent more than a few years grappling with the challenges of productivity improvement. His arguments are logically convincing, and the similarities of his examples to ones I have encountered over the span of my own career are striking.

Occasionally, propositions are overgeneralized. For instance, to say that "job accomplishments cannot be set in the absence of an understanding of the economics of the environment" is just not so. Job accomplishments can and are prescribed every day by managers without the least bit of interest in the economic realities of a secretary's job, or a research chemist's job, or even the process-design engineer's job as Gilbert himself so clearly illustrates. Every day, people perform in an exemplary fashion in jobs that do not pass the ACORN test, though differences can be seen in varying definitions of "exemplary."

The important issue is not whether Gilbert's model is the "right" one or not. Models do not change managers' behavior. A lot of convincing will have to be done "top-down" in our organizations before managers will see the needed links between employee performance standards and the paramount objectives of the organization. For those who see the light, Gilbert's LAMPS, MAPS, and PIPS will provide the tools to achieve this linkage. If enough managers and human resource professional become schooled in his approach and master the logic that underlies his model, they may be able to shift the practices in their organizations toward the higher levels of performance upon which corporate survival depends.

SUMMARY AND CONCLUSIONS

We began this book with a set of guiding principles and a conceptual framework for designing practically useful assessment methodologies. Eight independent assessment projects, widely disparate as to systems level, setting, and population, were then described. We now reach the task of determining whether any coherent synthesis can be derived from that mass of information.

In the following chapter, common elements among the various assessment models are identified, and the methodologies are examined in detail with regard to the sequence of phases through which a fully developed assessment system must pass, from conceptualization to full-scale dissemination. Although the several projects described in Chapters 3–8 have focused on different aspects of the process, all are consistent with the general conceptual framework we have outlined. A common strategy for the design of assessment systems can be clearly defined and appears to be generally useful, regardless of the setting, population, or organizational level for which the methodology is employed.

Relations between the research reported in this book and the body of research and theory on behavioral decision-making are then considered. Decision theory and decision-focused assessment are both concerned with decision-making, and some linkage between the two might reasonably be expected. Instead, theory-driven research on decision processes and applied research as demonstrated by the authors of this book have gone on in nearly total isolation. Review of the present work in reference to some classical issues in psychological assessment also shows that the issues as defined for formal research usually need to be reframed for practical application.

The gap between research and practice in psychology is attributed to the lack of a bridging technology, analogous to engineering in relation to physical science or medicine in relation to human biology. The contents of this book are offered as a guide for building part of the technology needed to bring psychological knowledge into more effective public use.

Chapter 11

On Getting the Right Information and Getting the Information Right

DANIEL B. FISHMAN and
DONALD R. PETERSON

This book addresses the challenge of designing psychological assessment systems so that they facilitate practical decision-making in natural settings of major social importance. Creating a conceptual foundation and framework to this end is the focus of the first two chapters. Chapter 1 reviews the history of assessment in psychology and its relevance to decision-making. The chapter concludes that past efforts in this area have been disappointing, and proposes a number of general principles to guide the development of improved applied assessment models. These include: (1) fundamental concern for the interests of consumers rather than the interests of the assessors in designing assessment programs; (2) linkage of assessment information to change; (3) study of psychological processes over time; (4) grounding assessment in the complexity of the real world so that no significant influences on function are ignored; (5) location of assessment systems in natural settings; (6) the use of multiple procedures in collecting assessment data; (7) relating assessment to functional conceptions of behavior that evolve by a "bootstrapping" process; and (8) sensitivity to societal goals and pressures in developing and managing assessment programs.

Chapter 2 builds upon these eight principles and probes more deeply into the "bottom-line" accomplishments and fundamental assumptions underlying applied psychological assessment. A review of the meager results of traditional, "theory-driven," basic research in psychological assessment, together with recent philosophical critiques of the logical positivist epistemology underlying this research, is argued to justify a different, technological-managerial paradigm for applied assessment. Called "Technological Assessment in Psychology," or the "TAP" paradigm, this model begins in the problems of the real world rather than the theories of investigators and leads to particular solutions to particular problems rather than general laws of nature. Although no universal principles are sought in the technological approach, strategies developed in solving one problem may be useful in solving others. Indeed, the authors propose that the problem-solving process in decision-focused assessment is much the same whether one is studying individuals, groups, or organizations. To elaborate this notion, a 25-step sequential process is set forth for the development, implementation, and dissemination of a decision-focused assessment system. These steps, summarized in Table 11.1, cluster into five major phases: conceptualizing the decision to be made; developing a data methodology linked to the decision; pilot-testing the methodology; implementing the methodology at full scale; and disseminating the methodology at full scale.

With the framework described in Chapters 1 and 2 in hand, the editors sought specific assessment models that fit within the general outlines of the TAP paradigm. Although the paradigm is new and has not been formally adopted as such by other researchers, we were able to find examples of outstanding work that is consistent with the TAP framework. We selected investigators whose work represented the highest excellence in regard to conceptual soundness, innovative quality, respect for data, and practical utility. Our goal in collecting this work was twofold. First we aimed to illustrate and explore the present status and scope of decision-focused assessment. Second, we wished to test the TAP assumption that there is a generic structure in decision-focused assessment by determining whether assessment methodologies in operation actually follow the 25-step sequential process outlined in Table 11.1. In line with these goals, we sought the most advanced available examples from applied researchers working a wide variety of decisional settings, with two examples each from four different levels of psychological processes: biopsychological, individual, interpersonal, and organizational. These eight models comprise Chapters 3–10 of this book.

TABLE 11.1
The Technological Process Model

A. *Conceptualizing the decision to be made*
 1. Identify type of decision to be made
 2. Describe decision context and decision-maker culture
 3. Summarize relevant research re. steps 1, 2, 4, and 5
 4. Construct a conceptual model of the decision

B. *Developing a data methodology linked to the decision*
 5. Develop model of data collection, scoring, and application, including:
    a. Types of data to collect and collection methods
    b. Procedure for data sampling
    c. How to score and summarize
    d. How to link to decision-making

C. *Pilot-testing the methodology*
 6. Select setting and collect data
 7. Score and summarize data for applying decision rules
 8. Evaluate data's quality—reliability and validity
 9. Use data for practical decisions
 10. Evaluate impact on decisions
 11. Employ evaluation for feedback and revision
 12. Conduct additional pilot tests if needed
 13. Replicate successful pilot test at least once

D. *Implementing the methodology at full scale*
 14. Develop operational plan
 15. Implement plan
 16. Evaluate plan
 17. Revisions if necessary
 18. Routinize the plan, with ongoing monitoring and evaluation

E. *Disseminating the methodology at full scale*
 19. Replicate full-scale implementation at least once
 20. Review professional literature on technology diffusion
 21. Develop a dissemination plan
 22. Implement the plan
 23. Evaluate the plan
 24. Complete revisions if necessary
 25. Routinize the plan, with ongoing monitoring and evaluation

VENTURES IN ASSESSMENT: A TECHNOLOGICAL PERSPECTIVE

Common Elements among the Assessment Models

Although the assessment models selected for the book were deliberately chosen to emphasize phenotypic diversity, a review of the substance of Chapters 3–10 reveals common elements among the models presented. These common elements are very much in accord with the eight "guiding principles" outlined in Chapter 1 and the TAP model described in Chapter 2.

Linkage of assessment to programmatic decisions. Table 11.2 summarizes some of the common elements. The first column lists the systems level, from the neuropsychological to the organizational, within which the work of each author is principally located. In addition to dealing with a particular systems level, each author's assessment model is linked to programmatic decisions in the larger organizational setting within which the model is embedded. These decisional settings are listed in the second column of Table 11.2. Although the types of programmatic decision questions addressed by the book's authors are varied, they all involve issues that are consistent with many of the eight guiding principles of Chapter 1. Thus, the assessment issues tend to be linked with programs of planned change, to involve assessment information collected in natural settings over time, to be grounded in the complexity of the real world, and to be sensitive to societal goals and pressures. For example, consider the following sample questions addressed by our authors.

Buffery: Can rehabilitative medical services to right-brain-injured, speech-impaired patients be made more effective and cost efficient by introducing home-based, self-administered, computerized programs for automated assessment and treatment delivery?

Katkin: Is business justified in using polygraphy to assess employee honesty, and then to base decisions upon these assessments? Likewise, is government justified in using polygraphy to assess employee security risk, for similar decisions about personnel?

Paul: Should the management and program content of residential mental health services be radically reorganized around the routine, scientifically rigorous collection and feedback of data directly summarizing ongoing staff and patient behavior?

Fowler: Should prison classification be changed to incorporate a more rational and deliberate rehabilitative thrust?

Patterson and Bank: Is it possible to assess parental behavior accurately in the areas of discipline and monitoring, to show that those behaviors are strongly related to childhood aggression, and if so, to design programs to change the parental behaviors so that the aggressions of the children will be reduced?

Hackman and Helmreich: Should the safety potential of airline crews be assessed in a very different manner from the present individually focused procedures by assessing a crew's ability to function effectively as a team?

Broskowski: To what extent are not-for-profit human service organizations (NPHSOS) most effectively and efficiently managed by decision-making that is closely linked to normative organizational performance indicators, such as the national Key Performance Indicator (KPI) system?

Gilbert: Can business and government organizations become more productive by applying the MAP-LAMP-PROBE assessment methodology to the design of (a) jobs in those organizations, (b) environmental supports for the jobs, and (c) performance standards by which job activity is judged?

Direct measurement of dysfunction. The last three columns of Table 11.2 illustrate additional common technological elements among the assessment models. Each selects target dysfunctions to measure (Column C), each measures these dysfunctions in a direct manner (Column D), and each provides ongoing feedback about variation in the level of dysfunction over time (illustrated in Column E for variation in the direction of improvement). Assessment procedures are directed toward two aims. One is to identify the degree of dysfunction present over an initial period of baseline performance. The second is to continue measurement of the target dysfunction over time. This ongoing measurement has in turn two purposes: To help remediate the dysfunction through feedback, and to evaluate the effects of various programmatic attempts to reduce the dysfunction.

The technological perspective's emphasis on the direct measurement of target dysfunctions is shared by the assessment tradition of program

TABLE 11.2
Characteristics of the Eight Assessment Models

A. Systems level (Author)	B. Type of decisional setting	C. Sample target dysfunction for identification and remediation feedback	D. Direct measure of target dysfunction	E. Sample type of feedback generated
Neuropsychological (Buffery, Chapter 3)	Medical (brain damage)	A stroke victim's language dysfunction	Model measures actual language functioning by the brain function therapy "probe"	Improvement in level of language dysfunction
Psychophysiological (Katkin, Chapter 4)	Medical (biofeedback)	An individual's experienced anxiety (via electrodermal responses)	Model involves measures of psychophysiological responses	Lowered electrodermal responses as an indicator of reduced anxiety
Individual (Paul, Chapter 5)	Mental health and mental retardation (residential service)	A residential patient's maladaptive behavior, and a staff member's inappropriate behavior	Direct observation of patient and staff appropriate and inappropriate behavior on the TSBC and SRIC	Increased levels of a patient's appropriate behavior in areas such as reduced hostility and improved self-maintenance
Individual (Fowler, Chapter 6)	Correctional (prison classification)	A prisoner's high level of dangerousness	Model makes primary use of formally documented acts of past violent and dangerous behavior	Reduced level of a prisoner's dangerousness, resulting in prison reclassification to a category of

ter 7)	vices for aggressive children)	and a child's aggression	and child behavior and monitors it by time-sampled, structured phone calls	priate discipline and monitoring of his/her child
Small group (Hackman and Helmreich, Chapter 8)	Business (functioning of work teams)	An airline crew's poor team functioning	Model directly observes an air crew's functioning in the LOFT simulation exercise	In a LOFT simulation, an air crew's improved communication and increased positive leadership by its captain
Organizational (Broskowski, Chapter 9)	Mental health and other human services (service delivery programs)	A mental health executive's inability to make routine organizational decisions efficiently and effectively	KPI model consists of summary indicators of organizational products directly linked to an agency's programmatic performance	A mental health agency's improvement on its Key Performance Indicators
Organizational (Gilbert, Chapter 10)	Business and government (employee productivity)	A used-truck department's poor "bottom line" in disposing of trucks	MAP-LAMP-PROBE model defines a business's key goals and directly measures ongoing degree of attainment by employees	A business department's improvement on its MAP indicators of productivity

evaluation. A major objective of program evaluation is to measure the impacts of human service interventions upon explicitly defined goal behaviors (Rossi et al., 1979). As Morell (1979) says, "whatever else evaluation may be, it must concern itself with outcome, i.e., with the influence of a social program on its clients and/or its societal context" (p. 1). Within the tradition of program evaluation, outcome measurement basically consists of the direct assessment of predefined target dysfunctions at baseline, during an intervention program, and at the end of the program.

The emphasis in the technological perspective on the direct measurement of target dysfunctions is also shared by the tradition of behavioral assessment, which has developed as a subdiscipline within behavior therapy. Nelson (1983) states that a major contribution of behavioral assessment has been the "recognition that behaviors are important to measure in and of themselves . . . as samples of what a person does in a particular situation, rather than as signs of what a person has" (p. 6).

Thus, behavioral assessment stresses the direct measure of target problem behaviors identified for change. In contrast, other assessment traditions, such as psychodynamic theory and trait theory, view personality as the central factor in understanding, predicting, or changing behavior. Trait theory holds that individual actions are primarily determined by stable, enduring, inner dispositional characteristics, such as aggressiveness, dependency, or honesty. Behavior is regarded not as a *sample* of a more general behavioral domain but as a *sign* of underlying personality traits, which are then presumed to determine behavioral effects. In line with this view, the emphasis in personality assessment is upon measuring various manifestations of these traits so as to infer their presence or their strength. The direct recording of presenting target dysfunctions displayed by an individual is of secondary concern, because those dysfunctions are considered only peripheral signs of the central dynamic dispositions that are seen as the causes for behavior.

The direct measures of target dysfunctions that our authors collect serve as performance indicators of the individual, group, and organizational systems they are assessing and about which they are providing feedback. In fact, the selection of these performance indicators from among large numbers of possible variables is an important function served by the conceptual model that each author constructs in his methodology (see Table 11.1, Step 4). The conceptual model provides a view of the decisions of interest that allows for a rational reduction of the vast complexity of the real world to a working conception of it, a working conception that focuses on a relatively few key variables. Ultimately, the assessment methodology can be judged by the extent to which it conceptually identifies and technically measures performance indicators in such a way as to improve decision-making in the organizational setting of interest.

Although all the eight assessment models emphasize the direct assessment of target dysfunctions for an individual, group, or organization, four of them also measure personality-related variables in more traditional ways. Fowler uses the Minnesota Multiphasic Personality Inventory (MMPI) to aid in assessing an inmate's need for psychiatric services. Hackman and Helmreich plan to use traditional personality questionnaires to assess the impact on group functioning of composing crews on the basis of personality and demographic variables. Patterson and Bank use a parent-child behavioral checklist reflecting aggressive or clandestine behaviors. Paul uses traditional self-report questionnaires, inventories, and checklists (QICS) to measure the relatively enduring and stable social and psychological characteristics of the patients and staff on a hospital ward. This information helps to provide an interpretive context for the actual behaviors and activities that are directly observed on the ward via Paul's TSBC and SRIC instruments.

Interconnections among system levels. A final common technological feature of the eight assessment models is the inclusion of interconnections among system levels within each model, although they vary as to the scope of intersystem inclusiveness. Each model was chosen in part because it focuses mainly on one particular systems level, as shown in the first column of Table 11.2. However, each model also accommodates the fact that in the real world, different system levels are always interconnected (Miller, 1978). Each human psychophysiological or neuropsychological subsystem is embedded in a whole functioning person; each person functions not only as an individual, but also as a member of numerous small groups, such as family units and work teams; all organizations are composed of individuals and small groups. Therefore, if a technology involving any one system level is to be effective in the natural environment, its concepts and procedures must include perspectives and implications from other systems levels. The assessment models discussed in Chapters 3–10 provide rich illustrations of such cross-level perspectives and implications. Some examples are listed in Table 11.3.

TABLE 11.3
Multiple System Levels Involved in Each Author's Assessment Model

| | Systems level of functioning | | | |
Author	Biopsychological	Individual	Interpersonal	Organizational
Buffery	Neurologically based language dysfunction[a]	The individual patient's sense of mastery by active participation in his/her rehabilitation program	The clinical "caring" team, consisting of a mix of professionals and the patient's family	Home-based computerized care calls for a department-wide service reorganization in the rehabilitation departments of general hospitals
Katkin	Physiological indicators of lying or stress[a]	Implications of a polygraph test for an individual job applicant	A polygrapher's and subject's social interaction, an important determinant of the polygrapher's final evaluation	Government agencies' and businesses' overvaluing and potentially misusing the results of polygraphy, in light of its scientific foundation
Paul	The TSBC behavioral profile used to monitor the effects of psychoactive drugs on patients	The weekly TSBC behavioral profile report of an individual patient[a]	Quality assurance summary report #1 for a particular ward, summarizing patient outcome by movement to and from the ward	Quality assurance summary report #1 for a whole mental hospital, summarizing patient outcome by movement to and from the hospital

		present the inmate's case to the classification board	mates classified as requiring maximum custody
Patterson and Bank	—	The antisocial behavior of an individual child	Parent-child interaction, with emphasis on parent monitoring and disciplining of the child[a]	Policy implications of the parental determinants of child aggression, e.g., parent training programs in areas with high juvenile crime rates
Hackman and Helmreich	—	The technical skill and personality of each airline crew member	The functioning of an airline crew as a group[a]	Viewing an air crew as a task group implies changes in policy of regulatory agencies, airline companies, and pilot unions
Broskowski	—	The decision-making behavior of the individual director of a community mental health center	Multiple small groups (board of directors, management, staff) who represent different constituencies for community mental health center decisions	A community mental health center using the KPI performance indicator system to help make its decisions[a]
Gilbert	—	An individual manager's LAMP specification of the desired accomplishments in his job	The PIP method for setting standards for workers engaging in a similar task (PIP ratio reflects the performance of exemplary vs. typical workers)	The MAP-LAMP-PROBE system leading to increases in a business's overall profitability and productivity[a]

[a] Primary systems level on which the author's assessment model is focused.

The "Phase" Emphasis of Each System

In line with "Phase A" in the technological process model summarized in Table 11.1, each author in Chapters 3–10 begins by presenting a description and conceptualization of an important type of decision that is being addressed. In addition, each author contributes to the technology of most, if not all, of the other phases. However, although we went looking for complete systems, we found very few in actual practice. Different phases are emphasized in the contemporary work of our authors, and the chapters vary in the phase or phases upon which they primarily focus. These foci are presented in Table 11.4. Katkin, Hackman and Helmreich, and Broskowski emphasize Phase A; Patterson and Bank, Phase B; Buffery, Phase C; Fowler, Phase D; and Paul and Gilbert, all the phases. We shall consider each of these groups in turn, together with the views of our discussants.

Phase A: Conceptualizing the decision to be made. Katkin and his discussant, Neigher, focus upon several types of target decisions (see Table 11.1, Step 1). Two of the major ones include how to decide, based upon polygraphic "lie detection" data, whether an employee is a security risk or dishonest, and how to decide, based upon electrodermal responses, whether a psychological anxiety reduction technique, such as systematic desensitization, is effective. Other researchers and practitioners have employed decision-focused psychophysiological assessment models to answer these questions. All of these models are based upon the following theoretical assumption: Because psychophysiological responses consist of "hard" biological processes, compared to the "soft" processes involved in self-report questionnaires and behavioral assessment, psychophysiological measures are more valid indicators of psychological processes such as lying, feeling anxious, and thinking schizophrenically. Utilizing his own and other research in this area (Table 11.1, Step 3), Katkin devotes much of his chapter to an empirical, theoretical, and methodological critique of this assumption.

Katkin's critique leads him to set forth an alternative theoretical assumption, namely, that psychological processes such as lying and feeling anxious are intrinsically psychological and do not have direct, clear, and defining representation in physiological responses. Thus, although we might discover physiological responses that correlate with psychological responses, the former will only be correlates and never as "real" or direct in measuring psychological processes as the psychological responses themselves. From this assumption, Katkin derives a different conceptual model (Table 11.1, Step 4) for decision-focused psychophys-

TABLE 11.4
Phase of Technological Process Emphasized

Author(s) and discussants	A. Conceptualizing the decision	B. Data methodology	C. Pilot-testing	D. Implementation at full scale	E. Dissemination	All phases
Buffery and Barbrack			X			
Katkin and Neigher	X					
Paul and Lieberman						X
Fowler and Rotgers				X		
Patterson/Bank and Wurmser		X				
Hackman/ Helmreich and Pallone	X					
Broskowski and Kamis-Gould	X					
Gilbert and Kline						X

iological assessment. The model states that psychophysiological responses are useful in assessing and monitoring those illnesses in which dysfunctional physiological processes are stimulated by psychosocial events.

Neigher, the discussant of Katkin's chapter, speaks from his experience as a health planner, marketer, and manager in a general hospital. Neigher provides some additional examples that are consistent with Katkin's model, for example, using psychological processes through biofeedback in efforts to change the physiological dysfunction underlying medical disorders such as vascular headaches, Raynaud's disease, myofacial pain and bruxism. However, speaking from his experience in the medical decision-making culture (Table 11.1, Step 2), Neigher points out two pressures to misuse psychophysiological methods by overselling them to the public despite their weak scientific research bases. First, because the provision of medical services is becoming more and more dominated by profit-making considerations, economic pressures encourage overselling psychophysiological methods, marketing them on the basis of profitability only. Second, because psychophysiological methods are a politically attractive way for the psychiatric profession to "remedicalize" the mental health field and thus to gain more political authority over that field, political pressures also encourage overselling psychophysiological methods.

The target decision for Hackman and Helmreich and their discussant, Pallone (see Table 11.1, Step 1), is how to evaluate the function of an airline crew for regulation and possible remediation. Based upon the group process and organizational behavior research literature (Table 11.1, Step 3), the authors first develop a conceptual model of the decision (Table 11.1, Step 4). The central theme of their conception is that the safety of the crew is a function of how well the crew works together *as a team*, and thus involves such psychosocial variables as the ability of the individual crew members to communicate with each other and the ability of the pilot to provide group leadership, especially in unpredictable crisis situations.

The Hackman/Helmreich conceptual model is in conflict with the one presently employed by government and industry, which focuses on the technical aeronautical ability of the individual members of the crew. This conflict is highlighted by Pallone, the discussant of Hackman and Helmreich's chapter, who points out that these authors' adoption of a group process model is in basic opposition to the values of our overall societal culture "that still preaches independence at the expense of interdependence" and that primarily rewards individual effort and accomplishment. It therefore comes as no surprise that the Hackman-Helmreich model has been resisted by decision makers in key positions in the pilot unions, in the airline companies, and in governmental regulations agencies. Before beginning the detailed development of data collection methods, Hackman and Helmreich therefore deemed it necessary to perform a detailed analysis of the culture of those key decision makers who presently evaluate airline crews, and an analysis of the context in which these decision makers now function (Table 11.1, Step 2). This analysis comprises the major portion of their chapter.

The target decisions for Broskowski and his discussant, Kamis-Gould (Table 11.1, Step 1), are the choices made by executive directors of community mental health centers (CMHCs) and other non-for-profit human service organizations (NPHSOS)—choices about how to collect the maximum amount of revenue given other constraints, what mix of clients to serve, what mix of professional staff to hire, what mix of services to provide, whether to move to different physical facilities, how to communicate a positive message about their center to the community they serve. As a social scientist, Broskowski was trained to support the use of formal, quantitative assessment models in CMHC decision-making. However, in his tenure as a CMHC executive director, Broskowski has been immersed in a decision context and culture (Table 11.1, Step 2) that is resistant to the use of formal assessment in decision-making.

In attempting to resolve the conflict between his experience as a social scientist and as a manager, Broskowski turns to research on organizational effectiveness (Table 11.1, Step 3). He uses this literature as a guide in developing criteria for judging the effectiveness of a CMHC director's decisions. These criteria help form the basis for a conceptual model (Table 11.1, Step 4) for deciding when a particular decision is amenable to formal assessment data input. The model is summarized in Broskowski's Table 9.2, entitled "Factors That Facilitate or Inhibit the Use of Formalized Data in the Decision-Making Process." For example, Broskowski points out that today's CMHC directors function in a very turbulent and reactive environment, where cost-cutting and "cutback management" are salient concerns. Efforts in this environment to validate formal assessment methodologies like the Key Performance Indicator (KPI) model "could easily become bogged down in a morass of political and economic agendas."

Kamis-Gould, the discussant of Broskowski's chapter, adds her own experience in elaborating the conditions under which formal assessment models are constructively adopted by decision makers. She illustrates her points by describing one such model, the Performance

Management System, which is in the process of being adopted by New Jersey's statewide system of CMHCS.

Phase B: Develop a data system linked to decision. The main target decision for Patterson and Bank and their discussant, Wurmser, is how to intervene to reduce aggressive, antisocial behavior in children (Table 11.1, Step 1), behavior like verbal and physical fighting, stealing, lying, and using illegal drugs. For over 20 years Patterson and his colleagues in Oregon have been developing a conceptual model that is relevant to this decision (Table 11.1, Steps 3 and 4). The model was developed in part out of extensive clinical experience working directly with antisocial children and their families, in part from observation of other intervention programs that attempt to socialize these children. Thus Patterson's model is embedded in the culture of those human service decision makers who have responsibility for dealing with children (Table 11.1, Step 2).

Patterson's model is a performance theory of children's antisocial behavior. The theory identifies an interrelated set of real-world measures of parent, child, peer, and setting variables that predict real-world, criterion measures of aggression across children and contexts. Patterson and Bank's chapter is devoted to the task of developing a measurement system (Table 11.1, Step 5) for indicators of three of the performance theory dimensions, namely, quality of parental discipline, quality of parental child monitoring, and the degree of the child's antisocial behavior. The authors' goal is to derive indicators of these dimensions that meet Paul's "Four Rs" of assessment utility: replicability, representativeness, relevance, and relatively low cost of data collection. Their strategy is to collect a wide diversity of measures that vary by agent (peers, teachers, parents, a "neutral" outside observer, and the child) and by mode (direct behavioral observation, interview with mother, ongoing parental telephone interviews, child interview, peer nomination, and questionnaires). The many measures that emerge are reduced to a smaller set by eliminating those with inadequate reliabilities. The surviving measures are then subjected to the statistical procedures of structural equation modeling to determine how many dimensions are required to accommodate intercorrelations among measures and to determine which measures are most closely intercorrelated within each dimension.

Wurmser, the chapter discussant, is executive director of a CMHC that focuses on family and child services. In this role, she is a typical decision-maker consumer of Patterson's assessment methodology. Because antisocial children are viewed as a very difficult clinical population for which effective methods have not yet been developed, Wurmser points out that decision makers in positions like hers can understand the need for a more psychometrically sophisticated approach than is currently available. Wurmser also notes the attractiveness to decision makers of the clinical experience and real-world embeddedness that underlies Patterson and Bank's model.

Phase C: Pilot-testing. The target decision for Buffery and his discussant, Barbrack (Table 11.1, Step 1), is how to improve the effectiveness and cost efficiency of rehabilitative services to individuals whose language functioning is impaired by damage in their left brain. Working from the field of neuropsychological theory and research (Table 11.1, Step 3), Buffery develops a conceptual model (Table 11.1, Step 4) which posits that, through a large number of precisely designed trials of Brain Function Therapy (BFT) in which the right brain is "bombarded" with language learning experience, the right brain can acquire the ability to take over language functioning from the damaged left hemisphere. The trials are so arranged that they can be delivered by a self-administering computer program, which uses assessment data from a patient's previous responses to tailor the next learning trial to the patient's present level of functioning. By tracking and summarizing the results of a patient's sequential responses to the learning tasks, the computer can also generate ongoing assessment feedback to monitor the progress of the patient. In developing his computerized model, Buffery analyzes the context and culture of neuropsychological rehabilitation and argues that computerized brain function therapy is well suited to meeting the needs of brain-injured patients, although he acknowledges cultural resistances to BFT that could emerge.

The major focus of Buffery's chapter is the presentation of a single, strikingly successful case study that ties together his conceptual model and most of his technology. (The major element lacking is that the learning trials were delivered by professionals in a hospital rather than by a computer in the patient's home.) Although the case study helps to establish the feasibility of Buffery's model, his discussant, Barbrack, points out the need for additional successful pilot studies involving a sizable number of patients before the model is ready for the next phase of implementation at full scale (Table 11.1, Phase D).

Phase D: Implementing the methodology. The target decision for Fowler and his discussant, Rotgers (Table 11.1, Step 1), is to classify prison inmates in a manner that is rational, valid, humane, and effective in promoting rehabilitation. Through a unique set of contextual and cultural circumstances (Table 11.1, Step 2) Fowler and his colleagues in the Psychology Department at the University of Alabama were presented with the task of developing and implementing at full scale an assessment system to classify over 3,000 inmates in the Alabama prison system. Fowler's chapter is a vivid description of the successful implementation of the assessment model he developed.

Fowler based his assessment approach upon a conceptual model (Table 11.1, Step 4). The model, which draws upon previous work in this area (Table 11.1, Step 3), is based upon a number of major premises. In line with the concepts of due process and the stimulation of positive motivation through participation, the inmate is viewed as a collaborator in collecting the basic assessment data, in drawing conclusions from those data, and in presenting conclusions to the classification board. Second, the data collected are as concrete and behavioral as possible. Third, inferences from the data are straightforward, at a low level, and oriented to pragmatic decision-making about the inmate's classification status and his potential needs for vocational, educational, medical, psychiatric, and related services.

Rotgers, Fowler's discussant, is a staff psychologist with the New Jersey parole board and a former chief psychologist in one of that state's maximum security prisons. Rotgers is enthusiastic about Fowler's model from a technical point of view. He considers the methodology highly rational and effective, and relatively simple and inexpensive to implement. However, Rotgers emphasizes the uniqueness of the political conditions that lead to Fowler's opportunity to carry out his work. Rotgers points out that such conditions are not likely to recur in today's correctional culture, which involves "a political climate that favors segregation and punishment rather than more creative and rehabilitative approaches to altering criminal behavior." It would seem that changes have to occur in the correctional culture before more pilot tests of Fowler's model can be completed, and thus before subsequent progression to the next stage, full-scale implementation, is possible (Table 11.1, Phase D).

All phases. The target decision for Paul and his discussant, Lieberman (Table 11.1, Step 1), is how to improve the quality, effectiveness, and cost efficiency of residential services for the mentally ill and retarded. In approaching this decision, Paul has developed a conceptual model (Table 11.1, Step 4) on the basis of both the research literature (Table 11.1, Step 3) and his own experience in designing, managing, and evaluating two research wards in a typical residential service culture and organizational setting (Table 11.1, Step 2).

Paul's conceptual model begins with an analysis of residential service programs in terms of the types of decisions they require and the logical interrelationships among these decisions. This analysis, which is presented in Table 5.1 in Paul's chapter, includes decisions in such areas as client admission, disposition, and treatment planning; the evaluation of client progress; staff hiring and firing; and program compliance with external regulatory standards. Paul then explores the nature of these decisions to derive the classes of information that are needed to aid each type of decision. His conclusions, summarized in Table 5.2 in his chapter, are that six classes of information are needed, three in the client domain and three in the staff domain.

The two most important classes of information in Paul's system are those involving client problem behaviors and staff treatment techniques. Both of these classes of information are best measured by ongoing, direct observation and coding of staff and client behaviors and interactions. Such Direct Observational Coding (DOC) is done at the time and place of the behavior's occurrence. This is in contrast to traditional Questionnaires, Inventories, Checklists, and Scales (QICS), in which retrospective, interpretive recordings of past observations are obtained on a single occasion.

Paul has developed two formal assessment instruments for implementing DOC in residential settings (Table 11.1, Phase B). These are the Time-Sample Behavior Checklist (TSBC), which employs "brief, discrete-momentary, hourly time-samples of [the behavior of] every client and staff member"; and the Staff-Resident Interaction Chronograph (SRIC), which employs "a continuous-chronographic, 10-minute observation period of a single staff member, systematically observing all staff members over time at the rate of one or two per hour within each treatment unit. . . . [and coding] all interactions with clients by the target staff member" (Chapter 5).

Paul has created a comprehensive data methodology (Table 11.1, Phase B) for implementing his conceptual model and assessment instruments. He calls the technology the Computerized TSBC/SRIC Planned-Access Observational Information System, or the TSBC/SRIC system for short. Its main components include: (a) the creation of a team of full-time, nonparticipating technician-level observers who are trained to operate the TSBC and SRIC on a treatment ward; (b) computer terminals for entry of the day's TSBC/SRIC data by night-shift clinical staff when clients are sleeping; (c) a main computer with special software for processing the TSBC/SRIC data and producing summary reports; and (d) a specially created and formatted series of reports, which are designed to summarize the basic data in different ways and at different levels of aggregation so that multiple decision questions can be addressed by multiple levels of decision makers.

For over 17 years, Paul and his associates have been developing the TSBC/SRIC system and extending its implementation. After a number of pilot tests (Table 11.1, Phase C), in the early 1970s they conducted a full-scale implementation of the system (Table 11.1, Phase D). The TSBC and the SRIC were used to collect ongoing and complete data on all clients and staff of two different 28-bed residential wards of a large community mental health center for nearly 4½ years. At first the data were used primarily for research purposes, but various components of the system were gradually added so that for the last 12 to 18 months of the project, the system was supporting all major clinical and administrative decision-making.

After this successful implementation, Paul and his associates began the process of dissemination (Table 11.1, Phase E). Preliminary dissemination has already taken place, involving additional full-scale implementations in five units in two different facilities over a three-year period, and in a third hospital for more than a year. In addition, normative data and interpretive users' manuals based upon full-week observational samples of more than 1,200 clients and 600 staff in 36 different treatment units located in 17 different institutions will soon be available.

The last part of Paul's chapter deals with the next step, expansion to dissemination at full scale (Table 11.1, Phase E). In spite of the fact that he has not yet explicitly marketed the system, there is strong interest in it in the United States and Canada. The last step before a major dissemination effort can take place is completion of all the written manuals, model videotapes, and computer programs needed to fully "package" the TSBC/SRIC.

Lieberman, the discussant of Paul's chapter, is a designer and administrator of residential services. In keeping with this professional background, Lieberman adopts a potential user's perspective toward the TSBC/SRIC system and presents a consumer-oriented commentary on Paul's chapter. Specifically, Lieberman provides an excellent contribution to the dissemination process by systematizing the questions a potential consumer brings to the decision about adopting such a complex and wide-ranging technology. Lieberman organizes his questions into several domains, including clinical factors, assessment tool factors, and administrative factors.

In his closing remarks, Lieberman suggests that any organization that is seriously considering the adoption of the TSBC/SRIC system should form a task force to do an implementation feasibility study. Such a group should analyze the target agency's operations in relation to the variables assessed by the TSBC/SRIC, should become familiar with forthcoming volumes describing the system, should visit at least two programs where the system has been implemented, should customize the list of Lieberman's evaluative questions to the target agency setting, and should make recommendations to the agency's senior management that heavily weight administrative factors.

The target decisions of Gilbert and his discussant, Kline (Table 11.1, Step 1), are how to design an organization's jobs and measure performance in them so as to maximize the organization's productivity and profitability. Gilbert has developed the MAP-LAMP-PROBE conceptual model (Table 11.1, Step 4), based on the organizational literature (Table 11.1, Step 3) and Gilbert's own experience as a successful, full-time organizational consultant to business and government. Because his livelihood has been dependent upon successful sale of his services to senior managers, Gilbert has a vital incentive to learn the culture of the senior managers to whom he offers his services and to embed his assessment model within that culture (Table 11.1, Step 2). The dramatic, vivid, clear, and personal style of Gilbert's chapter illustrates his sensitivity to presenting his ideas in a manner that is both interesting and professionally sound for a lay audience of managers.

Gilbert's model has three components: measures of attainable performance (MAP), leading-accomplishment models of performance (LAMP), and profiling behavior (PROBE). (He points out that these are the tools needed to seek gold in dark caves!) The first task in performance improvement is to develop appropriate measures and standards of job performance (the MAP). The key in this task is to select measures that are directly linked to the economic goals of the organization. In one illustration, an auto-door manufacturing supervisor appeared to be the poorest performer as judged by the labor cost of new, intact doors he produced, but he was found to be the best performer when judged on an alternative, economically more relevant outcome measure that also took into consideration the cost of scrapping doors with detectable defects. In another example, Gilbert describes a baseline condition he found when working with a group of chemical design-process engineers. In comparing the economic relevance of five variables of the engineers' performance with what management actually knew about these variables, Gilbert found a perfect negative correlation!

After measures and standards are set for monitoring job performance, the next step is to conceptualize the types of accomplishments most closely related to those measures and standards. A statement of these accomplishments, the LAMP, should be based upon the ultimate goals of the job. For example, Al, a used-truck manager, had a long detailed job description, which consisted of a list of 50 characteristics, many of them unmeasurable, like "taking initiative" and "being creative." However, missing from his job description was the act that was found to be economically most important in acquiring a used truck, especially on a trade-in, that is, establishing a price for it. Al's management had assumed that he was chiefly responsible for doing this, but had never put it in his job description. When Al's job description was restructured and simplified, with setting an acquisition price on each used truck as a very prominent accomplishment, his performance improved tremendously.

Once the economic context of a job is defined and the job designed to be consistent with that context, job behavior and its environmental setting must be assessed in order to ascertain the possible presence of behavioral barriers that are preventing exemplary performance. Gilbert's approach to this assessment process, the PROBE model, focuses on six variables. Three are in the environment and are predicated on the assumption that exemplary performance is facilitated when an employee receives clear and supportive feedback, when he or she has proper tools with which to perform, and when he or she is provided with attractive incentives. The other three variables are within the person. Paralleling the first three, these intraindividual variables are predicated on the assumption that exemplary performance is facilitated when an employee has proper knowledge and training for the job, along with appropriate capacity (mental, physical, and emotional) and adequate motivation.

Gilbert's data methodology (Table 11.1, Phase B) is not as strictly formalized as Paul's. This is to be expected. Paul's model assesses clients and staff in a single type of setting, namely residential programs for individuals with behavioral dysfunctions. For this reason, the model can be highly structured for those particular settings. In contrast, Gilbert's model addresses a wide range of job roles, as disparate as "laboratory technicians and design engineers, telephone company repair clerks and high-technology sales representatives, strategic analysts and financial planners, factory supervisors and meat inspectors, packaging-machine operators and insurance sales people, not to mention managers of almost every kind and level." Nevertheless, Gilbert's chapter is rich in examples of the ways he operationalizes the various factors in his model into quantifiable indicators for these diverse groups.

Two of Gilbert's particularly useful contributions in data methodology are his economic models, which link performance data with the economic success of an organization, and his PIP method (potential for improving performance) for evaluating the relative competence of different incumbents in the same type of job. PIP consists of a ratio between the accomplishments of an exemplary performer and that of a typical performer in a particular job; the larger the PIP, the more potential there is for the average performer to improve. Through the use of PIP, exemplary performers can be identified, and the ingredients of their success can be used to help other employees in similar positions to perform at higher levels.

Gilbert has been pilot-testing, implementing, and disseminating his ideas and methods for 23 years. Over that time he has worked with over 300 large organizations, with huge corporations and the federal government, involving employees in a wide diversity of jobs like those listed above. Although Gilbert does not discuss the dissemination process per se, it should be noted that his examples, which are presented in a lively and vivid style, illustrate an important component in the "marketing of sound assessment models to lay decision makers." Moreover, as his discussant, Kline, points out, Gilbert's 23 years of applied work in organizational settings have paid off in the "ecological validity" of his approach. In Kline's words, Gilbert's insights from his years devoted to grass roots performance engineering ring true for "those of us who have also spent more than a few years grappling with the challenges of productivity improvement."

Contributions of the Models across Steps

Each of the eight models we have been reviewing contains concepts, strategies, and procedures that contribute across assessment settings and systems levels to the general technology of decision-focused assessment. These components, together with the "common elements" among the assessment models that were discussed above, can be usefully summarized as a series of strategic guidelines for technologically focused assessment in a particular organizational setting. Examples of these guidelines, as suggested by our eight authors, are presented below. The examples are grouped in terms of the phases of technological development listed in Table 11.1

Phase A: Conceptualizing the decision to be made. Gilbert argues persuasively that a proper place to begin in developing a conceptual model for decision-focused assessment is the articulation of a clear mission and goals statement for the organizational setting in which the decision takes place. Productivity and profit in a corporate setting (Gilbert) and improvement in client functioning in a mental hospital (Paul) are examples of these general goals. In this context, Broskowski points out that a prior political step in the development process is to determine whether the decision makers in power are in actuality motivated to keep their goals unclear. He notes: "A wisdom commonly shared by many chief executives of large corporations is that to maintain their corporation's options and responsiveness to opportunities they should avoid a declaration of highly specific goals and objectives."

In a related way, Hackman describes negative incentives for airline unions and companies to increase reliable, accurate, and credible data about airline accidents. Such data can make these groups more accountable to outside agencies, causing them to give up some of their organizational control and flexibility. On the same point, Fowler warns that the existence of a nonformal assessment model can perform latent organizational functions that are in conflict with those of a proposed formal model. Before the Alabama prisons implemented Fowler's formal inmate classification model, classification was used in an informal and subjective manner as a principal form of punishment for minor inmate offenses.

Thus, the first task for the assessor is to establish that a decision maker's motivation for accurately assessing performance concerning clearly stated goals is present, and then to articulate those goals. Broskowski proposes that the next task is to analyze the decisions associated with the goals in order to identify characteristics of the decision and its setting that facilitate or inhibit the use of formalized data in the decision-making process. For example, other factors being equal, decisions are amenable to formal assessment to the extent that they are made frequently, involve a small number of clear options, and take place in an organization whose members are in substantial agreement about its goals and values.

If the decisions are amenable to formal decision-making, Paul illustrates how to analyze their logical interrelationships in order to determine if the same data base can be aggregated in different ways to address the needs of diverse decision makers at different systems levels, for example, the individual clinician whose needs may differ from those of the program administrator of a mental hospital ward.

When the variables being measured are process variables that are assumed to be causally related to a particular outcome, complexities may arise. Hackman and Helmreich point out two complications in linking air crew process variables to airline safety. The first is the systems theory concept of "equifinality," which says that "just as there are multiple routes one can fly and still get from New York to Chicago, so are there multiple ways that a crew can operate and still achieve essentially the same performance outcome." The second is Tyler's (1981) principle of "multiple possibilities," which states that there are many possible outcomes that can emerge in any given situation, and the particular one actualized is not completely determined by the causal factors that precede it. Buffery and Katkin underline a related complexity when causal interrelationships are being explored, namely individual differences in the way variables are causally linked. Buffery points out that "because of the idiosyncratic nature of the dysfunctioning subsequent upon similar CNS lesions in different people, the further the clinician moves from data derived from single case studies, the less relevance the neuropsychological measures have to the rehabilitation of the individual patient." Similarly, Katkin discusses the problem of generalizing across subjects in psychophysiological studies because of the phenomenon of "individual response stereotypy," which refers to the tendency of subjects to show maximum responsivity to stimuli in only one particular response modality.

In developing a model of the target decision and the related decision-making process, several authors remind us of the need to build in safeguards against the misuse of assessment data. For example, when data are being employed to make crucial decisions that affect an individual's liberty (as in correctional classification), Fowler emphasizes the need to build into the decision-making context the legal concept of "due process." Broskowski sensitizes us to the fact that when assessment data are being used by one organization to monitor and regulate others, we have to be alert to tendencies toward "gaming" on the part of the regulated agency, that is, the tendency of an organization to distort data reporting so as to "beat" the regulatory system. Broskowski gives the example of hospitals that are showing signs of "DRG creep," which means that they are assigning diagnoses based upon their profit margins, not upon patients' actual medical conditions.

Hackman and Helmreich note the conflict between assessment data being used for "formative" decisions about an individual employee's training and development in his or her job, and use of the same data to make "summative" evaluative decisions about the employee's promotion or retention in the job. In their work with the assessment of airline crew performance, these authors suggest the creation of two separate versions of the same flight simulation exercise, one to be used for regulatory evaluation only (LOFT), and the other for the evaluation of individual training and development needs only (LOCK).

Phase B: Developing a data methodology linked to the decision. After the target decision is properly conceptualized, a data methodology has to be developed. Patterson and Bank remind us that during this developmental process, the conceptual model of the decision is typically not fixed. Rather, there is a give-and-take, "bootstrapping" relationship between conceptualization and data collection. The assessor starts off with some sort of conceptual model of the decision. The variables in the model are then translated into particular measures, and data are collected on those measures. These data are then used to guide revision of the original conceptual model, which in turn generates a revised set of empirical measures. Structural equation modeling is only one of the procedures Patterson uses to aid the bootstrapping process. In deciding how to measure a particular conceptual variable, Patterson suggests collecting a variety of empirical indicators. In his own work he measures a child's antisocial behavior on the basis of scores from three agents—peers, teachers, and parents—and from three modes of assessment—questionnaires, peer nomination, and telephone interview. Patterson's rationale for collecting multiple measures of a construct is based on the assumption that any particular measure has three components: a "true" assessment of one aspect of the target construct, which is unique to that measure; an "artifactual," distorting indication of the construct, which is also unique to that measure; and a "true" assessment of the construct, which overlaps with the assessments of the other constructs. By including multiple measures, the overlapping true components and the uniquely true components add together to yield a broader, more accurate view of the construct, and the unique, artifactual components cancel themselves out.

Paul emphasizes another aspect of a data methodology, that is, the need to summarize data in such a way as to facilitate its use for practical decision-making. His work illustrates this by the development of standardized reports that are explicitly designed for operational use in residential settings. A principle used in organizing results is that of hierarchically ordered detail. Thus, the decision maker typically starts by scanning a report's broadest summary measures. If all is going well, no more analysis is needed. However, if problems emerge, other more detailed indicators are available in the report for rational hypothesis generation and testing based on objective data.

Phases C and D: Pilot-testing and implementing the methodology.
Buffery presents a good example of an effective pilot test: a detailed, graphic, and successful demonstration of the feasibility of a particular assessment model. Such a pilot test obviously has many unique features and, as indicated in Table 11.1, should be replicated at least once before proceeding to the next phase of implementation. It is important to note, moreover, that implementation also frequently takes place in a unique setting, so a successful implementation does not necessarily indicate the feasibility of dissemination to a variety of other sites. This fact is vividly illustrated in Fowler's successful implementation of a formal classification model in the Alabama prisons. This enterprise took place under a special set of judicial, geographic, and historical conditions, which seem in conflict with the political emphasis upon segregation and punishment in today's correctional culture.

Phase E: Disseminating the methodology at full scale. In planning for dissemination, Paul notes the importance of familiarity with the dissemination literature. He summarizes some of the salient points in this literature as follows. "For an innovation to be adopted in practice, it must be judged to be worthwhile by those who have the power to adopt, and the adopters must be informed about the need for the innovation and its availability and be willing and able to undertake its implementation." In this context, Paul points to a crucial organizational reality: Innovations requiring minimal change in organizational roles and functioning can frequently be disseminated rapidly, often being overadopted with respect to its scientific data base (computerized test interpretation and office-based biofeedback offer worrisome examples). "In contrast, those innovations requiring changes in roles, structures, and operating principles as well as organizational adoption decisions are . . . disseminated slowly, often being actively resisted or avoided." Unit-wide residential and community psychosocial programs display these characteristics and the histories of resistance Paul has noted.

Paul and Gilbert, the two authors whose work has involved active efforts in dissemination, both emphasize the importance of careful packaging and marketing in the dissemination process. Paul's chapter and Lieberman's commentary illustrate the extensive efforts that should be devoted to a full technical packaging of an innovation as complex and far-reaching as his TSBC/SRIC system. As a complement, Gilbert illustrates the importance of persuasive presentation of an assessment innovation.

These are only a few of the practical lessons the authors have to teach us. Collectively, their efforts are also interesting in regard to the general field of behavioral decision-making and to several issues in psychological assessment that have preoccupied methodologists over the years. To these matters we now turn.

DECISION THEORY IN THE WORLD OF PRACTICAL CONSEQUENCE

The Shape and Size of Research on Decision-Making

The topic of decision-making, about which this book is focused, has concerned scholars from many disciplines for many years. A large literature, generally identified as "decision theory" or "behavioral decision-making," has resulted from their efforts. Decision theory begins in the observation that people are constantly confronted with the need to make decisions that require forecasts of events and outcomes about which they have insufficient information. The earliest systematic formulations in the field did not appear in psychology but in economics and mathematics. Classical economic theories were dominantly concerned with the gains and losses of individual entrepreneurs in reference to economic philosophies of lofty moral tone and broadly general scope. In fact, most business decisions, at least in capitalist societies, are made by groups of people whose individual interests are often competitive and who must usually join in coalitions with others to resolve conflicts. This consideration led von Neumann and Morgenstern (1947) to study the ways individuals make decisions as participants in socially complex games and market operations. The resulting theory and research stimulated great interest not only among economists, but also among psychologists, sociologists, political scientists, and military planners.

Around the same time, Abraham Wald (1950) developed a general "statistical decision theory," instigated in part by problems of quality control in industrial production. Although the uncertainties facing decision makers on production lines arise more from random variations in physical events than from the predicted actions of human competitors, game theory and statistical decision theory shared many common features and tended to merge in the more general conceptions that followed their introduction.

The main ideas of decision theory were brought to bear on issues in psychological and educational assessment by several writers (e.g., Cronbach & Gleser, 1965; Edwards, 1954; Girschick, 1954). The most influential of these statements was Cronbach and Gleser's *Psychological Tests and Personnel Decisions*, originally published in 1957 and revised in 1965, which signalled a clear departure from classical measurement theory and offered psychologists a new way to think about the problems they faced in the design and application of assessment procedures. Early measurement theories (e.g., Hull, 1928; Thurstone, 1931) assumed that "the ultimate purpose of using aptitude tests is to estimate or forecast aptitudes from test scores" (Hull, 1928, p. 268). Later formulations (e.g., Gulliksen, 1950; Thorndike, 1949) accepted this basic premise and were devoted mainly to issues of reliability and validity of individual tests. As Cronbach and Gleser examined the problems faced by those who used psychological tests for such purposes as the selection and placement of people in jobs, however, they came to believe that the ultimate purpose of tests was to aid practical qualitative decisions rather than to estimate true, quantitative psychometric values from imperfect, error-ridden data.

This shift in perspective raised a new set of questions. In the field of personnel management, what kinds of decisions do administrators face? A taxonomy of decision problems followed that distinguished between individual and institutional decisions and among the special problems of classification, placement, and selection. What kinds of information are needed to guide the decisions? A taxonomy of procedures followed, along with explication of such concepts as the bandwidth-fidelity dilemma. How can one design the most useful batteries of procedures for the various decisions that have to be made? Problems of value and utility, cost and payoff, joined the traditional problems of reliability and validity as issues of concern in psychological assessment.

By now, the literature on decision-making is enormous. Beyond its start in economics, decision-making has been studied over an increasingly diverse range of disciplines including medicine, education, geography, engineering, political science, marketing, and management science, as well as psychology. Within psychology, its many facets have been examined with great energy and ingenuity by cognitive and social psychologists, in the laboratory and in the field, as a prescriptive discipline directed toward elucidating the rules of rational decision and as a descriptive enterprise designed to characterize the actual behavior of decision makers. Four chapters in the *Annual Review of Psychology* have been devoted to the topic, by Edwards in 1961, by Becker and McClintock in 1967, by Rapoport and Wallsten in 1972, and by Slovic, Fischhoff, and Lichtenstein in 1977. Some idea of the amount of accumulated material can be gained by noting that over 1,000 new references appeared between 1971 and 1975. It is also interesting to observe that the *Annual Review* chapters on decision theory moved progressively forward in successive volumes, from last in 1961 to first in 1977. Perhaps some doctoral student looking for a dissertation problem could determine whether the positions of chapters in bibliographic volumes of this kind have any utility for deciding about the importance of the topics.

A brief summary of some of the main issues and research trends considered in the most recent *Annual Review* chapter offers a sense of the range of activity in the field. The chapter is divided into two main sections, "descriptive research" and "decision aids," reflecting the common distinction between descriptive and prescriptive inquiries. Six major headings are required to accommodate a total of 21 subtopics in descriptive research. Among the fields of most vigorous activity are *heuristics and biases*, concerned with the implicit rules that people follow in reaching probabilistic judgments and the systematic errors to which people employing these heuristics are prone; *risky choice*, which began with simple experimental comparisons of risk-taking behavior in individual and group situations, but has now progressed into increasingly complex investigations of risk-taking and choice under conditions of risk; *regression approaches* to the development of algebraic models for describing the ways people weight and combine information in arriving at decisions; and studies of the *ecological representativeness* of decision research, aimed mainly toward examining the extent to which principles derived from laboratory research generalize to natural settings. *Dynamic decision-making*—the study of tasks in which (a) decisions are made sequentially over time, (b) task specifications may change over time, (c) information for later decisions may be contingent on outcomes of earlier decisions, and (d) implications of any decision may reach into the future—had been the subject of a great deal of research at the time of an earlier review, but has not seen much attention recently. Probably the models were so complex and required so many assumptions that experimental results were difficult to interpret and therefore difficult to publish.

The section on decision aids in the review by Slovic and his colleagues begins with a hypothetical conversation (p. 17):

"What do you do for a living?"

"Study decision-making."

"Then you can help me. I have some big decisions to make."

"Well, actually . . . "

The authors proceed, however, to review the efforts of numerous researchers and professional entrepreneurs to provide techniques that may help users make better decisions than they can make unaided. Most of the techniques rely on some form of "decomposition" as a response to the problem of information overload. The decision aid fractionates and thereby simplifies the problem into a series of structurally related parts, and requires subjective judgments for only small and manageable components at any given point in the process. Research showing that decomposition improves judgment is reported by several investigators.

Among the subtopics prominently considered in the review of decision aids is *multiattribute utility theory*, designed for use in decision problems in which one object or course of action must be chosen from a set. The approach outlines strategies for defining attributes and attaching values to them, and then combining the weighted utilities in systematic ways. Additional subtopics include the field of *decision analysis* and the rapidly growing field of *man/machine systems*, with special emphasis on the uses of computers to aid decisions.

To ease cognitive strain and stay within page allotments, Slovic, Fischhoff, and Lichtenstein focused on individual decision-making. They deliberately excluded work on group and organizational decision processes, as well as the extensive literature on Bayesian statistics and much of the work on axiomatic formulations of decision theory. Yet the review as it stands is long (319 references) and much more complex than the simple summary above might suggest. Clearly, the topic of behavioral decision-making has not been neglected by scientists in psychology and related fields.

The Isolation of Research and Practice in Decision-Making

Now we note a remarkable fact. Research and practice in decision-making have scarcely anything to do with each other. There, in the literature we have just described, stands a vast, rapidly growing body of elegant theory and sophisticated research on decision processes. Here, in the preceding chapters of our book, are efforts by psychologists to design assessment operations that work in the world of practical decision-making. Gordon Paul specifically credits Cronbach and his colleagues with providing part of the conceptual framework that guided his enterprise. The notions of representativeness, relevance, and relative cost among his "four Rs' will certainly sound familiar to anyone conversant with Cronbach's writings on generalizability and decision theory. Anthony Broskowski cites two analyses of the decision-making practices of mental health center administrators. In some loose way, a general interest in utility and rationality pervades the writing of all of our our authors. With those exceptions, however, formal research in decision theory and practical application as demonstrated by the authors of this book stand in total isolation.

This might not be surprising if our authors were a bunch of arty clinicians who never read a journal since they left graduate school and spent all their time practicing arcane psychotherapeutic mysteries in the privacy of their clinical offices. But these are all scientists, clearly literate in their own disciplines, many trained in the best traditions of the scientist-practitioner model of education, and several richly honored for their own scientific contributions. The separation of research and practice in decision-making might also excite no surprise if *some* formal decision theory and experimental research were seen as pertinent. But that is not what we find. Not *one* of our authors makes *one single reference* to the massive theoretical and experimental literature on formal decision-making. Wald, von Neumann, Morgenstern, Savage, Luce, Raiffa, Rapoport, Kahneman, Tversky, Slovic, Coombs, Simon— where are you?

One answer has to be, "We are right where we belong, in our laboratories and at the consoles of our computers, working out the theoretical puzzles that interest us. It is up to you applied psychologists to grasp the significance of our research and put it to work in prisons, mental hospitals, and other field settings."

There is merit in that view. Certainly any professional psychologist who pretends to know much about decision processes should be aware of the errors in judgment to which human beings are prone. The literature on decision theory is rich in demonstrations. Kahneman and Tversky's work on heuristics and biases, for example, shows that people in a wide range of situations are likely to judge the relative frequency of objects or the likelihood of particular events according to the relative *availability* of the objects or events, that is, their accessibility in perception, memory, or imagination. To the extent that availability is actually associated with objective frequency, the availability heuristic can be a useful judgmental tool. Often, however, the vividness with which an event can be perceived, the completeness with which it can be recalled, the ease with which it can be imagined, are poorly correlated with frequency or likelihood of occurrence, and in those cases the availability heuristic will be misleading.

The *representativeness* heuristic, in which simple criteria of resemblance are employed in problems of categorization, is also subject to bias when the attributes by which judgments are made are in fact irrelevant to the categorization required. The story is told that on the eve of World War I, Woodrow Wilson was obsessed by the prospect of war with *Great Britain.* What was his reasoning? The British had been illegally searching American ships, just as they had before the War of 1812. That set the stage for the fear. Wilson's agony mounted, however, when he began to dwell on the realization that in all of American history he and Madison were the *only Princeton men* ever to become president of the United States (May, 1973, cited in Nisbett & Ross, 1980).

A third heuristic described by Kahneman and Tversky is *anchoring and adjustment.* In their first pass at a judgmental problem, people "anchor" their estimates to the most credible information at their disposal. The initial estimates are usually sustained more rigidly than valid data would justify, and later adjustments to accommodate additional information are typically imprecise and insufficient. The influence of anchoring lends special importance to the "framing" of decisions. With or without Machiavellian intent, the way decision makers define problems and the information they present in introducing them are likely to have powerful effects on the directions decisions will take.

Other forms of error are equally serious and common. The persuasive dominance of vivid, concrete examples over "pallid statistics" has been repeatedly demonstrated (Nisbett & Ross, 1980). The dangers of "groupthink," in which administrative leaders gather like-thinking advisors about them, and then mistake the consensual agreement that derives from selection and group process for valid judgment, are well known to social psychologists (Janis & Mann, 1977). The dangers are less often perceived by administrators, however, including social psychologists themselves when they leave their laboratories to assume administrative responsibilities. Experts are not exempt from judgmental mistakes. Trained statisticians are as clearly subject as the laity to the "law of small numbers" that generates systematic errors in probabilistic estimation (Tversky & Kahneman, 1971). Expert clinicians are as subject as untrained college sophomores to "illusory correlations" among test cues and personality characteristics. Repeated experience does not dependably reduce error, and the illusory correlations are highly resistant to change (Chapman & Chapman, 1967; Golding & Rorer, 1972). Perhaps the most useful message decision makers can derive from research on the decision process is its clarion call for caution.

All of us in the arena of practical decision-making will do well to enter with a sad appreciation of the vulnerability of human judgment, yours and mine alike, to emotional bias and irrelevant information.

General calls for caution, however, provide thin comfort to those required to make publicly visible decisions in politically sensitive situations. They already know the price of error. They are all too keenly aware of the fallibility of human judgment. Practitioners and scientists alike need more than attitudes. The practitioners need to do their work effectively. Whatever they may say, most researchers would like to see their efforts lead to uses that benefit the public. In some way or other, both feel that benefits would improve if theory, research, and application were more closely unified.

The Call for Field Research

In many areas of psychology, respected investigators have questioned the returns that have been realized from years of laboratory investigation, and have recommended a more balanced blend of laboratory and field research. Robert Sommer (1982), for example, reviewed research on the prisoner's dilemma game, a laboratory analogue that had been employed in over 1,000 studies at the time his article was written but that had had no visible impact on the world of practical bargaining that inspired the research in the first place. The original "dilemma" involved two prototypic criminal suspects negotiating confessions and penalties with a district attorney. This is exactly the situation involved in legal plea bargaining, the most common method for settling court cases in the American criminal justice system. As laboratory research proceeded however, it became progressively more elegant and complex, but at the same time farther and farther removed from the realistic, practically important issues with which it began. "There is a hypnotic fascination with laboratory studies," says Sommer, "that enables small permutations of an original paradigm to become self-justifying as part of a larger search for knowledge. Carried to an extreme, such an attitude leads the investigator away from those questions that the original research was intended to answer" (Sommer, 1982, p. 531). Sommer recommends a return to an experimental paradigm that includes essential features of the plea-bargaining situation and a general methodology that integrates laboratory with field research. "The ideal research strategy is a dialectical process of studies in the real world, modeling in the laboratory, comparison with the real world, revised laboratory modeling, and so on" (Sommer, 1982, p. 531).

An emphasis on field research and clinical trial is also prominent in Janis and Mann's (1977) approach to decision-making. Subjects in experiments on decision processes are usually expected to make rational choices under the fundamentally safe conditions of the laboratory. In contrast, decision makers in life outside the laboratory are often beset by conflict, subject to pressure, prone to distortion, liable to irrationality, and not necessarily likely to behave as they do in the face of artificial laboratory demands. Janis and Mann do not propose cessation of laboratory research. They believe that its metaphors and models can provide a pertinent conceptual framework for analyses of many kinds. They argue, however, for a better balance of laboratory experimentation, field research, and practical application than the current literature provides, and their own analyses of defective appraisal under high conflict and defensive avoidance among policy makers exemplify the broad-based, ecologically relevant approaches they hope to find useful in the hurly-burly of practical decision-making.

The call for naturalistic research has been sounded for many years in psychology. Kurt Lewin's (1946) concepts of field theory and action research are widely known. Egon Brunswick's (1947) concept of representative design has found its way into many statements on methodology in psychological science. Barker (1968), Bronfenbrenner (1977), McGuire (1967), and Proshansky (1976) head a long list of distinguished investigators who have seen a need to complement laboratory experiment with field research if psychology is ever to build a base of knowledge that will interest anyone besides the experimentalists themselves.

Laboratory research can be defended for its own sake. Berkowitz and Donnerstein (1982) have argued that the demand for external validity is inappropriate as an evaluative criterion for laboratory research. Experiments are designed to test causal hypotheses under restricted, controlled conditions. Representative designs that encourage ecological validity are inadequate for testing causal hypotheses and are suited instead to the establishment of population estimates. The generalizability of laboratory results to other situations is an empirical question that does not require an affirmative answer. Douglas Mook (1983) extends a similar argument by noting that "artificial" findings may acquire interest by showing what can happen, even if it rarely does. Where generalizations are made, they may gain added force exactly because the sample or setting was artificial.

In sympathy with these authors and other proponents of basic science, we do not propose that all studies in psychology demonstrate immediate relevance to the societal concerns of the natural world. We certainly do not propose that controlled experimental investigations be abandoned. However, we do side with those who claim that the emphasis on laboratory research in decision-making is often stimulated more by convenience of method and the social acceptability (i.e., publishability) of results than by any deep and durable importance of the question under study, and we applaud those who are willing to face the frustrations and challenges of research in natural settings.

The Need for Direct Technological Innovation

Even field research, however, cannot provide the technology required for useful application of knowledge in the natural process of decision-making. No matter how thoroughly a representative design may sample natural conditions, no matter how carefully the study may be executed, field research by itself does not provide the technical armamentarium needed for assault upon problems of practical importance. Most field research, like laboratory experimentation, starts and ends in theory. It is designed to test the generalizability of a theoretical proposition and in that way to extend or limit the boundaries of the conceptual domain within which it is focused. Technically useful procedures may "spin off" from some of the activity but there is nothing in the design of field research to guarantee that they will, and even when some components of a practically useful methodology issue from field investigation, additional steps must be taken to bring them into full professional use and to derive from them the greatest possible public value.

Technological development resembles basic research in some regards, but it is also different from basic research in important ways, whether the scientific investigations are conducted in the laboratory or in the field. As we proposed in the second chapter of this book, as our authors have shown in their substantive contributions throughout the body of the book, and as we have reemphasized in the present chapter, the disciplined application of knowledge in the solution of human problems requires a distinctive orientation. The process begins in the particular problem itself. "Bridge this river. Cure this disease. Make better beer" (Ziman, 1974, p. 23). The importance of conceptualizing the decision to be made cannot be overstated. Paul's contribution to assessment in residential settings derives not only from the technical quality of his procedures but even more from their direction toward accomplishing the fundamental aim of any mental health organization, which is to help staff help clients get better rather than to infer personality traits, count contact hours, or meet any of the other aims toward which assessment and documentation are so often directed. The importance of understanding the context of decision, and particularly the political and economic culture of decision makers, is expressed throughout the book but is illustrated most vividly in the reports of Fowler, Hackman and Helmreich, and Broskowski. The need to carry well-conceptualized, technically adequate methodologies beyond simple demonstrations to implementation and dissemination at full scale is clear to anyone who is concerned about the public uses of assessment operations. As noted above, only Paul and Gilbert among the authors of this volume have advanced to this stage. That is not to derogate the work of the others, but only to insist that the returns of practical use will not accrue until all the steps of the technological assessment paradigm have been completed. Until then, the gap between science and practice will remain, and the full public benefits of our labors will not be realized.

OBSERVATIONS ON SOME FAMILIAR ISSUES
IN PSYCHOLOGICAL ASSESSMENT

Clinical and Actuarial Prediction

In 1954, Paul Meehl showed that statistical methods of combining data were superior to human judgment in predicting a wide range of socially important behavioral outcomes. This shocked many clinicians. The notion that sensitive, thoroughly trained, doctorally credentialed professional psychologists performed worse than statistical tables in predicting human behavior was insulting to some, threatening to others, and an intriguing intellectual issue to every psychologist concerned with assessment. Meehl's monograph aroused a storm of controversy. Opposing arguments (e.g., Holt, 1958), refinements (e.g., Gough, 1962; Sawyer, 1966), and qualifications of many kinds appeared. Actuarially based, automated systems for interpreting test data, especially the (MMPI), were developed by several psychologists in several locations (e.g., Finney, 1966; Fowler, 1966; Pearson et al., 1964). Controversy over the logic of clinical and statistical prediction, interpretation of data bearing on the issue, and the advantages and disadvantages of the two approaches continue into present times.

   It is interesting to observe how our authors actually behaved when they found themselves in situations that required the collection and integration of data to aid practical decisions. All of them were familiar with the clinical/statistical prediction argument. They knew what the data showed. Yet in actual practice most of them combined data in both mechanical and judgmental ways, and in no case was a purely actuarial formula used to derive a prediction that would affect a client's life. Even Fowler, author of one of the most widely used, actuarially based systems for interpreting the MMPI, only employed personality test information as a minor component in the matrix of information used to determine classification of Alabama prisoners. Histories of aggressive behavior figured far more prominently in gauging appropriate levels of security. Further, and more directly germane to the argument about clinical and statistical prediction, Fowler was never so foolish as to suggest that behavior records, test data, and other forms of information be fed into a computer in expectation that the most accurate possible prediction of violent behavior and a justifiable security classification would roll out the other side.

Instead, the entire procedure of data collection, data combination, and decision was embedded in the context of due process. Quasi-legal agreements as to burden of proof were required before assessment began. Instead of assuming that all prisoners required maximum security until proved otherwise, Fowler and his colleagues adopted the principle that prisoners were entitled to the least restrictive environment their behavior appeared to require. The kinds of data to be entered in the record and employed as bases for decision were carefully discussed before assessment could proceed. Data were clearly to be combined by human judgment, and the panels empowered with decisional responsibility were composed to balance the rights of prisoners and the rights of society in the most judicious possible manner. Even if the careful research required to support a statistical decision procedure had been available, no one would seriously have proposed its actual use in this situation. The political, ethical, and legal conditions that prohibit sole use of actuarial methods for combining data are not limited to the world of criminal justice; these conditions might affect assessment at any of the levels and in any of the settings in which the authors of this book are engaged.

The question our authors have had to confront is not whether mechanical data combinations or judgmental data combinations will win in horse-race competition. Their problem is an extension of the question Meehl raised after he presented his notorious box score of successes and failures for statistical and clinical predictions. It is a generalized and differentiated version of the question, "When shall we use our heads instead of the formula" (Meehl, 1957). For us, "What kinds of formal data systems, in reference to what kinds of decisions, combined in what ways with human judgment, will lead to the most judicious decisions?" No single answer to that question can be expected. In Chapter 9, Broskowski noted general conditions under which formal data systems are likely and unlikely to be used. More directly pertinent to narrower questions about statistical and judgmental data combination, our authors have demonstrated at least two cases in which one or the other mode of aggregation is appropriate.

Where amounts of data or speeds of data entry exceed the data-processing capacities of the human brain, and where the elements to be included and the weights or other modifiers attached to the elements in a predictive formula have been derived from systematic observations in controlled research, statistical attribution is *always* superior to judgmental attribution. The conditions imposed by large data masses that flow rapidly and that must often be aggregated in complex ways to guide decisions are frequently encountered in psychological assessment. This is where computers can help us, as they do, in fact, help Buffery, Paul, and others of our authors. Mere automation, however, without prior research to examine linkages among elements in the data mass and the criterion outcomes for which attributions are ultimately required only provides an illusion of accuracy—the appearance of scientific objectivity with none of the substance. It is the development of this data base that requires research on the correlates of psychophysiological responses as recommended by Katkin or the study of constructs in parental behavior as examined by Patterson, and that lends significance in the decision process to all careful research of this kind. Once the research is done and the correlational structures are known, a formal data system can be developed and its use can be justified. Indeed failure to employ accurate predictors when they are available can be as serious an error as their illegitimate use.

In the political-economic whirl of clinical-administrative decision-making, however, conditions often arise that have never been examined in previous research. In its general form, the actual situation practitioners commonly face most closely resembles that of "dynamic decision-making" as defined in a previous section of this chapter. That is, decisions are made sequentially over time, task specifications change over time, information for later decisions is contingent on outcomes of earlier decisions, and implications of any decision reach into the future. We noted that research on that process had been active for a time but had nearly stopped by the time of the review by Slovic and his colleagues. Possibly the research ceased not only because of the complexity of the issue, but because investigators realized that the most interesting questions in the natural ecology are unique. An administrator considering a complex decision may find that the conditions for which decisions are required have never occurred in just this pattern before, and will never occur in just this pattern again. In this situation, computer simulations of various options and outcomes can be of value, as Broskowski and Kamis-Gould suggest. Ultimately, however, there is no substitute for human intelligence. Data, both formal and informal, combine only as well as inherently fallible human judgment allows. Optimization is often out of the question; the best the administrator can do is satisfice. When public accountability is expected, requirements of political credibility may outweigh any concerns for scientific accuracy the decision maker may harbor. The challenge for assessment technology is not to determine whether actuarial prediction is better than clinical prediction or the other way around, but where and under what conditions statistical information and human judgment can be coordinated to improve particular decision-making procedures.

Idiography and Nomothesis

In 1937 Gordon Allport brought the ideas of idiographic and nomothetic inquiry from German philosophy into American psychology. The conceptions stimulated a good deal of discussion and instigated another controversy that has engaged theorists from that time forward. The issue is often framed as a distinction between two kinds of lawfulness. Nomothetic laws are conceived as universal. Idiographic laws are conceived as individual. The distinction gives rise to several debatable questions. Can truly idiographic "laws" be defined, or are they instead merely special cases of general principles (and if the latter, why do we need to talk about idiography in the first place)? Can general laws ever provide the detailed information required for thorough understanding and accurate prediction of individual behavior (and if not what is the point of seeking general principles)? Many resolutions of these issues have been proposed. Among the most widely accepted is Meehl's view that behavioral laws are nomothetic in form for any given group, but individualized as to parameters for separate members of the group, and entirely idiographic as to end terms defined by the actual behavioral topography that any particular individual displays. Thus response rates can be conceived as nomothetically lawful functions of reinforcement schedules, but parametric rates of change may vary among individuals, and the detailed pattern of behavior that constitutes expression of any generic response class may be perfectly unique for any individual (Meehl, 1954).

Insofar as idiography and nomothesis are proposed as alternatives, the weight of opinion in psychology has favored nomothesis (e.g., Eysenck, 1954; Falk, 1956; Holt, 1962; Nunnally, 1967). The arguments vary (almost idiographically) but center ideologically on the claim that only nomothetic inquiries are truly scientific and that nothing very orderly can come of individual description. "Idiography is an antiscience point of view: it discourages the search for general laws and instead encourages the description of particular phenomena . . . to accept an idiographic point of view in advance is to postulate that only chaos prevails in the description of human personalities" (Nunnally, 1967, p. 472). As noted in Chapter 2, this view still dominates scientific psychology, although returns from a century of search for universal laws of human behavior are meager.

As was true in regard to clinical and statistical prediction, the behavior of our authors is interesting to observe in light of the issues involved. For the most part, these investigators were not concerned with universal principles, and the linkage of their work with such "laws" as psychology may claim can only be seen at a broadly general level. The work of Paul and Patterson is grounded in the conceptual framework of social learning theory. Both investigators assume, and in fact have demonstrated, important practical consequences of general principles of social reinforcement. In his performance theory of aggression, Patterson is attempting to define lawful relationships that link parental behavior with the antisocial behavior of children. Gilbert conceptualizes his PROBE analyses for behavior modification in the familiar terms of discriminative stimuli, response patterns, and reinforcing contingencies, as combined with Lewinian concepts of transaction between person and environment.

For the most part, however, the descriptive activities of all investigators are clearly idiographic, both in intent and outcome. By means of a generally applicable technology and common strategy, Buffery seeks detailed, individualized data on brain function, and arranges the stimuli with which any patient is bombarded in a form designed to suit the particular pattern of disability and residual capability of each individual. The inquiries of Paul and Patterson also follow common strategies, but the resulting descriptions may be perfectly unique for any given client or family. Treatment regimes are designed to suit the behavioral topographies of individuals, and demonstrations of effect are shown by changes in individual response rates, although these may be aggregated in various ways to examine questions about the average effectiveness of one form of treatment or another. Gilbert's MAPS and LAMPS look different from one company to another, although the same general plan of inquiry can be employed across a wide range of settings. For any particular organization, what matters is clearly demonstrated effect *for that organization.* The Acme Widget Corporation will pay Gilbert for documented improvement in the economically relevant performance of its own employees. They will not pay him for general averages or universal laws.

Although some of the most heated controversies over idiography and nomothesis have concerned the nature of law in psychology, it is well to remember that Allport's original emphasis was not upon the philosophical character of psychological principles, but upon idiographic and nomothetic *modes of inquiry.* In this regard, our authors clearly operate in the idiographic mode, as is appropriate for investigators concerned with the practical uses of assessment. It is also important to note that there is nothing the least bit unscientific about the inquiries our authors report or recommend. Their work proceeds in the experimental tradition of Ebbinghaus and Skinner. Across a wide range of settings and over all the levels of organization with which the book is concerned, the careful descriptions and close controls of single-case design are emphasized. In this, our authors form a methodological partnership with Barlow et al. (1984) and a growing number of like-minded investigators who propose that exclusive concern with nomothetic principles leads only to broad abstractions of limited practical use or to progressively diverging qualifications of general principles, and that descriptive order must depend fundamentally on detailed, accurate, individualized description of each particular case.

Just as there is nothing unscientific about this work, neither is it inhumane. The word "technology" calls up images of stainless steel instruments, mysterious electronic gadgets, and totally impersonal treatment of the victims of a heartless, mechanistic society. In every case, however, the technology described in this book leads to more humane treatment of people than they enjoy without it. Buffery's "probes" and "bombardments," skillfully deployed by a well-managed "caring team," help patients lead more productive, more satisfying lives than they could without assistance. Fowler's prisoners were better off when they were classified by his procedures than when their fates depended on the mercies of guards and other prisoners. Many a hard-bitten business manager has shaken Tom Gilbert's hand in warm appreciation of the new sense of worth and accomplishment Gilbert's procedures have helped him attain. Our technologists do not spend much time weeping in sympathy over the plights of their miserable clients. Instead they get to work and help people, in technically effective, entirely humanitarian ways. And they do so by aiming toward the greatest possible benefit for each and every client, rather than attempting to demonstrate statistically reliable, but often tiny, changes in average performance.

In his concept of "idiothetic personality," Lamiell (1981) has proposed that personality description be approached in an explicitly idiographic way, and that the search for nomothetic principles be directed toward elucidating the process of personality development. Our authors offer living demonstrations of agreement with this view, not only for individual personality, but for the study of biopsychological functions and of groups and organizations as well.

Personality Assessment and Behavioral Assessment

For many years, psychological assessment was conceived mainly as a process of inferring constructs, especially personality traits and intellectual abilities, from more or less standardized observations, especially tests. Beginning in the late 1950s, at an accelerated pace through the 1960s, and into the present time, the view of assessment as inferential construction began to receive serious criticism from several quarters on several grounds. A series of investigations demonstrated shockingly low agreement among expert clinicians in attributing personality traits to the people who took part in their studies (e.g., Goldberg, 1959; Kostlan, 1954; Little & Schneidman, 1959). Two independent, simultaneous reviews showed that trait characterizations were not nearly as generalizable as most psychologists had assumed, that the situational specificity of behavior had been grossly underestimated in traditional personality theories, and that any formulation that did not take environmental determinants of behavior into systematic account was fundamentally incomplete (Mischel, 1968; Peterson, 1968).

Logical difficulties were seen in psychodynamic trait conceptions. Constructs were blatantly reified. "When pus accumulates and forms an abscess, the abscess must be opened and drained. If it isn't done the infection spreads. In the end, it may destroy the individual. Just so with feelings. The 'badness' must come out. The hurts and fears and anger must be released and drained" (Baruch, 1949, p. 38). Circular reasoning offered a pretense of explanation but no real gain in explanatory power. A youngster would be brought to a clinic because he had been beating up on smaller children on the playground. He would be given a Rorschach, on which he saw lots of knives and volcanoes and responded a couple of times to pure color as a determinant. The test report would emphasize deep-seated hostility and lack of impulse control, which were then employed as constructs to explain the aggression that brought the young fellow to the clinic in the first place. Some of us in the psychological assessment business began to wonder whether understanding of the problem had improved much through this exercise, and we definitely began to question whether we had gained any information that would help us do something about the aggressive behavior. These and other considerations led many psychologists to seek alternatives to the conceptions of traditional personality theory and the inferential, test-based process by which most psychological assessment was conducted.

The alternative that won the strongest following was behavioral assessment. Early formulations, based principally on the operant psychology of B. F. Skinner, usually excluded all considerations that smacked of mentalism, and restricted inquiry to the direct observation of explicit behavior, in conjunction with the stimulus conditions that preceded and followed the emission of behavior. Some early proposals, however (Peterson, 1968); and nearly all of the recent ones (e.g., Ciminero et al., 1977; Nelson, 1983) adopted a broader purview that included cognitive-affective functions and could readily be extended beyond the individual to the assessment of group and organizational behavior. The procedural repertoire was enlarged beyond direct observation of behavior *in situ* to include a range of analogues, records, self-reports, and guided interviews. The hallmarks of behavioral assessment in its more liberal forms are not rigid restriction to directly observable behavior or assumption of primary causal significance for the reinforcing consequences of behavior but (a) focus on behavior as worthy of study for its own sake rather than as a basis for inferring internal characteristics, (b) focus at the same time on the environmental conditions that envelop behavior, (c) interpretation of behavior as a sample of action in a particular situation rather than as a sign of some trans-situational internal quality, and (d) the study of behavior-in-situation as a process subject to change if either the situation or the way the situation is acted upon can be altered.

As noted above, the authors of this volume are clearly working in the behavioral mode. They do not exclude tests as procedures or inferences as logical operations. The MMPI was part of Fowler's battery. Paul uses questionnaires and inventories to estimate relatively enduring personal-social dispositions. However, the procedural advantages of direct observational coding of behavior are clear in Fowler's work as in Paul's and in most of the operations used or recommended by the other authors. Katkin questions the use of psychophysiological measures as signs of psychological deception and urges their more direct use as samples of physiological function in the treatment regimes of behavioral medicine. Patterson gauges parental discipline and monitoring through multiple operations that describe what parents do to and with their children. Gilbert's measures are based on performances, not upon traits.

The emphasis in the methodologies of our authors is not so much on behavior, narrowly defined, as on functional performance, broadly defined. In this regard, the aims, methods, and outcomes of assessment are closely in line with those of program evaluation, as conceived by Rossi et al. (1979), Morell (1979), Cronbach et al. (1980) and the many others who have established the discipline of program evaluation in recent years. Investigators examine how and how well a particular program works in a particular setting. Wherever possible, dysfunctions are identified and changes are introduced to improve effectiveness of performance. The immediate outcome is a technological case study rather than a theoretical generalization, although common strategies of inquiry and change may be useful for many kinds of functions in many kinds of settings.

The leaning of our authors toward behavioral rather than psychodynamic views, toward functional rather than structural concepts, toward observational rather than inferential procedures, is of course no accident. These considerations were on our minds as we chose participants for the symposium. Insofar as we can claim insight into our own preferences, however, they arise not so much from adherence to ideological behaviorism as from an interest in pragmatic effectiveness. We sought assessment systems that met the conditions of social value identified in the first two chapters of this book. We realize that the aims of psychodiagnostic inquiry within a psychodynamic conception of personality are not entirely the same as those of behavioral assessment. Psychodynamically oriented clinicians aim for understanding on their own part in the hope of encouraging insight on the part of their clients. Through observation, inquiry, and conjecture they develop a "working image" of each client and organize the complex of conceptions and hypotheses into an "emerging synthesis" (Sundberg et al., 1983; Sundberg & Tyler, 1962). We also appreciate that not all psychodynamically inclined clinicians are guilty of gross logical errors and that some of them (e.g., Schectman & Smith, 1984) are searching earnestly and intelligently for the linkage between assessment and change that we consider essential for any useful approach to assessment. But so far, we have not seen any psychodynamically based methodologies that meet the conditions of practical value outlined in the first chapters of this book.

The Uses of Assessment

The *American Psychologist* of October, 1981, is a special issue devoted to concepts, policy, practice, and research in psychological testing. The use of tests for educational placement, occupational access, and social determinations of many kinds gives rise to serious legal and political issues, as well as to scientific and professional ones. Articles on the scientific basis of ability testing, on testing and the law, on bias in testing (especially of linguistic minorities), on testing in educational classification and placement (including college admissions), on the realities of employment testing, on testing for licensure and certification, on federal guidelines and professional standards, and on the social context of testing, all in this one issue of the *American Psychologist*, suggest that the questions involved are wide-ranging, complex, and often hotly controversial. So far, discussions of these matters have centered on psychological tests, but the problems are not restricted to one class of procedures. Wherever systematic, professionally delivered assessment methods of any kind are used to guide socially important decisions, the same problems arise. The issues become especially sharp and public controversy most severe where economic, political, or legal consequences are involved.

If one general theme rises above others in the reports of the authors of this book, it is that processes going on at one level in our universe of living systems affect processes at other levels. Study of brain-behavior relationships expresses one linkage directly, but beyond that the design of an effective rehabilitation regime requires a "caring team" that includes the patient and his or her family as well as professionals. Neuropsychology, individual psychology, and social psychology are all inherently involved in the practical world of useful assessment and effective treatment, however discretely isolated they may be in the analyses of scientific research. The heavy force of judicial action instigated the Alabama prison project. The power of the correctional bureaucracy was equally at play in the design of the assessment system and in its operation. Human individuals were the subjects of study, but their evaluation was conducted by way of group process in an organizational context, forcefully surrounded by the political, legal, and judicial culture within which correctional institutions are located. The linkage of individual, group, and organizational function is equally apparent in Paul's work in residential treatment settings, in Hackman and Helmreich's work in the air transport industry, in Broskowski's reflections on the management of mental health centers, and in Gilbert's work as a performance engineer in commercial organizations. All these projects are embedded in a social community made up of people who would appreciate some honest help from professionals and scientists, but who are much more concerned with economic and political outcomes than with the technical and scientific merits of our devices.

Psychologists are only slowly growing mindful of these realities. There is still some sense that the public ought to take the quality and value of our work on faith. The authors of this book are more keenly aware of the constraints of public use than most. Any who may have been a bit naive going into the world of application seem sadder and wiser coming out. Even more than the authors, the discussants, working on the line of public policy and accountability, have brought home the realities of economic necessity and political limitation. Others involved in psychological assessment have much to learn from their experiences. From its beginning into the present time, the field of psychological assessment has changed radically in its position on the uses of assessment. The field will inevitably continue to change in the future. In this evolution, four main stages can be discerned.

The age of innocence. At the start, investigators who developed psychological tests were almost completely preoccupied with the scientific and technical merits of their instruments. Within the academy, controversies raged over the structure of intelligence, the distinction between aptitude and ability, and a host of other theoretical issues, but the test inventors and testers themselves assumed that only good could come of their efforts. Here at last, they thought, were scientific methods to replace the fallible judgments and outright skulduggeries of amateurs and charlatans. Surely everyone would be grateful for the boon to mankind a developing and useful psychological science could provide.

In fact the early contributions of systematic assessment were difficult to deny. Demonstrations by Terman and others of the predictive validity of intelligence tests showed that powerful instruments had been placed at our disposal. Batteries of tests for the selection of military pilots appeared to save thousands of lives and millions of dollars. But abuses inevitably occurred. IQ tests were used to deny immigrants who spoke little or no English access to American citizenship. The same kinds of tests were used to place children in institutions for the mentally retarded, whatever the error limits of the tests might be and whatever other information might have been required for decisions that determined the courses of entire lives. Testing did not escape public criticism. Walter Lippman published a series of articles in the *New Republic* blasting psychologists for the indiscriminate use of intelligence tests and questioning the assumption of hereditary determination on which many interpretations were based. Lippman wrote in his usual vigorous, often vituperative style, and drew a reply in kind from Lewis Terman. In this battle, in the journalist's arena, Professor Terman was hopelessly outmatched (Cronbach, 1975; Haney, 1981). Despite occasional attacks, however, psychologists who invented and used psychological tests continued to defend them on grounds of reliability and validity, and for the most part the general populace accepted the scientific view.

The age of utility. As noted before, the publication of Cronbach and Gleser's *Psychological Tests and Personnel Decisions* marked the beginning of a new era in assessment theory. No longer were instruments regarded as imperfect means for estimating "true" scores. Instead the tests were perceived as utilitarian devices to guide practical decisions. The value of a procedure resided not only in its accuracy but in its payoff. The effect of this view on psychological assessment has been profound. It continues to the present time, and it provides a general contextual and valuational framework for this book.

The age of awareness. Recently, a more disturbing note has been sounded. Not only must assessment procedures be scientifically accurate and economically useful, they must also be legally, politically, and morally beneficial. A single date for this transition is difficult to mark. Recognition of the political and moral consequences of psychological assessment can be found very early, in the writings of Galton and Binet, for example. Controversy over the uses of tests has continued as a kind of counterpoint to the major theme of technical development throughout the history of the psychometric movement (Cronbach, 1975). Full, deep realization of the political importance of assessment did not take hold, however, until the strident demands of the civil rights movement required attention to the matter. No longer could tests that systematically placed children with one skin color in mainstream classes and those with another skin color in special classes be used with impunity. No longer could tests that assumed fluency in one language be interpreted in quite the usual way for bilingual children. The political ramifications of psychological assessment, however, go beyond tests as procedures and beyond minorities as subjects. Any time any psychological method is systematically and professionally used to guide decisions that affect the lives of people, possible legal, economic, and political consequences of assessment need to be appreciated. This understanding has been forced upon us in the psychological testing of children and is beginning to take hold in the openly visible, politically sensitive field of program evaluation. We propose that the same awareness will necessarily make its way into the entire field of psychological assessment, whether we want it to or not.

It has been said that academics are allowed intellectual freedom not so much because the search for truth must proceed untrammeled, but because nothing most academicians say or do matters very much. As long as psychologists stay in their towers, deal only with esoteric issues, and exchange ideas only among themselves, nobody will bother them, though they might wonder how long society will continue to support them. The minute they bring their methods into the world of public action, however, they join a pluralistic community whose interests will not always coincide with their own. If nothing else, they need to be aware of that condition.

The age of involvement. In their book, *Toward Reform in Program Evaluation,* Lee Cronbach and his associates write:

Evaluation has vital work to do, yet its institutions and its ruling conceptions are inadequate. Enamored of a vision that "right" decisions can replace political agreements, some who commission evaluations set evaluators on unrealistic quests. Others among them see evaluation chiefly as a means to strengthen the hand of the commissioning authority. Evaluators, eager to serve and even to manipulate those in power, lose sight of what they should be doing. Moreover, evaluators become enthralled by technique. Much that purports to be theory of evaluation is scholastic; evaluations are endlessly categorized, and chapels are dedicated to the glorification of particular styles. Latter-day theologians discuss how best to reify such chimeras as "goals" and "benefits." . . . All too rarely does discussion descend to earthy questions such as, "Is worthwhile information being collected?" (Cronbach et al., 1980, pp. 1–2)

They proceed, in Lutheran tradition, to present 95 theses among which the following are especially pertinent to the argument we are now approaching:

The evaluator has political influence even when he does not aspire to it.

A theory of evaluation must be as much a theory of political interaction as it is a theory of how to determine facts.

The evaluators' professional conclusions cannot substitute for the political process.

The notion of the evaluator as a superman who will make all social choices easy and all programs efficient, turning public management into a technology, is a pipe dream.

An image of pluralistic accommodation more truly represents how policy and programs are shaped than does the Platonic image of concentrated power and responsibility.

The evaluator must learn to serve in contexts of accommodation and not dream idly of serving a Platonic guardian.

The view of the evaluator that follows from these arguments is very different from traditional views of the assessor in psychology. Isolation in the laboratory is obviously out of the question. Even the usual idea of a professional diagnostician, using technically advanced procedures to offer precise determinations of the parameters of a particular problem, is insufficient. Instead the evaluator is part of a team that serves the interests of a larger community. His main role in team activity is to seek information that will ultimately work to the benefit of the community. Diverging, sometimes antagonistic, social interests must often be taken into account. Compromises will sometimes be required. Political finesse may often be more important than technical adequacy in determining social effects. To accomplish these aims and still maintain a justifiable sense of personal and professional integrity is a far more difficult task than merely telling the "truth" wherever it may lead. Cronbach and his associates use the phrase "enlightened accommodation" to characterize both the process and the outcome of useful program evaluation in a pluralistic society.

The view carries direct implications for methodology, as further "theses" suggest.

Much that is written on evaluation recommends one "scientifically rigorous" plan. Evaluations should, however, take many forms, and less rigorous approaches have value in many circumstances.

A strictly representative sample may provide less information than a sample that overrepresents exceptional cases and deliberately varies realizations.

The symmetric, nonsequential designs familiar from laboratory research and survey research are rarely appropriate for evaluations.

External validity—that is, the validity of inferences that go beyond the data—is the crux; increasing internal validity by elegant design often reduces relevance.

Results of a program evaluation are so dependent on the setting that replication is only a figure of speech; the evaluator is essentially a historian.

In project-by-project evaluation, each study analyzes a spoonful dipped from a sea of uncertainties.

We believe that the general attitudes as well as the methodological guidelines that Cronbach and his associates propose for program evaluation are equally appropriate in other forms of psychological assessment. We might as well stop railing at employers who hire poorly trained polygraphers to identify dishonest employees. Instead, we need to realize that theft can be a ruinously expensive problem for a department store owner, and either develop better ways of spotting thieves or stay quiet about the problem. We might as well curb our peevishness toward mental hospital superintendents who fail to snap up our elegant methods, remember that their jobs are politically tenuous as well as legally vulnerable, and do our best to bring about the kind of enlightened accommodation that an improved methodology, adroitly delivered, may provide.

We need to present our methods in forms that will appeal to those who use them. Foundation in sound theory and thorough research is still required. Technical adequacy in the natural settings where the methods will be used is still essential. But beyond that, the methodology must be understandable and persuasive. To quote one final Cronbachian thesis, "Scientific quality is not the principle standard; and evaluation should aim to be comprehensible, correct and complete, and credible to partisans on all sides" (Cronbach et al., 1980, p. 11). We suggest that the emphasis on comprehensibility and credibility in Cronbach's "four Cs" be added to Gordon Paul's "four Rs" as necessary conditions for the public utilization of any assessment methodology.

SCIENCE, PRACTICE, AND THE NEED FOR A BRIDGING TECHNOLOGY

Throughout this book we have claimed that successful applications of psychology have been limited because the field lacks a technology that can provide useful means for solving human problems. Physical sciences must be complemented by engineering technology if bridges are to be built and space vehicles launched. Human biology must be complemented by medical technology if diseases are to be cured and prevented. A more active, more thoroughly developed discipline of applied psychology is needed if knowledge about human behavior is to be placed in the public benefit.

In the new technology, assessment will play a central role. We have proposed a general strategy, Technological Assessment in Psychology, to guide the development of useful assessment methodologies. The authors of this book provide examples of kinds of work that can be conceptualized within the framework, although the original aims of the investigators may not have been explicitly technological. As broad as the scope of their collective works may seem, the entire field of psychological technology, as we conceive it, is even broader. Among the many settings we have neglected, schools are an especially conspicuous omission. Powerful work has been done there (e.g., Kratochwill, 1981; Sulzer-Azaroff & Mayer, 1986), and clear opportunities can be seen for doing work of general and lasting public benefit by improving the psychoeducational process. The work of Azrin (1977) in such widely varied settings as the offices of personal managers, the back wards of mental hospitals, and the bathrooms where parents are toilet training their children suggests that the kind of "learning based, outcome oriented" activity we are proposing can be extended to any human function and any environmental situation. Our labors are only beginning.

The role of the applied psychologist is not that of a scientist who has done some practice, nor of a practitioner who has learned some science, but of a consulting engineer. Any particular problem is initially taken on the client's terms, though one of the professional's most useful contributions is often an alternative conception. The problem is addressed within the boundaries of the client's culture. The consultant joins a team, working to accomplish outcomes valued by those who pay the bills, whether the sources of funds are public or private. To gain an invitation to join the team, the consultant must be mindful of the forms in which methodologies are presented. Labels must be carefully chosen.

Deliberate marketing may be required. To help the team win, that is, to accomplish valued outcomes, the consultant must often be as knowing about coalitions, networks, and modes of conflict resolution as about the technical merits of procedures. In the face of actual complexities that may seem overwhelming, conceptual and technical simplifications may be required that are at once persuasive and justifiable. The challenges of maintaining professional integrity and at the same time accomplishing practical objectives are often vexing.

Preparation for the work of a consultant in applied psychology requires some modifications of traditional PhD curricula. Training in laboratory research is clearly insufficient. Training for direct, individual clinical practice is equally limited. Training for both of those is no good either, unless the linkage of research and application, from a managerial viewpoint, within the culture of the consumer, is clearly perceived and carefully taught. Professional models of education in psychology that are firmly grounded in disciplined knowledge and are sufficiently comprehensive to offer a reasonably broad sample of the range of situations encountered in practice are suited to the demand. So are the more progressive forms of education in the scientist-professional framework. In fact, comprehensive "professional" education as defined by Peterson (1976a, 1976b, 1982) and "scientist-professional" education as defined by Sundberg et al. (1983) or by Barlow et al. (1984) would probably not appear discriminably different to anyone outside our own field. Indeed, the view of clinical psychology expressed by Sundberg et al., with its emphasis on the linkage of assessment and intervention at various systems levels, and the view of Barlow et al., with its emphasis on systematic, case-oriented inquiry into complex human problems as they occur in nature, are entirely congruent with the view developed in this book. These conceptions are all suitable as general frameworks for professional education. Experience in administration and management, often lacking in traditional doctoral programs in psychology, is important. Above all, supervised experience in the kinds of inquiry considered in this book will prepare students to do the jobs they will be called upon to do later on. Expecting laboratory research, however elegant, and training in psychotherapy, however prolonged or profound, to prepare students for work in the useful assessment of human function is asking a little training in science and practice to go a long way.

Psychology is often seen to be composed of two cultures, one of science and the other of practice. The two are often at odds. Scientists complain that practitioners are not scientific. Practitioners complain that the science they have seen is not practical. We propose the creation of a third culture, technology—not just a blend of the other two, but a new creature that undoubtedly is just what those with the clearest visions of applied psychology and the scientist-practitioner model of education intended to encourage all along. So far, however, those visions have been poorly realized. We believe that the third culture we have described, whose outlines we have sketched in the technological assessment paradigm, and which is illustrated and extended by the authors of this book, will help bring psychology into effective public use.

REFERENCES

Allport, G. W. (1937). *Personality: A psychological interpretation*. New York: Holt.

Azrin, N. H. (1977). A strategy for applied research: Learning based but outcome oriented. *American Psychologist, 30*, 469–485.

Barker, R. G. (1968). *Ecological psychology: Concepts and methods for studying the environment of human behavior*. Stanford: Stanford University Press.

Barlow, D. H., Hayes, S. C., & Nelson, R. O. (1984). *The Scientist-practitioner: Research and accountability in clinical and educational settings*. New York: Pergamon.

Baruch, D. W. (1949). *New ways in discipline*. New York: McGraw-Hill.

Becker, G. M., & McClintock, C. G. (1967). Value: Behavioral decision theory. *Annual Review of Psychology, 18*, 239–286.

Berkowitz, L., & Donnerstein, E. (1982). External validity is more than skin deep: Some answers to criticisms of laboratory experiments. *American Psychologist, 37*, 245–257.

Bronfenbrenner, J. (1977). Toward an experimental ecology of human development. *American Psychologist, 32*, 513–531.

Brunswick, E. (1947). *Systematic and representative design of psychological experiments*. Berkeley: University of California Press.

Chapman, L. J., & Chapman, J. P. (1967). Genesis of popular but erroneous diagnostic observations. *Journal of Abnormal Psychology, 72*, 193–204.

Ciminero, A. R., Calhoun, K. S., & Adams, H. E. (Eds.). (1977). *Handbook of behavioral assessment*. New York: Wiley.

Cronbach, L. J. (1975). Five decades of public controversy over mental testing. *American Psychologist, 30*, 1–14.

Cronbach, L. J., Ambron, S. R., Dornbusch, S. M., Hess, R. D., Hornik, R. C., Phillips, O. C., Walker, D. F., & Weiner, S. S. (1980). *Toward reform in program evaluation*. San Francisco: Jossey-Bass.

Cronbach, L. J., & Gleser, G. C. (1965). *Psychological tests and personnel decisions* (2nd ed.). Urbana: University of Illinois Press.

Edwards, W. (1954). The theory of decision making. *Psychological Bulletin, 51,* 380–418.

Edwards, W. (1961). Behavioral decision theory. *Annual Review of Psychology, 12,* 473–498.

Eysenck, H. J. (1954). The science of personality: Nomothetic. *Psychological Review, 61,* 339–341.

Falk, J. (1956). Issues distinguishing idiographic from nomothetic approaches to personality theory. *Psychological Review, 63,* 53–62.

Finney, J. C. (1966). Programmed interpretation of MMPI and CPI. *Archives of General Psychiatry, 15,* 75–81.

Fowler, R. D., Jr. (1966). *The MMPI notebook: A guide to the clinical use of the automated MMPI.* Nutley, N.J.: Roche Psychiatric Service Institute.

Girschick, M. A. (1954). An elementary survey of statistical decision theory. *Review of Educational Research, 24,* 448–466.

Goldberg, L. R. (1959). The effectiveness of clinicians' judgments: The diagnosis of organic brain damage from the Bender-Gestalt Test. *Journal of Consulting Psychology, 23,* 25–33.

Golding, S. L., & Rorer, L. G. (1972). Illusory correlation and subjective judgment. *Journal of Abnormal Psychology, 80,* 249–260.

Gough, H. G. (1962). Clinical versus statistical prediction in psychology. In L. Postman (ed.), *Psychology in the making.* New York: Knopf.

Gulliksen, H. (1950). *Theory of mental tests.* New York: Wiley.

Haney, W. (1981). Validity, vaudeville, and values: A short history of social concerns over standardized testing. *American Psychologist, 36,* 1021–1034.

Holt, R. R. (1958). Clinical *and* statistical prediction: A reformulation and some new data. *Journal of Abnormal and Social Psychology, 56,* 1–12.

Holt, R. R. (1962). Individuality and generalization in the psychology of personality: An evaluation. *Journal of Personality, 30,* 377–402.

Hull, C. L. (1928). *Aptitude testing.* Yonkers, N.Y.: World Book.

Janis, I. L., & Mann, L. (1977). *Decision making.* New York: Free Press.

Kostlan, A. (1954). A method for the empirical study of psychodiagnosis. *Journal of Consulting Psychology, 18,* 83–88.

Kratochwill, T. R. (Ed.). (1981). *Advances in school psychology* (Vol. 1). Hillsdale, N.J.: Erlbaum.

Lamiell, J. T. (1981). Toward an idiothetic psychology of personality. *American Psychologist, 36,* 276–289.

Lewin, K. (1946). Action research and minority problems. *Journal of Social Issues, 2,* 34–46.

Little, K. B., & Schneidman, E. S. (1959). Congruencies among interpretations of psychological test and anamnestic data. *Psychological Monographs, 73,* (6, Whole No. 476).

Mathews, K. (1982). Psychological perspective on the Type A behavior pattern. *Psychological Bulletin, 91,* 293–323.

May, E. R. (1973). *"Lessons" of the past.* New York: Oxford University Press.

McGuire, W. J. (1967). Some impending reorientations in social psychology: Some thoughts provoked by Kenneth Ring. *Journal of Experimental Social Psychology, 3*, 124–139.

Meehl, P. E. (1954). *Clinical versus statistical prediction: A theoretical analysis and a review of the evidence.* Minneapolis: University of Minnesota Press.

Meehl, P. E. (1957). When shall we use our heads instead of the formula? *Journal of Counseling Psychology, 4*, 268–273.

Miller, J. G. (1978). *Living Systems.* New York: McGraw-Hill.

Mischel, W. (1968). *Personality and assessment.* New York: Wiley.

Mook, D. G. (1983). In defense of external invalidity. *American Psychologist, 38*, 379–387.

Morell, J. A. (1979). *Program evaluation in social research.* New York: Pergamon.

Nelson, P. R. (1983). Behavioral Assessment: Past, Present, and future. *Behavioral Assessment, 5*, 195–206.

Nisbett, R., & Ross, L. (1980). *Human inference: Strategies and shortcomings of social judgment.* Englewood Cliffs, N.J.: Prentice-Hall.

Nunnally, J. C. (1967). *Psychometric theory.* New York: McGraw-Hill.

Pearson, J. S., Swenson, W. M., Rome, H. P., Mataya, P., & Brannick, T. L. (1964). Further experience with the automated MMPI. *Proceedings of the Mayo Clinic, 39*, 823–829.

Peterson, D. R. (1968). *The clinical study of social behavior.* New York: Appleton-Century-Crofts.

Peterson, D. R. (1976a). Is psychology a profession? *American Psychologist, 31*, 572–580.

Peterson, D. R. (1976b). Need for the Doctor of Psychology degree in professional psychology. *American Psychologist, 31*, 792–798.

Peterson, D. R. (1982). Origins and development of the Doctor of Psychology concept. In G. R. Caddy, D. C. Rimm, N. Watson, & J. H. Johnson (Eds.), *Educating professional psychologists.* New Brunsick, N.J.: Transaction Books.

Proshansky, H. (1976). Environmental psychology and the real world. *American Psychologist, 31*, 303–310.

Rapoport, A., & Wallsten, T. S. (1972). Individual decision behavior. *Annual Review of Psychology, 23*, 131–176.

Rossi, P. H., Freeman, H. E., & Wright, S. R. (1979). *Evaluation: A systematic approach.* Beverly Hills, Calif.: Sage.

Sawyer, J. (1966). Measurement and prediction, clinical and statistical. *Psychological Bulletin, 66*, 178–200.

Schechtman, F., & Smith, W. H. (1984). *Diagnostic understanding and treatment planning: The elusive connection.* New York: Wiley.

Slovic, P., Fischhoff, B., & Lichtenstein, S. (1977). Behavioral decision theory. *Annual Review of Psychology, 28*, 1–40.

Sommer, R. (1982). The district attorney's dilemma: Experimental games and the real world of plea bargaining. *American Psychologist, 37,* 526–532.

Sulzer-Azaroff, B., & Mayer, G. R. (1986). *Achieving educational excellence using effective behavioral strategies.* New York: Holt, Rinehart & Winston.

Sundberg, N. D., Taplin, J. R., & Tyler, L. E. (1983). *Introduction to clinical psychology: Perspectives, issues, and contributions to human service.* Englewood Cliffs, N.J.: Prentice-Hall.

Sundberg, N. D., & Tyler, L. E. (1962). *Clinical psychology.* New York: Appleton-Century-Crofts.

Thorndike, R. L. (1949). *Personnel selection: Test and measurement techniques.* New York: Wiley.

Thurstone, L. L. (1931). *Reliability and validity of tests.* Ann Arbor, Mich.: Edwards.

Tversky, A., & Kahneman, D. (1971). Belief in the law of small numbers. *Psychological Bulletin, 76,* 105–110.

Tyler, L. E. (1981). More stately mansions: Psychology extends its boundaries. *Annual Review of Psychology, 32,* 1–20.

von Neumann, J., & Morgenstern, O. (1947). *Theory of games and economic behavior.* Princeton: Princeton University Press.

Wald, A. (1950). *Statistical decision functions.* New York: Wiley.

Ziman, J. (1974). What is science? In A. C. Michalos (Ed.), *Philosophical problems of science and technology.* Boston: Allyn & Bacon.

Name Index

Subject Index

457